Walk Worthily

A Commentary on Ephesians

Jeff Smelser

Walk Worthily: A Commentary on Ephesians
© 2017 by DeWard Publishing Company, Ltd.
P.O. Box 6259, Chillicothe, Ohio 45601
800.300.9778
www.deward.com

Cover design by Barry Wallace.

Unless otherwise noted, Old Testament quotations are taken from the New American Standard Bible®,Copyright © 1960, 1962, 1963, 1968, 1971, 1972, 1973, 1975, 1977, 1995 by The Lockman Foundation Used by permission (www.Lockman.org), while New Testament quotations are usually the author's own translation.

Nestle-Aland, Novum Testamentum Graece, 28th Revised Edition, edited by Barbara and Kurt Aland, Johannes Karavidopoulos, Carlo M. Martini, and Bruce M. Metzger in cooperation with the Institute for New Testament Textual Research, Münster/Westphalia, © 2012 Deutsche Bibelgesellschaft, Stuttgart. Used by permission.

Reasonable care has been taken to trace original sources for any excerpts and quotations appearing in this book and to document such information. For material not in the public domain, fair use standards and practices were followed. Should any attribution be found to be incorrect or incomplete, the publisher welcomes written documentation supporting correction for subsequent printing.

Printed in the United States of America.

ISBN: 978-1-936341-94-8

To my father, Dale Smelser,

who often taught about the "glorious church,"
and who imparted to his sons an appreciation for the sacrifice of Jesus
and for the body which was thereby sanctified.

CONTENTS

ABBREVIATIONS

ANF	*Ante Nicene Fathers*
ANRW	*Aufstieg und Niedergang der römischen Welt: Geschichte und Kultur Roms im Spiegel der neueren Forschung. Edited by H. Temporini and W. Haase, Berlin, 1972–.*
BAGD	Bauer, Walter. *A Greek-English Lexicon of the New Testament and Other Early Christian Literature.* Revised and augmented by F. Wilbur Gingrich and Frederick W. Danker, Second Edition. Chicago: University of Chicago Press, 1979
BDAG	Bauer, Walter. *A Greek-English Lexicon of the New Testament and Other Early Christian Literature.* Revised and edited by Frederick William Danker, Third Edition. Chicago: University of Chicago Press, 2000
BDF	Blass, F. and A. Debrunner, *A Greek Grammar of the New Testament and Other Early Christian Literature,* translated and revised by Robert W. Funk. Chicago: University of Chicago Press, 1961.
EM	*Etymologicum Magnum*
NA27	*Novum Testamentum Graece.* Edited by Barbara and Kurt Aland, Johannes Karavidopoulos, Carlo M. Martini, and Bruce M. Metzger, 27th rev. ed. Stuttgart: Deutsche Bibelgesellschaft, 1993
NA28	*Novum Testamentum Graece.* Edited by Barbara and Kurt Aland, Johannes Karavidopoulos, Carlo M. Martini, and Bruce M. Metzger, 28th rev. ed. Stuttgart: Deutsche Bibelgesellschaft, 2012, 4th corrected printing, 2015.

NPNF	*Nicene and Post-Nicene Fathers*
TDNT	*Theological Dictionary of the New Testament*, ed. Gerhard Kittel and Gerhard Friedrich, trans. Geoffrey W. Bromiley, 10 vols. Grand Rapids: Eerdmans, 1964–76.
LXX	*Septuaginta*. Edited by Alfred Rahlfs. Stuttgart: Deutsche Bibelgesellschaft, 1935.
PL	*Patrologia Latina*
PG	*Patrologia Graeca*
TDNT	*Theological Dictionary of the New Testament*, ed. Gerhard Kittel and Gerhard Friedrich, trans. Geoffrey W. Bromiley, 10 vols. Grand Rapids: Eerdmans, 1964–76.
TR	*Textus Receptus*
UBS4	*The Greek New Testament*, Edited by Barbara Aland, Kurt Aland, Johannes Karavidopopulos, Carlo M. Martini, and Bruce M. Metzger, 4th rev. ed. Stuttgart: United Bible Societies, 1993. 2001. Reprint (6th printing) 2002.
UBS5	*The Greek New Testament*, Edited by Barbara Aland, Kurt Aland, Johannes Karavidopopulos, Carlo M. Martini, and Bruce Metzger, 5th rev. ed. Stuttgart: United Bible Societies, 2014.
WH	Westcott, Brooke Foss, and Fenton John Anthony Hort. *The New Testament in the Original Greek*. New York: Macmillan, 1925.

PREFACE

The message of Ephesians is most particularly the message needed by so many of those who come to God through Jesus Christ today. Fifty years ago in the United States, someone who became obedient to the gospel most likely already had some knowledge of the Bible and probably even had some prior denominational affiliation. At the very least he or she had grown up in a culture whose underpinnings were in large part the stories and morals found in the Bible. This person had never known a time when the Bible was not thought of as God's word. Today, however, it is likely that people responding to the gospel have had no prior religious affiliation and did not grow up learning about the characters and stories of the Bible. These people are in a circumstance more similar to that of the Gentiles to whom Paul wrote.

And in truth, we all are. All we who have been saved by grace have come from a world characterized by conduct that is unworthy of the calling wherewith we have been called. This worldly standard of conduct has been so much a part of our culture that it has shaped our individual thinking, and made insensitive our own consciences to things that are works of darkness, even if we were raised by Christian parents. Paul implores the Gentiles of the first century, and us today, to understand the great blessing we have in Christ, and therefore to walk worthily of the calling wherewith we were called.

With a desire to impress this thought on the readers of this volume and at the same time to provide an exegesis of the text, I originally gave little thought to providing a typical introduction that would address the usual questions concerning authorship, recipients, date, and place of composition. What little thought I gave to such questions was that focusing on them might distract from the great message of the letter itself.

But in the course of preparing this work, I realized that especially the questions of authorship and recipients (*e.g.*, which Gentiles in particular were included in the original audience) are sufficiently important that they must be addressed. Other questions such as where and when this letter was written are also important, having some connection with how we view this letter in relation to Colossians and Philemon. For these reasons, an introduction wherein these questions are addressed is provided, with a hope that the reader will not lose sight of the great message of this epistle.

Another question of considerable significance has been to what extent and in what manner this work should consider the original language. There are too many nuances that cannot be explained, too many questions that cannot be answered, and too many conclusions that would seem to be nothing more than assertions, without discussion of the Greek text. But whereas many technical commentaries assume significant original language proficiency on the part of the reader, this work has been prepared having in mind the first or second year Greek student, and the erstwhile student who may have forgotten many of the features of Greek grammar. For such readers, fundamental grammatical explanations have been provided herein in order to help the reader understand the point of grammar at issue in a given passage.

Where the Greek text of the New Testament is quoted, it is from NA28 unless otherwise indicated. Quotations from the Greek translation of the Old Testament are from Rahlfs' *Septuaginta*. The translation of the Greek text of Ephesians is my own. I have not attempted to provide a fluid, easily readable translation. Rather, my goal has been to produce a translation that will facilitate ready comparison with the Greek text for those who have some knowledge of Greek.

It is truly a humbling thing to put forward such a work as this. In private discussion and correspondence, and even in public teaching, one may err and correct himself. But in such a work as this, one's errors are set in print, if not in stone, for as long as copies of the published work survive. In order to reduce the number of such errors, I have asked knowledgeable friends to review this work carefully. I am especially indebted to Rick Duggin, Scott Smelser, Gary Fisher and Nathan Smelser for providing criticisms. They have not always agreed with my conclusions, and I have not always accepted their advice, but this work has benefited from their efforts. I am also indebted to Josiah Peeler for providing transliterations of Hebrew words and phrases, and to Crystal Crawford and Danny Glover for proof-reading and editorial suggestions. Whatever errors remain are mine. I ask that the reader be aware of what I keenly perceive and have come to appreciate more keenly than ever through this effort, that being my own fallibility, and that the reader consider the pages of this work with that in mind.

INTRODUCTION

Author

The ancient evidence unanimously pointing to Paul as the author of Ephesians has been often revisited, and needs no more than a cursory review here. For a thorough discussion, consult van Roon, who also provides a very helpful description of the arguments against Pauline authorship, and Hoehner, who traced the testimony of the ancient writers and also tallied the views of modern scholars.

For our purposes, it will suffice to note the following:

In the first half of the second century, Polycarp acknowledged Ephesians as part of the body of literature which he called the "sacred writings" when he quoted Ephesians 4.26 and identified the passage as being part of "these scriptures."[1] If it had been supposed that Ephesians was written not by Paul but rather by an impostor—not to say an admiring protégé who merely desired to perpetuate Paul's teaching, but by one who was truly an impostor, one who claimed to be "Paul an apostle of Jesus Christ" (1.1) to whom "the mystery had been made known by revelation" (3.3), even claiming to be "in chains" (6.20)—would Polycarp have regarded the letter as belonging to the "sacred writings"? We may be confident that Polycarp understood that the letter was written by Paul.

Toward the end of the second century, Irenaeus cited Ephesians 5.30 saying, "even as the blessed Paul declares in his Epistle to the Ephesians, that 'we are members of His body, of His flesh, and of His bones.'"[2] Irenaeus also referred to the language of Ephesians 2.2, saying it was what "the Apostle Paul has declared in his Epistle to the Ephesians."[3]

---

[1] To the Philippians 12.1. This part of Polycarp's letter is not extant in the original Greek. As translated into Latin, the letter refers to the *sacris literas,* (sacred writings), and thereafter says, *ut his scripturis dictum est, Irascimini et nolite peccare, et sol non occidat super iracundiam vestram* (as has been said in these scriptures, Be angry and do not sin, and let not the sun go down upon your wrath).

[2] Adv. Her. 5.2.3, ANF vol. 1, 528.

[3] Adv. Her. 5.24.4, ANF vol. 1, p. 553.

Also near the end of the second century, Clement of Alexandria quoted Ephesians 4.13–15, attributing the words to the same apostle who wrote 2 Corinthians, from which he also quotes. As Clement continued, he explicitly named Paul. It can hardly be supposed that he believed the apostle who wrote 2 Corinthians and Ephesians was any other. Again in Stromata 4.8, Clement quotes 1 Corinthians 11.3, 8, and 11, attributing the passage to "the apostle," and shortly thereafter attributes Ephesians 5.22–29 to the same writer.

Ephesians was known to have been written by the Apostle Paul, and so the matter stood for 17 centuries. Unitarian Edward Evanson is credited with being the first to assert that Paul was not the author of Ephesians. In a work published in 1792, in a couple of paragraphs, he denounced both Ephesians and Colossians as having been "fabricated by the same opificer." Evanson argued that in view of the time Paul spent at Ephesus and in view of his parting words recorded in Acts 20, it is hardly possible that he could have written to the Ephesians as if he had not yet been there.[4]

Then came Usteri (1824), De Wette (1826), and F.C. Bauer (1845), all finding fault with the notion that Ephesians could have been written by Paul. De Wette found the similarities between Ephesians and Colossians problematic and dismissed Ephesians as "a transcription" and as "unworthy of an Apostle."[5] Edgar J. Goodspeed (1933) also appealed to the many similarities between Ephesians and Colossians, as well as similarities between Ephesians and other Pauline epistles (which similarities he exaggerated), as evidence that Ephesians was not written by Paul. After all, "Paul himself could hardly have so rigidly confined himself to what he had previously written."[6]

De Wette, Goodspeed, and others who have seen similarity between Ephesians and Colossians as suspicious have failed to recognize the distinctive purpose in each. They have failed especially to appreciate the sublime message of Ephesians undisturbed by forays into Gnostic and Judaistic error. In all the New Testament, Ephesians is the most direct, most eloquent, most thorough, and most compelling appeal to Gentiles that they recognize what God has done especially for them and that they therefore respond by walking worthily of their calling.

---

[4] Evanson, 2nd ed. 1805, p. 312f.

[5] De Wette, p. 283.

[6] Goodspeed, p. 9.

Colossians largely follows the general outline of Ephesians but focuses on the particular problem at Colossae. In Ephesians, Paul discussed the gifts God had bestowed on the church, that is, the apostles, prophets, evangelists, pastors and teachers from whom Gentiles would learn how to walk worthily of their calling, thus leading to a practical unity in the body of Christ. But in the corresponding section of Colossians, Paul's discussion of doctrinal error turns pointedly to Judaistic Gnosticism to such a degree that this becomes that for which that epistle is most readily remembered. So then in short, Ephesians is a general appeal to Gentile Christians to abandon the ways of the Gentile world, whereas Colossians is a similar appeal but with a special focus on a particular doctrinal error in a particular location.

Unless we are predisposed to believe Ephesians was written by someone other than Paul at a date later than Colossians, it would never occur to us that the similarities between the two belied the authenticity of the one. We would no more suppose similarity between Colossians and Ephesians discredited Ephesians than we would suppose similarity between Galatians and Romans discredited one or the other.

Regarding the time of composition, the *prima facie* evidence is that the two letters were written at very nearly the same time, both delivered by Tychicus on the same journey (Eph 6.21, Col 4.7–8). A personal letter to Philemon was also conveyed at this time. Onesimus traveled with Tychicus (Col 4.9), and was being sent back to Philemon (Phlm 12). That Philemon and Colossians were written at the same time is further evidenced by the fact that the same group of men (Epaphras, Mark, Aristarchus, Demas, and Luke) were with Paul as he wrote both letters (Phlm 23f, Col 4.10–14). Hence we conclude that all three letters, Ephesians, Colossians and Philemon, were sent at this time. Whether Paul penned Ephesians or Colossians first, surely he had both messages in mind, the general one for all Gentile Christians in the region to which the letters went, and the specific one to apply the same principles to the particular problem in the particular locale of Colossae. It requires a certain audacity to deny Paul the liberty of having proceeded precisely thus.

Nonetheless, it has become commonplace to suppose that Paul would not have written such similar letters at the same time, delivered by the same courier to people in one area. Moreover, the close personal relationship that Paul had with the church at Ephesus seems at odds with such an impersonal letter as Ephesians being sent by Paul to that church. This was Evanson's basis for rejecting the letter's authenticity, and it is why so many in subsequent years have been predisposed to believe Ephesians was written by a later author. As we shall see, the problem lies not in the identification of Paul as the author, but in the identification of the recipients.

Recipients

Comparing Ephesians and Colossians. Shortly, we will take up the matter of the phrase *in Ephesus* at the beginning of this letter. But let us begin discussion of the recipients where we left off in discussing the author. As discussed in the foregoing pages, the similarity between Ephesians and Colossians is seen by some as evidence that Ephesians is nothing more than an imitation of Colossians. There is a better interpretation of the similarity, in view of the differences. The similarity is consistent with the supposition that the letters were written at the same time and to similar audiences. But where there is great similarity, the differences are all the more significant. The primary differences are that Colossians includes a response to a Judaizing element with gnostic tendencies (Col 2.8–23), mention of various individuals at Colossae or known to the Colossians (1.7, 4.9–17), and a reference to Christians at nearby locations (2.2, 2.13–16). These are all local peculiarities. These differences are consistent with the supposition that Colossians was addressed to a specific church in a specific locality wherein there was a specific doctrinal error, while Ephesians, wherein we see no local peculiarities, was addressed to a wider audience.

In order to fully appreciate this point, it will be helpful to lay out the nature and degree of similarity between the two letters. First, the two letters can be usefully outlined in the same way. To be sure, this outline is a better reflection of the structure of Ephesians than of Colossians, partly because Colossians is more personal and less formally structured. But this is a serviceable outline for both letters.

	Ephesians	Colossians
Greeting	1.1–2	1.1–2
WHAT GOD HAS DONE FOR US IN CHRIST	**1.3–3.21**	**1.1–2.5**
All things are in Christ, who is the head of the body	1.3–2.10	1.9–2.5
Our prior condition	2.11–12	1.21
Our reconciliation through Christ	2.12–22	1.22–23
Paul's role in proclaiming the reconciliation	3.1–21	1.24–2.5
HOW WE SHOULD THEREFORE WALK	**4.1–6.20**	**2.6–4.6**
The body is to ber built up, free from error and doctrines of men	4.1–16	2.6–2.23
Put away sin; put on righteousness	4.17–5.21	3.1–17
Instructions to house hold members...	5.22–6.9	3.18–4.1
...to wives	5.22–24	3.18
...to husbands	5.25–33	3.19
...to children	6.1–3	3.20
...to fathers	6.4	3.21
...to servants	6.5–8	3.22–25
...to masters	6.9	4.1
Final exortation, especially to pray, particularly on Paul's behalf that he might speak as he ought	6.10–20	4.2–6
Tychicus to make known Paul's affiars to them	6.21	4.7–8

The similarity is even more striking when we consider the degree to which phrasing found in one letter is also found in the other, often word for word. Passages included in the table below show similarity both in vocabulary, meaning, and context. In one instance, I have regarded a single verb as parallel because it is found in parallel contexts with obviously similar meaning.[7]

---

[7] There are other verbal parallels of vocabulary, and even phrases, that are not included in this list because the similar language is used to make significantly different points in the respective letters. For example, in Eph 1.20 we see καθίσας ἐν δεξιᾷ αὐτοῦ and in Col 3.1 we see ἐστιν ἐν δεξιᾷ τοῦ θεοῦ καθήμενος, but in Colossians the phrase is used of what we should seek whereas in Ephesians it is simply about Christ's exaltation. Again, in both Ephesians 3.19 and Colossians 1.9 we have ἵνα πληρωθῆτε, but in Ephesians it is that they might be filled with all the fulness of God while in Colossians it is Paul asking that they might be filled with the knowledge of God's will, similar ideas to be sure, but not quite

	Ephesians		Colossians
1.1f	Παῦλος ἀπόστολος Χριστοῦ Ἰησοῦ διὰ θελήματος θεοῦ τοῖς ἁγίοις τοῖς οὖσιν [ἐν Ἐφέσῳ] καὶ πιστοῖς ἐν Χριστῷ Ἰησοῦ, χάρις ὑμῖν καὶ εἰρήνη ἀπὸ θεοῦ πατρὸς ἡμῶν	*1.1f*	Παῦλος ἀπόστολος Χριστοῦ Ἰησοῦ διὰ θελήματος θεοῦ...τοῖς ἐν Κολοσσαῖς ἁγίοις καὶ πιστοῖς ἀδελφοῖς ἐν Χριστῷ, χάρις ὑμῖν καὶ εἰρήνη ἀπὸ θεοῦ πατρὸς ἡμῶν
1.4	ἁγίους καὶ ἀμώμους κατενώπιον αὐτοῦ	*1.22b*	ἁγίους καὶ ἀμώμους καὶ ἀνεγκλήτους κατενώπιον αὐτοῦ
1.7a	Ἐν ᾧ ἔχομεν τὴν ἀπολύτρωσιν	*1.14a*	ἐν ᾧ ἔχομεν τὴν ἀπολύτρωσιν
1.7b	διὰ τοῦ αἵματος αὐτοῦ	*1.20*	διὰ τοῦ αἵματος τοῦ σταυροῦ αὐτοῦ
1.7c	τὴν ἄφεσιν τῶν παραπτωμάτων	*1.14b*	τὴν ἄφεσιν τῶν ἁμαρτιῶν
1.8	ἐν πάσῃ σοφίᾳ καὶ φρονήσει	*1.9c*	ἐν πάσῃ σοφίᾳ καὶ συνέσει πνευματικῇ
1.9	τὸ μυστήριον τοῦ θελήματος αὐτοῦ	*1.9b*	τὴν ἐπίγνωσιν τοῦ θελήματος αὐτοῦ
1.10	τὰ ἐπὶ τοῖς οὐρανοῖς καὶ τὰ ἐπὶ τῆς γῆς	*1.20*	εἴτε τὰ ἐπὶ τῆς γῆς εἴτε τὰ ἐν τοῖς οὐρανοῖς
1.13	ὑμεῖς ἀκούσαντες τὸν λόγον τῆς ἀληθείας, τὸ εὐαγγέλιον τῆς σωτηρίας ὑμῶν	*1.5*	ἣν προηκούσατε ἐν τῷ λόγῳ τῆς ἀληθείας τοῦ εὐαγγελίου

---

similar enough to be included in this list. Also in Eph 4.13 we have εἰς ἄνδρα τέλειον, εἰς μέτρον ἡλικίας τοῦ πληρώματος τοῦ Χριστοῦ and in Col 1.28 we have ἄνθρωπον τέλειον ἐν Χριστῷ, similar language. But in Ephesians, the reference is to the body of Christ maturing whereas in Colossians the words are used of individual Christians maturing.

1.15	ἀκούσας τὴν καθ᾽ ὑμᾶς πίστιν ἐν τῷ κυρίῳ Ἰησοῦ καὶ τὴν ἀγάπην τὴν εἰς πάντας τοὺς ἁγίους	1.4	ἀκούσαντες τὴν πίστιν ὑμῶν καὶ τὴν ἀγάπην ἣν ἔχετε εἰς πάντας τοὺς ἁγίους
1.16	οὐ παύομαι εὐχαριστῶν ὑπὲρ ὑμῶν μνείαν ποιούμενος ἐπὶ τῶν προσευχῶν μου	1.9a	οὐ παυόμεθα ὑπὲρ ὑμῶν προσευχόμενοι καὶ αἰτούμενοι
1.18	τίς ὁ πλοῦτος τῆς δόξης	1.27	τί τὸ πλοῦτος τῆς δόξης
1.21	ὑπεράνω πάσης ἀρχῆς καὶ ἐξουσίας καὶ δυνάμεως καὶ κυριότητος	1.16	εἴτε θρόνοι εἴτε κυριότητες εἴτε ἀρχαὶ εἴτε ἐξουσίαι
1.22f	καὶ αὐτὸν ἔδωκεν κεφαλὴν ὑπὲρ πάντα τῇ ἐκκλησίᾳ, ἥτις ἐστὶν τὸ σῶμα αὐτοῦ	1.18	καὶ αὐτός ἐστιν ἡ κεφαλὴ τοῦ σώματος, τῆς ἐκκλησίας
2.1	Καὶ ὑμᾶς ὄντας νεκροὺς τοῖς παραπτώμασιν	2.13a	καὶ ὑμᾶς νεκροὺς ὄντας τοῖς παραπτώμασιν
2.2f	ἐν αἷς ποτε περιεπατήσατε...κατὰ τὸν ἄρχοντα τῆς ἐξουσίας τοῦ ἀέρος, τοῦ πνεύματος τοῦ νῦν ἐνεργοῦντος ἐν τοῖς υἱοῖς τῆς ἀπειθείας· ἐν οἷς καὶ ἡμεῖς πάντες ἀνεστράφημέν ποτε...καὶ ἤμεθα τέκνα φύσει ὀργῆς	3.6f	δι᾽ ἃ ἔρχεται ἡ ὀργὴ τοῦ θεοῦ [ἐπὶ τοὺς υἱοὺς τῆς ἀπειθείας] ἐν οἷς καὶ ὑμεῖς περιεπατήσατέ ποτε
2.5	καὶ ὄντας ἡμᾶς νεκροὺς τοῖς παραπτώμασιν συνεζωοποίησεν τῷ Χριστῷ	2.13	καὶ ὑμᾶς νεκροὺς ὄντας τοῖς παραπτώμασιν...συνεζωοποίησεν ὑμᾶς σὺν αὐτῷ
2.11f	ποτὲ ὑμεῖς τὰ ἔθνη ἐν σαρκί...ἀπηλλοτριωμένοι	1.21	καὶ ὑμᾶς ποτε ὄντας ἀπηλλοτριωμένους

2.13ff	ἐγενήθητε ἐγγὺς ἐν τῷ αἵματι τοῦ Χριστοῦ. Αὐτὸς γάρ ἐστιν ἡ εἰρήνη ἡμῶν, ὁ ποιήσας τὰ ἀμφότερα ἓν…ἵνα τοὺς δύο κτίσῃ ἐν αὐτῷ εἰς ἕνα καινὸν ἄνθρωπον ποιῶν εἰρήνην καὶ ἀποκαταλλάξῃ τοὺς ἀμφοτέρους ἐν ἑνὶ σώματι τῷ θεῷ διὰ τοῦ σταυροῦ	1.20ff	καὶ δι' αὐτοῦ ἀποκαταλλάξαι τὰ πάντα εἰς αὐτόν, εἰρηνοποιήσας διὰ τοῦ αἵματος τοῦ σταυροῦ αὐτοῦ…νυνὶ δὲ ἀποκατηλλάγητε ἐν τῷ σώματι τῆς σαρκὸς αὐτοῦ διὰ τοῦ θανάτου
2.15	τὸν νόμον τῶν ἐντολῶν ἐν δόγμασιν	2.14	χειρόγραφον τοῖς δόγμασιν
3.2	τὴν οἰκονομίαν τῆς χάριτος τοῦ θεοῦ τῆς δοθείσης μοι εἰς ὑμᾶς	1.25	τὴν οἰκονομίαν τοῦ θεοῦ τὴν δοθεῖσάν μοι εἰς ὑμᾶς
3.4f	τῷ μυστηρίῳ τοῦ Χριστοῦ, ὃ ἑτέραις γενεαῖς οὐκ ἐγνωρίσθη	1.26a	τὸ μυστήριον τὸ ἀποκεκρυμμένον ἀπὸ τῶν αἰώνων καὶ ἀπὸ τῶν γενεῶν
3.5	ὡς νῦν ἀπεκαλύφθη τοῖς ἁγίοις ἀποστόλοις αὐτοῦ	1.26b	νῦν δὲ ἐφανερώθη τοῖς ἁγίοις αὐτοῦ
3.7a	οὗ ἐγενήθην διάκονος	1.23	οὗ ἐγενόμην ἐγὼ Παῦλος διάκονος
3.7b	κατὰ τὴν ἐνέργειαν τῆς δυνάμεως αὐτοῦ	1.29	κατὰ τὴν ἐνέργειαν αὐτοῦ τὴν ἐνεργουμένην ἐν ἐμοὶ ἐν δυνάμει.
3.16	τὸ πλοῦτος τῆς δόξης αὐτοῦ	1.27	τί τὸ πλοῦτος τῆς δόξης
3.17	ἐν ἀγάπῃ ἐρριζωμένοι καὶ τεθεμελιωμένοι	2.7	ἐρριζωμένοι καὶ ἐποικοδομούμενοι ἐν αὐτῷ
4.1	ἀξίως περιπατῆσαι τῆς κλήσεως	1.10	περιπατῆσαι ἀξίως τοῦ κυρίου
4.2	ταπεινοφροσύνης καὶ πραΰτητος, μετὰ μακροθυμίας, ἀνεχόμενοι ἀλλήλων	3.12f	ταπεινοφροσύνην, πραΰτητα, μακροθυμίαν, ἀνεχόμενοι ἀλλήλων

4.16	ἐξ οὗ πᾶν τὸ σῶμα συναρμολογούμενον καὶ συμβιβαζόμενον διὰ πάσης ἁφῆς τῆς ἐπιχορηγίας κατ' ἐνέργειαν ἐν μέτρῳ ἑνὸς ἑκάστου μέρους τὴν αὔξησιν τοῦ σώματος ποιεῖται	2.19	πᾶν τὸ σῶμα διὰ τῶν ἁφῶν καὶ συνδέσμων ἐπιχορηγούμενον καὶ συμβιβαζόμενον αὔξει τὴν αὔξησιν τοῦ θεοῦ
4.22ff	ἀποθέσθαι ὑμᾶς κατὰ τὴν προτέραν ἀναστροφὴν τὸν παλαιὸν ἄνθρωπον τὸν φθειρόμενον... ἀνανεοῦσθαι δὲ τῷ πνεύματι τοῦ νοὸς ὑμῶν, καὶ ἐνδύσασθαι τὸν καινὸν ἄνθρωπον τὸν κατὰ θεὸν κτισθέντα ἐν δικαιοσύνῃ καὶ ὁσιότητι τῆς ἀληθείας	3.9f	ἀπεκδυσάμενοι τὸν παλαιὸν ἄνθρωπον σὺν ταῖς πράξεσιν αὐτοῦ, καὶ ἐνδυσάμενοι τὸν νέον τὸν ἀνακαινούμενον εἰς ἐπίγνωσιν κατ' εἰκόνα τοῦ κτίσαντος αὐτόν
4.25	ἀποθέμενοι	3.8a	ἀπόθεσθε
4.29	πᾶς λόγος σαπρὸς ἐκ τοῦ στόματος ὑμῶν μὴ ἐκπορευέσθω	3.8b	αἰσχρολογίαν ἐκ τοῦ στόματος ὑμῶν
4.32	χαριζόμενοι ἑαυτοῖς καθὼς καὶ ὁ θεὸς ἐν Χριστῷ ἐχαρίσατο ὑμῖν.	3.13	καθὼς καὶ ὁ κύριος ἐχαρίσατο ὑμῖν οὕτως καὶ ὑμεῖς
5.3	πορνεία δὲ καὶ ἀκαθαρσία πᾶσα ἢ πλεονεξία	3.5a	πορνείαν ἀκαθαρσίαν πάθος, ἐπιθυμίαν κακήν, καὶ τὴν πλεονεξίαν
5.5	πλεονέκτης, ὅ ἐστιν εἰδωλολάτρης	3.5b	πλεονεξίαν, ἥτις ἐστὶν εἰδωλολατρία
5.6	διὰ ταῦτα γὰρ ἔρχεται ἡ ὀργὴ τοῦ θεοῦ ἐπὶ τοὺς υἱοὺς τῆς ἀπειθείας.	3.6	δι' ἃ ἔρχεται ἡ ὀργὴ τοῦ θεοῦ [ἐπὶ τοὺς υἱοὺς τῆς ἀπειθείας]
5.15f	Βλέπετε οὖν ἀκριβῶς πῶς περιπατεῖτε μὴ ὡς ἄσοφοι ἀλλ' ὡς σοφοί, ἐξαγοραζόμενοι τὸν καιρόν	4.5	Ἐν σοφίᾳ περιπατεῖτε πρὸς τοὺς ἔξω τὸν καιρὸν ἐξαγοραζόμενοι

5.19f	λαλοῦντες ἑαυτοῖς [ἐν] ψαλμοῖς καὶ ὕμνοις καὶ ᾠδαῖς πνευματικαῖς, ᾄδοντες καὶ ψάλλοντες τῇ καρδίᾳ ὑμῶν τῷ κυρίῳ, εὐχαριστοῦντες πάντοτε ὑπὲρ πάντων ἐν ὀνόματι τοῦ κυρίου ἡμῶν Ἰησοῦ Χριστοῦ τῷ θεῷ καὶ πατρί	*3.16f*	διδάσκοντες καὶ νουθετοῦντες ἑαυτούς, ψαλμοῖς ὕμνοις ᾠδαῖς πνευματικαῖς ἐν [τῇ] χάριτι ᾄδοντες ἐν ταῖς καρδίαις ὑμῶν τῷ θεῷ· καὶ πᾶν ὅ τι ἐὰν ποιῆτε ἐν λόγῳ ἢ ἐν ἔργῳ, πάντα ἐν ὀνόματι κυρίου Ἰησοῦ, εὐχαριστοῦντες τῷ θεῷ πατρὶ δι' αὐτοῦ
5.22	αἱ γυναῖκες τοῖς ἰδίοις ἀνδράσιν ὡς τῷ κυρίῳ	*3.18*	Αἱ γυναῖκες, ὑποτάσσεσθε τοῖς ἀνδράσιν, ὡς ἀνῆκεν ἐν κυρίῳ
5.25	Οἱ ἄνδρες, ἀγαπᾶτε τὰς γυναῖκας	*3.19*	Οἱ ἄνδρες, ἀγαπᾶτε τὰς γυναῖκας
5.27	ἵνα παραστήσῃ αὐτὸς ἑαυτῷ ἔνδοξον τὴν ἐκκλησίαν... ἵνα ᾖ ἁγία καὶ ἄμωμος.	*1.22a*	παραστῆσαι ὑμᾶς ἁγίους καὶ ἀμώμους
6.1	Τὰ τέκνα, ὑπακούετε τοῖς γονεῦσιν ὑμῶν [ἐν κυρίῳ]· τοῦτο γάρ ἐστιν δίκαιον	*3.20*	Τὰ τέκνα, ὑπακούετε τοῖς γονεῦσιν κατὰ πάντα, τοῦτο γὰρ εὐάρεστόν ἐστιν ἐν κυρίῳ
6.4	Καὶ οἱ πατέρες, μὴ παροργίζετε τὰ τέκνα ὑμῶν	*3.21*	Οἱ πατέρες, μὴ ἐρεθίζετε τὰ τέκνα ὑμῶν
6.5fff	Οἱ δοῦλοι, ὑπακούετε τοῖς κατὰ σάρκα κυρίοις μετὰ φόβου καὶ τρόμου ἐν ἁπλότητι τῆς καρδίας ὑμῶν ὡς τῷ Χριστῷ, μὴ κατ' ὀφθαλμοδουλίαν ὡς ἀνθρωπάρεσκοι ἀλλ' ὡς δοῦλοι Χριστοῦ ποιοῦντες τὸ θέλημα τοῦ θεοῦ ἐκ ψυχῆς, μετ' εὐνοίας δουλεύοντες, ὡς τῷ κυρίῳ καὶ οὐκ ἀνθρώποις, εἰδότες ὅτι ἕκαστος, ἐάν τι ποιήσῃ ἀγαθόν, τοῦτο κομίσεται παρὰ κυρίου	*3.22ff*	Οἱ δοῦλοι, ὑπακούετε κατὰ πάντα τοῖς κατὰ σάρκα κυρίοις, μὴ ἐν ὀφθαλμοδουλίᾳ ὡς ἀνθρωπάρεσκοι, ἀλλ' ἐν ἁπλότητι καρδίας, φοβούμενοι τὸν κύριον. ὃ ἐὰν ποιῆτε, ἐκ ψυχῆς ἐργάζεσθε ὡς τῷ κυρίῳ καὶ οὐκ ἀνθρώποις, εἰδότες ὅτι ἀπὸ κυρίου ἀπολήμψεσθε τὴν ἀνταπόδοσιν τῆς κληρονομίας. τῷ κυρίῳ Χριστῷ δουλεύετε·

6.9a	Καὶ οἱ κύριοι, τὰ αὐτὰ ποιεῖτε πρὸς αὐτούς, ἀνιέντες τὴν ἀπειλήν, εἰδότες ὅτι καὶ αὐτῶν καὶ ὑμῶν ὁ κύριός ἐστιν ἐν οὐρανοῖς	4.1	Οἱ κύριοι, τὸ δίκαιον καὶ τὴν ἰσότητα τοῖς δούλοις παρέχεσθε, εἰδότες ὅτι καὶ ὑμεῖς ἔχετε κύριον ἐν οὐρανῷ
6.9b	προσωπολημψία οὐκ ἔστιν	3.25	καὶ οὐκ ἔστιν προσωπολημψία
6.18ff	διὰ πάσης προσευχῆς καὶ δεήσεως προσευχόμενοι ἐν παντὶ καιρῷ ἐν πνεύματι, καὶ εἰς αὐτὸ ἀγρυπνοῦντες ἐν πάσῃ προσκαρτερήσει καὶ δεήσει περὶ πάντων τῶν ἁγίων καὶ ὑπὲρ ἐμοῦ, ἵνα μοι δοθῇ λόγος ἐν ἀνοίξει τοῦ στόματός μου, ἐν παρρησίᾳ γνωρίσαι τὸ μυστήριον τοῦ εὐαγγελίου, ὑπὲρ οὗ πρεσβεύω ἐν ἁλύσει, ἵνα ἐν αὐτῷ παρρησιάσωμαι ὡς δεῖ με λαλῆσαι	4.2ff	Τῇ προσευχῇ προσκαρτερεῖτε, γρηγοροῦντες ἐν αὐτῇ ἐν εὐχαριστίᾳ, προσευχόμενοι ἅμα καὶ περὶ ἡμῶν, ἵνα ὁ θεὸς ἀνοίξῃ ἡμῖν θύραν τοῦ λόγου λαλῆσαι τὸ μυστήριον τοῦ Χριστοῦ, δι' ὃ καὶ δέδεμαι, ἵνα φανερώσω αὐτὸ ὡς δεῖ με λαλῆσαι
6.21f	Ἵνα δὲ καὶ ὑμεῖς εἰδῆτε τὰ κατ' ἐμέ, τί πράσσω, πάντα γνωρίσει ὑμῖν Τυχικὸς ὁ ἀγαπητὸς ἀδελφὸς καὶ πιστὸς διάκονος ἐν κυρίῳ, ὃν ἔπεμψα πρὸς ὑμᾶς εἰς αὐτὸ τοῦτο, ἵνα γνῶτε τὰ περὶ ἡμῶν καὶ παρακαλέσῃ τὰς καρδίας ὑμῶν	4.7f	Τὰ κατ' ἐμὲ πάντα γνωρίσει ὑμῖν Τυχικὸς ὁ ἀγαπητὸς ἀδελφὸς καὶ πιστὸς διάκονος καὶ σύνδουλος ἐν κυρίῳ, ὃν ἔπεμψα πρὸς ὑμᾶς εἰς αὐτὸ τοῦτο, ἵνα γνῶτε τὰ περὶ ἡμῶν καὶ παρακαλέσῃ τὰς καρδίας ὑμῶν
6.24	ἡ χάρις μετὰ πάντων τῶν ἀγαπώντων τὸν κύριον ἡμῶν Ἰησοῦν Χριστὸν	4.18	ἡ χάρις μεθ' ὑμῶν

Now with the remarkable similarity clearly in mind, we may well say Colossians is a version, or variation, of Ephesians, and we can give attention to the particular difference that accounts for a distinct letter being sent to the church at Colossae.

In both letters, the second part focuses on the practical matters of walking in accordance with the grace of God in Christ. In Ephesians, this begins with the words, "Therefore I, the prisoner in the Lord, beseech you to walk worthily of the calling with which you were called" (4.1). In Colossians, this begins with the words, "Therefore as you received Christ Jesus the Lord, in him walk" (2.6).

In both letters, Paul indicates that this walk comes about as the result of teaching. In Colossians, the very next verse speaks of how they had been taught. In Ephesians, Paul brings into view the work of the apostles, prophets, evangelists, and pastors who are teachers.

But in Colossians, the teaching is immediately contrasted with a particular error that had arisen at Colossae and those who would promote it, thus making spoil of the saints through a vain and deceitful philosophy. This philosophy was characterized by Judaistic (2.16) and gnostic (2.17–23) elements. In Ephesians, Paul indicates that the teaching will prevent being tossed to and fro and carried about with every wind of doctrine (4.14), but no particular error is addressed.

Thereafter, particularly beginning in Colossians 3.5, the teaching in Colossians addresses the same topics as does that in Ephesians, and these are the same kinds of things that all people coming out the world need to be taught.

So then in Colossians, this attention to a particular doctrinal error, along with the geographically specific references to nearby Laodicea and Hierapolis, and the mention of various individuals in Colossae or known to the Colossians, are the kinds of things we might expect to see in a letter to one specific church. But none of these things are found in Ephesians, though in all other respects the two letters are very similar.

Rather than indicating that Ephesians was a late imitation of Colossians written by an impostor, we may interpret these facts as indicating that the two letters were written at the same time, but that Ephesians was written to Christians in many churches throughout the region, and that a variation of that letter with content specific to a local audience was written to the Colossians.

An Impersonal Letter. The fundamental objection so many have had to attributing the letter to Paul is the impersonal nature of the letter. Paul was at Ephesus for three years, admonishing "every one night and day with tears,"[8] and yet it seems that the letter's intended audience was made up largely of people whom Paul did not know personally, and who did

---

[8] Acts 20.31.

not know him personally. He speaks only of having heard of their faith (1.15). Paul writes to them not as people with whom he had spent three years, people who certainly would have been familiar with his mission as an apostle to the Gentiles, but rather says, "if you heard about the stewardship of the grace of God that was given to me on your behalf."[9]

Furthermore, missing from the letter is any mention of people at Ephesus, greetings from people who knew the Ephesians, or events associated with Paul's time at Ephesus. Those inclined to deny that Paul wrote Ephesians point to the particularly strong ties between Paul and the church at Ephesus. Of all churches, it is hard to imagine Paul would have written to the Ephesian church without mentioning either individuals there or his activities there.

In Colossians, a letter addressed to Christians who, for the most part, had not seen Paul in person (Col 2.1), a letter very similar to Ephesians in content, written at the same time and delivered by the same courier on the same journey, we see personal greetings from Aristarchus, Mark, Jesus who is called Justus, Epaphras, Luke, and Demas. Ephesians includes none. Colossians includes Paul's particular greeting to Archippus, whereas Paul sends no greeting to any particular individual in Ephesians. Paul had made two visits to Ephesus and had spent three years there. Thereafter at Miletus, he met with the elders of the church at Ephesus and they, supposing they would not see his face again, "wept sore, and fell on Paul's neck and kissed him."[10] And yet it is in the letter we know as Ephesians that there are no personal greetings.

To be sure, Ephesians is not unique in this aspect. Neither of Paul's letters to the church at Thessalonica mention anyone at Thessalonica by name. Nor do we find such in 2 Corinthians. It is the absence of such personal touches in Ephesians contrasted with what we see in the companion letter to the Colossians that is striking.

But perhaps even more striking than the absence of any mention of or greetings to particular individuals is the absence of any reference at all to Paul's time at Ephesus. Excluding the letter known as Ephesians, in every case where we have a known letter of Paul to a church that he had visited, we see allusions to his time there.[11] But in Ephesians, there is no mention

---

[9] See the remarks on Eph 3.2.

[10] Acts 20.37.

[11] See 1 Cor 1.14–16, 3.2, 3.2–15, 11.23, 15.1, 2 Cor 1.12, 2.1, 11.2–10 (verse 9, "even when I was present with you") 12.11–14, 13.1–2, Gal 4.12–15, Phil 1.30, 2.12, 1 Th 1.5–6, 1.9, 2.1, 2.6–12,

of, indeed, no hint of, Paul's visit to Ephesus. Aside from the words, "in Ephesus," there is nothing in the letter connecting it uniquely with the church at Ephesus nor with any single church.

There is another letter written by Paul that was intended for a region rather than one specific church, namely, the letter to the Galatians. And therein, as in Ephesians, we find no mention of individuals. As we shall see, like Galatians, the letter known to us as Ephesians was intended for Christians throughout a region, many of whom Paul had never met. And as we shall see, it was addressed especially to Gentile Christians, possibly including those in the churches of Galatia.

So far, then, we have seen that two of the primary arguments lodged against Pauline authorship, namely, the impersonal nature of the letter and the similarity to Colossians, no longer weigh against Pauline authorship. Moreover, the latter argument, in view of the differences between Ephesians and Colossians, is in fact better explained if we understand Ephesians to have been intended for a broader audience that needed to hear the same fundamental message as did the Colossians but without the foray into the specific error that had arisen at Colossae.

But there is evidence even more compelling that this letter was not written uniquely to the church at Ephesus. The same evidence will lead us to conclude that while all the saints at Ephesus could benefit from the letter, not all of them were part of the primary target audience.

A Letter Written to Gentiles. At its founding, the church at Ephesus consisted largely of Jews.[12] There is no mention of Greeks, or even proselytes, among those who heard Paul when he first visited Ephesus. We read only that Paul entered the synagogue and reasoned with the Jews. Though they asked him to stay longer, he did not. But he did leave Aquila, a Jew, and his wife, Priscilla, there.

Apollos, a Jew, visited Ephesus, teaching only the baptism of John until further instructed by Aquila and Priscilla.[13] When Paul returned,[14] the "disciples" whom he found there were no doubt Jews inasmuch as they were men who surely had been influenced by Apollos' teaching either directly or indirectly. This seems to be the reason Luke inserts the account of Apollos at Ephesus prior to discussing Paul's arrival there in about AD

2.17, 3.4, 2 Th 3.7–10. I am indebted to Scott Smelser for this observation.

[12] Acts 18.19*ff.*

[13] Acts 18.24*ff.*

[14] Acts 19.1*ff.*

52. Acts 19.2 may be interpreted as indicating that they were men who were anticipating the pouring out of God's Spirit in accordance with OT prophecies[15] but were unaware that the Spirit had already come.

After enlightening these men, Paul was teaching in the synagogue three months, and he and the rest of the disciples only separated themselves from the unbelieving Jews when the latter began to speak evil of the believing Jews.[16] At this point, the church there seems to have consisted entirely or almost entirely of Jews.

While we know Gentiles came to be included among the saints at Ephesus,[17] it is unlikely that this church had come to consist almost entirely of Gentiles in a half dozen years.[18] But the letter known to us as Ephesians was written specifically to a Gentile audience.

The most conspicuous evidence of this fact is Ephesians 2.11*ff.* But also see 1.13, where the "you also" is in contrast to the "we who had previously hoped in Christ"—that is, the Jews who for generations had hoped in a coming Messiah. If the "we" refers to Jews, then the "you also" refers to the Gentiles.[19] Again in 2.1*ff*, Paul distinguishes between "you," *i.e.*, the Gentiles, and "we also," *i.e.*, the Jews.[20] In 2.17, Paul's readers are addressed in the second person, "you who were far off" (*i.e.*, Gentiles) while the Jews are mentioned obliquely, "those who were near." And again, in 3.1 Paul addresses his audience as Gentiles and speaks of "the dispensation of the grace of God that has been given me toward you," a clear reference to his particular mission to preach to Gentiles.

So then, inasmuch as the letter was written to Gentiles, its primary recipients could hardly have been the entire church at Ephesus wherein there were surely many Jews. And given the absence of individual greetings and more especially the absence of any mention of Paul's time at Ephesus, as well as the indications that the letter was written to an audience made up in large part of many whom Paul did not know, the letter can hardly have been written solely to the entire church at Ephesus.

---

[15] Cf. Acts 1.6, Ezek 36.27, 37.14, Joel 2.28*f.*

[16] Acts 19.8–9.

[17] Acts 19.10,17,26; 20.21.

[18] This assumes Paul left Ephesus no earlier than AD 55, and wrote "Ephesians" about AD 61. See the discussion of the date of the letter below.

[19] See the notes on 1.13. That the "we" and "you" referred to Jews and Gentiles respectively was the understanding of Terullian, (Adv. Marcionem, 5.17). Chrysostom's remarks on the passage seem to presuppose the same understanding, (Homily 2 on Ephesians).

[20] See the notes on 2.1–5.

"In Ephesus"? In the early centuries, Irenaeus, Clement of Alexandria,[21] and Basil all recognized the letter as having been addressed to the Ephesians. Irenaeus referred to it as the "epistle to the Ephesians" three times[22] and once cited a passage from the letter as what "the apostle says to the Ephesians."[23] Only the speculation of Marcion, that it was written to the Laodiceans, comes down to us as an opposing view.

Some manuscripts, very few to be sure, omit the words "in Ephesus" in Ephesians 1.1. The extant manuscript evidence is heavily in favor of the reading "to the saints in Ephesus." Ninety-nine percent of the manuscripts that include verse one have "in Ephesus."[24]

At this point we might be inclined to ask, τί ἔτι χρείαν ἔχομεν μαρτύρων (*what need do we yet have of witnesses?*), supposing the textual question to be settled. But in the early centuries, manuscripts that omitted the words "in Ephesus" were more prevalent, such that some well learned men understood the true reading of the text to exclude the words. One ancient writer seemed to be unaware of manuscripts that included the words. Among all manuscripts extant today that include Ephesians 1.1, among those that lack the words ἐν Ἐφέσῳ are the three oldest.[25]

We can be more confident of any conclusion about the reading of Ephesians 1.1, either retaining or omitting the words ἐν Ἐφέσῳ, if we can account for the existence of the alternative reading. If the words ἐν Ἐφέσῳ were original, what can account for the omission of the words in those earliest manuscripts? This is a more difficult question than the alternative one, that being, what accounts for the presence of the words in so many manuscripts if the letter was not uniquely addressed to the church at Ephesus? As we shall see, there are reasonable explanations for the presence of the words ἐν Ἐφέσῳ in so many later manuscripts even if the letter was not intended especially for the church at Ephesus, but rather for a larger, primarily Gentile, audience.

The Greek behind the traditional text is τοῖς ἁγίοις τοῖς οὖσιν ἐν

---

[21] Strom. IV.8 (64.1-GCS II, P. 277), Paed. i.5 (18.3= GCS I, p. 100).

[22] Adv. Her. v.2.3, v.8.1, v.24.4.

[23] Adv. Her. v.14.3.

[24] This statement is derived from Kurt Aland's tally of MSS readings for Eph. 1:1 in Text und Textwert der Griechischen Handschriften des Neuen Testaments, 2, Die Paulinischen Briefe, Band 3: Galaterbrief Bis Philipperbrief, p. 356f, Walter De Gruyter:Berlin, 1991.

[25] 𝔓46 (c. AD 200), and the fourth century uncials Sinaiticus and Vaticanus, both of which have ἐν Ἐφέσῳ added in the margin by a later hand.

Ἐφέσῳ καὶ πιστοῖς ἐν Χριστῷ Ἰησοῦ, *to the saints the ones being in Ephesus and faithful in Christ Jesus.* Approximately 580 manuscripts have τοῖς οὖσιν ἐν Ἐφέσῳ, and another eighteen have variations of this phrase, all of which include the words ἐν Ἐφέσῳ.[26] Five manuscripts in their original form lacked the words ἐν Ἐφέσῳ, and in a sixth, the words were marked as inauthentic.[27]

If we suppose the words ἐν Ἐφέσῳ ought not be there and then try to translate the phrase, the critical issue involves the participle οὖσιν (*being*). *Being* what? Do we attempt to find something else in the passage that tells us what they were being, other than *"in Ephesus"*? Do we suppose it means *"to those being saints and faithful in Christ Jesus,"* or *"to the saints, the ones who are being also faithful in Christ Jesus"*? Or does οὖσιν stand alone as some sort of existential affirmation, *"to the saints, those existing, and to faithful ones in Christ"* i.e.,*"to the existing saints and faithful ones in Christ Jesus"*?[28]

Origen (third century) appears to have been unaware of a text that included the words ἐν Ἐφέσῳ and grappled with the meaning of the text as he had it. He went the existential route, taking οὖσιν in an absolute sense. He alluded to Exodus 3, supposing that just as God's name was *the one who is* (Ex 3.14), perhaps so also those who partake of his being become *the ones who are*.[29] But the significant thing here is not so much Origen's attempt at explaining the meaning in the absence of the words

---

[26] This tally is based on Kurt Aland's collation of MSS readings for Eph. 1.1 in Text und Textwert der Griechischen Handschriften des Neuen Testaments, Vol. 2 Die Paulinischen Briefe, Band 3: Galaterbrief Bis Philipperbrief, p. 356f , Walter De Gruyter:Berlin, 1991.

[27] The five are the very early 𝔓[46] (c. AD 200), the fourth century uncials Sinaiticus and Vaticanus (both of which have the words added in the margin by a later hand), the sixth century Claromontanus, and the tenth century minuscule 1739. A corrector of the eleventh century minuscule 424 marked the words as inauthentic.

[28] An absolute use of the participle is certainly possible in some contexts. We see it in 1 Cor. 1.28, τὰ μὴ ὄντα... τὰ ὄντα, *"the things that are not...the things that are."* But Paul's formulaic greetings argue against understanding the participle in such an absolute sense in Eph. 1.1.

[29] Lightfoot, 378. Not only is this absolute use contrary to Paul's usage in the greetings in his various epistles, but it can also be said that expecting a prepositional phrase following the participle and indicating where the saints are is consistent with usage elsewhere here in Ephesians. In Ephesians 4.18, τὴν ἄγνοιαν τὴν οὖσαν ἐν αὐτοῖς is structurally parallel to τοῖς ἁγίοις τοῖς οὖσιν ἐν Ἐφέσῳ. In both phrases we have an articular substantive followed by an attributive phrase involving a participle of εἰμί with a prepositional phrase introduced by ἐν explaining wherein the substantive resides: the ignorance that is *in them*, and the saints who are *in Ephesus*.

ἐν Ἐφέσῳ as it is simply the fact that in the letter as he knew it, the words ἐν Ἐφέσῳ were absent.

In the fourth century, as the debate concerning the nature of the Father and the Son raged, the word οὐσία in the sense of "substance" was much discussed. Writing in opposition to the Arian views of Eunomius and charging him with denying the οὐσία of the Son, Basil cited a version of Ephesians 1.1 which he said was found in the old manuscripts, and which he thought helped his case in that it lacked the words ἐν Ἐφέσῳ, leaving what he interpreted as Paul's description of the saints as *the ones who are*, just as Christ is *the one who is*.

> But also writing to the Ephesians as truly having been united through knowledge with the one who is, he named them particularly as *being*, saying, "To the saints who *are*, and are faithful in Christ Jesus." For thus also those before us have handed it down, and thus we have found it in the old samples of the copies.[30]

Basil reasoned much as Origen did a century earlier. But again, what is valuable here is not the meaning Origen and Basil ascribed to the text absent the words ἐν Ἐφέσῳ, but simply the fact that in the third and fourth centuries it was supposed that the original reading of the text lacked the words ἐν Ἐφέσῳ.

At about the time that Basil wrote this, Codex Sinaiticus and Codex Vaticanus were produced, both of which originally lacked the words ἐν Ἐφέσῳ at Ephesians 1.1.[31]

Clearly, even though Origen and Basil supposed the authentic reading of Ephesians 1.1 did not include the words "in Ephesus," they nonetheless understood the letter to have been written to the Ephesians. But one may make the case that the epistle was not universally reckoned to have been addressed to the Ephesians until late in the second century. The earliest reference to the letter as having been written to the Ephesians comes from Irenaeus near the end of the second century. Before that, the only explicit mention of a destination for the letter is that of Marcion who speculated that it was written to the Laodiceans.

---

[30] Adv. Eunomius. ἀλλὰ καὶ τοῖς Ἐφεσίοις ἐπιστέλλων ὡς γνησίως ἡνωμένοις τῷ ὄντι δι' ἐπιγνώσεως ὄντας αὐτοὺς ἰδιαζόντως ὠνόμασεν, εἰπών· Τοῖς ἁγίοις τοῖς οὖσι καὶ πιστοῖς ἐν Χριστῷ Ἰησοῦ. Οὕτω γὰρ καὶ οἱ πρὸ ἡμῶν παραδεδώκασι, καὶ ἡμεῖς ἐν τοῖς παλαιοῖς τῶν ἀντιγράφων εὑρήκαμεν.

[31] In both codices, the words ἐν Ἐφέσῳ are added in the margin.

The letter written by Ignatius to the Ephesian church contains one hint suggesting that in Ignatius' day (or in the day of whomever may have been the author if its authorship is questioned), the letter we know as Ephesians may not have been universally recognized as having been addressed to the Ephesians. Ignatius urges them to pray without ceasing, using exactly the same wording as that found, not in Ephesians 6.18 (προσευχόμενοι ἐν παντὶ καιρῷ), but rather in 1 Thessalonians 5.17 (ἀδιαλείπτως προσεύχεσθε). If Ignatius had understood our letter to have been written to the Ephesians, and if writing to that same congregation he had desired to urge them to pray without ceasing, and if he were inclined to quote from one of Paul's letters in so urging them, would it not seem likely that he would have quoted the words from the very letter Paul himself had sent them?[32]

Well then, if we find reason to doubt that the text originally said ἐν Ἐφέσῳ but reject the explanations of the text as explained by Basil and Origen absent the words ἐν Ἐφέσῳ, is there a better explanation of the meaning of the text sans ἐν Ἐφέσῳ?

Some suggest τοῖς ἁγίοις τοῖς οὖσιν is *to those who are holy i.e., to the saints*.[33] οὖσιν is indeed used of a person or persons being (or not being) characterized by some trait e.g., *being Romans* (Ac 16.21), *being called* (Rom 8.28), *not being gods* (Gal 4.8).

But in Ephesians 1.1, we must understand οὖσιν to anticipate some location. That is because the wording of the greeting is very similar to Paul's greetings in other epistles.[34] Where we see this similar greeting, the addressees are always described as being in some location. Philippians is addressed to "all the saints in Christ Jesus τοῖς οὖσιν ἐν Φιλίπποις." 1 Corinthians was addressed to "the church of God τῇ οὔσῃ ἐν Κορίνθῳ." In 2 Corinthians 1.1 the participle *being* occurs twice, once in the singular and once in the plural: "to the church of God τῇ οὔσῃ ἐν Κορίνθῳ with all the saints τοῖς οὖσιν ἐν ὅλῃ τῇ Ἀχαΐᾳ." Similarly, Romans was addressed to πᾶσιν τοῖς οὖσιν ἐν Ῥώμῃ. And besides the greetings, we should note

---

[32] That Ignatius was familiar with this letter may be evidenced by his description of those in the church at Ephesus as "being imitators of God" (μιμηταὶ ὄντες Θεοῦ, Ad Eph. 1.1), language perhaps based on Ephesians 5.1 (μιμηταὶ τοῦ θεοῦ), and perhaps also by his letter to Polycarp (Ad Poly. 6.2) wherein he uses metaphors of armor similar to, though not identical to, Paul's metaphors in Ephesians 6.13*ff*.

[33] *e.g.*, Schnackenburger, p. 41. Schnackenburger concedes this is not in keeping with Paul's usual greeting, but he believes the letter was written by a pseudonymous author.

[34] Compare also Luke's τῆς ἐκκλησίας τῆς οὔσης ἐν Ἰερουσαλὴμ (Acts 11.22).

1 Thessalonians 2.14, τῶν ἐκκλησιῶν τοῦ θεοῦ τῶν οὐσῶν ἐν τῇ Ἰουδαίᾳ ἐν Χριστῷ Ἰησοῦ. Galatians, Colossians, and 2 Thessalonians all include a mention of the location of the recipients in the greeting, though without the participle *being*. We may say that, excluding the letters to individuals, all of Paul's letters include a mention of the location of the recipients, unless this letter labeled Ephesians is the sole exception.

We must, therefore, expect that the greeting provides an answer to the question, "being where?" But is the answer necessarily, or only, Ephesus?

An Encyclical. Paul's letter was carried by Tychicus (6.21–22). The letter to the church at Colossae was also carried by Tychicus (4.7–8).[35] Accompanied by Onesimus (Col 4.7–9), Tychicus also carried the letter to Philemon at this time.

Tychicus was a native of Asia.[36] He was mentioned in connection with Trophimus who was an Ephesian, suggesting the possibility that Tychicus also was from Ephesus. It may also be noted that Paul would later send Tychicus to Ephesus again, not merely en route to other places, but as a destination (2 Tim 4.12). If indeed Tychicus were an Ephesian, it might be especially likely that, traveling from Rome to Colossae, he would make port at Ephesus and travel inland from there.

In any event, one writer has noted that a popular route for those traveling from Rome to the East was to take the Appian Way across Italy, then sail across the Adriatic Sea, then follow the Egnatian way to Thessalonica, and then sail to Ephesus from whence they could continue to points throughout the East. Whether Tychicus took this route, or sailed from Italy directly to Asia, Ephesus would have been a likely jumping off point to begin his travel across the Anatolian peninsula, and all the more so if he were indeed a native Ephesian.

From Ephesus, he would have traveled southeast a short distance to Magnesia and the road that ran eastward along the Maeander River. Not far beyond Magnesia was Tralles, each of these cities being the location of a church in the early part of the second century. Were there already Christians in these cities as Tychicus passed through them? Luke tells us that during Paul's stay in Ephesus, "all they that dwelt in Asia heard the word

---

[35] This is stated in almost identical words in the two letters. In Ephesians, there is an introductory "and that you also might know," and Paul adds the two words τί πράσσω (*what I do*), while in Colossians, Paul adds the two words καὶ σύνδουλος (*and fellow-slave*). Otherwise, the passages are identical.

[36] Acts 20.4.

of the Lord."[37] He further reports Demetrius' complaint that "not alone at Ephesus but almost throughout all Asia, this Paul hath persuaded and turned away much people, saying that they are no gods, that are made with hands."[38]

Continuing east along the road through the Maeander Valley, Tychicus would have come to the point where the Lycus River joined the Maeander. From there continuing east along the Lycus River, he would arrive at Laodicea. Just a few miles to the north, across the valley, lay Hierapolis. And then no more than a dozen miles upstream, he would come to Colossae, just about 100 miles from Ephesus. Carrying with him not only a letter specifically addressed to the church at Colossae in which Paul had confronted the particular errors afflicting the saints there (and a personal letter to Philemon), Tychicus also had copies of this similar but more general letter, copies to be distributed to the various churches along the way. No doubt he left one at Ephesus, and in that copy, there were the words, τοῖς ἁγίοις τοῖς οὖσιν ἐν Ἐφέσῳ καὶ πιστοῖς ἐν Χριστῷ Ἰησοῦ. Did he also leave a copy at Magnesia and another at Tralles? Or if indeed those churches already existed at that time, did he suppose that they were close enough to Ephesus that it would be easy for them to get access to the copy at Ephesus? After all, it was an expensive process to make multiple copies, and where proximity allowed sharing, that would be desirable.[39]

But Laodicea was too far inland to make it easy for the brethren there to readily and frequently consult the copy at Ephesus. And so a copy of the same letter left at Ephesus was delivered to the church at Laodicea. And their copy may well have had the words τοῖς ἁγίοις τοῖς οὖσιν ἐν Λαοδικείᾳ καὶ πιστοῖς ἐν Χριστῷ Ἰησοῦ, thus giving rise to Marcion's later insistence that what we know as Ephesians was actually written to the Laodiceans. But Colossae was only a dozen miles away, and the saints

---

[37] Acts 19.10.

[38] Acts 19.26.

[39] I am not enamored of the theory that a blank space was left in the greeting and that Tychicus was expected to fill in the name of each city where he delivered a copy of the letter. It seems more likely to me that Tychicus left Rome with just a few copies, each already addressed to the saints in a particular city. Probably he had one addressed to Ephesus, most likely one addressed to Laodicea, and perhaps a very few others. But it would have been cumbersome to have carried many copies all the way from Rome. In most instances, it would have been expected that unaddressed churches would gain access to the copy at a nearby church (as the Colossians were instructed to read the letter that was in the Laodiceans' possession), or that copies would be made from one delivered by Tychicus and further distributed.

there, as well as the saints at Hierapolis, could easily have access to the copy that was left at Laodicea. And in any event, a separate, similar letter (known to us as Colossians), was being delivered especially to the Colossian brethren. Still, the more general letter would be of value to them as well, and Paul told the Colossians that they should "read the epistle from Laodicea," not meaning a letter written by the Laodiceans, but meaning a letter that the Colossians could obtain from the Laodiceans.[40]

If we grant that "from Laodicea" refers to the location of the letter and not to the writers of the letter, we are compelled to understand this to be a letter sent by Paul. If Paul did not have in mind a letter that he himself was sending to Laodicea by the hand of Tychicus, how was it that Paul, nearly a thousand miles away in Rome, knew at the time he was writing Colossians that when Tychicus would arrive in Colossae, there would be a letter at Laodicea which the Colossian saints should also read? Even if he had been made aware of some letter already in the possession of the Laodicean saints, how could he know it would still be in their possession weeks later when Tychicus would arrive in Colossae? If it were a letter suitable for circulating, how could he know it would not have been sent over to Hierapolis, or up to Philadelphia, by the time Tychicus arrived? Paul's certainty that the letter from the Laodiceans would be available to the Colossians when Tychicus arrived is a strong indication that the letter "from the Laodiceans" was one he himself was sending to the Laodiceans by Tychicus.

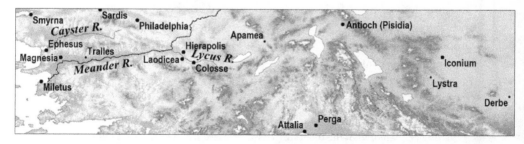

In Ephesians, Paul tells his readers that he has previously written to them about the mystery having been made known to him by revelation, and that he was charged especially with the responsibility of preaching to the Gentiles (Eph 3.1–4). Unless we can suppose that Paul refers to

---

[40] Col 4.16. For a thorough discussion of the various theories that have been proposed for the identity of the letter "from Laodicea," see J. B. Lightfoot, Saint Paul's Epistles to the Colossians and to Philemon, a Revised Text, pp. 274–300.

something he wrote earlier in Ephesians (and I think we cannot[41]), we must suppose that many among the recipients of Ephesians had read or could read an earlier letter written by Paul. The following scenario could identify a readership of Ephesians who would have also read such a previous letter.

If Tychicus continued eastward following the road from Colossae, he would have passed through the great market city of Apameia, and shortly thereafter he would have crossed into the province of Galatia where were the cities of Antioch, Iconium, Lystra, and Derbe.[42] Ramsay described this route as one of only two that traversed Asia Minor:

> Now the centre of Asia Minor is occupied by a great salt lake and a salt desert, and there are only two routes across the plateau from east to west, one south and the other north of the desert....The southern route is the great highway of the Graeco-Roman period....It is a far shorter way from Ephesos to the Cilician Gates than the northern route, which involves an immense détour. It is also by far the easier.[43]

And Ramsay added this: "It is an interesting and suggestive detail that the gate of Laodiceia ad Lycum, through which this road issued, was called the 'Syrian Gate.' The custom of naming city-gates according to the chief object of the road which issued through them is well known."[44] Clearly, had Tychicus intended to travel from Ephesus to the cities of southern Galatia, this would have been his route, and just as clearly, Laodicea lay in his path. Of course, we know that he intended to go to Colossae, just beyond Laodicea, but we are now suggesting that he intended to go further, and carry copies of Paul's letter to churches in Galatia.

Antioch, Iconium, Lystra, and Derbe were cities where many Gentiles had become Christians and where Jews had opposed the gospel from the beginning.[45] At Antioch, Gentiles "glorified the word of God" while Jews stirred up persecution. At Iconium, both Jews and Greeks believed, but

---

[41] See the comments on 3.1–4.

[42] Ramsay described this route in reverse: "The ordinary route for trade between Antioch and the west coast passed through Apameia and Colossae and Laodicea." The Church in the Roman Empire, p. 93.

[43] Ramsay, The Historical Geography of Asia Minor, p. 27.

[44] Ibid. p. 35.

[45] Acts 13.45–48, 14.19, 14.27.

others among the Jews worked to undermine the work of Paul and Barnabas. In Lystra, Paul and Barnabas had so greatly impressed the pagan Gentiles that they were deemed gods. It appears some became believers, because when Paul was resuscitated after having been stoned nearly to death by Jews who came from Antioch and Iconium, there were disciples standing around him. When Paul and Barnabas returned to Antioch of Syria, they described the events of the journey, reporting that God had opened a door of faith unto the Gentiles.[46] The letter we know as Ephesians, written as it was to Gentile Christians, would have been a very appropriate message for Christians in these cities.

This could account for Paul's apparent reference in Ephesians 3.3 to an earlier letter. Paul had indeed written an earlier letter to these Christians, the letter to the churches of Galatia. Therein he had indeed described how that by revelation the mystery had been made known to him and that he had been sent to the Gentiles, and he had described all of this in "a few words." Galatians 1.11–16 may be the few words Paul references in Ephesians 3.3.

Why would Paul make reference to a previous letter as if all the recipients of the present letter had read it when in fact the previous letter was only sent to the churches of Galatia, a mere subset at best, of the recipients of the present letter? We may only suppose Paul was aware that his letters were being circulated beyond their original audience, and that so many years after the composition of Galatians, that letter had been read by Christians throughout the Anatolian peninsula.

But this conjecture that Paul intended the present letter for the churches of Galatia as well as those of Asia runs up against another problem. If the phrase "as I wrote before in few words" refers to something in the letter to the churches of Galatia, then in that very same breath to say, "If then you heard about the dispensation of the grace of God that has been given me toward you" would seem to cast doubt on the Galatian brethren's knowledge of Paul's mission. That the Galatian Christians could have been ignorant of Paul's particular mission to the Gentiles would have been inconceivable at one point in history.

However, if we consider the fact that a dozen years passed between Paul's last visit to any of the Galatian churches and the writing of the present letter, it could be assumed that there might be many new converts

---

[46] Acts 14.27. Cf. 15.12.

among the churches of Galatia, people who had never met Paul. Surely even they were familiar with his letter to the churches of Galatia. But in writing to people whom he has never met, while supposing that they may well have read what he had written about his particular mission to the Gentiles, Paul's manner of referring to this is exactly what one would expect: "If then you heard about the dispensation of the grace of God that has been given me toward you, namely that according to revelation the mystery was made known to me..." There is no presumption, but there is recognition that they likely are aware of these things.

So who were the intended recipients of the letter we know as Ephesians? We have already shown that they were a large audience, not limited to one church. We have already shown that they included many whom Paul had not personally met. But they were people whom Tychicus could and would visit, and so we understand that this letter was sent to a specific geographic destination, but an area wherein were churches made up largely of Gentiles.

It is reasonable to conclude that the intended recipients were the Gentiles among the churches of Asia and Galatia, especially those along the route one would traverse from Ephesus to Derbe. Multiple copies of this same letter were conveyed by Tychicus, one saying, "to the saints in Ephesus," one saying "to the saints in Laodicea," and so on.[47] Not every church along this route received its own copy, with the name of its city in the introduction. The church at Colossae was referred to the copy that went to the Laodiceans. The church at Hierapolis may also have been referred to the copy that went to the Laodiceans inasmuch as Hierapolis was even closer to Laodicea than was Colossae. Hierapolis was just a half dozen miles across the valley from Laodicea.

Though each copy might bear the name of the city to which it was delivered by Tychicus, these would be re-copied, and then these second generation copies would be distributed to an even larger audience. The copy that went to Ephesus, that rightly contained the words ἐν Ἐφέσῳ,

---

[47] Or is it possible that Paul's original letter said, τοῖς ἁγίοις τοῖς οὖσιν ἐν τοῖς ἔθνεσι καὶ πιστοῖς ἐν Χριστῷ Ἰησοῦ (cf. Acts 1523)? Given what we see to be the manifest purpose of the letter, this is a very attractive thought. However, two points are to be urged against it: 1) No extant manuscript has this reading nor is there any mention in any of the ancient writers of any manuscripts ever having had this reading, and it is a dangerous thing to conjecture readings for which there is no manuscript evidence, and 2) had this been the original reading, it would be difficult to explain the prevalence of manuscripts that substitute the name of a city for τοῖς ἔθνεσι.

must have been the copy from whence most second generation copies were made for posterity. Why did this come to be?

Why Did the Letter Come To Be Associated with Ephesus? If Tychicus followed the route suggested above, the saints at Ephesus would have become the first recipients of the letter. Word of the letter's contents and its existence at Ephesus might have spread from that prominent city before Tychicus had even delivered copies to some cities. It may well be that as Tychicus continued along the Maeander toward the Lycus River valley, scribes were already busy making copies of the original letter left at Ephesus, and these copies were being disseminated throughout Asia, bearing the name of the city that was found in the original. Thus even though Smyrna, Pergamum, Thyatira, Sardis, and Philadelphia did not lay along Tychicus' route, churches in those cities could have received copies containing the words "in Ephesus." It is worth mentioning that all of these cities were closer to Ephesus than was Laodicea. So then very early on, even before Tychicus had completed his trip, a version of this letter with the words "in Ephesus" could have become widespread.

Besides the likelihood of copies being distributed from Ephesus to the churches of Asia not visited by Tychicus, there are other factors that could have contributed to the eventual preponderance of manuscripts wherein the letter is addressed to the saints "in Ephesus." Perhaps Tychicus was indeed from Ephesus as suggested earlier. If he ultimately returned to Ephesus after Paul's death, his close relationship with Paul and his part in the dissemination of the letter could have enhanced the standing of the version of the letter that went to the church there.

Perhaps the church at Ephesus was especially diligent in maintaining the original writings of the apostles. There is the claim that as late as the seventh century, the church in Ephesus still held the autograph of the gospel of John.[48] If what Tychicus had delivered remained at Ephesus for some centuries, conceivably this too could have enhanced the standing of the reading, ἐν Ἐφέσῳ.

It may also be noted that Ephesus had been designated the capital of proconsular Asia during the reign of Augustus, and it is not inconceivable that the copy that went to the capital city, more so than any other copy circulated among the intended audience at least in Asia, would on

---

[48] Chronicon Paschale, vol. 1 ed. Ludwig August Dindorf, Impensis ed. Weberi:Bonnae 1832.

that account be the copy to which later generations would appeal. But in addition to the secular status of the city, already in the second century the church at Ephesus was reckoned as famous in its own right. Ignatius referred to the church there as "famous unto all the ages."[49]

Perhaps the most compelling factor of all is the same dynamic that led to the development of a hierarchy of bishops. It should be remembered that in the early centuries, in the face of gnostic heresy there was a conscious effort to hold up certain churches as being the standard bearers of orthodoxy. The church at Ephesus was among these churches. Late in the second century, in his effort to undermine the influence of gnostic teachers, Irenaeus wrote, "Suppose there arise a dispute relative to some important question among us, should we not have recourse to the most ancient Churches with which the apostles had constant intercourse, and learn from them what is certain and clear in regard to the present question?"[50] At that time, which churches were especially so regarded? They were those that had come to be recognized as "apostolic mother churches," namely, the churches in Jerusalem, Antioch of Syria, Alexandria, Ephesus, Corinth and Rome.[51] Misguided as it was to appeal to *who* says what rather than to *what God* said, this was the state of affairs; it was urged that appeal be made to the practice of these churches in testing competing doctrines. Of all the churches in Asia Minor that might have been original recipients of a copy of the letter we know as Ephesians, only the church at Ephesus attained the dubious distinction of being an "apostolic mother church." Is it surprising then that a letter originally sent in various forms, each with a different city identified in the greeting, would eventually be preserved for posterity in the form containing the name of Ephesus rather than, say, Lystra? And is it surprising that even in those few existing manuscripts where the words ἐν Ἐφέσῳ are absent in Paul's greeting, the title nonetheless says "Ephesians"?

The evidence indicates that Paul intended something, some phrase indicating the intended audience, to follow τοῖς οὖσιν. The evidence also indicates that it was not necessarily Ephesus. But the evidence for ἐν Ἐφέσῳ is very strong, even compelling. So what could account for all of

---

[49] To the Ephesians, 8, transl. by Lightfoot.

[50] NPNF. Adv. Her. III.iv.1

[51] Schaff, vol 2, p. 153.

this evidence? The foregoing explanation accounts for all of this, as well as Paul's reference in Ephesians 3.4 to a previous letter.

I believe the foregoing also addresses some of the objections some have had to one theory or another. Meyer offered two choices: Either we accept that the letter was specifically written to the church at Ephesus, or we suppose the letter was "a *catholic* one, without any limitation whatever of locality or nationality of the readers."[52] The latter alternative is of course untenable. Whoever the intended recipients were, they were sufficiently local and identifiable that Tychicus could be sent to them (Eph 6.21*f*). And they were sufficiently identifiable that Paul could say he had heard of their faith and love (Eph 1.15). So then the letter cannot be supposed to have been catholic, that is, written in the first place to all the body of Christ at large (though certainly the Spirit intended that ultimately it would benefit the body of Christ at large). But we are only forced to accept the alternative, that it was written only to the church at Ephesus, if we suppose that is the only alternative. And as we have seen, it is not. The letter was addressed to churches throughout a limited area, the area that Tychicus would visit.

Again, Meyer offered only two possibilities concerning the text of verse one. Either we must admit that ἐν Ἐφέσῳ is the original reading, or we must strike it altogether and derive some sensible meaning out of τοῖς ἁγίοις τοῖς οὖσιν καὶ πιστοῖς, an unenviable task indeed as Meyer well shows. But again, as we have seen, these are not the only two possibilities. An original version of Paul's letter did contain the words "in Ephesus." But versions of the letter that went to some other churches contained the names of other cities.

By accepting a false dilemma, Meyer was forced to suppose that by the time Paul wrote this letter, the church at Ephesus had come to be primarily Gentile.[53] On the theory we have put forward herein, there is no need to make such an assumption.

Best finds fault with any theory that both reckons the letter to be authentically Pauline and also accepts the phrase "in Ephesus" as authentic on the grounds that the letter in no way acknowledges Paul's evangelistic work with that church.[54] (As noted earlier, this was the basis for the origi-

---

[52] Meyer, p. 291.

[53] Ibid., p. 287.

[54] Best, "Recipients and Title of the Letter to the Ephesians" ANRW Band II.25.4 p. 3248.

nal repudiations of Pauline authorship.) However, such acknowledgement is only to be expected if the letter were uniquely addressed to the church at Ephesus. Such an acknowledgement would be less likely if it was Paul's aim to address Gentiles throughout Asia, and perhaps also Galatia.

And so I think we have herein put forward a theory that does not run up against the difficulties felt by many. To be sure, we cannot with certainty perfectly explain the circumstances of this letter, to whom it was written, and what variations there were in the introductions of the original versions of the letter. We can only put forward a reasonable explanation that accounts for the facts we have, thus demonstrating the unnecessary impatience of those who are quick to conclude that Paul did not write this letter.

And yet, even in view of the necessity of maintaining some reservation, the theory put forward herein has been put forward not merely as one speculative possibility among many, but in the hope that the reader might find it as compelling as has the author. This much we can say with some measure of confidence: Paul composed the letter we know as Ephesians having in mind a larger audience than just the church at Ephesus. There need be little doubt that it was intended for Gentile Christians in multiple churches, and especially those of the Lycus and Maeander valleys.

That copies of the letter received at Ephesus were promptly distributed among all the churches of Asia other than those visited by Tychicus seems very likely inasmuch as that would go far in explaining why later manuscripts containing the words "in Ephesus" predominate. That Tychicus continued eastward from Colossae into Galatia to deliver copies of the letter to Antioch, Iconium, Lystra and Derbe and that Paul had in mind Christians in those cities when he composed the letter is less certain. But this scenario is a reasonable explanation of Paul's reference to an earlier letter, in which case we would understand that earlier letter to be Galatians.

Remaining Difficulties. Even so, uncertainties remain. If the letter was written to Gentiles, and if the church at Ephesus was largely made up of Jews, how could a version of Paul's letter be addressed simply to the "saints in Ephesus" as if to the whole church there? And if the letter was an encyclical, why not address the letter "to the churches of Asia," or "to the churches of Asia and Galatia," just as Paul had previously written a letter to "the churches of Galatia"? And again, if Tychicus delivered versions to various churches with the name of the respective city included in the greeting, why did some early manuscripts have no mention of any city, whether Ephesus or some other? And finally, why would Paul refer to a previous letter as if all the recipients of the present letter had read it when in fact the previous letter was only sent to the churches of Galatia, a subset at most of the recipients of the present letter? Though we cannot with certainty answer these questions, a few thoughts may be considered.

If the letter was written to Gentiles, and if the church at Ephesus was largely made up of Jews, how could a version of Paul's letter be addressed simply to the "saints in Ephesus" as if to the whole church there? That Paul wrote having especially the Gentiles in mind would have been evident from the contents of the letter itself. But we may suppose Tychicus delivered the letter to the whole church (all the saints would benefit from reading it), and verbally communicated the fact that Paul had especially intended it for the Gentiles among the churches generally throughout the region.

If the letter was an encyclical, why not address the letter "to the churches of Asia," or "to the churches of Asia and Galatia," just as Paul had previously written a letter to "the churches of Galatia"? We may note that Paul did vary the means by which he addressed an audience, writing to the "church of God at Corinth," to "the church of the Thessalonians," and to "all that are in Rome" (though in this latter instance, the difference may be due to the existence of multiple churches in Rome). Moreover, if we are correct in supposing that intended recipients were in Galatia as well as Asia, that fact alone may have been enough to move Paul to address them in a different manner than when he wrote to churches in only one province.

Why did some early manuscripts have no mention of any city, whether Ephesus or some other? Some scribal errors and alterations will always remain inscrutable, and such may be the case in this instance. But we may have a clue in that it was a Cappadocian that said the older manuscripts omitted all mention of a city in the greeting. To the east of Galatia, copies of Paul's letter eventually arrived in Cappadocia. It is easy to suppose that in this region, copies of Paul's letter would more likely have been made from the originals among the Galatian churches than from the various copies that had become well known among the churches of Asia. As described above, many copies in Asia likely were made from the original at Ephesus and contained the words "in Ephesus" as part of Paul's greeting. But if Marcion's testimony indicates that the greeting in the version delivered to Laodicea said ἐν Λαοδικείᾳ, we may well suppose that any delivered by Tychicus to the Galatian churches also had some reading other than "in Ephesus." Even though the association of the letter with Ephesus may have taken hold early on, scribes in Galatia would have been well aware that not all of the original letters delivered by Tychicus said "in Ephesus." And this could account for the fact that in the fourth century Basil of Caesarea *in Cappadocia* was familiar with old manuscripts that lacked mention of any city in Paul's greeting. Perhaps, as copies were made for further distribution to churches in Cappadocia, rather than putting either the name of Ephesus, or Laodicea, or Antioch, in Paul's greeting, the mention of a location was left out all together.

Place of Composition

The letter pictures Paul as being a prisoner (δέσμιος, 3.1, 4.1) and constrained by a chain (6.20). We see a similar picture in Colossians (Col 4.18) and Philemon (Phlm 1,9,23), letters that we have already said were delivered by Tychicus at the same time as Ephesians. Also note that those whom Paul mentions as being with him when he wrote Philemon (Epaphras, Mark, Aristarchus, Demas, and Luke) are the same men mentioned as being with him when he wrote Colossians. We are led to the conclusion that Ephesians, Colossians, and Philemon were all written from the same location at about the same time.

It is often said tradition holds that Rome was that location. However, the sub-apostolic writers of the early centuries are mostly silent on the question. In regard to Colossians, Chrysostom was no more specific than to say the letter was written some time after Paul wrote Romans and some time before he wrote 1st and 2nd Timothy. In regard to Ephesians, what early tradition there is consists primarily of comments prefixed or appended to these letters in the manuscripts.

Alternative views are that Paul wrote these letters while imprisoned at Caesarea (Acts 23–26), or that he wrote them during an imprisonment at Ephesus not described by Luke.

Ephesus? A strong argument can be made for an Ephesian imprisonment based on evidence both in the NT itself and in later writings.[55] Evidence is seen especially in Paul's mention, when writing from Ephesus,

---

[55] See Bowen, St. Paul's Ephesian Ministry, pp. 66–71; Duncan, "Are Paul's Prison Letters from Ephesus?" *The American Journal of Theology* Vol. 24, No. 1 (Jan., 1920), pp. 112–135.

of having been "doomed to death" (1 Cor 4.9), and his reference to having "fought with beasts at Ephesus" (1 Cor 15.32).[56] It is also significant that Paul writes from Macedonia (his brief visit there noted in Acts 20.1) saying that he has been "in prisons more abundantly" (2 Cor 11.23). Luke records only one of Paul's imprisonments prior to Acts 20, that being at Philippi (Acts 16). Ephesus, from whence Paul had come to Macedonia, would be a logical setting for one or more of the abundant imprisonments not chronicled by Luke.

But affirming that Paul was imprisoned while at Ephesus and saying that it was during such an imprisonment that he wrote some or all of the prison epistles are two different things. An imprisonment of a man condemned to death and thrown to the wild beasts hardly seems like the sort of imprisonment described in the prison epistles.

The attempt to connect the prison epistles with a putative Ephesian imprisonment usually starts with the thought that Onesimus, a runaway slave, would more likely have fled to Ephesus, a mere 100 miles from Colossae, than to distant Rome. With such evidence and more, Duncan especially made a circumstantial case for Ephesus as being the place from which Paul wrote. But this is a subjective argument,[57] ignoring a runaway's desire to create distance from those who might be searching for him, the facility with which people traveled in those days, and the attraction that a very large city such as Rome would naturally have for someone who wished to get lost in the crowds.

---

[56] For discussion of 1 Cor 15.32 and references to relevant literature, see Fee, page 770f, including notes 50–54.

[57] Truly, the force of some of the arguments advanced is really a function of predisposition. Arguing for Ephesus rather than Rome as the place of the relevant imprisonment, Bowen pressed the case that it was much less likely that Paul would have received relief from the Philippians if he were in Rome than if he were in Ephesus. Bowen asked, "Is it really plausible that in Rome, surrounded by a large church to which he had recently written the Epistle to the Romans...where he had had means enough at his disposal to hire a house for two years, the apostle fell into such dire need that it could not be relieved there, but is heard of and after some delay relieved by a church 800 miles away?" But one could as well ask, "Is it really plausible that in Ephesus, surrounded by a large church among whom Paul spent three years and developed such a bond that his eventual farewell would elicit hugs and kisses as they escorted him to his ship, that while there he could not be relieved by the church in Ephesus but would have to receive help from a church 460 miles away?" Wherever Paul was imprisoned, whether in Rome or Ephesus or Caesarea, the Philippians sent gifts to him notwithstanding the assistance that might have been provided by the brethren where Paul was. Regarding the house Paul rented in Rome for two years, who is to say that the funds provided by the Philippians did not help make that possible?

There is one piece of extra-Biblical evidence that should be mentioned. Some Latin manuscripts, the earliest of which (Codex Fuldensis) dates from the sixth century, include an introductory paragraph for each of Paul's epistles. The prevailing theory is that these prologues originated much earlier among the Marcionites, if not from Marcion himself, and hence they are called the Marcionite prologues. The Marcionite prologue to Colossians says, *apostulus iam ligatus scribit eis ab Epheso*, "the apostle writes to them from Ephesus already in custody." But this testimony is undermined by the Marcionite prologues to Philemon and Ephesians, both of which place Paul in Rome.[58] We have already established that the three letters must have been written about the same time and delivered by the same courier on the same journey.

For whatever it may be worth, Chrysostom's assertion that Ephesians was written after Paul wrote Romans runs counter to the theory that Paul wrote Ephesians during an Ephesian imprisonment. Paul's three-year stay in Ephesus (described in Acts 19) preceded his visit to Greece (mentioned in Acts 20.2f) during which he wrote the letter to the saints at Rome.

We may miss a clue when we analyze the writings of the New Testament as if they came together by happenstance, forgetting that the Holy Spirit inspired them and intended them to function collectively. Surely it is no accident that the book of Acts provides an illuminating backstory to Paul's letters to churches. We can identify at what point in Luke's narration Paul wrote Romans, 1 Corinthians, 2 Corinthians, and 1 Thessalonians, and we have a pretty good idea as to about where 2 Thessalonians fits. If this is intentional, and I believe it is, should we be surprised if the imprisonment Paul mentions in his letters is one Luke describes? This would argue against Ephesus as the locale from which Paul wrote the prison epistles.

However, the greatest shortcoming of the theory of Ephesus as the locale from which Paul wrote these letters is the letter of Ephesians itself. If we were to suppose the letter was addressed specifically and peculiarly to the church at Ephesus, we cannot imagine that Paul, right there in Ephesus as he wrote, with access to audiences (Eph 6.20), would have said such things as, "having heard of your faith in the Lord Jesus" (1.15), "if indeed

---

[58] The prologue to Philemon says *scribit autem ei a Roma de carcere*, "He writes to him from Rome, from prison." The prologue to Ephesians says, *hos conlaudat apostolus scribens eis ab urbe Roma de carcere per Tychicum diaconum*, "The apostle writes to them with praise from the city of Rome, from prison, by Tychicus the deacon."

you heard about the stewardship of the grace of God that has been given me toward you" (3.2), and especially, "In order that you also might know the things according to me, what I do, Tychicus, the beloved brother and faithful servant in the Lord, will make known all things to you, whom I sent to you unto this end, in order that you might know the things concerning us" (6.21*f*)! On the other hand, if, as argued in the present work, this letter was addressed to churches throughout Asia, and if Ephesus were the place of composition, it is difficult to imagine that the words "in Ephesus" would have entered the text as an indication of the destination, let alone become the dominant reading in the manuscript tradition.

If we can rule out Ephesus as the setting from which Paul wrote Ephesians, then appealing again to the clear evidence that Ephesians, Colossians, and Philemon were all written at about the same time and delivered by the same courier on the same journey, we can say that none of these letters were written from Ephesus.

Caesarea? It is often noted that Paul's freedom to interact with the Praetorian Guard and to serve as an ambassador in chains is in keeping with the picture Luke gives us of Paul's Roman imprisonment. However, it must be granted that this picture is not necessarily at odds with Paul's Caesarean imprisonment. During that imprisonment, Paul had the opportunity to speak before Felix and his Jewish accusers (Acts 24), and was allowed to entertain guests (Acts 24.23). He preached to Felix and his wife, Drusilla, of righteousness, self-control, and judgment to come (Acts 24.24*f*), and subsequently appeared often before Felix (Acts 24.26). He spoke to Festus, Agrippa and Bernice along with the chief captains and principal men of the city (Acts 25.23–26.29).

Still, there is no good evidence in support of dating these letters during the Caesarean imprisonment that would not equally suit the Roman imprisonment. Usually, the case for Caesarea is based on weak inferences from Philippians and Philemon. In regard to Philemon, some have thought it more likely that Onesimus would have run away to Caesarea than to Rome. In regard to Philippians, some have imagined the distance between Philippi and Rome was too great for the events described in Philippians 2.25–30 to have occurred during the time of Paul's Roman imprisonment. Neither of these objections are founded on anything factual.

Rome? The traditional view that Paul wrote Ephesians during his first Roman imprisonment is the one most easily defended. At the end of the book of Acts, we see Paul a prisoner (δέσμιος, Acts 28.17) in Rome, bound by a chain (Acts 28.20). Even so, Luke tells us that Paul lived in a hired dwelling and was receiving audiences during this time (Acts 28.17*ff*, 30). The language of Ephesians 6.19–20 is consistent with having access to audiences. Paul asks that his readers pray on his behalf that "utterance might be given me in opening my mouth in boldness, to boldly make known the mystery of the gospel." He describes himself as "an ambassador in chains."

If Philippians was written from the same location as Ephesians (and Colossians and Philemon), the case for Rome as the location of all of these letters is strengthened. Philippians almost certainly was written from Rome and not during the Caesarean imprisonment, nor during some Ephesian imprisonment. The mention of the Praetorian Guard is not in itself conclusive—there was a πραιτώριον at Jerusalem (Mt 27.27), and at Caesarea (Acts 13.5).[59] But the greeting from those of Caesar's household (Phil 4.22) is strong indication that Paul wrote Philippians from Rome.

It does seem most likely that Philemon and Philippians were written during the same imprisonment. In both Philippians and Philemon, Paul expresses an expectation that he will soon be free and will be able to visit his readers (Phil 1.25–27, 2.24, Phlm 22). If Paul had so surmised during his Caesarean imprisonment, he would have been mistaken. Of course, it was possible for Paul to be mistaken about future events, when he spoke from his own surmising rather than from divine revelation as he did in Acts 27.10 (cf. 27.22–25). But if Paul was correct about being able to soon visit Philemon and the saints at Philippi, the end of his Roman imprisonment, not the Caesarean imprisonment, must have been approaching.

There is also this: In Ephesians 3.1, Paul identifies himself as *the prisoner of Christ on behalf of you Gentiles*. Those words, *on behalf of you Gentiles*, are most appropriate in connection, not with any Ephesian imprisonment, but with the long series of imprisonments that began in Jerusalem and continued in Caesarea and then Rome. Paul was assaulted when certain Jews from Asia supposed he had taken a Gentile into the temple. When Claudius Lysias gave him the chance to speak to the people, they listened to him up until he talked about being sent to the Gentiles. At that point, "they lifted up their voice and said, 'Away with such a fellow from the

---

[59] Duncan argued that Paul used the word πραιτώριον of those associated with the official residence of the proconsul of Asia.

earth: for it is not fit that he should live.'" While Paul was at sea enroute to Rome, an angel of God told him that he would arrive safely in Rome and stand before Caesar, and thus Paul came to understand that this imprisonment was going to be the means whereby Gentiles in Rome would hear the gospel.

The evidence from early tradition, such as it is, carries some weight, and points to Rome rather than Caesarea as the place from which Paul wrote Ephesians. This tradition is evidenced, for example, in the subscriptions of various manuscripts.[60] While these subscriptions are unreliable as far as establishing the fact of the location from which a given letter was written, the near unanimity[61] with which they identify Rome as the place from which Paul wrote all of the prison epistles indicates this was the early consensus. Conversely, consider Dunn's observation regarding the plausibility of Ephesus as the place from which Paul wrote Philemon: "The problem is that the more that is attributed to an Ephesian imprisonment...the more surprising it is that the imprisonment seems to have made so little lasting impact in the Christian memory."[62]

Evidence Regarding Paul's Circumstance from Mention of His Companions. In an effort to gain insight concerning the setting from which Paul wrote these letters, we may consider information gleaned from Colossians and Philemon concerning Paul's companions.

Aristarchus is a *fellow prisoner* (συναιχμάλωτος, Col 4.10), as is Epaphras (Phlm 23). Not so much can be learned from this fact as we might have hoped, for Paul also refers to Andronicus and Junias as his *fellow prisoners* when he is writing from Corinth (Rom 16.7). We do not know of an imprisonment at Corinth, and in any event, Andronicus and Junias were not with Paul at the time he so describes them. They were in Rome.

The significance of συναιχμάλωτος in Paul's letters is uncertain. An αἰχμάλωτος was not just any prisoner, but specifically a prisoner of war, which Paul was not, at least certainly not in a literal sense, neither in Caesarea, nor in Rome (nor for that matter, in Ephesus). Lightfoot entertained

---

[60] In the extant mss, the earliest subscription for Ephesians is from Codex Vaticanus (fourth century), which says, προς εφεσιους εγραφη απο ρωμης (*To Ephesians, It was written from Rome*). Among the other mss that include similar inscriptions, a few of the earlier ones that may be mentioned are Claromontanus (sixth century, in the Latin, not in the Greek of this diglot), Codex Mosquensis (ninth century). Codex Angelicus (ninth century).

[61] The Marcionite prologue to Colossians being an exception.

[62] P. 308.

the possibility that συναιχμάλωτος is used by Paul metaphorically and is equivalent to σύνδουλος (*fellow slave*).[63] Kittel favored this view. Kittel however saw it as "no accident that it is during his prison days" that Paul used the word συναιχμάλωτος,[64] the literal imprisonment suggesting the spiritual figure.

Others have supposed that while αἰχμάλωτος referred to a prisoner of war, συναιχμάλωτος does indeed refer to the literal imprisonment that some shared with Paul, but that they did so voluntarily for brief periods of time.[65] Aristarchus accompanied Paul when he left Caesarea (Acts 27.2). It is most likely that Aristarchus was traveling as a companion to Paul, and not actually as a fellow prisoner. Luke portrays the Caesarean imprisonment as arising out of a personal vendetta against Paul on the part of the Jews. Why would Aristarchus (or, for that matter, Epaphras) have been caught up in that? They were not transferred to Felix' custody along with Paul—Claudius Lysias mentioned only "this man" in his letter to Felix, not "these men" (Ac 23.26–30). Nor does it appear that Aristarchus and Epaphras were prisoners with respect to the same case as Paul at the time that Festus succeeded Felix. Festus laid Paul's case, not the case of several prisoners, before Agrippa (Ac 25.14). So then Aristarchus must have accompanied Paul to Rome as a free man, a companion, just as did Luke.

While it may seem strange to us that a prisoner could have traveling companions, Pliny the younger (late first, early second century) gives an account of one Paetus who was being sent to Rome by ship as a prisoner, whose wife wanted to accompany him, and who therefore reasoned, "as he is of consular rank, you will assign him some servants to serve his meals, to valet him and put on his shoes. I will perform all these offices for him."[66] Though her request was refused, this attests to the practice of allowing a Roman citizen of some rank to be accompanied by attendants when being transported as a prisoner to Rome.

Paul identifies Aristarchus, Jesus, and Mark as being of the circumcision and also his only co-workers (Col 4.10–11). Undoubtedly he means

---

[63] Lightfoot, Philippians, p. 11, n. 6

[64] Kittel in TDNT, vol 1, p. 197.

[65] See in Alford, vol III, p. 243*f.*

[66] Though she was not permitted to join her husband aboard ship, Pliny reports, "she hired a fishing-boat and in that tiny vessel followed the big ship." Letters of Pliny the Younger 3.XVI, To Marcilius Nepos. Translator unknown.

these are his only co-workers from among the Jews,[67] especially given that he mentions Epaphras and Luke separately. It is difficult to imagine that Paul could speak of these three as his only co-workers from among the Jews if he were in Caesarea, especially given Philip's residence in that city (Acts 9.40, 21.8).

If we were to understand "Babylon" in 1 Peter 5.13 as standing for Rome, then we would have Mark in Rome, and the mention of Mark's presence with Paul in Colossians 4.10 would lend some support to the view that Colossians, Philemon and Ephesians were written from Rome. But it is not certain that we should identify Babylon in 1 Peter 5.13 with Rome.

Given that Justus, who was of the circumcision, had a perfectly good Hebrew name (Jesus), it seems less likely that he would have been called by his Roman name if he were in Caesarea rather than Rome.

Demas is present, and later we see him having forsaken Paul when Paul was subsequently imprisoned at Rome (2 Tim 4.9, if we can place Paul in Rome when writing 2 Timothy), thus giving us reason to suppose it was not unexpected for Demas to be in Rome.

Luke was present both when Paul left Caesarea (Acts 27.1) and when Paul arrived in Rome (Acts 28.14), and therefore little can be learned from the mention of his name.

Consideration of Paul's companions does not contribute much to our understanding of Paul's location at the time he wrote these letters. But after weighing all of the evidence, seeing little to support Caesarea as the setting, and seeing significant evidence against Ephesus as the setting, Rome seems to be the most likely setting from which Paul wrote Ephesians, Colossians, and Philemon, just as it was the place from which he wrote Philippians.

Date of Composition

Having settled on Rome, and particularly, Paul's time there during his first imprisonment, we only have to determine when that imprisonment was, and at what point during that imprisonment Paul wrote Ephesians.

The discovery of an inscription bearing the name of Gallio, the proconsul mentioned in Acts 18, provides us with a starting date.[68] Luke in-

---

[67] So Lightfoot, Colossians and Philemon, p. 238 and Dunn, p. 279.

[68] Prior to the 20th century, commentators worked out the dates of Paul's travels and writings from Luke's account starting with the eviction of the Jews from Rome mentioned in Acts 18.2. But the date of this event is less certain than the date of Gallio's tenure as

dicates Gallio was proconsul during Paul's year and half at Corinth. De-issmann reasoned that Luke must mean that "a new proconsul arrived in the person of Gallio, with whom the Jews then proceeded to try their luck."[69] Deissmann noted the parallel to Acts 24.27–25.2 wherein we read that as soon as Festus came into office, the Jews took opportunity to press their case against Paul.[70] Hence we take the events of Acts 18.12–17 to correspond to the beginning of Gallio's term.

In the late 19th century,[71] an inscription was found near Delphi that included the text of a letter from Claudius, wherein Claudius mentioned Lucius Junius Gallio, identifying him as proconsul. The letter was sent after the 26th acclamation of Claudius as Imperator, which most probably corresponds with the 12th year (less likely, the 11th year) of his tribunician power. With this information, Diessmann, with the assistance of Hermann Dessau, calculated that the letter represented in the inscription was most probably written between the beginning of the year 52 and August 1 of the same year.[72]

Given that a proconsul's term was usually one year,[73] the window for the beginning of Gallio's term would be from the beginning of AD 51 to August 1 of 52. But the term of a proconsul generally began in the summer, perhaps near the first of July.[74] Given that Gallio was already in office at the time of the writing of the letter represented in the Delphi inscription, then he most likely came to office in the summer of 51, or possibly in the summer of 52. Haenchen explains the difficulty involved in assuming that Gallio came to office in 52, describing the various events that would have had to occur in a very short timeframe prior to the 27th acclamation of Claudius as imperator, which took place on August 1, 52.[75] Therefore, we place the events of Acts 18.12–17 in the summer of 51.

After Gallio's intervention, Luke says Paul was "yet many days" in Corinth before setting sail (Acts 18.18). How long is "many days"? Were it

---

proconsul.

[69] Deissmann, St. Paul, A Study, p. 238*f.*

[70] Diesmann, 239 n. 1.

[71] The first published account of this inscription seems to have been that of Alexander Nikitsky in 1894 or 1895, but its significance for the chronology of Acts does not seem to have been considered in a published work until A. J. Reinach took note of it in 1907.

[72] Deismann, 248–250.

[73] Deismann 238,252.

[74] Deissmann, 254.

[75] Haenchen, 66, n.3.

something approaching a year or more, we would expect language such as we see in Acts 19.10, 20.31, 24.27, 28.30, as well as 18.11. The language sounds like something less than a year, probably something less than six months (cf. Acts 27.7).[76] But the reference to "many days" must have been even less than that, for anything more than 90 days would have resulted in sailing during the dangerous late fall or winter months. So then Paul must have left Corinth in the late summer or early fall of AD 51.

Luke's language suggests that Paul stopped at Ephesus only briefly before sailing on to Caesarea.[77] After arriving in Caesarea, he visited the church at Jerusalem, and then returned to Antioch, arriving there in the fall of 51. But he seems not to have spent a great amount of time there before embarking upon another journey.[78] The language is consistent with a departure the following spring after good weather had arrived. That would put the beginning of the next journey early in 52.

Paul seems to have come to Ephesus in fairly short order. Acts 18.23 has him passing through Galatia and Phrygia "one place after the other."[79] Luke's Greek is διερχόμενος καθεξῆς τὴν Γαλατικὴν χώραν καὶ Φρυγίαν. Then Luke tells us Paul was three months in the synagogue at Ephesus, and then another two years at the school of Tyrannus. Paul would later describe the total duration as three years (Acts 20.31). This brings us to sometime in 55. At this time he traveled to Macedonia and then to Achaia where he spent three months, presumably the winter months, just as he had suggested he might do.[80] Now this means his departure from Achaia through Macedonia must have been in the spring

---

[76] Something less than six months makes sense in each of the other places (Acts 9.23, 9.43, 27.7) where Luke uses the expression *many days* (ἡμέραι ἱκαναί), most especially so in Acts 27.7 where the phrase is used to describe the slow progress of the ship as it sailed along the coast near Cnidus. Surely this was a matter of days rather than months, days rather than even weeks. In any event, Luke's ἡμέραι ἱκαναί seems usually to be a shorter period than his ἱκανὸς χρόνος (Lk 8.27, 20.9, 23.8, Ac 8.11, 14.3, 27.9). Notice that in Acts 27, the ἱκαναῖς ἡμέραις (*many days*) of verse 7 is just a part of the ἱκανοῦ χρόνου (*much time*) of verse 9. Slingerland ("Acts 18.1–8, The Gallio Inscription," p. 443), in downplaying the chronological value of Luke's account, either confuses the two expressions or treats them as being identical, lumping all the occurrences in Acts of both phrases together indiscriminately.

[77] Acts 18.20, ἐρωτώντων δὲ αὐτῶν ἐπὶ πλείονα χρόνον μεῖναι οὐκ ἐπένευσεν.

[78] Compare ποιήσας χρόνον τινά—"having spent some time" (Ac 18.23)—with the similar expression in 15.33, ποιήσαντες χρόνον.

[79] BDAG, s.v. καθεξῆς, p. 490.

[80] 1 Cor 16.6, "perhaps I shall stay wth you, or even spend the winter."

of 56. He left Philippi after the days of unleavened bread,[81] which would have been late March of 56.

Paul, now once again accompanied by Luke, sailed from Philippi and arrived at Troas in five days, where he tarried seven days. From Troas, Paul made the short trip to Assos by land (16 miles), where he rejoined Luke and others who had sailed around the point (about 35 miles). Then they sailed across the strait to Mitylene, about 30 miles, then the next day came near Chios, and the next day ported at Samos, and the next day at Miletus. They must have been in Miletus a couple of days, maybe three, just long enough to send word 30 miles to Ephesus that Paul wished to speak with the elders of the church there and for them to then arrive in Miletus. Luke tells us Paul was hastening to arrive at Jerusalem before Pentecost (Acts 20.16), and it was Paul's haste that had prevented him from stopping at Ephesus. Therefore we can be sure that his stay in Miletus was very brief. After he spoke with the Ephesian elders, he stayed no longer. Indeed they saw him to his ship. So then his departure from Miletus was about twenty days after leaving Philippi, or four weeks after Passover, allowing a week for the days of Unleavened Bread mentioned in Acts 20.6. So with three weeks remaining till Pentecost, Paul set sail from Miletus.

This leaves Paul three weeks to accomplish the transit to Ceasarea by ship and then overland to Jerusalem, the overland portion being easily accomplished in two days. Therefore, we will assume that Paul did in fact achieve his purpose and arrived in Jerusalem before Pentecost, which falls in late May or early June. This puts Paul's arrival at Jerusalem sometime in the late spring of 56.

The day after his arrival, he was asked to purify himself with and be at charges for certain men who had taken a vow. So the very next day he began the seven day process of purifying himself according to the law.[82] Near the end of those seven days, he was arrested (Acts 21.27). The next events are carefully chronicled: One day after his arrest Paul stood before the council (Acts 22.30); the following night the Lord told him he would go to Rome (Acts 23.11); the next day the plan to murder Paul was hatched (Acts 23.12); that night Paul was whisked away to Caesarea (Acts 23.20–33); and five days later Paul stood before Felix as he was accused by Tertullus and the Jews. Only seven days had passed from the time that Paul went

---

[81] Acts 20.6.

[82] Numb. 6.9f.

into the temple until the time that he stood before Felix in whose custody Paul remained for two years (Acts 24.27). So then we are at the late spring or early summer of 58 when Festus comes to office. This fits nicely with the fact that a coin minted by Festus for Judea is imprinted with the date of Nero's fifth year, which would be 58 or 59.

Thereafter, Luke's timeline again moves quickly: Three days after having come into office (Acts 25.1) Festus went up to Jerusalem and declined a request to bring Paul to Jerusalem; then after another "eight or ten days" he returned to Caesarea and had Paul brought to him. "Some days" passed (25.13) and then Agrippa and Bernice arrived at Caesarea. At this point the timeline slows a bit as they tarried there "many days" (Acts 25.14). During this time, Festus told Agrippa about Paul and the next day, Paul stood before Agrippa, Berenice, and Festus, and laid out his story. It seems Paul's departure for Rome was shortly thereafter. It must have been within a few months of Festus' arrival in office, no more. So then Paul's departure for Rome was in the same year that Festus became procurator of Judea.

Luke mentions "the Fast" as having already passed by the time Paul reached Crete. This would have been the Day of Atonement which falls in October. Paul's voyage took an unintended turn at this point, and he was shipwrecked at Melita where he and the rest spent the winter. So Paul's arrival in Rome would have been in the spring of 59.

The problem we now encounter is that we do not know how long Paul's imprisonment lasted or exactly how it ended. Luke tells us Paul lived in his own hired dwelling, under house arrest, for two whole years. But the account comes to a conclusion without telling us the outcome of Paul's appeal. Paul's imprisonment must have continued for some period of time after the two years or Luke would surely have described his release.[83] That his first Roman imprisonment ended in release at some point is indicated by Paul's letters to Timothy and Titus. They show that Paul was able to visit Macedonia, Troas, Miletus, and Crete before being again imprisoned. Later tradition indicates that Paul was able to accomplish what he had long desired to do, travel to Spain. But nothing, either in scripture or in later tradition, tells us when his first Roman imprisonment ended.

We can say with confidence his release must have occurred no earlier

---

[83] One reason different writers come to different conlusions about the date of the prison epistles is that some assume the two years mentioned by Luke is the totality of Paul's first Roman imprisonment. So, for example, Thiessen, p. 233.

than the spring of 61 for he arrived in Rome in the spring of 59 and Luke has him there "two whole years" (διετίαν ὅλην). And we can be confident his release was before July 64, for that is when Rome burned, an event for which Christians were made scapegoats. Had Paul still been a prisoner at that time, it is doubtful he would have been spared. So he was released sometime between the spring of 61 and the summer of 64. Paul's significant activity after being released and before being again imprisoned while Nero was yet emperor may point to a release earlier in this window rather than later.

Paul's request that Philemon prepare him a lodging suggests that Paul was writing toward the end of his Roman imprisonment when release was imminent. Ephesians, Colossians and Philemon all must have been delivered by the same courier on this same journey. If Paul was correct in believing that release was imminent, this could have been no earlier than late in the year AD 60 and no later than AD 64. If there is validity to our speculation that his release was earlier rather than later, this would point to a date for the composition of Ephesians closer to 60 than to 64.

It should be noted that the foregoing chronology is based on certain assumptions, probabilities, and inferences. These include the inference and likelihood that Gallio had newly arrived in office when the Jews in Corinth brought charges against Paul, the probability that Gallio's term was only one year, and the probability that there was insufficient time for communications between Gallio and Claudius to have resulted in the Delphi communication before Claudius' 27th acclamation as Imperator if Gallio had only become proconsul in the summer of 52. Nonetheless, if all of these assumptions were incorrect, it would throw the calculation off by no more than a year.

Of course, if we suppose Paul wrote from Caesarea, the date was between 56 and 58, and if from Ephesus, it would have been as early as 52 and no later than 55. But for the remainder of this work, we will assume Paul wrote from Rome between AD 60 and no later than AD 64, probably closer to 60.

Historical Background and Purpose

Properly understood, Ephesians is perhaps the greatest call in the New Testament to first century Gentiles (and also to 21st century Gentiles) to respond to God's grace by walking worthily of their (and our) calling.

Written by Paul less than two dozen years after the first Gentiles became Christians, it is an intensely motivating reminder to Gentiles of what God has done for them in accordance with his eternal purpose, and it is a clarion call to abandon the lifestyle of their peers, and we our peers, to bring our lives into harmony with God's will, that the body of Christ, which includes both Jews and Gentiles, can truly be united not only in theory but in practice.

But for the commentator who supposes it was not written by the apostle and was not written early in the seventh decade of the first century, it is an enigma. "Who wrote it?" and "Why was it written?" are questions that confound him. It seems to him little more than an impoverished imitation of Colossians, an amalgamation of Pauline expressions, a pious fraud. It loses cogency, urgency and current relevance.

Some who have denied Pauline authorship, including Schnackenburg[84] and Goodspeed[85], suppose that our understanding of who the author was and when the letter was written affects our perception of the message. And they are correct.[86] The letter was written to remind Gentiles of the great grace of God toward them such that they are fully citizens of the household of God and that they therefore must walk worthily of their calling so that the body of Christ might truly be united. But Goodspeed felt the need to dismiss this self-evident purpose as a mere "form" under which a later writer really meant to call for unity "in the face of rising sects" of a later era. Thus study of the meaning of Ephesians has suffered over the past century due to the increasing conviction among scholars that it was not written by Paul.

But is it also the other way around? Has failure to discern the message of Ephesians hindered some from attributing the letter to Paul? When Lincoln assessed the writer's humility (3.8, "the least of all saints") as "exaggerated" and "lacking the spontaneity of 1 Cor 15:9,"[87] was it because he failed to discern that the writer was expressing his profound gratitude for being the one vested with the privilege of telling the Gentiles of the great grace of God that was available to them, even though he

---

[84] p. 25.

[85] p. 15.

[86] Goodspeed's oft-quoted remark that "Ephesians is the Waterloo of commentators" was intended to characterize the difficulty that results from ignorance of "the situation that called" for the writing of Ephesians. Goodspeed, 15.

[87] Lincoln, lxiii.

himself had failed his God so miserably? Apparently seeing neither the grandeur of the message to Gentiles nor understanding what a privilege it was to inform them of the great blessing available to them in Christ, Lincoln does not believe the sentiment rings true and seems rather to see this as a gratuitous humility that reflects the efforts of a pseudepigrapher imitating Paul.[88]

Rudolf Schnackenburg tells us, "The Pauline thrust against the Jewish idea of the way to salvation through the works of the law is gone without a trace," and, "The Law (the νόμος) is only mentioned once," and cites these facts as evidence against Pauline authorship.[89] However, if as the present work argues, Ephesians is a letter written particularly to Gentile Christians with the specific goal of urging them to walk worthily of their calling in Christ Jesus, there is little reason to expect a treatise against the Jewish idea of salvation through works of the law. Again, failure to discern the purpose of Ephesians has contributed to rejection of Paul as the author.

Others have otherwise misconstrued the purpose of the letter. One writer supposed it was written "to urge the Gentile Christian majority to accept a Jewish Christian minority and to retain its ties with the ancient Hebrew tradition."[90]

It was rather a reminder to Gentile Christians of the great grace that God had bestowed upon them, the standing before God they had acquired, a standing that put them on equal footing with their spiritual patrons, the Jews, and in view of these things, a call to Gentile Christians to abandon the immorality of their larger culture with the goal of bringing about a practical unity in the one faith of Jesus Christ.

Paul's letter naturally falls into two parts. In the first part, chapters one through three, Paul addresses Gentile Christians, people who could easily have felt they were second class citizens in the kingdom of God, having been previously "separate from Christ, excluded from the com-

---

[88] Compare Mitton, whom Lincoln later quotes, "This sounds a little like false modesty" (Ephesians, p. 125). Mitton went on to describe 1 Cor 15.9 as "a cry of genuine remorse," but in contrast thought the words in Ephesians 3.8 sounded "artificial and exaggerated," and said they "are more easily understood as those of the later disciple who wished to make his master appear as excelling in penitence and humility" (Ephesians, p. 125).

[89] Rudolf Schnackenburg, Ephesians, A Commentary, (translated by Helen Heron from Der Brief an die Epheser, Evangelisch-Katholischer Kommentar zum Neuen Testament, Benziger/Neukirchener, 1982) T&T Clark Edinburgh, 1991, p. 27.

[90] Käsemann, as summarized by Yee, p.4.

monwealth of Israel, and strangers to the covenants of promise." He tells them they are not only "fellow citizens with the saints," but have been made the very "dwelling of God in the Spirit." He tells them that their inclusion is no afterthought, but is in accordance with the eternal purpose of God. The second part of Paul's letter, chapters four through six, is an exhortation to these Gentile believers in view of the glorious standing they have through the grace of God. The exhortation is that they now walk worthily of their calling.

Gentile Christians, the Intended Audience. Essential to recognizing the plan of the letter is a clear perception that Gentile Christians comprise the intended immediate audience. Each of Paul's other letters was directly addressed to an immediate audience, whether a church, a group of churches, or an individual, even though in each case the Lord intended Paul's letter to be instructive throughout the ages. In the case of Ephesians, the immediate audience is Gentile Christians, and as previously discussed, not only those in the church at Ephesus. The immediate audience seems to have been Gentile Christians throughout a region Tychicus was to visit.

That Paul was writing to Gentile Christians is first indicated in Eph 1.12*f.* Paul writes, "…we who had previously hoped in the Christ would be to the praise of his glory, in whom you also, having heard the word of the promise, the good news of your salvation, in whom you, having also believed, were sealed by the promised Holy Spirit." Notice the distinction between *we* and *you*. Paul says, "*we* who had before hoped in Christ," in contrast to, "*you* also, having heard the word of the promise, the good news of your salvation." Who is it that had "previously hoped in the Christ"? Who is it that was looking for a Christ, that is, a Messiah, one who would sit on the throne of David and be the Savior of Israel? It was, of course, Israel. Paul was among the Jews who had looked for the Christ to come, and who had recognized Jesus as that Christ. But now, Paul writes to Gentiles who also have heard the word of the truth.

Paul describes these Gentile believers as having been previously dead by means of their trespasses and sins (2.1–2), but before he gets around to saying what he wants to say, namely that God has now made them alive by Christ, he is compelled to acknowledge that the Jewish believers ("we also") formerly walked in the desires of the flesh (2.3). So it is that once again we see this interplay between *you* and *us,* you the Gentile believers in contrast to us the Jewish believers.

And of course, especially in 2.11 Paul explicitly identified his audience as Gentiles. Thereafter, the point is that though they were far off in contrast to the Jews who were near, they now with Jewish believers have come to comprise the very house of God.

Again in 3.1 Paul explicitly addresses his audience as Gentiles, calls to mind his special mission to them, and thereafter rejoices that he has been graced with the privilege of preaching the gospel to them. Clearly, this is a letter written to Gentile believers.

Paul's point in the first three chapters is ultimately to show that in Christ, that distinction between Jews and Gentiles has been eliminated. Just how magnificent an accomplishment that was, and how joyous it would have been to Gentile believers, can only be appreciated if we reflect upon the circumstances of Gentile believers in the first century.

Consider a Gentile and how he was regarded by the Jews in his city. When Peter entered Cornelius' house, he noted the irregularity saying, "You yourselves know how unlawful it is for a Jew to associate with or to visit anyone of another nation" (Acts 10.28). Though Peter himself had come to understand that God is no respecter of persons, the other apostles and the brethren in Jerusalem did not yet share that understanding. Upon his arrival in Jerusalem, they indicated their dismay, saying, "You went to uncircumcised men and ate with them" (Acts 11.3). Their attitude toward Gentiles was that of Jews generally. It is the attitude Jesus alluded to in explaining how to treat the sinner who will not heed the church's warning: "Let him be to you as a Gentile and a tax collector."

It was with some justification that Jews viewed Gentiles as depraved. Paul's characterization of the sin at Corinth as being "such fornication as is not even among the Gentiles" is a testament to the low expectations of Gentile morality. While the law of Moses was not to be imposed upon Gentiles, James did feel the need to remind Gentiles coming to Christ that they must "abstain from the things polluted by idols, and from sexual immorality, and from what has been strangled, and from blood."

While the Jews were themselves guilty of many of the things practiced by Gentiles, as Paul attests both in Ephesians 2.3 and in his scathing indictment in Romans 2, coming out of the exile they did learn to abhor idolatry and its licentious accoutrements. So from the Jewish perspective, it was not they themselves who were depraved, but the Gentiles.

From the perspective of Gentiles, this Jewish standoffishness seemed haughty and arrogant. Tacitus' summary of the Jewish attitude toward others was simply this: "toward every other people they feel only hate and enmity."[91] Diodorus Siculus says the Jews "avoided dealings with any other people and looked upon all men as their enemies," "had made their hatred of mankind into a tradition," were forbidden "to break bread with any other race" or "to show them any good will at all," and had "misanthropic" customs and "xenophobic" laws.[92] While Diodorus is describing the Jews from the perspective of the Seleucid kings (including the notorious Antiochus Epiphanes) and their advisors who could hardly be characterized as unbiased commentators, the historian clearly shared their perspective. Hecataeus, as communicated by Diodorus, described the Jews as having derived from Moses "a somewhat isolated and xenophobic life."[93] Hecataeus' various historical assertions are woefully in error (he supposed Israel was divided into 12 tribes in keeping with the 12 months of a year, that Moses founded Jerusalem, and that Jews never have a king because Moses appointed judges) such that it is clear his description of the Jews is not so much historical but is rather in accordance with the perceptions of his own time.

Josephus endeavored to counter negative attitudes toward Jews. In an effort to prove that the kings of both Asia and Europe appreciated the Jews for their civic zeal, bravery and fidelity,[94] and more especially to demonstrate friendship between the Jews and the Romans,[95] Josephus cited various official acknowledgements of privileges granted to the Jews such as exemption from military service and freedom to worship according to their customs. These were decrees made in the first century BC during the time of Hyrcanus.

However, in those various proofs, we also see evidence of the tension that existed between Gentiles and Jews, most notably in Asia. A proconsul named Publius Servilius Galba had indicated that the Jews' observance of their customs was not to be forbidden, but he found it necessary to write a letter reiterating that policy to the rulers, council, and people

[91] Histories, 5.5 (15). Loeb, transl. by Clifford H. Moore.

[92] DS XXXIV/XXXV.1.1–4 LCL DS vol XII, fragments of books XXXIII-XL, transl. Francis R. Walton, Cambridge Mass, Harvard University Press, 1967

[93] διὰ γὰρ τὴν ἰδίαν ξενηλασίαν ἀπάνθρωπόν τινα καὶ μισόξενον βίον εἰσηγήσατο ("For on account of their own deportation, he led them into a somewhat isolated and xenophobic life"), DS XL.3.4.

[94] *Ant. XIV.186.*

[95] *Ant. XIV.266.*

of Miletus when he received a report that they were "hindering the Jews from keeping the Sabbaths and from performing their native rituals and from managing their produce according to their customs."[96] Miletus was a coastal city on the Aegean Sea just about 30 miles south of Ephesus.

In Tralles, a city on the Meander River about 50 miles inland from Miletus and, as argued above, one of those cities in the region where lived the intended recipients of Paul's letter, the citizens at first objected to the proconsul's decrees that they permit the Jews to observe their customs and refrain from doing them injury.[97]

Gruen describes Jews in the Province of Asia as "conspicuous," stubbornly holding "to practices and beliefs that set them apart from Gentile neighbors." He says, "Jewish communities in the cities of the Hellenistic world and the Roman Empire were readily identifiable." The Jews "never disappeared into a melting pot."[98] In Rome, at least, and probably in most cities, this separation was manifest geographically. During the reign of Augustus, the Jews in Rome inhabited a section on the opposite side of the Tiber River.[99]

So then Paul's reminder that Gentile believers had been "separated from Christ, alienated from the commonwealth of Israel and strangers to the covenants of promise, having no hope and without God in the world" (2.12) was a theological statement, but not merely so. And in every city where there was a Jewish enclave, the Gentiles knew how they were regarded by the Jews.

Now consider the Gentile who heard the gospel and came to believe that his salvation was dependent upon a Jewish Messiah, who confessed Jesus and understood his need to assemble with other believers, other believers who happened to be—Jews. He found himself compelled to walk across town and seek acceptance among those by whom he reckoned himself to be despised. While he had been alienated from the commonwealth of Israel, the mutual enmity may have seemed to be no great problem, at least practically. They did not like him, and he did not care for them, but they were the minority and could be ignored. But now, as he endeavors to

---

[96] *Ant. XIV.*245. The terms ἄρχων, βουλή, and δῆμος probably refer to three entities of municipal governance, with the term δῆμος here used of a town meeting, more or less, as in Acts 17.5, 19.30,33.

[97] *Ant. XIV.*241–242.

[98] Gruen, p. 84.

[99] Philo, The Embassy to Gaius, 155.

worship their God and his, together with them, he could easily see himself as being something of a second class citizen among them, a tolerated but not entirely worthy member of their number.

To such Gentile believers, Paul writes, "now in Christ Jesus you who once were far off have been brought near by the blood of Christ. For he himself is our peace, who has made us both one." Paul says that both Jew and Gentile are reconciled "in one body through the cross," that through Jesus, "we both have access in one Spirit to the Father." There is no back alley entrance through which Gentiles must enter. Gentiles and Jews alike have the same access to the Father. Paul says to them, "you are no longer strangers and aliens, but you are fellow citizens with the saints and members of the household of God."

Indeed, whereas before, Gentile visitors to the temple in Jerusalem had been kept at a distance from the house of God,[100] Gentile believers are now themselves "being built together into a dwelling place for God by the Spirit."

In chapter three, Paul expresses his great pleasure at being the one who gets to deliver this joyous message to Gentiles, this mystery now revealed, that they "are fellow heirs, members of the same body, and partakers of the promise in Christ Jesus through the gospel." He marvels that he, who is "the very least of all the saints," is the one chosen to give them this message. And he underscores the magnitude of the message, saying that in the church, this one body wherein both Jew and Gentile are reconciled to God through the cross, "the manifold wisdom of God" is "made known to the rulers and authorities in the heavenly places." And the inclusion of the Gentiles was no afterthought. This was all "according to the eternal purpose" of God "in Christ Jesus our Lord."

The Requisite Walk. Chapter four begins with a "therefore." The word translated "therefore" is actually the second word of the chapter in the Greek text, as is "therefore" in most English translations. But it is an inferential conjunction and logically ties what has been said previously to what follows. What has been said is the basis for what Paul is about to say. And what he is about to say is that his readers should "walk in a manner worthy of the calling to which you have been called." You are fel-

---

[100] The meaning of "the middle wall of partition" will be discussed in the commentary. But let it be noted here that the great landmarks of the world were familiar to people throughout the Roman Empire. Many people traveled, and for those who did not, there were writers such as Strabo who provided an armchair view of the world.

low citizens with the saints, a dwelling place for God in the spirit, God's eternal purpose; Therefore, I, a prisoner for the Lord, urge you to walk in a manner worthy of that calling. His appeal to them is on the basis of their exalted standing as God's inheritance and his own willingness to suffer hardship on their behalf.

Walking worthily is going to require living in such a manner as to facilitate a unity within the body. That cannot happen in reality if the Gentiles continue to live as they have in the past. Paul first calls attention to the unity: "There is one body and one Spirit—just as you were called to the one hope that belongs to your call—one Lord, one faith, one baptism, one God and Father of all, who is over all and through all and in all."

This is not to be a salad dressing of oil and vinegar poured into one bottle. Jew and Gentile comprise one body, not two. They are called to one hope, not two. They worship one Lord, hold one faith, share one baptism.

Then Paul introduces the gifts the Lord has provided, the offices through which the teaching will be done that will accomplish a true unity of faith and walk, and not merely a union of diverse and incompatible groups.

And then Paul reiterates, "This, therefore, I say and testify in the Lord, that you no longer walk, as the Gentiles walk." Three times more, Paul will call them to walk worthily: "walk in love" (5.1), "walk as children of light" (5.8), "look carefully how you walk" (5.15). This is to be contrasted with the Gentiles' walk, which had been in trespasses and sin (2.1–2).

PART ONE

Chapters 1–3

Paul Sets Forth the Great Blessings
God Has Bestowed upon the Gentiles in Christ

1.1–2 Greeting

Paul, an apostle of Christ Jesus through God's will to the holy ones who are [in Ephesus] and who are faithful in Christ Jesus; grace to you and peace from God our Father and the Lord Jesus Christ.

See the introduction for a discussion of the intended recipients and of the authenticity of the words ἐν Ἐφέσῳ. The evidence discussed there points to the conclusion that this letter was written to Gentile Christians, and not only to those at Ephesus, but to all those within an area through which Tychicus would travel, both those in the churches that Tychicus would visit and also those in other nearby churches.

Given the similarity between Ephesians and Colossians, it should be noted that when Paul wrote to the church at Colossae, Timothy was included as sender along with Paul (καὶ Τιμόθεος ὁ ἀδελφός, exactly as in 2 Corinthians), while there is no mention of Timothy in Ephesians. Inasmuch as these two letters were written at the same time, the absence of Timothy's name in one is significant. Apparently, Timothy's name would be recognized by the church at Colossae, but perhaps it was not known to all the recipients of the present letter we know as Ephesians. Based on Luke's record, we can say that the church at Ephesus almost certainly knew Timothy at this time. Timothy had rejoined Paul at Corinth[1] from whence Paul traveled to Ephesus the first time. And during Paul's subsequent stay at Ephesus, it seems that Paul sent Timothy, along with Erastus, to Macedonia from Ephesus.[2] Given that Timothy was with Paul when Colossians

---

[1] Acts 18.5.

[2] Acts 19.22.

and Ephesians were written, and especially in view of Timothy's inclusion as sender of the letter to the Colossians, if Ephesians had been written to the Ephesians uniquely just as Colossians was written to the Colossians uniquely, we would expect to see Timothy's name included as sender. This further supports our understanding that what we know as Ephesians was not written only to the church at Ephesus, but to a larger audience.[3]

The greetings we see in the New Testament letters represent an elaboration upon the greetings that were typical of the time. Many letters began simply with the name of the sender, the name of the recipient, and the word χαίρειν (*greeting*). For example, Ἀπολλώνιος Ζήνωνι χαίρειν, (*Apollonios to Zenon, greeting*).[4] But occasionally, especially in a less personal and more formal letter, something more descriptive was necessary. So Athenagoras began a letter, Ἀθηναγόρας ὁ ἀρχίατρος τοῖς ἱερεῦσι τῶν ἐν τῶ[ι] Λαβυρίνθωι στολιστῶν καὶ τοῖς στολ[ισ]ταῖς χαίρειν, (*Athenagoras, the chief physician, to the priests of the stolistae at the Labyrinth and to the stolistae, greeting*).[5]

The self-identification Παῦλος ἀπόστολος Χριστοῦ Ἰησοῦ διὰ θελήματος θεοῦ (*Paul an apostle of Christ Jesus through God's will*) is typical of Paul, and is identical to what we see in 2 Corinthians, Colossians, and 2 Timothy. χάρις ὑμῖν καὶ εἰρήνη (*grace to you and peace*) replaces the simple but ubiquitous χαίρειν. In letters generally, we occasionally see the more effusive πλεῖστα χαίρειν, and sometimes χαίρειν καὶ ἐρρῶσθαι. "Grace and peace" was a distinctively Christian greeting.[6] Χαίρω is *rejoice*. We see the infinitive form χαίρειν used imperatively as a greeting in a letter in Acts 15.23, Acts 23.26, and James 1.1 just as it was used in letters generally. χαίρειν and χάρις (*grace*) are from the same family. It has been suggested that in the Pauline greetings, χάρις "echoes...the key-term χαίρειν in the greeting in Gk. letters."[7] We can add that in substituting χάρις for χαίρειν, Paul (and also Peter in both his epistles) used a word reminiscent of the typical greeting but bringing into view a higher joy, joy created by God's gracious love bestowed upon the recipients through Christ Jesus.

---

[3] See Ramsay's slightly different reasoning, but with the same conclusion, in A Historical Commentary on St. Paul's Epistle to the Galatians, pp 238–241.

[4] P. Cairo Zen. 59154.

[5] Select Papyri, Vol. I, Non-Literary Papyri, Private Affairs, translated by A.S. Hunt and C.C. Edgar, Loeb Classical Library, 1988, pp. 292–294.

[6] Hoenher, 149.

[7] TDNT, vol. 9, p. 394.

εἰρήνη represented a typical oriental greeting[8] which we see, for example, in Daniel 4.1 where the Theodotian text of Daniel has Nebuchadnezzar beginning his address with the words, "Nebuchadnezzar the King to all the peoples, tribes, and tongues who dwell in all the land, May peace to you be multiplied (Εἰρήνη ὑμῖν πληθυνθείη)."

So then in the greeting χάρις ὑμῖν καὶ εἰρήνη (*grace to you and peace*), we see a new take on the typical Greek greeting, χαίρειν, using χάρις instead and thus calling to mind God's grace, and that combined with the oriental greeting now embued with a greater, more profound meaning, *viz.* peace with God.

Grace to you from God our Father and the Lord Jesus Christ. The whole phrase χάρις ὑμῖν καὶ εἰρήνη ἀπὸ θεοῦ πατρὸς ἡμῶν καὶ κυρίου Ἰησοῦ Χριστοῦ is the greeting found in Romans 1.7, 1 Corinthians 1.3, 2 Corinthians 1.2, Galatians 1.3, Philippians 1.2, and 2 Thessalonians 1.2 according to the NA28 and USB5 text, although some minor variants in some of the Greek manuscripts are noted for Galatians 1.3 and 2 Thessalonians 1.2.

Any ambiguity in the significance of genitive κυρίου Ἰησοῦ Χριστοῦ is removed by comparing this greeting with Paul's greeting in Titus 1.4, χάρις καὶ εἰρήνη ἀπὸ θεοῦ πατρὸς καὶ Χριστοῦ Ἰησοῦ τοῦ σωτῆρος ἡμῶν. There, clearly, genitive Χριστοῦ Ἰησοῦ is an object of ἀπό just as is θεοῦ. Grace and peace are from both God the Father and Christ Jesus our Savior. So also in Ephesians 1.1, Paul is not saying God is both the father of us and of Jesus Christ. Rather, he is saying grace and peace are from both God our Father and Christ Jesus our Lord.

1.3–14 Blessed Be God Who Provides Everything in Christ

Blessed is the God and Father of our Lord Jesus Christ who has blessed us in every spiritual blessing in the heavens in Christ just as he chose us in him before the foundation of the universe, that we would be holy and blameless before him in love, having foreordained us to adoption through Jesus Christ unto himself according to the good pleasure of his will, unto praise of the glory of his grace which he gave us in the Beloved One, in whom we have the redemption through his blood, the forgiveness of the trespasses, according to the wealth of his grace, which he abundantly supplied to us in all wisdom and insight, having made known to us the mystery of his will, according to his good pleasure, which he planned in him unto a dispensation of the fullness of the times, to sum up all things in the Christ,

---

[8] *Ibid.*

the things in the heavens and the things upon the earth in him, in whom we were allotted, having been predetermined according to a plan of the one who works all things according to the counsel of his will, such that we who had previously hoped in the Christ would be to the praise of his glory, in whom you also, having heard the word of the promise, the good news of your salvation, in whom you, having also believed, were sealed by the promised Holy Spirit, which is a seal of our inheritance, unto redemption of the possession unto praise of his glory.

The primary thought of the sentence beginning in verse three is "Blessed is God who has blessed us in Christ." But Paul piles relative clause on top of prepositional phrase on top of participial phrase until the sentence extends all the way through our verse fourteen. To say that in Christ, God has given us "every spiritual blessing" is not sufficient. Paul elaborates, explaining that even before the foundation of the world, God had purposed to bless us in Christ and, in particular, to make us holy and blameless in Christ, sons even. Grace, redemption, forgiveness are all ours through Christ. Again in verse four, the point of emphasis is that God chose us *in him,* that is, in Christ.

All of this is couched in language emphasizing that the recipients are the beneficiaries of God's good will toward them. Twice Paul mentions that all this was God's "good pleasure" (1.5, 9). Paul emphasizes the liberality of God's kindness as he says God graced us with his grace (1.6), and forgave us in accordance with the riches of his grace (1.7), which he caused to abound toward us (1.8). Paul's aim is to move his readers to gratitude and, by means of that gratitude, to a walk worthy of their calling.

We ought not overlook Paul's indication that these blessings had been ordained before the foundation of the world. Paul will return to this idea in chapter three as he assures Gentile Christians that their inclusion is not an afterthought, but is in accordance with God's eternal purpose.

However, one misses the point if he looks at this through the prism of Calvinism and supposes Paul is asserting the choosing of each particular individual before the foundation of the world. Rather, Paul is further explaining what God has done for us *in Christ*: Before the foundation of the world, he chose us "to be holy and blameless before him in love," and he determined that this would be accomplished *in Christ.* Thirteen times in eleven verses, Paul makes it clear that these blessings are accomplished in, or through, Christ, sometimes saying "Christ," sometimes using a pronoun for Christ, once referring to Christ as the Beloved, and once saying "through Christ's blood."

1.3	ἐν Χριστῷ	in Christ
1.4	ἐν αὐτῷ	in Him
1.5	διὰ Ἰησοῦ Χριστοῦ	through Jesus Christ
1.6	ἐν τῷ ἠγαπημένῳ	in the Beloved
1.7	ἐν ᾧ	in Whom
	διὰ τοῦ αἵματος αὐτοῦ	through His blood
1.9	ἐν αὐτῷ	in Him
1.10	ἐν τῷ Χριστῷ	in the Christ
	ἐν αὐτῷ	in Him
1.11	ἐν ᾧ	in Whom
1.12	ἐν τῷ Χριστῷ	in the Christ
1.13	ἐν ᾧ	in Whom
	ἐν ᾧ	in Whom

Paul's extolling of what God has accomplished in Christ rises to a climax in the affirmation that he has summed up all things in Christ, all things in the heavens and in the earth, including even allotting to himself a people for his own possession.

Subsequent to the greeting of verse 2 and prior to verse 12, Paul has consistently spoken of what God has done for *us*, including himself with his readers as beneficiaries of God's blessings in Christ. But right here in verses 12–13, for the first time Paul distinguishes between Jews and Gentiles, identifying the Jewish believers in verse 12 (those who had before hoped in Christ),[9] and then the Gentiles in verse 13, when he says "you also." In order to rightly understand this letter, it is critical that we understand this distinction.

1.3 *in the heavens* (ἐν τοῖς ἐπουρανίοις) In 2 Maccabees 3.39 ἐπουράνιος characterizes the dwelling place of God (ὁ τὴν κατοικίαν ἐπουράνιον ἔχων, *the one who has a heavenly dwelling*). There it is an adjective characterizing κατοικίαν such that κατοικίαν ἐπουράνιον means "heavenly dwelling place." In Ephesians, it is used as a substantive. In English, we might supply a noun, "heavenly *realms*" or "heavenly *places*." But this is unnecessary—as a substantive, ἐπουράνιος can be synonymous with οὐρανός. Paul's declaration that Christ has been seated at the right hand of God in the ἐπουρανίοις (Eph 1.20) means simply "in the heavens."

---

[9] The Jews are distinctly indentified, if not in the phrase εἰς τὸ εἶναι ἡμᾶς εἰς ἔπαινον δόξης αὐτοῦ, then certainly in the phrase τοὺς προηλπικότας ἐν τῷ Χριστῷ. See the notes on the Greek text.

And similarly in verse 3, God has blessed us with every spiritual blessing in the heavens.

While some have sought significance in the use of ἐπουράνιος rather than οὐρανός—some seeing a reference to Gnosticism, some perceiving a reference to a particular one of the several heavens identified in Rabbinic writings—the point is probably simply exaltation. David wrote, "For as high as the heavens are above the earth,[10] so great is His lovingkindness toward those who fear Him" (Ps 103.11). And again, God's "lovingkindness is great to the heavens" (Ps 57.10). Is this really a very different idea than "Thy lovingkindness, O Lord is *in* the heavens"[11] (Ps 36.5), which the NAS translates as "extends to the heavens"? In the Septuagint, the parallel phrase is "Your truth is unto the clouds" (ἡ ἀλήθειά σου ἕως τῶν νεφελῶν). There is no distinction to be sought between ἐν τῷ οὐρανῷ (*in the sky*) and ἕως τῶν νεφελῶν (*unto the clouds*). Whether "clouds" or "sky," the point is exalted height, and whether "unto" or "in," the point is that God's kindness and truth belong to an exalted realm.

In Ephesians, the exalted Christ is seated ἐν τοῖς ἐπουρανίοις (1.20). Our exaltation is also described in terms of being raised and seated ἐν τοῖς ἐπουρανίοις ἐν Χριστῷ Ἰησοῦ (2.6). "In the heavens" does not mean the spiritual blessings are located geographically in some distant realm, removed from and having little to do with ourselves. After all, we have been raised and seated there! Rather, we are to understand that the spiritual blessings of God are themselves exalted, being derived from an exalted source.

This understanding is not undermined by the reference to the spiritual beings of the evil one that are said to be ἐν τοῖς ἐπουρανίοις (6.12). As did the King of Babylon (Is 14.10) and the King of Tyre (Ezek 28.5, 17), as did the Devil himself, they have exalted themselves. But they will be brought down.

But the point of emphasis, here as throughout verses 3–14, is that God has done this *in Christ*.

1.4 *just as he chose us in him before the foundation of the universe that we would be holy and blameless before him in love* (καθὼς ἐξελέξατο ἡμᾶς ἐν αὐτῷ πρὸ καταβολῆς κόσμου εἶναι ἡμᾶς ἁγίους καὶ ἀμώμους κατενώπιον αὐτοῦ ἐν ἀγάπῃ) Ninth century codices Augiensis (F) and Boernerianus (G) have ἐν ἑαυτῷ (*in himself*), rather than ἐν αὐτῷ (*in him*),

---

[10] LXX (Ps 102.11) has ὅτι κατὰ τὸ ὕψος τοῦ οὐρανοῦ ἀπὸ τῆς γῆς.

[11] LXX (Ps 35.6) has κύριε, ἐν τῷ οὐρανῷ τὸ ἔλεός σου.

but this seems to be a misguided scribal attempt at clarification. Metzger supposes these two manuscripts have a common archetype.[12] The manuscript evidence is overwhelming in support of ἐν αὐτῷ (*in him*).

WH had a comma after κόσμου as if the thought had been completed in merely saying that the choosing was before the foundation of the world, and the Nestle Aland text, through the 25th edition, retained the comma. But in the 26th and successive editions, the comma was rightly removed, thus recognizing that Paul's thought continues and explains what God chose us to be. Before the foundation of the world, God's plan was to accomplish this in Christ, namely, that we would be holy and without blemish before him in love. God did not merely choose people to be saved, but he predetermined that they would be holy and blameless.

ἐν ἀγάπῃ (*in love*) is perhaps to be understood as an adverbial modifier of ἐξελέξατο, that is, God chose us in love, motivated by love. On the other hand, Paul may have meant to explain in what we are to be holy and blameless, *viz.*, in love. This would be reminiscent of Jesus' teaching when he taught love toward our enemies, that we might be perfect as our heavenly father is perfect (Mt 5.43–48). Paul himself reckons love to be fulfillment of the law (Rom 13.8–10, Gal 5.14, cf. Mt 5.40).

Some commentators have supposed that ἐν ἀγάπῃ should be read with the following words, προορίσας ἡμᾶς. Thus ἐν ἀγάπῃ προορίσας ἡμᾶς would be "having foreordained us in love…" Against them, Alford aptly noted that

in the whole construction of this long sentence, the verbs and participles, as natural in a solemn emphatic enumeration of God's *dealings* with His people, *precede* their qualifying clauses: e.g. εὐλογήσας ver. 3, ἐξελέξατο ver. 4, ἐχαρίτωσεν ver. 6, ἐπερίσσευσεν ver. 8, γνωρίσας ver. 9, προέθετο ib., ἀνακεφαλαιώσασθαι ver. 10. In no one case, except the necessary one of a *relative* qualification (ver. 6, and again ver. 8), does the verb follow its qualifying clause: and for this reason, that the verbs themselves are emphatic, and not the conditions under which they subsist.[13]

1.5a *having foreordained us to adoption through Jesus Christ unto himself* (προορίσας ἡμᾶς εἰς υἱοθεσίαν διὰ Ἰησοῦ Χριστοῦ εἰς αὐτόν) Here, αὐτόν is used where we might have expected the reflexive

---

[12] The Text of the NT, p. 53.
[13] Alford's Greek Testament, v. III, p. 71.

pronoun, ἑαυτόν. Robertson tells us that originally, there were no distinct reflexive forms of pronouns, and that even after distinctly reflexive forms developed, the reflexive use of the personal pronouns persisted in a number of writers.[14] In the New Testament, we see evidence of this, e.g., at John 2.24, Ἰησοῦς οὐκ ἐπίστευεν αὐτὸν αὐτοῖς, *Jesus was not trusting himself to them.*

WH, as well as earlier editions of NA, have αὐτὸν, which is an abbreviated form of ἑαυτόν. The distinction between αὐτόν and αὑτόν would have been absent in the early manuscripts, where breathing marks were not regularly used.[15] If there is anything to be debated, it is only whether we should read αὐτόν or αὑτόν; either way the meaning is "himself," i.e., God the Father. We have been adopted through Jesus Christ unto God the Father.

1.5b-6a *according to the good pleasure of his will, unto praise of the glory of his grace* God's choice to adopt us as sons was something he was pleased to do, and not something he did reluctantly or begrudingly. And this fact should result in our perceiving and esteeming the glory of his grace.

1.6 *which he bestowed on us in the Beloved One* (ἧς ἐχαρίτωσεν ἡμᾶς ἐν τῷ ἠγαπημένῳ) The genitive ἧς is not to be understood as "of which" as if to say God parceled out *some of* his grace, but rather ἧς is genitive due to attraction to its antecedent, χάριτος. English convention almost requires that we depart from Greek syntax by adding a preposition somewhere in this construction. We may say, "his grace, *with* which he graced us," or "his grace, which he bestowed *on* us," or "...gave *to* us." Perhaps the English wording that would be most true to the Greek structure is "his grace, which he gave us," but *gave* hardly suffices to convey fully the thought of ἐχαρίτωσεν. ἐχαρίτωσεν, from χαριτόω and obviously cognate to χάρις (*grace, favor*), occurs in the New Testament only here and in Luke 1.28 where Mary is addressed as the one who has been favored. Not only was the adoption of ourselves accomplished through Christ, but it was a work of God's grace, grace he bestowed on us, with which he favored us, in the Beloved, that is, in Christ.

The use of perfect tense ἠγαπημένῳ rather than present tense ἀγαπωμένῳ is curious. We see the perfect participle used of Christians

---

[14] Robertson, A Grammar of the Greek New Testament, p. 680.
[15] Robertson, p. 226, 688.

in Romans 9.25, Colossians 3.12, 1 Thessalonians 1.4 and 2 Thessalonians 2.13. Used of Christians, the perfect tense points to a status as beloved that results from the act of love accomplished in the sacrifice of Jesus (cf. Rom 5.8, Eph 5.25). But to what event does Christ's status as "beloved" point?

1.7 *according to the wealth of his grace* (κατὰ τὸ πλοῦτος τῆς χάριτος αὐτοῦ) Some form of πλοῦτος (*wealth*) or a congate occurs six times in Ephesians, all in the first three chapters (πλοῦτος in 1.7, 1.18, 2.7, 3.8, 3.16; πλούσιος in 2.4). Twice, Paul speaks of the wealth of grace, and twice, the wealth of glory. Once he speaks of God being rich in mercy. The thought being developed in the first three chapters is the exceeding generosity God has bestowed upon us who are Gentiles, and this thought is being developed with a purpose, namely, to motivate us to walk as he would have us walk, which will be the theme of chapters four through six.

1.8 *which he abundantly supplied to us* (ἧς ἐπερίσσευσεν εἰς ἡμᾶς) Apart from contextual considerations, the verb ἐπερίσσευσεν might be understood intransitively (abounded) or transitively (caused *something* to abound, abundantly supplied *something*). The relative pronoun ἧς argues for the latter. The case of a relative pronoun reflects its function in its own clause unless it has been attracted to the case of its antecedent. Here, there is no means of explaining genitive case ἧς based on its function in its own clause. However, the genitive case can readily be explained as being due to attraction to the antecedent χάριτος which is genitive. That is, ἧς is genitive so as to agree with its antecedent, genitive χάριτος. But then we must ask, had attraction to the case of the antecedent not occured, what would have been the case of the relative pronoun? Or, in other words, what is the function of the relative pronoun in its own clause? Is it the subject ("which abounded" = "grace abounded") or the object of the verb ("which he abundantly supplied" = "he abundantly supplied grace")? Generally, attraction occurs when the relative pronoun functions as an object of a verb in its own clause. Robertson said, "no instance of attraction of a nominative to an oblique case occurs in the N.T. though this idiom is found in the ancient Greek."[16] So then if we suppose attraction has occurred, as must be true, we should suppose the relative pronoun functions not as the subject in its own clause, but as the object of the verb. Necessarily then, the verb must be understood as transitive, for an intransitive verb has no object. For this reason, we understand that

---

[16] p. 715.

"he [God] caused to abound grace," and we translate, "which he caused to abound" or "which he abundantly supplied."

1.9 *having made known to us the mystery of his will, according to his good pleasure, which he planned in him* (γνωρίσας ἡμῖν τὸ μυστήριον τοῦ θελήματος αὐτοῦ κατὰ τὴν εὐδοκίαν αὐτοῦ ἣν προέθετο ἐν αὐτῷ) The antecedent of ἣν (*which*) is εὐδοκίαν (*good pleasure*); God planned what he pleased, or thought good, to do. But then does ἣν προέθετο ἐν αὐτῷ mean *which he planned in himself,* or *which he planned in him* (i.e., *Christ*)? Were the former intended, we might have expected the reflexive pronoun ἑαυτῷ rather than αὐτῷ. In fact, ἑαυτῷ shows up in at least one manuscript.[17] But without assuming the epsilon, αὐτῷ written without diacriticals could represent αὑτῷ, the abbreviation for ἑαυτῷ. (See the note on verse 5a, and Robertson, p. 226.) And in any event, we have already established that αὐτόν may be used reflexively (see on vs. 5). So then, the wording would not preclude our understanding the phrase to mean *which he planned in himself.* But the theme of this section is what God has done in Christ. Thirteen times (twelve instances other than this one) in a passage of 203 words, Paul uses some phrase such as ἐν Χριστῷ, ἐν αὐτῷ, διὰ Ἰησοῦ Χριστοῦ, ἐν τῷ ἠγαπημένῳ, διὰ τοῦ αἵματος αὐτοῦ, ἐν ᾧ, etc. These assertions about all that God has done *in Christ* are regular enough that to understand ἣν προέθετο ἐν αὐτῷ otherwise would leave the middle of this passage void of reference to Christ in a striking way. God planned this in Christ.

1.10 *unto a dispensation of the fullness of the times* (εἰς οἰκονομίαν τοῦ πληρώματος τῶν καιρῶν) οἰκονομία is described in Xenophon's Oeconomicus. In response to Socrates' question concerning the nature of estate management (οἰκονομία), Cristobulus says, "The work of a good estate manager (οἰκονόμου) at least then seems to be to manage his own house well."[18] To which Socrates is said to have replied, "And might it be also the house of another, if someone permits it to him, would he not be able, if he desired, to manage it well, just as also his own?"[19] Cristobulus replies in the affirmative.

Shebna, who was "in charge of the royal household" (Is 22.15), was warned that he was about to be deposed from his οἰκονομίας, i.e., his of-

---

[17] the ninth century Codex Porphyrianus, P 025.

[18] Δοκεῖ γοῦν, ἔφη ὁ Κριτόβουλος, οἰκονόμου ἀγαθοῦ εἶναι εὖ οἰκεῖν τὸν ἑαυτοῦ οἶκον.

[19] Ἦ καὶ τὸν ἄλλου δὲ οἶκον, ἔφη ὁ Σωκράτης, εἰ ἐπιτρέποι τις αὐτῷ, οὐκ ἂν δύναιτο, εἰ βούλοιτο, εὖ οἰκεῖν, ὥσπερ καὶ τὸν ἑαυτοῦ;

fice, his stewardship (22.19, LXX). Jesus speaks of the faithful οἰκονόμος whom the Lord puts over the service of dispensing appropriate food allowances (Lk 12.42).

An οἰκονομία is a responsibility for managing one's own or another's wealth and transactions, appropriately allocating and distributing resources (Lk 16.2–4; cf. 16.5–7). Our English word *economy*, for which one meaning is "a system of producing, distributing, and consuming wealth," comes from οἰκονομία. One may speak of the economy of a household, of a city (Erastus was the οἰκονόμος of the city of Corinth, Rom. 16.23), or of a country. Josephus uses this word in describing the responsibility given to Joseph by Pharaoh (Ant. 2,89).[20]

Paul, as did Jesus, uses this vocabulary to speak of the distribution of God's wealth to those of his household. Paul speaks of the stewardship of evangelists (1 Tim 1.4) and overseers (Tit 1.7), who are responsible for distributing the wealth in God's house. He also uses it in speaking of his own responsibility to preach the gospel (1 Cor 9.17). But right here in Ephesians 1.10, if we are to think of a particular οἰκονόμος (*steward*) who is responsible for distributing the wealth, we should think of the Lord (whether specifically God the Father or Jesus himself). It is he who makes available the aforementioned wealth of grace (1.7).[21]

The phrase "dispensation of the fulness of the times" brings into view a planned distribution that was to occur at the culmination of a defined time period. At the appointed time God's grace, which was planned in Christ, would be distributed. This anticipates the point Paul will more fully develop in Ephesians 3.1–11. There Paul will speak of his own οἰκονομία, namely, his privilege to preach even to the Gentiles the unsearchable riches of Christ, thus making known what had previously been a mystery, although it was part of God's eternal purpose.

Mitton cited οἰκονομία as an example of vocabulary used differently in Ephesians than in Colossians and therefore as evidence that Paul did not write Ephesians, saying, "in Colossians, as in other Pauline writings, the Greek word *oikonomia* is used to mean 'stewardship' or 'an assign-

---

[20] αὐτῷ τὴν οἰκονομίαν παραδίδωσιν, ὥστε πράττειν ἃ καὶ τῷ πλήθει τῶν Αἰγυπτίων καὶ τῷ βασιλεῖ συμφέροντα ὑπολαμβάνει, τὸν ἐξευρόντα τὴν τοῦ πράγματος ὁδὸν καὶ προστάτην ἄριστον αὐτῆς ὑπολαβὼν γενήσεσθαι.

[21] See MaGee's comments (p. 138) wherein he distinguishes between God as the one in charge of the distribution in Eph 1.9–10 and Paul "as God's agent" who is the one making the distribution in 3.2–3.

ment,' a special task entrusted to someone. In Ephesians, however, it is used quite differently to mean 'God's own strategy', his broad statesmanship" [12]. However, in truth, *oikonomia* is used in Ephesians just as it is used in Paul's other writings.

τοῦ πληρώματος τῶν καιρῶν (*the fulness of the times*) should not lead us to think that God was waiting for some time when everything would be just right, but rather that God had ordained a time when the Christ would come into the world and the mystery would be revealed, and when that time had fully come, the dispensation or distribution of God's grace was made. This is the same idea as in Galatians 4.4. The dispensation τοῦ πληρώματος τῶν καιρῶν is "the dispensation peculiar to the fulness of the times."[22]

On the word καιρῶν, see the comments on 5.16.

to sum up all things in the Christ, the things in the heavens and the things upon the earth in him (ἀνακεφαλαιώσασθαι τὰ πάντα ἐν τῷ χριστῷ, τὰ ἐπὶ τοῖς οὐρανοῖς καὶ τὰ ἐπὶ τῆς γῆς ἐν αὐτῷ)   What God has accomplished for us, he has accomplished in the Christ. ἀνακεφαλαιώσασθαι, *to sum up*, aorist middle infinitive of ἀνακεφαλαιόω. Paul uses this word in Romans 13.9, "if there be any other commandment, it is summed up in this saying..."

Why does he say ἐπὶ τοῖς οὐρανοῖς rather than ἐν τοῖς οὐρανοῖς as in verse 3? The TR, with the support of several uncials, does have ἐν τοῖς οὐρανοῖς. Compare Colossians 1.20.

It is difficult to decide whether the words ἐν αὐτῷ (*in him*) go with what precedes or with what follows. At first glance, they seem unnecessary with either phrase. The preceding phrase already has the words ἐν τῷ χριστῷ (*in the Christ*), and the following phrase begins with ἐν ᾧ (*in whom*). The various forms of the Greek text handle these words in a variety of ways. The UBS5 and NA28 put them at the end of verse 10, followed by a period, "to sum up all things in the Christ, the things in the heavens and the things on the earth *in him*." The TR puts them in verse 11, and punctuates so as to make these words an introduction to what follows: "*In him* in whom also we were allotted." Either way, the words must be understood as an emphatic repetition (Alford), and we should not allow our quest for the appropriate placement of a punctuation mark to distract us from this thoroughgoing point: It is in Christ that all these things are

---

[22] Meyer, p. 321, quoting Calovius.

accomplished. However many times Paul must say that in order to make that abundantly clear, he will.[23] But as to the proper punctuation, I would put a comma after ἐν αὐτῷ, letting ἐν αὐτῷ stand with the foregoing. Then the whole phrase τὰ ἐπὶ τοῖς οὐρανοῖς καὶ τὰ ἐπὶ τῆς γῆς ἐν αὐτῷ is seen as an emphatic repetition of and explanation of the phrase τὰ πάντα ἐν τῷ χριστῷ. Thus we would have, "to sum up all things in the Christ, the things in the heavens and the things upon the earth in him."

1.11 *in whom also we were allotted* (ἐν ᾧ καὶ ἐκληρώθημεν) The καὶ (*also*) serves to include the action of allotting in the previously described summing up. In Christ, all things are summed up, also/even our being made an allotment, *i.e.,* an inheritance.

The force of the passive ἐκληρώθημεν is the question that needs attention here. The question is basically this: Does Paul speak of God's people as receiving something, an inheritance (as in the KJV, NAS, ESV, NLV), or does he speak of God's people as being something God receives, as being God's inheritance (as in the ASV, NIV, NET)?

κληρόω is *assign by lot*, or simply, *allot*. ἐκληρώθημεν is a passive form of this verb. The passive voice would seem to mean *be assigned by lot*. The first person plural ἐκληρώθημεν would mean *we were allotted*, not meaning something was allotted to us, but rather meaning we are the thing that was allotted.[24] That is, God inherited us by lot.

Paul explains the result of our being allotted in verse 12, εἰς τὸ εἶναι ἡμᾶς εἰς ἔπαινον δόξης αὐτοῦ, *unto our being for the praise of his glory.* Alford rightly observes that inasmuch as the result is our "being" something, we have confirmation that ἐκληρώθημεν should be understood in "the strict passive sense," and concluded that the meaning is *"we were made an (God's) inheritance."*[25]

---

[23] So also there is a redundant δι' αὐτοῦ (*through him*) in Col 1.20 which, perhaps on account of its redundancy, was omitted in numerous manuscripts. See the note in Metzger, A Textual Commentary on the Greek New Testament.

[24] Aristot. Const. Ath. 43.2, Demosthenes; Against Timocrates, 24.89; Lucian, De Luctu 2.

[25] Meyer argued that just as πιστεύομαι may mean *I trust* rather than *I am believed*, so also ἐκληρώθημεν may mean *we inherited* rather than *we were inherited*. He argued this must be the meaning because to be chosen by lot is to be chosen by chance, and of course, we were not chosen merely by chance, but by God's will. And so Meyer concluded the meaning is "we inherited," or "we were made partakers of the inheritance." Meyer cited two passages, Pind. Ol. viii.19 and Thuc. vi. 42, in support of construing the passive voice in this manner. Alford contradicted Meyer. Acknowledging only the Pindar passage, Alford disputed Meyer's use of it and dismissed its relevance, and then concluded that the true meaning is "we were made an inheritance."

The significance of *allotted* is not that God's people are chosen by chance. Rather, the language is reminiscent of the OT language wherein God's people are his *naḥalah*, *(inheritance)*.[26] In the LXX, *naḥalah* is usually translated by κληρονομία *(inheritance)*. But it is represented by κλῆρος *(lot)* in more than three dozen instances.

Considering specifically those many contexts wherein Israel was described as a *naḥalah*, most often the LXX has κληρονομία. But in two instances (Dt 9.26,29), the word κλῆρος is used,[27] and in one instance (Dt 4.20), ἔγκληρον is used.At the end of verse 14, Paul will speak of the redemption of the περιποιήσεως. The word περιποιήσεως might refer to *the act of acquiring* or to *the thing acquired*, a *possession* (see comments on verse 14). If we take ἐκληρώθημεν in verse 11 to mean *we were allotted* and περιποιήσεως in verse 14 to mean *possession* or *acquisition*,[28] we see a continuity in the metaphor.

This idea of inheritance will be carried forward into verse 14, where the Holy Spirit is said to be a pledge of our inheritance, that is, of our being inherited. Then again in verse 18, we will see Paul speak of God's "inheritance in the saints." We who are God's people comprise an allotment, an inheritance, something designated as belonging to God, having been so foreordained. God had been deprived of this allotment because of our sin. However, in Christ, God has redeemed his possession, regained it.

having been predetermined according to a plan of the one who works all things according to the counsel of his will Chrysostom saw in these words a clarification of the preceding statement that we were chosen by lot. Whereas the lot is presumed to determine outcomes by chance, Chrysostom supposed that Paul here corrects that notion, saying this was all predetermined by God in accordance with his plan.[29] But I think such

---

[26] Dt 4.20, 9.26,29, 1 Sam 10.1, 1 Ki 8.51,53, 2 Ki 21.14, Ps 33.12, 68.10 (68.9 in English), 106.5, Is 19.25, Mic 7.18, *et al.*

[27] On the relationship between κλῆρος *(lot)* and κληρονομία *(inheritance)* in the LXX, see the discussion in TDNT, vol. 3, p. 759.

[28] So BDAG, p. 804. See below on vs. 14.

[29] Chrysostom, Homily II, "Inasmuch as a lot is a matter of chance, not of deliberate choice, nor of virtue, (for it is closely allied to ignorance and accident, and oftentimes passing over the virtuous, brings forward the worthless into notice,) observe how he corrects this very point: 'having been foreordained,' saith he, 'according to the purpose of Him who worketh all things.' That is to say, not merely have we been made a heritage, as, again, we have not merely been chosen, (for it is God who chooses,) and so neither have we merely been allotted, (for it is God who allots,) but it is 'according to a purpose.'" NPNF vol. 13, transl. by Gross Alexander.

clarification is hardly needed. Yes, many things were decided by lot and thus by chance, but God also used the lot as a means of revealing his will where the outcome certainly was not by chance (e.g. Acts 1.24–26). In effect, to be allotted was to be appointed, to be ordained by God.

1.12 *such that we who had previously hoped in the Christ would be to the praise of his glory* (εἰς τὸ εἶναι ἡμᾶς εἰς ἔπαινον δόξης αὐτοῦ τοὺς προηλπικότας ἐν τῷ Χριστῷ)   τοὺς προηλπικότας ἐν τῷ Χριστῷ (*who had previously hoped in the Christ*) does not refer to "believers in general"[30] or "all Christians"[31], but rather to the Jewish believers in contrast to the Gentile believers.[32] Those who had previously hoped in Christ, in a coming Messiah,[33] were the Jews. προηλπικότας is *having previously hoped.* τῷ χριστῷ is *in the Christ = in the Messiah.* Jews had long hoped in a coming Messiah.

Hoehner argues against this understanding in part because he believes ἡμᾶς in verse 12 must have the same meaning as in verses 5 and 8 where it refers to "all Christians."[34] But could not Paul choose to talk about "us" who are Christians, and then subsequently speak of an "us" that is a smaller group? And if he were to do so, how might he indicate that the "us" in verse 12 is a smaller group? Perhaps by using some sort of qualifying phrase, like, "us…who had previously hoped in the Christ"?

While it should be clear that Paul distinguishes between Jew and Gentile here in verses 12–13, it is not so easy to discern what he means by ἡμᾶς (*us*) near the beginning of verse 12. Grammatically, τοὺς προηλπικότας ἐν τῷ Χριστῷ is an attributive descriptor of ἡμᾶς whereas the phrase referring to Gentiles (ἐν ᾧ καὶ ὑμεῖς…, *in whom you also…*) is not. So then if we see only the phrase τοὺς προηλπικότας ἐν τῷ Χριστῷ as pointing back to ἡμᾶς (*us*), ἡμᾶς would be understood as referring specifically to Jewish believers. If that is what was intended, the sense of the whole verse is εἰς τὸ εἶναι ἡμᾶς εἰς ἔπαινον δόξης αὐτοῦ, namely, τοὺς προηλπικότας ἐν τῷ

---

[30] Lincoln, p. 37.

[31] Schnackenburg, p. 64.

[32] See Introduction p. 27n19.

[33] Some commentators have concluded that in Paul, Χριστός may be nothing more than a surname, and in any event does not stress Jesus' identity as the Messiah. See especially Dahl, *"The Messiahship of Jesus in Paul."* Others have gone so far as to deny that Jesus' identity as the Messiah was of any concern to Paul. See for example, McRae and more emphatically, Gaston. But against all of these, and especially countering Dahl's arguments, see Novenson. More recently, N.T. Wright sees an *"a priori* case for assuming a messianic reference" in Paul's writings (Paul and the Faithfulness of God, p. 818).

[34] Hoehner, p. 232.

Χριστῷ. That is, *unto our being for the praise of his glory*, namely, *those who had previously hoped in the Christ.* This is not to say that only Jewish believers are to the praise of God's glory, but merely to say that the mention of being to the praise of God's glory happens to be part of what Paul says when he is speaking of Jews who had previously hoped in Christ.

However, because the message of Ephesians has to do most especially with what God has done for the Gentiles and this is part of that which extols God's glory (1.18, 3.21), a case can be made for taking ἡμᾶς (*us*) as meaning *all Christians* and then understanding that Paul subsequently subdivided "us" into two groups, those who had previously hoped in the coming Messiah (Jewish believers) and Gentile believers who have now also been sealed with the Holy Spirit. Reading it this way, we would take τοὺς προηλπικότας ἐν τῷ Χριστῷ as parallel to καὶ ὑμεῖς ἀκούσαντες τὸν λόγον τῆς ἀληθείας.. (*you also having heard the word of the truth…*) and reckon both to be subcategories of the *us* who are *unto the praise of his glory.* Thus it would not be only Jewish believers but also Gentile believers who are said to be to the praise of God's glory here in 1.12*f.*

But regardless of the precise signficance of ἡμᾶς (*us*) in verse 12, it is clear that Paul speaks specifically of Jewish believers in verse 12, and then in the next verse, he directly and distinctly addresses the Gentiles for the first time.

To reinforce the conclusion that these are the two groups in view, notice that again in 2.1*ff*, there is a *you* and a *we.* There, Paul first speaks of *you being dead by your trespasses and sins,* and then acknowledges that *we also…were children by nature of wrath even as the rest.* The *we* is not "we who write," namely, Paul.[35] Clearly the *you* refers to the Gentiles as is explicitly stated in 2.11, and therefore the *we* certainly refers to Jews. "We Jews were also children of wrath." So too in 1.12–13, the meaning is, "the Jews who had previously hoped in the Christ, and you Gentiles also."

The whole theme of chapter two is encouragement to Gentiles, reminding them of God's great gifts to them who had been so far removed from God, in contrast to Jews who could be described as having been "near" (2.17). Paul reminds them that Jewish believers had also had the same need as did the Gentiles (2.3), and that Gentile believers now have equal standing in the house of God along with Jewish believers (2.13–22). Again in chapter three, Paul will affirm that the Gentiles have equal

---

[35] Hoenher supposes that Paul here again merely means himself, p. 317.

standing as "fellow heirs and fellow members of the body and fellow partakers of the promise" (3.6). And then in 3.18, he will pray that they, along "with all the saints,"may be strong to apprehend the things of God. This message to Gentiles of belonging, of being beneficiaries of God's great kindness, does not begin suddenly, without prelude, in 2.11.[36] It is the point of the letter from the beginning. It is Paul's purpose from the beginning to emphasize to Gentile believers what God has done for them, so that in chapters four through six he might emphasize to those same Gentile believers how they must respond. Those who fail to see a distinct reference to Gentile believers in 1.13 fail to see the unity of the theme of the letter from beginning to end. This whole letter is an appeal to Gentile Christians to understand how great is the blessing they have in Christ, and to understand that they fully have the same status before God as Jewish believers, and therefore to walk accordingly.

And so it is that we must understand the words of 1.12, τοὺς προηλπικότας ἐν τῷ Χριστῷ, as a reference to Jewish believers in contrast to Paul's Gentile audience whom he addresses as *you also*.

In what sense are they to the praise of God's glory? Perhaps we can appreciate the meaning of this by considering some who were the opposite. When the spies returned from Canaan with a fearful report convincing the congregation that they would fall by the sword, God spoke of dispossessing them and starting over with Moses (Num 14.1–12). But Moses interceded on Israel's behalf, arguing that mankind's understanding of God's power was at stake.[37] When Israel went away into exile, God's name was profaned because "it was said of them, 'These are the people of the LORD; yet they have come out of His land'" (Ezek 36.20). In both instances, the unfaithfulness of the people cast doubt on God's glory. In both instances, God had concern for his holy name. And for this reason, in the second instance, he promised that he would bring his people out of captivity, thus vindicating the holiness of his great name (Ezek 36.21–23).

Now, Paul writes to those who through Christ have been allotted to God as his possession, just as he had predetermined and in accordance with his plan, and says that they are to the praise of his glory. God's plan

---

[36] Contrary to Hoehner, who wrote, "It is not until [chapter two] verse 11 that Paul makes a distinction between Jews and Gentiles" (p. 318).

[37] Nu. 14:15f, "…then the nations who have heard of Thy fame will say, 'Because the LORD could not bring this people into the land which he promised them by oath, therefore He slaughtered them in the wilderness.'"

has been accomplished. In truth, it is the culmination of all that God did throughout history, including his longsuffering with faithless Israel. Now, as Paul says in 3.10, the wisdom of God is manifest. The gloriousness of God includes his great mercy and his ability to transform a rebellious people into beloved sons, and when he does so, their redemption is to the praise of his glory.

1.13 *in whom you also*   Now he is addressing, not the Jews who had before hoped in Christ, but the Gentiles who also have been sealed by the Holy Spirit. Here, the significance of καὶ is *also*. In addition to us Jewish believers, now also you Gentiles heard the word of the truth; you also have believed.

having heard the word of the truth, the good news of your salvation, in whom also having believed   The Jews had been looking for the Christ. The gospel had been preached to them beforehand. But now Gentiles have heard the good news of salvation and have believed in the Christ.

These facts regarding the Gentiles are introduced by means of participles, ἀκούσαντες (*having heard*) and πιστεύσαντες (*having believed*), adverbial qualifiers explaining the circumstances of their sealing, which Paul is about to describe.

You (that is, the Gentiles to whom Paul writes) *were sealed by the promised Holy Spirit* (ἐσφραγίσθητε τῷ πνεύματι τῆς ἐπαγγελίας τῷ ἁγίῳ,)   There are at least three ideas associated with the language of sealing. First there is the idea of identification. Something is sealed with a mark indicating to whom it belongs. If a decree was sealed, the seal served as an authenticating signature (1 Ki 21.8, Neh 10.1, Est 3.10, 8.8, 8.10, *et al.*). The seal was formed by means of a cylinder that was rolled on a clay surface leaving an impression, or by means of a ring that was pressed into the surface.

But we see another idea when sealing refers to something that has been so marked consequently spared some coming destruction (Rev 7.3*f*). Such securing by sealing was not always connected with a literal identifying seal, even though the words used in the various contexts are the same (Hebrew noun *ḥotam* and verb *ḥatam*, and Greek noun σφραγίς and verb σφραγίζω).

Then as Fitzer noted, "The fact that the contents of a sealed vessel or purse were inaccessible gave σφραγίζω the further sense 'to close.'"[38] So

---

[38] TDNT, vol. 7, p. 945. After discussing the wide variety of uses of the word group, Fitzer summarized:

"The seal thus yields a complex nexus of relations. Mixed in it are the motifs of power

we see Jesus' tomb being sealed (Mt 27.66). Compare Job 14.17, Deuteronomy 32.34, and Daniel 12.4.

It is the first of these ideas, the idea of identification, that is prominent in Ephesians 1.13. This is consistent with the language of *possession* (περιποίησις) and *inheritance* (κληρονομία). God has identified the saints from among the Gentiles as part of the possession that constitutes his inheritance, or as Peter says, "a people for God's own possession (περιποίησιν)...you once were not a people, but now you are the people of God" (1 Pt 2.9f). But the idea of protection is not far behind inasmuch as the sealing results in the redemption of those sealed (vs. 14, cf. 2 Cor 5.4–5). So also at 2 Timothy 2.19, the seal identifies those who belong to the Lord, but the result is that the firm foundation of God stands. This is the point Paul is making in Ephesians 1.13. His readers have been identified as belonging to God, *sealed by the promised Holy Spirit*.

Much of the attention given to this phrase seems to derive from the notion that Paul is talking about the Spirit doing something in us in such a way that *we can discern* the sealing and thus be assured of our salvation. Whatever one may think of that idea, the point of *this* passage is that God's inheritance in the saints is assured to *him*, that he has assured it to *himself*, having sealed it such that "the Lord knows them that are his" (2 Tim 2.19).[39]

The words τῆς ἐπαγγελίας (*of the promise*) should be understood in light of Ezekiel 36.27, 37.14, 39.29, Joel 2.28, Matthew 3.11, Luke 3.16, John 7.38f, 20.22, Acts 1.4f, 2.16f,33,38. From the days of the OT prophets, God's people had anticipated a pouring out of God's Spirit that would accompany the restoration of the kingdom. For this reason, when Jesus spoke of the promise of the Father, telling the apostles they would be baptized in the Holy Spirit "not many days hence," Peter responded, "Do you at this time restore the kingdom to Israel?" While Peter may have misunderstood the nature of the restored kingdom, he was right to connect the promise of the Spirit with the restoration of the kingdom. In the

---

and authorisation, of legal validity and reliability, of the inviolate, closed and secret, of the costly and valuable." (p. 946).

[39] With this understanding in mind, an intriguing alternate translation possibility arises. While it seems most likely that τῷ πνεύματι τῆς ἐπαγγελίας τῷ ἁγίῳ means *by the Holy Spirit of promise*, is it possible that τῷ ἁγίῳ is not an attributive modifier of τῷ πνεύματι but is rather a true dative, the indirect object of ἐσφραγίσθητε, such that we should translate ἐσφραγίσθητε τῷ πνεύματι τῆς ἐπαγγελίας τῷ ἁγίῳ as *you were sealed by the Spirit of promise to the Holy One*?

messianic kingdom, God's people are identified as his inasmuch as they are led by his Spirit. "As many as are led by the Spirit of God, these are the Sons of God" (Rom 8.14).

1.14 *which is a seal of our inheritance* (ὅ ἐστιν ἀρραβὼν τῆς κληρονομίας ἡμῶν)   Neuter ὅ (*which*) agrees with its antecedent, neuter πνεύματι (*spirit*), but the Received Text (as well as Nestle Aland as recently as the 25th edition) has masculine ὅς in place of ὅ. Hoehner accepts ὅς and explains the masculine pronoun as agreeing with ἀρραβών[40], but in a footnote, indicates that the evidence favors ὅς only with "a slight edge" and then rightly concludes, "Either way the sense remains the same."[41]

ἀρραβών is a Hebrew loanword. It is used in Genesis 38 (vss. 17,18, 20) for the collateral Judah provided to Tamar, assuring payment would be forthcoming.

In many extra-biblical contexts, it is an initial payment, a down payment constituting a part of the full payment.[42] In this sense, it is explained as "πρόδομα. καὶ ἄγκιστρον."[43] But whether the ἀρραβών is part of the final payment or not, its purpose is to provide assurance.

Were we to construe genitive ἡμῶν subjectively as indicating possession (*our inheritance*) it would seem that in the middle of talking about *God's* inheritance (vs. 11, 18), also described as God's acquisition in the very next phrase after the words *our inheritance*, Paul would have interjected an unrelated and unexplained reference to a different inheritance, something *we* inherit. But the genitive case need not be construed as indicating possession. In general, the genitive is the case of kind, and possession is only one way of describing kind. Here we probably do better to understand the genitive case as being objective, specifying content and thus describing the kind of inheritance. It is God's inheritance, an inheri-

---

[40] p. 241.

[41] *Ibid.*, n. 1. Whether we ought to reckon ὅς, or ὅ, to have the slight edge is debatable.

[42] In AD 99, a young woman named Thenetkouis in the Faiyum Oasis in Egypt was hired to load olives into a press during the coming harvest. She was given 16 silver drachmas as an ἀρραβονα with the understanding that this prepayment would be deducted in installments from her daily wage during the coming weeks. Moreover, should she have failed to honor her obligation, she was to repay her employer the ἀρραβονα times two. An intriguing epilogue to this story is that two years later, the owner of the press appended a statement to the document indicating that he had received the aforementioned 16 drachma and made no further claim. Does this mean Thenetkouis failed to fulfill her obligation under the contract? And if so, did the owner release her for half of what she was obligated to pay? Had he patiently waited for two years to get back even the 16 drachma? (P. Faya, 91).

[43] HESYCHII ALEXANDRINI.

tance *of us*, just as a man may have an inheritance *of money*. The money does not inherit. The man inherits the money. So also κληρονομίας ἡμῶν (*inheritance of us*) does not mean *we inherit*. God inherits us.

To be sure, in every other NT passage where κληρονομία is associated with a genitive personal pronoun, the genitive is to be understood subjectively (Mt 21.38, Mk 12.7, Lk 20.14, Eph 1.18). But three of these are parallel accounts of one incident, and the other, Ephesians 1.18, serves to confirm that in the present context, Paul is not talking about something we inherit, but about us as God's inheritance.

We may also acknowledge that in the LXX a genitive associated with κληρονομία is almost always subjective. But at Psalm 110.6 (111.6 in MT) κληρονομίαν ἐθνῶν means the inheritance that consists of the nations. Isaiah 49.8 has κληρονομίαν ἐρήμου which means an inheritance of desolation, or a desolate inheritance.

The noun κληρονόμος (*heir*) is used with an objective genitive to describe what is inherited in Romans 4.13 (*heir of the world*), Hebrews 1.2 (*heir of all things*), 6.17 (*heirs of the promise*), 11.7, and James 2.5 (*heirs of the kingdom*).

The use of a genitive personal pronoun to describe the content of the inheritance is unusual, but not because it is genitive. It is the personal pronoun as the content that is unusual. People inherit more often than people are inherited. But clearly in Ephesians 1, the context has to do with people who are inherited, which is incontrovertibly shown by 1.18 even if there is debate about the significance of ἐκληρώθημεν in 1.11.

unto redemption of the possession unto praise of his glory (εἰς ἀπολύτρωσιν τῆς περιποιήσεως, εἰς ἔπαινον τῆς δόξης αὐτοῦ) The noun περιποίησις (*possession*) can refer to the act of preserving (Heb 10.39), or to the act of acquiring (1 Th 5.9, 2 Th 2.14), or it may be a name for the thing that is acquired (1 Pt 2.9). The first meaning makes no sense in the present context. If we were to suppose the second meaning is what Paul had in mind, we would understand ἀπολύτρωσιν τῆς περιποιήσεως as *redemption of the acquiring* which also fails to make sense in this context. But it suits the context very well, for the reason mentioned above (see comment on verse 11), to understand ἀπολύτρωσιν τῆς περιποιήσεως as *redemption of the acquisition*, namely that acquisition that belongs to God.

This idea is derived from the OT (Ex 19.5, Dt 7.6, 14.2, 26.18, Ps 135.4, Mal 3.17). In the LXX, in these passages where God speaks of defining a people for his own possession, the word s*egullah* (*possession, valued property, peculiar treasure*) is usually represented by περιούσιος (περιουσιασμόν at Ps 134.4). But at Malachi 3.17 (*'And they will be Mine,' says the Lord of hosts, 'on the day that I prepare My own possession'*), the Greek is περιποίησιν, the word that Peter uses (1 Pt 2.9) as he alludes to those OT passages, and the word that Paul uses here in Ephesians with the same meaning. So then εἰς ἀπολύτρωσιν τῆς περιποιήσεως is *unto redemption of the possession*. We who are God's people comprise an allotment, something designated as belonging to God. God had been deprived of this allotment because of our sin, but in Christ, God has redeemed his possession, regained it.

It is also worth noting the verb cognate in Acts 20.28. Luke records Paul's speech to the Ephesian elders wherein Paul spoke of the church as that which the Lord acquired (περιεποιήσατο).

1.15–21   Paul's Thankfulness for the Gentiles

On account of this, I also, having heard of your faith in the Lord Jesus and the love for all the saints, cease not giving thanks for you, making remembrance in all my prayers, that the God of our Lord Jesus Christ, the father of glory, might give to you a spirit of wisdom and revelation in his knowledge, the eyes of your heart having been enlightened unto your perceiving what is the hope of his calling, what is the wealth of the glory of his inheritance in the saints, and what is the surpassing greatness of his power unto us who believe according to the working of the might of his strength, which he worked in the Christ, when he raised him from the dead and seated him at his right hand in the heavens above every rule and authority and power and lordship and every name that is named, not only in this age but also in the coming age.

Here we have another long sentence, not as long as the sentence that runs from verse 3 to verse 14, but a bit more complex. Perhaps it will help to arrange the text in a manner that will help show how the various clauses are related to one another.

ON ACCOUNT OF THIS,

> having heard of your
>
> - faith in the Lord
> - and love unto all the saints

I ALSO CEASE NOT GIVING THANKS ON BEHALF OF YOU

MAKING REMEMBERANCE UPON MY PRAYERS

> *that the God of our Lord Jesus Christ, the father of glory, might give to you a spirit of wisdom and revelation in his knowledge*

THE EYES OF YOUR HEART HAVING BEEN ENLIGHTENED

> *unto your knowing*
>
> - what is the hope of his calling
> - what is the wealth of the glory of his inheritance in the saints,
> - and what is the exceeding greatness of his power unto you who believe
>
>> *according to the working of the might of his strength which he worked in the Christ*
>>
>> - when he raised him from the dead
>> - and seated at his right hand in the heavens above every ruler and authority and power and lordship and every name that is named not only in this age but in the coming one.

1.15 *On account of this, I also, having heard of your faith*[44] *in the Lord Jesus and the love for all the saints* There are several variations in the manuscripts, most including the word ἀγάπην (*love*) at one place or another. Following the καὶ we see

> τὴν εἰς πάντας τοὺς ἁγίους (the reading of ℵ*, B)
> *the (faith) unto all the saints*

---

[44] In τὴν καθ᾽ ὑμᾶς πίστιν, we see the prepositional phrase καθ᾽ ὑμᾶς in the attributive position, *the according-to-you faith = your faith*. Cf. Zerwick, p. 131, §130.

τὴν ἀγάπην εἰς πάντας τοὺς ἁγίους
the love unto all the saints

τὴν εἰς πάντας τοὺς ἁγίους ἀγάπην
the unto-all-the-saints love = the love unto all the saints

εἰς πάντας τοὺς ἁγίους ἀγάπην
unto all the saints, love

τὴν ἀγάπην τὴν εἰς πάντας τοὺς ἁγίους (the reading of NA28 and UBS5)
the love that is unto all the saints

If the original reading were the shortest reading, τὴν εἰς πάντας τοὺς ἁγίους, that being the one found in Vaticanus and in the original hand of Sinaiticus, we might suppose the presence of τὴν ἀγάπην in many mss (or simply ἀγάπην in some) came about due to assimilation to the parallel passage in Colossians 1.4. Why some scribes would have then moved ἀγάπην to the end of the phrase (mss 81, 104, 326) is a mystery.

But there is a greater problem with accepting the shortest reading. Both τὴν καθ' ὑμᾶς πίστιν ἐν τῷ κυρίῳ Ἰησοῦ and τὴν ἀγάπην τὴν εἰς πάντας τοὺς ἁγίους are objects of the verb ἀκούσας, that is, Paul has heard both of their faith (in the Lord Jesus) and their love (unto all the saints). If we accept the shortest reading, which omits τὴν ἀγάπην, then the second object of ἀκούσας, that is, the second thing that Paul has heard, is merely "the [something] unto all the saints." What had he heard that was unto all the saints? Given that the article is feminine, we might suppose we are to infer a repetition of πίστιν (*faith*) and understand that Paul is saying he has heard of their faith in the Lord Jesus and their faith to all the saints. But were that the case, we would really expect dative ἐν πᾶσιν τοῖς ἁγίοις (*among all the saints*), or with a different meaning, perhaps genitive πάντων τῶν ἁγίων, rather than accusative εἰς πάντας τοὺς ἁγίους. The problem is not that πίστιν cannot have an accusative object—it can, as in Acts 20.21, 24.24, Colossians 2.5—but rather that if the faith is followed by an accusative object, we would expect that object to be Christ, as in Colossians 2.5.

If the original reading were τὴν εἰς πάντας τοὺς ἁγίους ἀγάπην, with ἀγάπην at the end of the phrase, it is not clear what would account for the origin of the other readings.

But if the original reading were τὴν ἀγάπην τὴν εἰς πάντας τοὺς ἁγίους, it is possible that ἀγάπην τὴν was omitted in some manuscripts due to homoeoarcton. A scribe copied up to the first occurrence of τὴν, and then when his eye returned to his exemplar, it fell on the second occurrence of the word and he resumed copying at εἰς, thus omitting ἀγάπην τὴν.

This may be one of those passages where WH relied too heavily on the great codices Sinaiticus and Vaticanus, failing to consider sufficiently the weighty evidence that runs counter to the original reading of those two manuscripts.

1.15–16 In saying *having heard of your faith* (ἀκούσας τὴν καθ' ὑμᾶς πίστιν), Paul here, as in 3.2, leaves the impression that he is writing to people whom he knows by reputation more so than by personal contact. See the discussion of Recipients in the Introduction.

After the insertion of the adverbial clause wherein Paul explains the circumstance of his giving thanks, namely, that he had heard of their faith and love, the words οὐ παύομαι (*I cease not*) resume the thought begun in verse 15 with κἀγώ (*I also*).

I cease not giving thanks for you, making remembrance in all my prayers As he often does in his letters, Paul tells his readers of his prayers on their behalf. See the very similar sentiment and language at Philemon 4, 1 Thessalonians 1.2 and Philippians 1.3–4, as well as a similar sentiment expressed in slightly less similar language at Romans 1.8, Colossians 1.3, and 1 Corinthians 1.4.

1.17 *that the God of our Lord Jesus Christ, the father of glory, might give to you a spirit of wisdom and revelation in his knowledge* (ἵνα ὁ θεὸς τοῦ κυρίου ἡμῶν Ἰησοῦ Χριστοῦ, ὁ πατὴρ τῆς δόξης, δώῃ ὑμῖν πνεῦμα σοφίας καὶ ἀποκαλύψεως ἐν ἐπιγνώσει αὐτοῦ) In his letter to the church at Corinth, Paul mentioned his prayer that they too, "in every thing were enriched in him (i.e., Christ) in every word and all knowledge (ἐν παντὶ λόγῳ καὶ πάσῃ γνώσει)…so that you are not lacking in any gift." And thereafter (chapters 12–14), Paul discussed at length the use of spiritual gifts in the church at Corinth. Particularly named among these were λόγος σοφίας (*word of wisdom*) and λόγος γνώσεως (*word of knowledge*).[45] Particularly when used in the church, it was important to use these gifts rationally, in a manner that yielded instruction, and for this reason speaking ἐν ἀποκαλύψει ἢ ἐν γνώσει (*by revelation or by knowledge*) was valuable,

---

[45] 1 Cor. 12.8.

whereas speaking in an untranslated tongue was not.[46] Notice the terms σοφία (*wisdom*), ἀποκαλύψις (*revelation*), γνῶσις (*knowledge*) in these contexts. In Ephesians 1.17, when Paul prays that his audience might receive *a spirit of wisdom and revelation* (πνεῦμα σοφίας καὶ ἀποκαλύψεως), he has in mind guidance by means of such spiritual gifts.

Where WH have δῴη the NA28 has δώῃ. This is not so much a question of different manuscript readings (although Vaticanus has ΔΩ where most other uncials have ΔΩΗ) as it is in part a question of where to infer the iota subscript and then a question about whether ΔΩΗ was intended to be optative or subjunctive. First, it should be kept in mind that iota subscripts did not appear in the oldest manuscripts. If we see ΔΩΗ, it might represent either δῴη[47] (which would be optative) or δώῃ.[48] But if we suppose it is δώη we have a form that is neither the proper optative form nor the proper subjunctive form. However, as Robertson noted, in the New Testament, "The subjunctive active third singular shows great variation between δοῖ, δῷ..., and δώῃ (especially in Paul's Epistles)."[49]

1.18 *the eyes of your heart having been enlightened* (πεφωτισμένους τοὺς ὀφθαλμοὺς τῆς καρδίας [ὑμῶν][50]) When Paul speaks of his readers' enlightenment, he uses this intriguing expression, combining two seemingly unrelated features of the anatomy so as to connect the inner man with the avenue through which information and guidance can reach him. The mantra of our age has been "go with your heart," meaning do what you want to do regardless of evidence that would lead you in a different direction. But Paul would have his readers have hearts that are illuminated by divine input that enters by the eyes of the heart.

The enlightenment is interpreted by some as something for which Paul prays,[51] and by others as something Paul mentions as having already occurred.[52] That is, it may be construed as a desired consequence of the blessing for which Paul prays (*e.g.*, I pray that God may give you a spirit

---

[46] 1 Cor. 14.6*ff*.

[47] For 2nd aor. optative δοίη, after subordination of the *iota* to *omicron* that has lengthened to *omega*.

[48] For 2nd aor. subjunctive δῷ, and found in *Iliad* 16.725.

[49] Robertson, p. 308.

[50] We will assume the authenticity of ὑμῶν, the question of its actual authenticity being immaterial.

[51] So Caldwell, p. 53.

[52] So Lincoln (p. 58). Clinton describes the options: This is either "a prayer request or a spiritual experience they have already received and in which Paul roots his prayer request" (p. 105).

of wisdom, etc., that having thus been enlightened, you may know…). Or πεφωτισμένους could be construed as referring to an enlightenment in which his readers already stand (I pray that God may give you, who have already been enlightened, a spirit of wisdom, etc.).

What one thinks about the enlightment is related to one's understanding of the grammatical structure. We well might explain this phrase as an accusative absolute, a participial phrase grammatically independent of the rest of the sentence. But accusative absolutes are rare in the NT, some doubting that they are present at all.

On the other hand, we might see accusative πεφωτισμένους τοὺς ὀφθαλμοὺς as being an object of an earlier verb. One thought is that it could be an additional object of ἀκούσας in verse 15. Thus we would understand Paul to say, *Having heard of* three things: (1) *your faith in the Lord Jesus*, (2) *the love for all the saints—I cease not giving thanks on behalf of you…—* (3) *the eyes of your heart having been enlightened.* But this treats Paul's prayer as a mere parenthesis oddly inserted between the second and third items in the list of things Paul has heard.

Or we might suppose accusative ὀφθαλμοὺς is an additional object of δῴη (πνεῦμα being the first). Taking it so, Paul would have prayed that God would give them a spirit (of wisdom and revelation) and enlightened eyes (of their heart). The phrase would run, *might give to you a spirit of wisdom and revelation in his knowledge, (and) enlightened eyes of your heart…* But this is exceedingly awkward, both because of the absence of a conjunction between the two objects and because of the perfect tense πεφωτισμένους. If the intent had been to speak of two things that God would do for them, the second could have been more easily and more clearly indicated by the phrase καὶ φωτίσῃ τοὺς ὀφθαλμοὺς τῆς καρδίας ὑμῶν, the word φωτίσῃ (*might enlighten*) functioning as a parallel to δῴη. Then the meaning would be *might give to you a spirit of wisdom and revelation in his knowledge and might enlighten the eyes of your heart.*

It seems better to suppose that what we have here is, after all, an accusative absolute.[53] Paul is neither saying he heard of their enlightened

---

[53] Hoehner enumerates six explanations for πεφωτισμένους, three of which suppose it is something for which Paul prays and three of which suppose it describes a previously existing enlightenment. As he notes, the perfect tense of the participle is problematic for the three explanations in the first category. In the second category, the first explanation is that "πεφωτισμένους τοὺς ὀφθαλμοὺς is in apposition to ὑμῖν (v. 17)," but Hoenher objects, questioning why we see the accusative case rather than the dative case. However, we would only expect dative πεφωτισμένοις in agreement with ὑμῖν if indeed the read-

eyes, nor is he saying he prayed that God might give them enlightened eyes. He is simply acknowledging that the eyes of their heart have been enlightened.

The having been enlightened is unto their *perceiving what is the hope of his calling, what is the wealth of the glory of his inheritance in the saints, and what is the surpassing greatness of his power unto us who believe according to the working of the might of his strength, which he has worked in the Christ.* Although perfect tense πεφωτισμένους points to an existing enlightenment that has already yielded a perception of these things, in chapters two and three Paul will nonetheless endeavor to enhance his readers' appreciation for what God has done and the extent to which God has graced them.

unto your perceiving what is the hope of his calling The enlightenment had resulted in their perceiving three things: (1) *what is the hope of his calling,* (2) *what is the wealth of the glory of his inheritance in the saints,* and (3) *what is the surpassing greatness of his power unto us who believe.* It seems better to take these as the result of the enlightening mentioned at the beginning of this verse than as the result of the spirit of wisdom and revelation. εἰδέναι (*to perceive*) is the natural consquence of πεφωτισμένους (*having been enlightened*).

what is the wealth of the glory of his inheritance in the saints Again, as noted above (see comments on 1.11,14), Paul is describing the saints as God's inheritance. He is not discussing something the saints inherit. The idea of God's people having an inheritance will appear in Ephesians 5.5, but that is not the thought here. Extolling God's people, including Paul's readers, as being a glorious possession belonging to God is part of Paul's effort to lead his readers to appreciate their place in God's plan, and thus motivate them to walk worthily of this calling (4.1*ff*).

---

ers themselves were said to have been enlightened. But grammatically, this is not the case. Grammatically, it is the eyes of the their hearts that have been enlightened. We would certainly not expect τοὺς ὀφθαλμοὺς to be dative, and πεφωτισμένους must agree with τοὺς ὀφθαλμοὺς and is therefore accusative. So while πεφωτισμένους τοὺς ὀφθαλμοὺς is logically in apposition to ὑμῖν, it is not grammatically in apposition to ὑμῖν, and therefore the accusative absolute is a necessity. Understanding the matter in this manner, Hoehner's first and second explanations in this second category are essentially the same, and are probably more to the point than the third explanation he describes which ties πεφωτισμένους to accusative ὑμᾶς later in the verse. Were that explanation correct, the accusative participle would not be absolute. The problem with this third explanation is that it again is looking for an explanation of accusative πεφωτισμένους when in fact, πεφωτισμένους is accusative in order to agree with τοὺς ὀφθαλμοὺς.

1.19 *and what is the surpassing greatness of his power unto us who believe according to the working of the might of his strength* It is not the saints themselves who have made themselves glorious. They have been made glorious by the great power of God. This anticipates the thought that will be further developed in 2.8–10.

1.20 *which he worked in the Christ, when he raised him from the dead and seated him by his right hand in the heavens* The UBS5 (and similarly, the NA28) has ἦν ἐνήργησεν[54] ἐν τῷ Χριστῷ ἐγείρας αὐτὸν ἐκ νεκρῶν καὶ καθίσας ἐν δεξιᾷ αὐτοῦ ἐν τοῖς ἐπουρανίοις. The two participles, ἐγείρας (*raising* or *having raised*) and καθίσας (*seating* or *having seated*) are adverbial modifiers of ἐνήργησεν (*he worked*). They serve to explain how or when God worked in the Christ. In the translation, *when he raised him from the dead and seated him*, the adverb *when* governs both *raised* and *seated*. The *when* is part of the interpretation of the participles.

But the TR has the finite verb ἐκάθισεν (aorist indicative, *he seated*) rather than the participle καθίσας (*having seated*). Were we to follow the TR, we should have the relative clause end with the words "having raised him from the dead." Then we ought to understand καὶ ἐκάθισεν (*and he seated*) as the beginning of a new independent clause. In saying καὶ ἐκάθισεν (*and he seated*), Paul would not be continuing with the adverbial thought implied by the participle but would be introducing a new thought.

It could be argued that the manuscript evidence favors the reading ἐκάθισεν inasmuch as it has the support of the Western tradition as well as the Byzantine tradition. Furthermore, the Alexandrian witnesses are split between those that have καθίσας αὐτόν (*having seated him*)[55] and those that have merely καθίσας (*having seated*).[56] But the text reads much more smoothly if we accept the participle καθίσας, for then "having seated" and "having raised" are parallel ideas, both explaining what God has worked in Christ, and all of that being part of what Paul's readers knew about the exceeding greatness of God's power, the eyes of their hearts having been enlightened.

Often, the fact that one variant enhances the smooth reading of the text is evidence against it, the supposition being that this very fact ac-

---

[54] Alexandrinus, Vaticanus, and 11th century minuscule 81 have perfect tense ἐνήργηκεν, and this is the reading found in the WH with alternate reading ἐνήργησεν occupyng the place in the margin.

[55] These include Sinaiticus.

[56] These include Vaticanus.

counts for the existence of the variant as some scribe had endeavored to clean up a difficult passage. From that perspective, it might be thought that the participle was substituted for an original finite verb as a fix to an awkward transition. But here, the sentence is long enough and complex enough, and the "fix" is subtle enough (even increasing the length and complexity of the sentence), that it seems less likely that a scribe would have hit upon this solution had the finite verb been the original reading. For this reason, the participle is accepted herein as the reading that is more likely authentic.

ἐν δεξιᾷ αὐτοῦ could be construed as instrumental, *by means of his right hand*, with the focus being on God's power in accordance with the preceding language *according to the working of the might of his strength which he has worked in the Christ.* The point of the passage would be that the resurrection from the dead and subsequent seating in the heavenly realms was accomplished by God's strong right hand. But the background of this expression is the 110th psalm (as will become apparent in the following remarks), where clearly the Messiah is seated *at* the right hand of God, not *by means of* the right hand of God. So too in Matthew 26.64, Hebrews 8.1, 10.12, and 12.2, the meaning is clearly locative. And most significantly, in Colossians 3.1 Paul uses the expression ἐν δεξιᾷ τοῦ θεοῦ καθήμενος where, due to the introductory οὗ and its connection with the preceding phrase—"seek the things above, where Christ is"—it can only be speaking of the place where Jesus sits and not the means of his arriving there. For these reasons, we understand the present passage to say that God seated Christ at his right hand.

While rooted in the literal notion of the strong right hand, the expression καθίσας ἐν δεξιᾷ αὐτοῦ is symbolic, not literal. It indicates an abstract truth, not a concrete spatial relationship. Hence *YHWH* can be described as being at the Messiah's right hand (Ps 16.8, Acts 2.25) just as surely as the Messiah is at the right hand of *YWHW* (Ps 110.1 *et al.*) And, in fact, Peter demonstrated the reciprocal validity of the right hand status in his sermon on the day of Pentecost when he quoted both Psalm 2 (wherein the Messiah says of *YHWH*, "he is on my right hand") and Psalm 110.1 (wherein *YHWH* says to the Messiah, "sit thou on my right hand").

The right hand, being the strong hand for most people, indicates strength (Ps 60.5, 63.8, 108.6, 118.16*f*) and being the favored hand, indicates honor (Gen 48.13–19, 1 Ki 2.19, Ps 45.9, Eccl 10.2, Mt 25.33, Gal 2.9).

Perowne cited both Pindar and Callimachus to show that in antiquity, being at the right hand of a god was to share in his power.[57] In his Hymn to Apollo, Callimachus wrote of Apollos, "He is mighty, because he is at the right hand of Zeus."[58] In the 110th psalm, the Messiah, being at the right hand of *YHWH*, is not merely in a position of honor but of authority; he rules over his enemies, shatters kings, and judges nations. In Genesis, the Messiah is foreshadowed by Joseph who received the ring from Pharaoh's right hand and who was next to Pharaoh himself in authority (Gen. 41.40*ff*). When Jesus responded to the high priest, he said, "hereafter you will see the Son of Man sitting at the right hand of Power."

Throughout the NT, the imagery of the Christ at the right hand of God is connected to Psalm 110. As already noted, Peter quoted the psalm on the day of Pentecost, using David's own words to affirm that it was Jesus, not David, who had been exalted at the right hand of God. The psalm is not quoted in Matthew 26.64, Mark 16.19, or Colossians 3.1. But the language of Hebrews 1.3, 8.1, 10.12 and 12.2 must have Psalm 110.1 in view, given the extensive treatment of that psalm in Hebrews 5 and 7.

Lincoln says, "There is no firm evidence that before the time of the NT the imagery of the psalm was given a messianic interpretation."[59] But the evidence that it was indeed given a messianic interpretation is the Pharisees' inability to answer Jesus' question, "If David then calleth him [*i.e.*, the Messiah] Lord, how is he his son?" (Mt 22.45). The Pharisees had acknowledged that the Messiah would be the son of David. Jesus replied by quoting Psalm 110.1 wherein David referred to the Messiah as "my Lord." If the Pharisees had not already understood Psalm 110 to be Messianic, they could easily have replied, "David did not refer to the *Messiah* as his lord; David was talking about someone else!"

We conclude that the Jews did indeed understand the 110th Psalm to speak of the Messiah sitting at the right hand of God, and that this understanding lay behind the various NT passages that speak of the right hand in connection with his seating.

1.21 *Far above every ruler and authority and power and lordship and every name that is named not only in this age but also in the coming one* (ὑπεράνω πάσης ἀρχῆς καὶ ἐξουσίας καὶ δυνάμεως καὶ κυριότητος

---

[57] Perowne, p. 304.

[58] δύναται γάρ, ἐπεὶ Διὶ δεξιὸς ἧσται, To Apollo, 29.

[59] Lincoln, p. 62.

καὶ παντὸς ὀνόματος ὀνομαζομένου, οὐ μόνον ἐν τῷ αἰῶνι τούτῳ ἀλλὰ καὶ ἐν τῷ μέλλοντι) The words ἀρχη, ἐξουσία, and perhaps also δύναμις, are capable of being used either in a concrete sense of a person or in an abstract sense. ἀρχη can be used of a person who rules (e.g., Lk 12.11) or of the jurisdiction or authority of one who rules (*e.g.*, Jd 6). ἐξουσία can be used of a person who has authority (e.g., Lk 12.11) or of the authority he wields (e.g., Mt 10.1). δύναμις is perhaps the word least likely to be used of a person, but it is found at 1 Peter 3.22 along with ἄγγελος (as well as ἐξουσία), suggesting that it may be being used of one who has power, and of course it is used of the power one has.

But the word κυριότης seems only to mean *lordship* and not *lord*. Paul uses it twice, once here and once in Colossians 1.16, and it is also found at Jude 8 and 2 Peter 2.10. Feminine nouns in -ότης with genitive ending ότητος indicate quality.[60] Given this fact, it may be that Paul is using each noun abstractly, saying Jesus is above every rule, authority, power, and lordship, rather than every ruler, authority figure, etc.

However, whether he is speaking abstractly of power wielded or concretely of those who wield it, there is little difference in the meaning of the passage. If Jesus is above every abstract realm of authority, then of course he is above every being who holds any sort of authority.

Other questions that arise have more significant implications. Two questions in particular concern us, the first being whether or not supernatural powers are included in this list and the second being whether these powers are good or evil.

The answer to the first question is yes, supernatural powers are included. In Ephesians 3.10, Paul will speak specifically of rulers and authorities ἐν τοῖς ἐπουρανίοις (*in the heavens*), and in 6.12, Paul contrasts the rulers (ἀρχάς) and authorities (ἐξουσίας) in the heavens with "flesh and blood," saying our wrestling is not against the latter but is against the former.

δύναμις (and its cognate δυνάστης), and ἐξουσία had come to be used of spiritual entities prior to the NT. δύναμις is used to translate ṣaba' (*host, i.e., an army*) "about 130 times"[61] in the LXX. In particular we see the expression śar ṣaba' (*commander of the host*) used in Genesis 21.22 *et al.*, of Phicol (ὁ ἀρχιστράτηγος τῆς δυνάμεως), in Judges 4.2 of Sisera (ὁ ἄρχων τῆς δυνάμεως), and of others. But it is also used of the heavenly host, the

---

[60] Cf. ἁγιότης, ἁγνότης, ἁπλότης, θειότης, θεότης, ἰσότης, λειότης, ματαιότης, μεγαλειότης, νεότης, πιότης, σεμνότης, τελειότης, τιμιότης, χρηστότης.

[61] Hoehner, p. 268.

Lord's angelic army. In Joshua 5.14, Joshua encountered the "captain of the LORD's host" (*śar ṣ^eba' YHWH*, LXX has ἀρχιστράτηγος δυνάμεως κυρίου). The plural version of this expression, "Lord of Hosts" *i.e.*, LORD *Sabaoth* (*YHWH ṣ^eba'ot*) "is often rendered κύριος τῶν δυνάμεων."[62]

ἐξουσία is used of spiritual powers in conjunction with δυνάστης, a cognate of δύναμις, in 2 Maccabees 3.24. There, Heliodorus' attempt to confiscate the treasure from the temple is thwarted when "the Power (δυνάστης) of the spirits and of all authority (ἐξουσίας) appeared."[63]

It is doubtful that ἀρχή for a non-earthly being can be conclusively illustrated from the OT, though Delling supposed a close connection between the ἀρχή of Daniel 7.14 (Theodotian) and those beings of Daniel 10 "who wield power in the supraterrestrial sphere,"[64] and even supposed that in Daniel 7 (apparently vs. 25), the Theodotian mention of ἀρχαί "is perhaps to supraterrestrial and demonic powers which are subdued by the Messiah."[65] But the context in Daniel 7 requires nothing more than a general reference to rule and those who exercise it, whether earthly or heavenly.

However, it is the ἄρχων who holds ἀρχή, and we can demonstrate the use of ἄρχων for spiritual beings from Daniel 10, where the idea of such beings associated with nations is developed. There are those who assist God's people, and there are those who oppose those who assist God's people. The conflicts between these beings correspond to earthly conflicts, much as the war in heaven between Michael the archangel and the devil with his angels (Rev 12.7*ff*) corresponded to the earthly opposition to the Christ (Rev 12.3*ff*).[66] In Daniel 10, the word *śar* (*general, prince,* or *captain*) is used for each of these spiritual beings. To translate this, the LXX uses στρατηγός (10.13,20) or ἄγγελος (10.21), while Theodotion (*ca.* AD 150) uses ἄρχων. There is a prince (*śar*, LXX has στρατηγός, Theodotion has ἄρχων) of Persia who had opposed the angelic being who spoke with Daniel. But then Michael, "one of the chief princes" (εἷς τῶν ἀρχόντων τῶν πρώτων), came to the aid of the one who spoke with Daniel. Michael is identified as "your (i.e., Israel's) prince" (ὁ ἄρχων ὑμῶν). Michael assists the one speaking with Daniel in opposition to the prince of Persia and

---

[62] Grundmann, Walter, TDNT, vol. 2, p. 292.

[63] ὁ τῶν πνευμάτων καὶ πάσης ἐξουσίας δυνάστης, 2 Macc. 3:24. δυνάστης is used of God himself in 1 Tim. 6:15.

[64] TDNT, s.v. "ἀρχή," vol. 1, 481.

[65] Ibid., 483.

[66] We may well suppose it is this same Michael who is mentioned in Daniel 10.

also in opposition to "the prince of Greece" (LXX, στρατηγὸς Ἑλλήνων; Theodotion, ὁ ἄρων τῶν Ἑλλήνων) who is about to come. Finally, we ought not overlook Paul's mention of the devil himself (Eph 2.2), whom he describes as *the ruler* (ἄρχοντα) *of the power of the air.*

Though there is no Greek or Hebrew text extant for 1 Enoch 61 and the date is uncertain (though likely prior to AD 70), it is worth noting that 1 Enoch 61.10 reads,

> And He will summon all the host of the heavens, and all the holy ones above, and the host of God, the Cherubic, Seraphin and Ophannin, and all the angels of power, and all the angels of principalities, and the Elect One, and the other powers on the earth (and) over the water.

Not only can we say spiritual powers are included in Paul's list at Ephesians 1.21, but given the use of some of these terms in 3.10 and 6.12, it is probably best to understand that spiritual powers are most especially those that Paul had in view. The more difficult question is whether or not earthly rulers are in view at all. But it is at least doubtful that they are.

The answer to the question as to whether the rulers, authorities, powers, and lordship represent good or evil forces is probably "both." Certainly evil powers are in view inasmuch as Paul says our war is "against the rulers, against the authorities, against the world rulers of this darkness, against the spiritual beings of evil in the heavens."[67] On the other hand, it seems that the rulers and authorities in Ephesians 3.10 are at least as likely to be good as evil, considering the context there.

Like the phrase *every name that is named*, the phrase *not only in this age but also in the coming one* seems intended to cover all the bases, to make it clear that Jesus' authority is supreme and cannot successfully be challenged anywhere, anytime.

1.22–23 The Church, Christ's Body

And he subjected all things under his feet, and gave him as head over all things to the church, which is his body, the fulness of the one who fills all things in all things.

For the first time in Ephesians, Paul introduces the concept of the church as a body. But it is not a new concept in Paul's writings (See 1 Cor 12). It is, of course, the whole church that is described as a body. The vari-

---

[67] On the question of such evil forces being ἐν τοῖς ἐπουρανίοις, see the comments on 6.12.

ous congregations are never referred to as bodies respectively in scripture; that figure is reserved for the universal church.

Paul will return to the image of a body in 2.15–16 (where there seems to be a double meaning), in 4.12–13, and then again in 5.23*ff.*

The church is the body, which is the fullness of the one who fills all things. In other words, the church is the body, which is the fullness of Christ. In chapter five, Paul will have the church correspond to the wife who is the body of the husband, and who completes him. The thought is that found in Genesis 2.23 (she was taken out of man; the two become one flesh), further developed in Ephesians 5.28–31, but already anticipated here at Ephesians 1.23, that the church is the fullness of Christ. This sets up what Paul now wants to do, and that is expound upon the glorious blessing that God has bestowed upon this Gentile audience, affirming that in every way and with all the prerogatives of those who were saints before them, they are part of the body that is the fullness of Christ.

Grammatically, the definite article τοῦ goes with πληρουμένου (*the filling one*) which we must understand as middle, for the passive voice here yields no comprehensible meaning. The phrase τὰ πάντα ἐν πᾶσιν, *all things in all things*, functions as an attribute of πληρουμένου. To show the grammatical construction, we can represent it in English as "the fullness of the all-things-in-all-things filling one," which means *the fullness of the one who fills all things in all things.*

2.1–7 You (And We Also) Who Were Dead Are Made Alive

And you being dead by your trespasses and sins, in which you formerly walked according to the age of this world, according to the ruler of the power of the air, the spirit now working in the sons of disobedience, among whom we also all formerly went about in the desires of our flesh, doing the will of the flesh and of the thoughts, and were children by nature of wrath even as the rest; but God, being rich in mercy on account of his great love with which he loved us, and us being dead by the trespasses, he made us alive together with Christ—by grace you have been saved—and he raised us together and made us sit together in the heavenly realms in Christ Jesus that he might show in the coming ages the surpassing wealth of his grace in kindness toward us in Christ Jesus.

2.1 *And you being dead by your trespasses and sins* (Καὶ ὑμᾶς ὄντας νεκροὺς τοῖς παραπτώμασιν καὶ ταῖς ἁμαρτίαις ὑμῶν) The simple sentence in verses 1–5a is, "God made you/us alive together by Christ." The subject is God, not identified until verse 4, and the verb, "made alive," is not supplied until verse 5. The passage begins with the words, Καὶ ὑμᾶς ὄντας νεκρούς, *and you being dead*. The word *you* represents ὑμᾶς, accusative case and accordingly understood to be the object of the verb. However, before we get to the verb of which it is the object, a participial modifier is added, and then much more is added.

And in fact, Paul ends up re-stating the object as "us" rather than "you" before he ever gets around to telling us what was done to us/you. He changes the object of the verb from *you Gentiles* to *all of us, whether Jew or Gentile, who are in Christ*.

ὄντας (*being*) is a participle (masculine accusative plural, pres. act. participle of εἰμί), and is not the main verb of the passage. Paul does not say, "you were dead" (as in the NAS). The whole phrase, ὄντας νεκρούς τοῖς παραπτώμασιν καὶ ταῖς ἁμαρτίαις ὑμῶν, describes the erstwhile circumstances of ὑμᾶς (*you*), viz., *being dead in your trespasses and sins*. Or might it be better to understand the datives τοῖς παραπτώμασιν and ταῖς ἁμαρτίαις as instrumentals rather than locatives? Then it would be translated, *you, being dead by your trespasses and sins*. Either way, the English *in* or *by* is merely an attempt to represent the force of the case of the words παραπτώμασιν and ἁμαρτίαις. But I am inclined to favor the instrumental idea here, *being dead by your trespasses and sins*.

2.2 Having turned his attention to the circumstances of ὑμῶν (*you*), Paul elaborates before completing the sentence he has begun: *in which formerly you walked* (ἐν αἷς ποτε περιεπατήσατε). περιεπατήσατε (*you walked*) is aor. act. ind., 2nd pers. pl., of περιπατέω (cf. the English "peripatetic"). The former manner of walking is expressed globally by the aorist tense. Paul encapsulates the whole former way of life as a simple past event.

Two phrases are introduced to further characterize the former walk: κατὰ τὸν αἰῶνα τοῦ κόσμου τούτου (*according to the age of this world*), κατὰ τὸν ἄρχοντα τῆς ἐξουσίας τοῦ ἀέρος (*according to the ruler of the power of the air*). If it were not for the fact that "spirit" is the word we will need to use to translate πνεύματος in the coming phrase, we could translate the first phrase, *according to the spirit of this world* (though αἰῶνα itself does not mean *spirit*). Alternatively, we might say, "according to the zeitgeist."

τοῦ ἀέϱος (*of the air*) is a genitive of kind, not ablative indicating source. The power (ἐξουσίας) is ephemeral and pervasive. The evil influence is not localized in a particular region, or in a particular temple, or in a particular school—it is rather the predominate mentality that envelops all of this world.

τοῦ πνεύματος (*the spirit*) is genitive in order to agree with τῆς ἐξουσίας (*the power*) to which it is in apposition. That is, the power is further explained as a spirit, namely, the spirit that now works in the sons of disobedience. The construction τοῦ πνεύματος τοῦ νῦν ἐνεϱγοῦντος is attributive, the words νῦν ἐνεϱγοῦντος being in the place of the modifier. Paul's wording is, *the spirit, the now-working-in-the-sons-of-disobedience (one),* or said another way, the spirit that is now working in the sons of disobedience.

2.3 ἐν οἷς = *among whom*   οἷς is masculine plural to agree with its antecedent, υἱοῖς (*sons*). We might be tempted to translate otherwise—*in which* rather than *among whom*—and thus see a parallel between verse two, *in which you formerly walked,* and verse 3, *in which we also all formerly went about.* Rather than being construed as masculine, οἷς would be considered neuter (*which things*) and its antecedent would be the combined τοῖς παϱαπτώμασιν καὶ ταῖς ἁμαϱτίαις ὑμῶν (*your trespasses and sins*) in verse one. This is how Robinson understood the passage.[68] But the problem with this is that in the first part of the putative parallel, the relative pronoun is feminine αἷς. When Paul says ἐν αἷς ποτε περιεπατήσατε (*in which you formerly walked*), the grammatical referent of the feminine relative pronoun seems to be only feminine ταῖς ἁμαϱτίαις (*the sins*), and does not include masculine τοῖς παϱαπτώμασιν (*the trespasses*). But in verse three, Paul would use neuter οἷς to refer back to verse one only if he intended to include both masculine τοῖς παϱαπτώμασιν and feminine ταῖς ἁμαϱτίαις as referents. And yet then the parallel is destroyed. Therefore we do best to take οἷς as masculine and understand Paul to mean *among whom,* i.e., among the sons of disobedience.

One additional consideration is the parallel in Colossians 3.6–7. If we accept the authenticity of the phrase ἐπὶ τοὺς υἱοὺς τῆς ἀπειθείας in that passage, the most natural understanding of ἐν οἷς καὶ ὑμεῖς περιεπατήσατέ ποτε there is *among whom you also formerly walked,* refer-

---

[68] Robinson, *St Paul's Epistle to the Ephesians,* p. 155.

ring to the sons of disobedience, not *in which you also formerly walked.*[69] This would lend support to the idea that here too in Ephesians, following the mention of the sons of disobedience, Paul's meaning is, *among whom.*

among whom we also all formerly went about (ἐν οἷς καὶ ἡμεῖς πάντες ἀνεστράφημέν ποτε) ἡμεῖς (*we*) is in contrast to the ὑμᾶς (*you*) of verse 1. Here Paul strays further from the sentence he began, now intending to make it clear that what he says of the former walk of the Gentiles is also true of the former walk of the Jews. καὶ ἡμεῖς is *we also,* not only you Gentiles but *all* (πάντες) of us (Jews) as well.

ἀνεστράφημέν is a 2nd aorist passive form of ἀναστρέφω. It is classified as passive in accordance with traditional paradigms, but ought to be understood as middle in force—*conducted ourselves* or *went about.* ἀναστρέφω is a compound of στρέφω = *turn,* and ἀνα = *again,* the meaning then being to go back and forth, or to go about one's activities, to conduct oneself.

in the desires of our flesh (ἐν ταῖς ἐπιθυμίαις τῆς σαρκὸς ἡμῶν) Whether we should regard τῆς σαρκὸς as genitive (specifying the kind of desires, those pertaining to the flesh) or ablative (indicating the source of the desires) is difficult to decide. In this instance, the two ideas practically amount to the same thing. Paul goes on to indicate that the flesh is the source of the desires inasmuch as they are in accordance with the will of the flesh (τὰ θελήματα τῆς σαρκὸς), though not only of the flesh but also τῶν διανοιῶν, *of the thoughts.* Why did Paul use the plural διανοιῶν in contrast to the singular σαρκὸς? There is a flesh common to man according to which we walked, and there is also a mind common to man that Paul might have mentioned (indeed, has essentially mentioned in the phrase τοῦ πνεύματος τοῦ νῦν ἐνεργοῦντος ἐν τοῖς υἱοῖς τῆς ἀπειθείας). But what Paul mentions instead are the διάνοιαι plural.

Of course, one possibility is that Paul means to speak of various thoughts, various ideas, from which desires arise. This meaning is said to be illustrated in a few instances, though in at least some of the passages cited, the idea really seems to be *opinion, belief.*[70]

Perhaps plural διανοιῶν is in contrast to singular σαρκὸς both qualitatively and quantitatively. Qualitatively, the appetites of the flesh may

---

[69] However, both Lightfoot and Alford argued for understanding οἷς in Colossians 3.7 to mean *in which.*

[70] E.g., Plato Phaedo, 63.c, Plutarch, Generation of the Soul, 1014c.

be distinguished from philosophy (which Paul mentions in Col 2.8).[71] Quantitatively, while all men are of the same flesh and are in danger of being slaves to the same desires of the flesh, they may hold to different philosophies. We might translate, the desires of their flesh and of the minds, supposing that Paul is hereby indicting all men, both those who admittedly are slaves to base desires and also those who reckon themselves to be thinking men.

Behm said "there are no echoes of philosophical usage" of διανοία in the NT.[72] But it is possible that Paul's use of διανοιῶν here is the exception to Behm's statement. In Colossians, Paul pointedly confronted the gnostic attitudes and practices. There is comparatively little of that in Ephesians, but here we perhaps see a hint, a vague allusion. In Colossians, the gnostic influence seemed to have come from Judaizing teachers. Here in Ephesians, it is when Paul is speaking of what the Jewish believers formerly did that he alludes to philosophies. Perhaps there is an allusion to the gnostic speculations of some elements of Judaism.

and were children, by nature, of wrath (καὶ ἤμεθα τέκνα φύσει ὀργῆς) in other words, *devoted to destruction.* Particularly in Romans, Paul often used the word ὀργή (*wrath*) of God's judgment (Rom 1.18, 2.5 2x, 2.8, 3.5, 5.9, 12.19 and 9.22f). In Romans 13.4 it is used of God's wrath as executed by human rulers. Romans 9.22f is of special interest. There we see two phrases that are parallel to τέκνα ὀργῆς (*children of wrath*). Paul speaks of σκεύη ὀργῆς (*vessels of wrath*) and σκεύη ἐλεους (*vessels of mercy*). In these instances as in Ephesians 2.3, the genitive indicates the ultimate end of the preceding noun.

Meyer noted that the presence of φύσει (*by nature*) in this passage "has been employed in defence of *original sin* as an *inborn* condition of culpability (*inborn peccatum vere damnans*, 'sin truly condemning')."[73] But φύσει need not mean congenital. Josephus described David as ὄντι φύσει δικαίῳ καὶ θεοσεβεῖ (*being by nature righteous and devout*).[74] He described the Pharisees as by nature (φύσει) having leniency in the matter of punishments.[75]

---

[71] Not suprisingly, διάνοια and φιλοσοφία are connected, e.g., in Plato Phaedrus, 279b, ἔνεστί τις φιλοσοφία τῇ του ἀνδρὸς διανοίᾳ, *there is something of philosophy in the mind of the man.*

[72] TDNT, s.v. "διάνοια."

[73] Meyer, p. 365.

[74] Ant. 7.7.1 §130.

[75] Ant. 13.10.6 §291.

We see also this use of the word in 1 Corinthians 11.14, "does not nature (φύσις) itself teach you that if a man should wear long hair, it is dishonorable to him?" The meaning there cannot be something innate, but that which by longstanding practice has come to be the characteristic norm. As to the meaning of the word in Ephesians 2.3, we can hardly improve upon Meyer's comments: "the context points, in vv. 1–3, as again also in ver. 5, to an *actually produced*, not to an *inborn* state of guilt."[76] Meyer also questions the propriety of the word order if Paul had intended to introduce the notion of an inborn depravity:

> ...if Paul had wished, after touching on the sinful *action*, to bring into prominence the *inborn* state of culpability, and so had taken the course *ab effectu ad causam*, "from the effect to the cause," φύσει would have an emphasis, which would make its critically assured position, as it stands in the *Recepta*, appear simply inappropriate; in fact, not even the position in Lachmann (ἦμεν φύσει τέκνα ὀργῆς) would be sufficiently in keeping, but we should be obliged logically to expect: καὶ φύσει ἦμεν τέκνα ὀργῆς, "and (already) by birth were we children of wrath."[77]

And finally, against the doctrine that man is born already subject to God's wrath, Meyer rightly appeals to the consistent teaching of Paul that "man by his *actual* sin falls under the wrath of God (Rom. i.18, ii. 8, 9, vii. 7 f., *al.*)."[78]

as also the rest (ὡς καὶ οἱ λοιποί). With these words, Paul concludes the detour he began at the beginning of verse 3 designed to show that Jews as well as Gentiles were dead in trespasses and sins.

2.4 He now brings in the subject of this long sentence, the one who did something to the "you" of verse one, which was revised to "us" along the way: ὁ δὲ θεὸς πλούσιος ὢν ἐν ἐλέει, **but God, rich being, in mercy**. Now as he comes to the point where he stipulates the subject, θεός, Paul has to verbally regroup, so long was the detour. He starts the sentence over again, this time leading with the subject. And once again, there is a detour, this time to elaborate on God's mercy and love. διὰ τὴν πολλὴν ἀγάπην αὐτοῦ = **on account of his great love**. God's mercy

---

[76] Meyer, p. 366.

[77] Ibid. Note that Meyer is quoting the TR and therefore has active form ἦμεν rather than ἤμεθα.

[78] Ibid.

comes out of his love. ἣν ἠγάπησεν ἡμᾶς, *(with) which he loved us.*[79] The accusative ἡμᾶς (*us*) now includes both ὑμᾶς (*you*, i.e., the Gentiles) and ἡμᾶς (*us*, i.e., the Jews).

2.5   *and us being dead by the trespasses*   In verse 1, it was *you being dead by trespasses*. Now instead of ὑμᾶς ὄντας νεκροὺς τοῖς παραπτώμασιν (*you being dead by the trespasses*), he says, καὶ ὄντας ἡμᾶς νεκροὺς τοῖς παραπτώμασιν (*and us being dead by the trespasses*), now including Jews along with Gentiles.

He made us alive together with Christ (συνεζωοποίησεν τῷ Χριστῷ) συνεζωοποίησεν is aor. act. ind. 3rd sing., apparently from συζωοποιέω but unknown other than here and in Colossians 2.13. Hoehner said "Paul created the word."

How should we regard τῷ Χριστῷ? Given that in Colossians 2.13, Paul writes συνεζωοποίησεν ὑμᾶς σὺν αὐτῷ (*made you alive together with him*), we should look to the prefixed preposition in the verb and translate τῷ Χριστῷ "with Christ" rather than construing τῷ Χριστῷ as either locative (*in Christ*) or instrumental (*by Christ*).

One may ask how it can be said that we have been raised with Christ given that we have not yet been raised physically as Christ was raised physically. And it may seem odd to suggest that we have been made alive spiritually "together with" him who was raised bodily. Some solve the dilemma by supposing the aorist here is not a reference to our past resurrection, but to our future resurrection, thus having Paul speak of our bodily resurrection in similitude to Christ's resurrection. But the connection between Christ's physical resurrection and our spiritual resurrection is seen not only in Colossians 2.12, but also in Romans 6 where Paul explained that we are baptized into Christ's death so that "as Christ was raised from the dead through the glory of the Father, so we also might walk in newness of life." Moreover, the believer's past spiritual resurrection is what assures that his future physical resurrection is indeed of life (Jn 5.29); the latter will not be without the former. This was well expressed by Alford in his comments on this passage:

---

[79] We would say "he loved us *with* his great love," but the ἦν reflects the fact that the verb ἀγαπάω can take the object ἀγάπη much as the English "give" can take the object "gift" such that we might say, *his great gift which he gave us*. So then the Greek would be, *his great love which he loved us*. But in English, for the verb "loved" and its cognate noun "love," we must use the word "with"—*his great love with which he loved us*. This ἀγάπην αὐτοῦ ἣν ἠγάπησεν ἡμᾶς is reminiscent of the phrase χάριτος αὐτοῦ ἧς ἐχαρίτωσεν ἡμᾶς in 1.6.

The disputes about the meaning of ἐζωοποίησεν have arisen from not bearing in mind the relation in N.T. language between natural and spiritual death. We have often had occasion to observe that spiritual death in the N.T. includes in it and bears with it natural death as a consequence, to such an extent that this latter is often not thought of as worth mentioning: see especially John xi. 25,26, which is the key-text for all passages regarding life in Christ. So here—God vivified us together with Christ: in the one act and fact of His resurrection He raised all His people—to spiritual life, and in that to victory over death, both spiritual, and therefore necessarily physical also. To dispute therefore whether such an expression as this is past (spiritual), or future (physical), is to forget that the whole includes its parts. Our spiritual life is the primary subject of the Apostle's thought: but this includes in itself our share in the resurrection and exaltation (ver. 6) of Christ.[80]

So then the basic sentence Paul set out to write was Καὶ ὑμᾶς ὄντας νεκροὺς τοῖς παραπτώμασιν καὶ ταῖς ἁμαρτίαις ὑμῶν ὁ θεὸς ἐζωοποίησεν τῷ Χριστῷ, "And you being dead by your trespasses and sins, God made alive with Christ." But as revised to include the Jews, the basic sentence ends up being καὶ ἡμᾶς ὄντας νεκροὺς τοῖς παραπτώμασιν καὶ ταῖς ἁμαρτίαις ἡμῶν ὁ θεὸς συνεζωοποίησεν τῷ Χριστῷ—"And us being dead by our trespasses and sins, God made alive together with Christ."

The thought of being made alive τῷ Χριστῷ elicits the interjection, *by grace you have been saved* (χάριτί ἐστε σεσῳσμένοι).[81] The construction is periphrastic. The present tense copulative ἐστε (*you are*) is combined with the perfect participle σεσῳσμένοι (*having been saved*) to convey one verbal thought, *you are having been saved*, or simply, *you have been saved*.

2.6 *And he raised us together* (with Christ) ***and made us sit together*** (with Christ) ***in the heavenly realms.*** The Greek text is simply, καὶ συνήγειρεν[82] καὶ συνεκάθισεν ἐν τοῖς ἐπουρανίοις, *he raised us together and made us sit together in the heavenlies.* Whereas ἤγειρεν is *he raised*, the word used here, συνήγειρεν, is *he raised with*, or *he raised together.*" Similarly, whereas ἐκάθισεν is *he seated*, the word used here,

---

[80] Alford, vol. III, p. 92.

[81] Knox saw this phrase as evidence that Ephesians was written not by Paul but by a continuator, who felt "that grace and works must be dragged in at all costs" even though, according to Knox, the thought is foreign to the context. (Knox, 182).

[82] συνήγειρεν, aor. act. 3rd sing. of συνεγείρω, used only here and in Col 2.12 and 3.1.

συνεκάθισεν, is *he seated with* or *he seated together*. The two verbs, prefixed as they are with συν-, continue the association between saints and Christ that was explicitly expressed by τῷ Χριστῷ in verse 5, though the τῷ Χριστῷ is not repeated here.

Because Paul has Jews and Gentiles in mind and will shortly be emphasizing the uniting of both Jew and Gentile in one body, it is tempting to understand the verbs συνήγειρεν (*raised together with*) and συνεκάθισεν (*made to sit together with*) as especially emphasizing the idea of Jews and Gentiles being united together. But as with the earlier verb συνεζωοποίησεν, here again the focus is not so much on Gentiles being joined with Jews, but upon all of us being joined with Christ. And again this is made clear by the less ambiguous expression in Colossians. There, at 3.1, Paul also writes of being raised and seated; *you were raised together with Christ* (συνηγέρθητε τῷ Χριστῷ).

We must see here a connection with what was said in the preceding chapter. God demonstrated his power when he raised Jesus from the dead and seated him at his right hand in the heavenlies (1.20). Now Paul affirms that we who were dead in our trespasses have also been raised and made to sit with Christ in the heavenlies.

The reference to being *raised* probably ought to be understood as encompassing a bit more than the *made alive* of the previous verse. *Made alive* is a reference to our spiritual resurrection, made alive after having been dead in sin. In close connection with that but encompassing a further accomplishment, Paul now affirms that God raised us with Christ.

The verb ἐγείρω (without the prefixed συν) is used of resurrection from the dead in numerous passages.[83] In Colossians 2.12 where Paul affirms that his readers were raised with (συνηγέρθητε, aor. pass of συνεγείρω) Christ, whom God had raised (ἐγείραντος, gen. participle of ἐγείρω) from the dead, it seems clear enough that Paul's use of συνεγείρω there is intended to connect his readers' spiritual resurrection at baptism with Christ's resurrection.

But ἐγείρω is used in Acts 13.22 of the exaltation of David to the throne, and the compound ἐξεγείρω is used similarly of Pharaoh in Romans 9.17. The idea of being raised up in the sense of being exalted well suits the context of Colossians 3.1, for there Paul argues that inasmuch as his readers have been raised with Christ, they ought to seek things that are above.

---

[83] Mk 12.26, Lk 7.22, 20.37, 1 Cor 15.15f,29,32,35, 52, κ.τ.λ.

Seeking things that are above is commensurate with *being* above, having been exalted. Of course Colossians 3.1 (*if then you were raised together with Christ*) seems to be predicated upon Colossians 2.12, the unusual word συνεγείρω being used in both passages. But also in view at Colossians 3.1 must be the implication that the saints are no longer living in the world (2.20, *why as though living in the world*). The idea seems to be, "If then you were raised with Christ and exalted so that you are no longer living in the world, seek the things that are above."

So then while we should understand "made alive" in Ephesians 2.5 with reference to the spiritual resurrection at baptism, we should probably understand the "raised with" of 2.6 to encompass both this spiritual resurrection and the accompanying exaltation to the heavenlies, wherein Paul then affirms his readers have been made to sit with Christ.

in the heavenlies (ἐν τοῖς ἐπουρανίοις) The word ἐπουρανίοις (dative, plural) is an adjective, here used as a substantive. We might supply a noun in English, "heavenly realms." Every spiritual blessing in the heavenly realms is in Christ (1.3), and through Christ (ἐν Χριστῷ Ἰησοῦ) God has made Jew and Gentile sit together in the heavenly realms.

Sitting with Christ in the heavenlies while yet walking this earth evokes the notion of a conquering people who through their victorious king reign with him (Dan 7.27, Rev 5.10). Those who have been made alive have also been exalted and, through Christ, presently sit in a position of glory and honor and power.

This is all part of Paul's effort to instill in his readers an appreciation for the exalted state they have attained in Christ, with a view to motivating them to walk worthily of this great calling.

2.7 *that he might show in the coming ages the surpassing wealth of his grace in kindness toward us in Christ Jesus* While it is certainly true that God made both Jew and Gentile alive in Christ and raised them and seated them in the heavens *because he loved them* (Jn 3.16), here Paul has in mind another purpose that pertains to posterity. It is God's desire that in the coming ages, all sentient creation in the heavens (cf. 3.10) and on earth might be able to look back at what God accomplished in Christ and thus perceive his grace and kindness.

2.8–10 Salvation by Grace, God's Gift

For through faith you have been saved by the grace, and this not of yourselves, it is God's gift; not of works, that no one should boast. For we are his doing, created in Christ Jesus for good works which God prepared that we might walk in them.

2.8 for by the grace (τῇ γὰρ χάριτι). The word γάρ (*for*) indicates that what follows is the reason for the foregoing. The reason God's kindness toward us in Christ Jesus can be spoken of as an example of the surpassing riches of his grace is that it is God's gift to those who have faith and is not the result of our works. We are his work, his doing. The 100th Psalm comes to mind: "It is he who has made us and not we ourselves." That's true of mankind, it was true of Israel as a nation, and here in Ephesians it is said to be true of the church, those in Christ Jesus.

χάριτι is articular, *the grace*. The definite article serves to specify the grace as that previously mentioned in verse 5—"the aforementioned grace."[84]

χάριτι, dative in form, is instrumental, indicating the means of our being saved. Notice that Paul returns to using the second person rather than the first person. He began these remarks saying, "you, being dead by your trespasses and sins," but then modified his remarks to say that "we also" were dead by trespasses and sins. Now here in verse 8 he once again says, "you," directly addressing the Gentiles. He says ἐστε σεσωσμένοι (*you have been saved*, cf. vs. 5) rather than ἐσμεν σεσωσμένοι (*we have been saved*). And he will go on in verses 11–22 to address the Gentiles and further develop the idea of their participation together with Jews in the household of God. Paul has had the Gentiles in mind as his audience all along.

The new thought in the clause is that this salvation is **through faith** (διὰ πίστεως). *For through faith you have been saved by the grace.* That is, "It is through faith that you are being saved by the aforementioned grace."

And this not of yourselves, it is God's gift (καὶ τοῦτο οὐκ ἐξ ὑμῶν, θεοῦ τὸ δῶρον). The word "this" (τοῦτο) is anaphoric, carrying along the idea of what is already in view, namely ἐστε σεσωσμένοι (*you have been saved*). It is not pointing to πίστεως (*faith*), which is feminine, for if that were the intended meaning, we would expect the feminine αὕτη. Paul does not affirm that God's gift is faith, but rather that God's gift is our being saved; it

---

[84] Zerwick, however, supposed that in verse 8, articular χάριτι, by virtue of the article, is not to be regarded in the abstract as in verse 5, but instead means "the entire work of redemption, that concrete historical fact." p. 57, §176.

is God's gift inasmuch as it is by Christ and thus by grace rather than of ourselves. Nor does "this" refer to "grace," for χάριτι (*grace*) is also feminine. While it is true that God's grace is a gift, here, in saying καὶ τοῦτο οὐκ ἐξ ὑμῶν (*and this is not of yourselves*), Paul "refers to the whole conception, not to χάριτι."[85]

Examples of neuter τοῦτο referring to an abstract verbal idea are numerous (cf. Mt. 1.22, 8.9, 9.28, 13.28, 16.22, 19.26, 21.4, 26.56, 28.14, Mk. 9.21, 11.3, Lk. 1.18, 1.34, 5.6, and many more, including many occurrences of the phrase διὰ τοῦτο="on account of this"). In Ephesians in particular, see 6.1, "For this (τοῦτο) is right," where "this" refers to obeying one's parents.

2.9 *not of works that no one should boast* (οὐκ ἐξ ἔργων, ἵνα μή τις καυχήσηται). The phrases οὐκ ἐξ ὑμῶν (*not of yourselves*) and οὐκ ἐξ ἔργων (*not of works*) are parallel, both pointing to the conclusion that no one can boast. Man's pride gets in the way of his dependence on God. Inasmuch as our salvation requires that we have faith, i.e., trust, in God and is not of our own works, boasting is precluded.

2.10 *for we are his doing* (αὐτοῦ γὰρ ἐσμεν ποίημα). Paul now uses the first person. All of us, you Gentiles and we Jews, together in Christ are God's doing.

created in Christ Jesus for good works (κτισθέντες ἐν Χριστῷ Ἰησοῦ ἐπὶ ἔργοις ἀγαθοῖς). Though aorist in tense, the participle κτισθέντες (*created*) does not necessarily indicate prior time, "having been created." However, if in referring to this creation in Christ, Paul had meant to call attention to an ongoing process of men responding to the gospel, the present tense ("being created") would have been the appropriate choice. The fact that he used the aorist tense indicates that he viewed the creation of God's people globally. This creation was accomplished in Christ in accordance with God's eternal purpose (cf. 3.11). Our salvation is something God did, not something we are doing. And God did this, created us in Christ Jesus, *for* good works. ἐπί is here used in a final sense.[86]

which God prepared (οἷς προητοίμασεν ὁ θεὸς). The relative pronoun οἷς (*which*) is dative, having been attracted to the case of its antecedent ἔργοις (*works*). οἷς functions as the direct object of the verb προητοίμασεν and therefore might be expected to be accusative. How-

---

[85] Robertson, p. 1182. Cf. p. 704.
[86] Zerwick, p. 130, §129.

ever, when a relative pronoun would be accusative in its own clause and has an antecedent that is either genitive or dative, the relative pronoun is typically attracted to the antecedent so as to agree with it in case.

For προητοίμασεν (*prepared*), the ASV has "afore prepared," the KJV has "before ordained," and the NIV has "prepared in advance." Again, the eternal purpose of God is in view. The verb is the aorist active indicative third person singular form of προετοιμάζω, which is a compound of the preposition πρό (*before*) and ἑτοιμάζω (*make ready*). The idea of prior readying is already inherent in the English "prepare" (pre-pare), but perhaps we use "prepare" often enough without conscious emphasis on the prior aspect of the verb that additional language is deemed necessary by some translators to emphasize the prior idea in προετοιμάζω.

that we might walk in them (ἵνα ἐν αὐτοῖς περιπατήσωμεν). περιπατήσωμεν is aorist act. subjunctive. The word *might* is an attempt to represent the subjunctive mood (something that has largely passed out of common use in modern English). The clause indicates the purpose of God's having prepared the good works; He did so that we might walk in them. This phrase anticipates much of the message of the rest of Ephesians. Walking in the good works God has prepared for us is in contrast to walking according to the course of this world (vs. 2). Paul will have much to say about the walk of those saved by grace (4.1, "walk worthily of the calling"; 4.17, "not as the Gentiles walk"; 5.2, "walk in love"; 5.8, "walk as children of light"; 5.15, "walk as wise"). All of this is a call to the Gentiles to leave behind the sinful practices of their pagan background and walk worthily as fellow members with believing Jews of the household of God.

2.11–12 The Former State of Gentiles as Aliens

Wherefore remember that then, you, the Gentiles in flesh, those called uncircumcision by those called circumcision, in flesh, wrought by hands, that you were at that time without Christ, alienated from the polity of Israel, and estranged from the covenant of the promise, not having a hope, and godless in the world.

Paul begins this section with the inferential conjunction διό, *wherefore*. The expression is elliptical. The preceding was that they are God's work and cannot boast. Fully stated, Paul's thought seems to be something like this: "It is important that you understand this (that you are God's work) lest you fail to give God the credit and the glory, wherefore, I remind you of the condition in which you were."

While the form μνημονεύετε (*remember*) might be either indicative or imperative, in this context it only makes sense as an imperative. Paul calls upon his readers to remember, not affirming that they do remember. He is calling upon them to remember their previously estranged condition in order to highlight hereafter the magnitude of God's grace toward them and then call upon them to walk worthily of the high calling that is in Christ.

Paul specifies τὰ ἔθνη ἐν σαρκί. Among Greeks, ἔθνος simply meant "nation." It is the word from which comes the English "ethnic." People of a particular ethnicity are people of a particular national origin. The plural expression τὰ ἔθνη was used much as we might say, "the nations" meaning "the (other) nations," and thus was equivalent to "foreigners." But being "foreign" truly is in the eye of the beholder. For the Roman Appian, τὰ ἔθνη were those who were not Italian.[87] For Aristotle, τὰ ἔθνη were those who were not Greek.[88] But from the Jewish perspective, τὰ ἔθνη, "*the (other) nations*" were non-Jews. By the time Paul writes this letter, among Christians τὰ ἔθνη had also acquired a spiritual connotation, indicating people outside the kingdom of God, as evidenced by Paul's language in Ephesians 4.17 as well as by Peter's language in 1 Peter 4.3. But Paul does not so use the word here. Rather, here he is addressing those who have been saved by Christ, though they are indeed Gentiles *in the flesh*.

those called uncircumcision (οἱ λεγόμενοι ἀκροβυστία).   In verse 12, Paul will not only remind his readers that they had been without Christ, but also that they had been ἀπηλλοτριωμένοι τῆς πολιτείας τοῦ Ἰσραήλ, *alienated from the polity of Israel*. Paul aims to remind the Gentiles of where they had stood in relation to the people of God.

To the Jew—and it is important to remember that for some years after the resurrection the church was almost entirely Jews—a Gentile was not merely a foreigner; he was ἀκροβυστία, *uncircumcised*.

ἀκροβυστία is apparently a compound of two words, the first of which is clearly either the noun ἄκρον, meaning *endpoint*, as in the top of Jacob's staff (Hb 11.21), or the cognate adjective ἄκρος. Several suppose the other part is derived from the verb βύω, which can mean "stop up" or "close."[89] The combined idea would be a very literal reference to the

---

[87] Bell Civ. 1.0.6.

[88] Pol. Vii.2.5.

[89] *e.g.*, Hoehner p. 354, Schmidt in TDNT, vol. 1, p. 225.

"closed endpoint" of the uncircumcised man. This was the derivation postulated in Etymologicum Magnum.[90] In LSJ this derivation is said to be wrong, and the word is rather explained as a combination of ἄκρος and a Semitic root pertaining to shame.[91] However, the formulation in Acts 11.3, ἄνδρας ἀκροβυστίαν ἔχοντας (*men having uncircumcision*), may lend credence to the etymology long ago given in EM. To speak of *having* ἀκροβυστίαν would be consistent with understanding the word to mean *closed end*.

The word used among Greeks for the foreskin was the similar sounding ἀκροποσθία, and it has been suggested that ἀκροβυστία was "an intentional reconstruction of ἀκροποσθία."[92] Cr.-Kö supposes this formulation may have developed "with a view to expressing the matter in a decorously indirect and veiled manner."[93] But the opposite is probably true.

ἀκροβυστία is found several times in the LXX including five times in Genesis 17 where we first read of the covenant of circumcision. In the New Testament, the word is found only in Paul's writings and in Acts 11.3. It is not found outside of Biblical and ecclesiastical writings. Whatever the origin of ἀκροβυστία may have been, the significant fact here is that prior to the New Testament we do not find the term in use among non-Jewish writers. As Paul says, the Gentiles were called ἀκροβυστία ὑπὸ τῆς λεγομένης περιτομῆς, *i.e.*, they were so called by the Jews. And among the Jews, the term came to have a connotation that was anything but decorous. Although in many contexts the word is used with no hint of condescension,[94] in Acts 11.3 it is easy to hear the word as something of a slur.[95] While Paul

---

[90] EM 53.47–52. ἈΚΡΟΒΥΣΤΙΑ Ἐκ τοῦ ἀκρόβυστος ἀκροβυστία, ὃ σημαίνει τὸν κεκαλυμμένον, παρὰ τὸ βύω τὸ καλύπτω, βύσω βέβυκα βέβυσμαι βύστης καὶ ἀκρόβυστος. Ἐντεῦθεν καὶ ἄβυσσος, ἄβυστος, καὶ τροπῇ τοῦ Τ εἰς Σ, ἄβυσσος, μετὰ τοῦ ἐπιτατικοῦ ἄλφα, ὁ τόπος ὁ ὑπὸ πλήθους ὑδάτων καλυπτόμενος.

[91] p. 56.

[92] Cr.-Kö according to Schmidt in TDNT, also BDAG. Cr.-Kö is H. Cremer, Biblisch-theologisches Wörterbuch des nt.lichen Griechisch, revised by J. Kögel, 1923.

[93] Schmidt, TDNT, vol. 1 p. 225.

[94] E.g., Gal 2.7, 1 Cor 7.18f, throughout Romans. Although even in Romans, there are hints of a negative connotation. In Romans 2.25, the words "your circumcision has become uncircumcision (ἀκροβυστία)" are an an indictment. Then in verse 26, the phrase "if therefore the uncircumcision keeps the righteousness of the law" can be understood as ironic. The uncircumcision of the Gentile corresponds to the transgressing of the law on the part of the Jew.

[95] Cf. Joel Marcus, p. 77f, "The Circumcision and the Uncircumcision in Rome," New Testament Studies, 35(1989):1, pp. 67–81.

may have intended to use a derogatory term for Gentiles, in fact it is the only term for uncircumcision used in the NT. In any event, Paul used the word not out of hatred for Gentiles, but to emphasize the estranged condition of Gentiles apart from Christ, and thus to highlight the magnificence of the grace of God bestowed upon them in Christ.[96]

by those called circumcision, in flesh, wrought by hands (ὑπὸ τῆς λεγομένης περιτομῆς ἐν σαρκὶ χειροποιήτου). When referring to his readers as τὰ ἔθνη, Paul had specified ἐν σαρκί, and he now does the same thing when speaking of those who were circumcised. He says, you were called ἀκροβυστία by those who are called circumcised, but their circumcision is only in the flesh, made with hands. Jeremiah 9.25 comes to mind, where the Lord warned those who were "circumcised and yet uncircumcised," that is, as explained in vs. 26, "uncircumcised of heart." Their ears were uncircumcised and thus we could say, closed up, such that "they are not able to hear" (Jer 6.10). So while Paul is reminding the Gentiles of the spiritual desert in which they were, he at the same time acknowledges that the Jews who despised them were different only outwardly, only in the flesh.

that you were at that time without Christ, alienated from the polity of Israel (ὅτι ἦτε τῷ καιρῷ ἐκείνῳ χωρὶς Χριστοῦ, ἀπηλλοτριωμένοι τῆς πολιτείας τοῦ Ἰσραὴλ). πολιτεία is *citizenship* in Acts 22.28. But here, the word is used not in the technical sense of legal status. Paul may use the word in the practical sense of social and civic intercourse,[97] or perhaps in a corporate sense such that πολιτεία is another name for Israel.

Josephus went to great lengths to describe the high esteem in which Jews were held by various rulers of other nations. But in doing so, he made mention of one occasion, just a decade or so before Jesus' birth, when there was an attempt to deny πολιτεία to the Jews of Asia. According to Josephus, the Ionians of the region had petitioned Marcus Agrippa that they alone, and not the Jews, might enjoy the rights of citizenship.[98] Ralph

---

[96] The competing readings among the manuscripts of the Septuagint at Leviticus 19.23, most having ἀκαθαρσίαν (*uncleanness*) where others have ἀκροβυστίαν, may offer some evidence of the stigma associated with the word ἀκροβυστίαν. See Septuaginta, Vetus Testamentum Graecum, vol II, 2, Leviticus, Göttingen, Vandenhoeck & Ruprecht, 1986. P. 216, note in critical apparatus on vs. 23. Although to be sure, uncircumcision by any name would have been considered unclean among the Jews.

[97] *Cf.* Polybius 18.43.6

[98] *Antiq.* xii.125, p. 63 in Loeb. A more complete account of the same incident, including the case made on behalf of the Jews, is found at *Antiq.* xvi.27–65. It seems this took place on

Marcus opined that Josephus was confusing "citizenship with privileg-es and grants of religious freedom,"[99] and that it was the Jews' freedom to practice their religious customs that Ionian Greeks wished to revoke. Nonetheless, it can be said that not long before the time of Paul's writ-ing, there was current the idea that in Asia Greeks had attempted to deny πολιτεία to the Jews of Asia. And while the question of legal citizenship may not have hung in the balance, clearly the Ionians did not desire that the Jews should enjoy the privileges they had been granted. The impetus behind this animosity was the Jews' novel religion.[100]

Whether or not Paul was aware of this history, there is an irony in his characterization of the Gentiles of the region as having been alienated from the citizenship of Israel. And one would think that among Paul's audience, there would be those who would sense the irony. For further insights into the relationship between Jews and Gentiles, see the Intro-duction, under the heading "Gentile Christians, the Intended Audience."

and estranged from the covenant of the promise (καὶ ξένοι τῶν διαθηκῶν τῆς ἐπαγγελίας)   Paul's speeches recorded in the book of Acts help to clarify the meaning of this phrase. "The promise" is the messianic promise God made to the fathers, unto which the twelve tribes hoped to attain (Acts 26.6f, cf. Acts 13.23, 32f). The covenants of the prom-ise are the decrees made to the patriarchs, e.g., those made to Abraham (Gen 12.3), Isaac (26.4), and Jacob (28.14). From these the Gentiles had been estranged, even though they explicitly spoke of the inclusion of the Gentiles. That is, while the covenants spoke of the Gentiles, they were covenants God made with the patriarchs and their descendants, the na-tion of Israel (Rom 9.4). But now in Christ, the Gentiles have heard the word of the promise which is the good news of their salvation (Eph 1.13), that is, the proclamation of the means whereby Gentiles would become participants in the promised blessing (Eph 3.6).

not having a hope, and godless in the world (ἐλπίδα μὴ ἔχοντες καὶ ἄθεοι ἐν τῷ κόσμῳ)   This is reminiscent of 1 Thessalonians 4.13 where Paul describes "the rest" as οἱ μὴ ἔχοντες ἐλπίδα, *the ones not having hope.*

---

the island of Samos and in the presence of King Herod the Great.

[99] Ibid., p. 741–2, Loeb, Appendix C.

[100] Cf. Haman's description of the Jews to Ahasuerus, Esther 3.8.

2.13–18 In Christ, Gentiles and Jews Have Equal Standing

But now in Christ Jesus, you who were formerly far off became near in the blood of the Christ. For he himself is our peace, he who made both one and destroyed the middle wall of partition, the hostility, in his flesh, thus abolishing the law of commandments in ordinances, that in himself he might make the two into one new man, thus making peace, and might reconcile them both in one body to God through the cross, in it having killed the hostility. And having come, he proclaimed peace to you who were far off, and peace to those who were near, because through him we both have access in one Spirit to the Father.

The imagery is provided by the barrier in the temple. Gentiles' spiritual separation from God was represented in a very literal way by their lack of access to the temple. They could enter the outer courts, but compared to the access enjoyed by Jews, they were "far off." This idea is further developed in the next verse.

But now, by the blood of Christ, the Gentiles are also near. Indeed, Paul will shortly say they are much more than near.

In his letters, Paul uses νυνὶ δὲ (*but now*) both temporally and logically. The same can be said of νῦν δέ. But in regard to νυνὶ δέ, interestingly, whether by happenstance or simply due to the nature of a given letter's content, Paul is fairly consistent within a given letter in using the expression one way or the other. In Romans, νυνὶ δὲ is almost always temporal (6x), the only exception being Romans 7.17. In 1 Corinthians νυνὶ δὲ is always logical (4x), never temporal. Both occurrences in 2 Corinthians are temporal, as are both occurrences in Philemon, as are both occurrences in Colossians.

Here in Ephesians. 2.13, νυνὶ δὲ is in contrast to the preceding ποτὲ ὑμεῖς τὰ ἔθνη ἐν σαρκί (vs. 10) and τῷ καιρῷ ἐκείνῳ (vs. 11), *then, you, the Gentiles in flesh…at that time.*

The structure of the clauses in 2.14–15 is shown on the opposite page.

Paul's point here is to declare the fact and explain the means whereby Christ Jesus creates peace between Jew and Gentile, and ultimately, peace with God. He begins with a statement which he will explicate: Αὐτὸς γὰρ ἐστιν ἡ εἰρήνη ἡμῶν, *For he himself is our peace*. While nominative αὐτὸς is not necessarily intensive, here it is best to understand it to be so as it is resumptive, refocusing the reader's attention on him who was the object of the preposition in the previous sentence (ἐν Χριστῷ Ἰησοῦ) but is now the subject of the new thought: He himself is the one who is our peace.

Αὐτὸς γὰρ ἐστιν ἡ εἰρήνη ἡμῶν,	For **He himself** is our peace,
ὁ	**He**
(a) ποιήσας τὰ ἀμφότερα ἓν	(a) who made both one
καὶ	and
(b) τὸ μεσότοιχον τοῦ φραγμοῦ λύσας, τὴν ἔχθραν	(b) who destroyed the middle wall of partition, the hostility
ἐν τῇ σαρκὶ αὐτοῦ,	in his flesh,
τὸν νόμον τῶν ἐντολῶν ἐν δόγμασιν καταργήσας,	abolishing the law of commandments in ordinances
ἵνα τοὺς δύο κτίσῃ ἐν αὐτῷ εἰς ἕνα καινὸν ἄνθρωπον ποιῶν εἰρήνην	that in himself he might make the two into one new man, making peace.

Structure of Ephesians 2.14–15

Two participial clauses are introduced by and share one definite article. They are coordinated by καὶ. ὁ ποιήσας...καὶ...λύσας. They form two attributive modifiers of the subject, αὐτός, *i.e.*, Christ. He himself is our peace, the one who made and destroyed. Made what and destroyed what? Christ is the one *who made both one*, that is, made both Jew and Gentile one, and *who destroyed the middle wall of partition*.

Then, before stating the means whereby, or location in which, Christ did this, Paul renames the wall, calling it τὴν ἔχθραν, *the hostility*. The wall of estrangement, represented by the physical barrier in Jerusalem, was not merely an aloofness toward Gentiles; it was hostility toward the Gentiles on the part of the Jews. But Christ made them both one and destroyed this barrier, this hostility in his own flesh.

The words τὸ μεσότοιχον τοῦ φραγμοῦ are of special interest. Understanding the allusion here will help us more accurately understand the circumstance that gives rise to Paul's overall message. That circumstance was the low esteem in which Gentiles were held by Jews, and those Gentiles now seeking a place in a body that had previously been comprised entirely by Jews.

In the temple at Jerusalem, Gentiles were permitted to enter the outermost areas. But there was a barrier beyond which Gentiles were not permitted to go. Josephus described it as a δρύφακτος περιβέβλητο λίθινο, but others describe it as a sort of lattice work, or a "reticulated fence of sticks."[101] Perhaps the variation in the descriptions reflects changes made during Herod's vast renovation and expansion of the temple complex. Josephus gives its height as three cubits (BJ 5.193), about 4.5 feet. In the Mishna,[102] the height is given as "ten handbreadths." Signs were placed along this barrier with a warning of lethal consequences for Gentiles who ventured beyond it.[103]

The words τὸ μεσότοιχον τοῦ φραγμοῦ have in view this barrier in the temple, but as a symbol of the enmity that existed between Jews and Gentiles, and also a symbol of the Gentiles' relative remoteness from God.[104] Its destruction is an apt figure for the uniting of Jew and Gentile as one people, reconciled to God.

But not all are ready to acknowledge an allusion to this dividing wall. Alford saw in this phrase a reference to the veil that was torn when Jesus died on the cross. He acknowledged the fact that that veil did not separate Jew and Gentile, but pointed out that it symbolized separation from God and argued that its removal was the "admission to Him of that one body into which Christ made Jew and Gentile." In this indirect manner, Alford supposed reference to the veil was connected with the words "made both one," words which Alford rightly recognized as describing the uniting of Jew and Gentile.[105]

Hoehner lays out four arguments against understanding Paul's words to be a reference to the well-known barrier in the temple: (1) He does not see a reference to the wall in this context, (2) "the Jerusalem

---

[101] Jewish Encyclopedia, s.v. Temple, Plan of Second. In tractate Middoth 2.3.a, the Hebrew word used is *soreg*, from the root word *sarag, to entwine*.

[102] Middoth 2.3.a.

[103] Josephus, A.J. 418 [15.11.5], p. 203 in Loeb. In footnote *d*, Marcus and Wikgren give the text of one of the inscriptions as follows: Μηθένα ἀλλογενῆ εἰσπορεύεσθαι ἐντὸς τοῦ περὶ τὸ ἱερὸν τρυφάκτου καὶ περιβόλου. ὃς δ' ἂν ληφθῇ ἑαυτῷ αἴτιος ἔσται διὰ τὸ ἐξακολουθεῖν θάνατου.

[104] Chrysostom saw the wall here in Eph 2.14 as representing separation from God, but attested to fact that others saw it as representing the separation between Jews and Gentiles: "Some indeed affirm that he means the wall of the Jews against the Greeks, because it did not allow the Jews to hold intercourse with the Greeks"(Homily 5 on Ephesians). But the two interpretations are not mutually exclusive.

[105] Alford, p. 97.

wall is never called by the designation given in the present context," (3) "the wall in Jerusalem was still standing when Paul wrote this letter," and (4) "it was probably unfamiliar to the average person in the churches around Ephesus."

The first three objections are trivial. Regarding the first, how can one say there is no reference to the well-known barrier in Ephesians 2 before determining if the words τὸ μεσότοιχον τοῦ φραγμοῦ themselves refer to that barrier?

Regarding the second objection, the absence of confirmation that μεσότοιχον τοῦ φραγμοῦ was a phrase used for the barrier, the fact is there are very few references of any sort to the wall in contemporaneous literature. In Hebrew, the wall was the *soreg*. It may be that if there was a special Greek term for the wall, it was δρύφακτος.[106] But it seems that what was notable was not so much the wall itself as the effect of the wall. Philo mentions the penalty of death for one not of the Jewish nation who might pass into the inner courts, but does so without specifically mentioning the dividing wall at all.

So then there is little evidence to support the notion that among Greeks there was a stereoptyped name for the wall. To the readers of Paul's letter, the phrase τὸ μεσότοιχον τοῦ φραγμοῦ would not be understood as a technical term for the barrier, but a descriptive phrase suited to the context, highlighting the fragmentation of mankind into the categories of Jews and Gentiles, with Gentiles having been far off, unable to approach the presence of God.

Nor is Hoehner's third objection, the fact that the wall was still standing when Paul wrote, conclusive against our understanding. Paul refers to the barrier only as a figure for the spiritual estrangement of Gentiles apart from Christ. The house of God in which Jews and Gentiles would be joined was not the physical one. And therefore the destruction of

---

[106] Josephus twice refers to the wall using the word δρύφακτος (A.J. 15.417, B.J. 5.193). The alternate spelling, τρύφακτος, was found on one of the signs warning Gentiles not to enter. This was a word used of a railing or latticed partition serving as a bar in a court of law. (See Apollodorus of Damascus, Πολιορκητικά "Seige Engines," 172.1, and also Aristophanes Vespae (Wasps) 386, where Lovecleon, afflicted with an addiction to jury duty, attempts to escape the house where he has been imprisoned so that he can join his fellow jurors, and says to them that if he dies in the process, they should bury him under the δρυφάκτοις, i.e., under the court railings.) δρύφακτος was also used more generally, as in Polybius 1.22.6 where it refers to the railings on either side of a corvus, a device for boarding enemy ships.

the spiritual barrier was not predicated on the literal destruction of the physical barrier. Though the physical barrier would be destroyed soon enough, the destruction of which Paul speaks is that which was accomplished by the work of Jesus, not the work of the Roman armies. Prior to the cross, Jews were "near" inasmuch as they had been entrusted with the oracles of God, and this was symbolized by their access to the physical temple. But Gentiles were "far off." Now in Christ, that distinction has been abolished.

Hoehner's fourth objection was that the barrier to Gentiles in the Jewish Temple "was probably unfamiliar to the average person in the churches around Ephesus."[107] There is, however, reason to believe that Greeks in foreign lands had some familiarity with the temple. Strabo alluded to the temple at Jerusalem as if his readers were familiar with it (16.2.34), though without mentioning the middle wall of partition in particular. Hecataeus (fourth/third century BC) described the temple in detail, though without mentioning this partition which well may not have existed in his time. Josephus quotes Hecataeus' description in Contra Apion I.198–199. These references establish the fact that the temple in Jerusalem was not unknown to the Greek world.

But especially among the churches to whom Paul was writing, the allusion to the wall would have been understood. After all, Paul writes this letter as a prisoner in Rome, his original arrest having been due to an accusation that he had taken a Gentile into the inner court. Moreover, it was an Ephesian that Paul was accused of having taken into the temple. Even if Luke had not yet immortalized that incident in the book of Acts,[108] it is difficult to imagine that the churches of Asia to whom Paul writes were not already aware of it. So then Hoehner's fourth objection falls by the side.

τὴν ἔχθραν must be understood in apposition to τὸ μεσότοιχον. It is another way of speaking of the middle wall of partition, again, not the physical barrier itself, but that which it represented, namely, the hostility inherent in the estrangement of the Gentiles. This was a hostility on the part of the Jews.

---

[107] O'Brien also considers this to be a problem for the view that Paul does indeed have in mind the wall in the temple at Jerusalem: "whether Gentile readers of this letter, living in Asia Minor, would have recognized such an allusion is questionable." p. 195.

[108] Ephesians was written sometime between AD 60 and AD 62, the same window of time in which Luke must have composed Acts. It is impossible to say whether Acts or Ephesians was composed first.

Some have understood ἐν τῇ σαρκὶ αὐτοῦ to be directly related to τὸν νόμον τῶν ἐντολῶν ἐν δόγμασιν καταργήσας.[109] That is, he abolished the law of commandments in ordinances by means of his flesh. Structurally, I think we should rather understand ἐν τῇ σαρκὶ αὐτοῦ as describing the foregoing words, ὁ ποιήσας τὰ ἀμφότερα ἓν καὶ τὸ μεσότοιχον τοῦ φραγμοῦ λύσας. That is, Christ made both one and destroyed the middle wall of partition by means of his flesh. The phrase ἐν τῇ σαρκὶ αὐτοῦ may be understood as having either locative force ("in his flesh") or instrumental force, *i.e.*, it was by means of his flesh, his body that hung on the cross, that he accomplished this. In fact, both in Greek and in English, we easily blur the distinction between location and means, using one for the other. "*In* writing this commentary, I hope to promote a greater understanding of the book of Ephesians."

The two attributive participles are followed by a clause anchored by an adverbial participle, τὸν νόμον τῶν ἐντολῶν ἐν δόγμασιν καταργήσας (*abolishing the law of commandments in ordinances*). καταργήσας is not to be understood consecutively, as subsequent to ποιήσας τὰ ἀμφότερα ἓν and τὸ μεσότοιχον τοῦ φραγμοῦ λύσας. It is rather an adverbial statement indicating the action that was associated with Christ's becoming our peace. He himself is our peace, having set aside the law of the commandments in ordinances. This corresponds to Paul's phrase in Colossians 2.14, ἐξαλείψας τὸ καθ' ἡμῶν χειρόγραφον τοῖς δόγμασιν ὃ ἦν ὑπεναντίον ἡμῖν. Whereas here in Ephesians Paul uses the participal καταργήσας, in Colossians he chose the participle ἐξαλείψας and then further explained this by the phrases αὐτὸ ἦρκεν ἐκ τοῦ μέσου and προσηλώσας αὐτὸ τῷ σταυρῷ.

A difficulty may be perceived here inasmuch as Paul elsewhere insists that he does not nullify law by proclaiming justification by faith, (νόμον οὖν καταργοῦμεν διὰ τῆς πίστεως; μὴ γένοιτο, *therefore do we nullify law through the faith? Let it not be!* Rom 3.31), and there uses the same verb, καταργέω, as he uses here where he says Christ has indeed nullified the law of commandments in ordinances. The explanation is to be found in distinguishing between nullifying for us the effect of the law (condemnation) and nullifying law itself. Law (in the abstract, though not in the specific requirements of the Mosaic law) persists. But because the requirement of law is satisfied in Christ, the condemnation that God's people

---

[109] e.g., Stoeckhardt, p. 147; Schnackenburg.

would otherwise face under law is nullified. So then the requirement of the law is fulfilled (Rom 8.4), and thus Paul can say law is actually established by faith (Rom 3.31). That is to say, trusting in Jesus' death as the satisfaction of the requirement of the law is tacit acknowledgment of the validity of the law.

in order that he might make the two into one new man, making peace (ἵνα τοὺς δύο κτίσῃ ἐν αὐτῷ εἰς ἕνα καινὸν ἄνθρωπον ποιῶν εἰρήνην) Although τοὺς δύο is accusative and an object of κτίσῃ grammatically, Paul is not here saying Jesus created the two, Jew and Gentile. Rather the creation in view is the making of one out of the two. A very similar construction, though absent the preposition, is seen in Jn 4.46, ἐποίησεν τὸ ὕδωρ οἶνον. In Paul's construction, we see the predicate use of εἰς. Compare Matthew 19.5, 2 Corinthians 6.18, and Hebrews 1.5, Ἐγὼ ἔσομαι αὐτῷ εἰς πατέρα, καὶ αὐτὸς ἔσται μοι εἰς υἱόν. An example cited by Robertson where the verb is not a copulative is Acts 7.53.[110]

2.16 *and might reconcile them both in one body to God through the cross.* The verb ἀποκαταλλάξῃ (*might reconcile*) is subjunctive and is grammatically parallel to κτίσῃ (*might create*) in the preceding verse, both verbs being introduced by the conjunction ἵνα (*in order that*, or simply, *that*). So then, it is *that he might create…and reconcile.*

There is a twofold meaning here, both in the significance of ἑνὶ σώματι (*one body*) and in the function of ἐν (*in*), as well as in the meaning of ἀποκαταλλάξῃ (*might reconcile*). The one body is both the phyical body of Jesus *by which means* (instrumental function of ἐν with dative) both Jews and Gentiles are reconciled to God. But the one body is also the spiritual body *in which* (locative function of ἐν with dative) Jews and Gentiles are reconciled to each other, that is, in the church which is his body (Eph 1.22–23). While the reference to the cross brings to mind Jesus' physical body, the stress on the singularity of the body makes it clear that Paul does indeed have in mind the spiritual body, the church wherein there is no more Jew and Gentile, but one new man in Christ.

reconciled to God	reconciled to one another
by means of	in
(the sacrifice of) his body on the cross	the spiritual body, i.e., the church

---

[110] Robertson, A Grammar, p. 596.

in it having killed the hostility ἀποκτείνας τὴν ἔχθραν ἐν αὐτῷ   Does αὐτῷ refer to himself (*having killed the hostility in himself*) or to the cross (*having killed the hostility in it*)? Already in this sentence we have seen αὐτῷ used reflexively (vs. 15). And yet "the cross" could easily be understood to be the antecedent of αὐτῷ.

More critical to gaining an accurate understanding of Paul's meaning is the significance of ἔχθραν here. Previously (2.14), this word was used of the hostility of Jews toward Gentiles and was symbolized by the middle wall of partition. But the significance of ἔχθραν in verse 16 will best be understood if we remember that the entire thought, beginning in verse 14, is a grammatically independent clause setting forth the explanation for the statement made in verse 13. There, Paul stated that the Gentiles, who had been far off, have been made near through the blood of Christ. Verse 14 begins with the word *for*[111]—*For he is our peace, he who made both one.* We should, therefore, expect to find in verses 14–16 an explanation of the Gentiles being brought near to God. Along the way, it is evident that Paul brings the Jews into the picture, the Gentiles being united with them in one body, before arriving at his point, which is that Christ has put to death the hostility that existed between all men and God.

Were we to understand ἔχθραν otherwise, were we to suppose it is yet again a reference to hostility between Jew and Gentile, it would be inappropriately anticlimactic, or so it seems to me. After wending his way through a discussion of Jews and Gentiles brought together in one body in order to arrive at his point that Gentiles, in this one body and along with Jews, have been reconciled to God, for Paul to then append the phrase "having put to death the hostility between Jew and Gentile" would only detract from the point he set out to make, namely to explain how Gentiles had been brought near *to God*.

That is not to say that destroying the hostility between Jew and Gentile was a minor thing. It was not. Indeed, the circumstance that gives rise to this letter is that very hostility. But Paul's desire is that his Gentile readers see what God has done for them by reconciling them to himself, by making them his house, and that they are no less so than Jewish believers.

---

[111] In Greek, the word γάρ ("for") is actually in the second position in the clause. γάρ is one of several words described as postpositive in Greek, that is, they are never the first word in a clause though logically are conjunctions joining their clause to a preceding clause. We may compare our use of "therefore" in English, e.g., Franklin D. Roosevelt said, "The real safeguard of democracy, therefore, is education."

Essential to understanding this is that they with the Jews comprise one body, not two separate bodies. But it is the reconciliation to God that is the ultimate point.

Notice this structure:

An assertion about Gentiles

An acknowledgment that Jews and Gentiles are in the same state

A conclusion relative to the initial assertion about Gentiles, but that also applies to Jews

We saw this in Ephesians 2.1–5. There, Paul began his discussion of Gentiles being dead in their trespasses in verses 1–2, then in verse 3 added that the Jews were in the same condition, and finally in verse 5 arrived at his conclusion that God in his mercy had made them (both) alive in Christ:

You (Gentiles) being dead in your sins (2.1–2)

We (Jews) were too (2.3)

God made us (both Jews and Gentiles) alive in Christ (2.4–5)

So here Paul declares the Gentiles' improved access to God in verse 13, then in verses 14–15 begins his explanation of the same by adding that they are no longer separated from that to which Jews had access, and that they with the Jews have become a single body, before finally in verse 16 stating that this one body has been reconciled to God, the hostility (between man and God) having been destroyed:

You (Gentiles) were far off but have been made near (2.13)

For Christ made both (Jew and Gentile) one (2.14–15)

And reconciled both in one body to God through the cross (2.16)

Finally, after considering the structure of this passage and noting that the first element included the words "made near *in the blood of Christ*," it seems best to me to understand the final words "having put to the death the hostility ἐν αὐτῷ" as meaning *in the cross* rather than *in himself*. In this way, Paul closes the loop. The making near by means of the blood of Christ was accomplished when God destroyed the hostility between man and himself, the hostility which existed because of man's sin (Is 59.2), but which was eliminated when man's sin was punished in the cross (Isaiah 53, 1 Peter 2).

2.17 *And having come, he proclaimed peace to you who were far off, and peace to those who were near* Hoehner thinks this must refer to a proclamation that was made after Christ's crucifixion, "for that served as the basis of the peace proclaimed" (p. 385). Hoehner further argues, "In his earthly ministry Christ preached almost entirely to the Jews." He therefore concludes that the proclamation was made "by means of the Holy Spirit through his apostles (cf. Eph. 3:5–6)."

However, Christ preached peace prospectively before his crucifixion (Jn. 14.27, 16.33). And we ought not forget that Jesus' teaching prior to his crucifixion offered hope to Gentiles as well as to Jews. It is true that he himself preached primarily to the lost sheep of the house of Israel (Mt 15.24), but on more than one occasion he managed to say enough about Gentiles being welcomed into the kingdom to offend the Jews (Lk 4.24*ff*, Mt 21.43). If not to everyone at the time, at least to us today it is evident that his gospel was that which had been anticipated in the prophetic expectation of a light for the Gentiles (Is 9.1–2, Mt 4.15). He spoke of the salvation of Gentiles both explicitly (Mt 8.5–13) and in parables (Mt 21.43, Lk 14.23), and his actions were interpreted as being in fulfillment of OT prophecy pertaining to the salvation of Gentiles (Mt 12.18–21). The entirety of Jesus' incarnation, beginning with the angelic "peace among men," constituted such a proclamation as Paul describes. Perhaps an attempt to identify a particular occasion of proclamation to a Gentile audience, for example, the household of Cornelius or the audience at Antioch, encumbers εὐηγγελίσατο with a more formal sense than is necessary for Paul's purpose here.

We ought to notice that once again we see how clearly Paul addresses this letter specifically to Gentiles. Whereas he writes to Gentiles, addressing them directly—*he proclaimed peace to you, the far off ones*—Paul writes about Jews obliquely, *and peace to the near ones.*

Finally, Paul's teaching here in 2.14–17 fundamentally undermines the doctrine of a raptured Gentile church distinct from a later millennial Jewish kingdom. That theory has Jews and Gentiles being reconciled to God in two distinct entities. Moreover, that theory regards the church of Jesus Christ as a mere placeholder, counting time till an intended (Jewish) kingdom is reinstated. But Paul will say the church's existence was *according to a purpose from eternity which he accomplished in Christ Jesus our Lord* (3.11).

2.18 *because through him we both have access in one Spirit to the Father* (ὅτι δι' αὐτοῦ ἔχομεν τὴν προσαγωγὴν οἱ ἀμφότεροι ἐν ἑνὶ πνεύματι πρὸς τὸν πατέρα) ὅτι is a conjunction that connects εὐηγγελίσατο εἰρήνην with δι' αὐτοῦ ἔχομεν τὴν προσαγωγήν. But the nature of the connection is the question. Does ὅτι introduce the cause of the foregoing, or does ὅτι introduce a result of the foregoing? That is, is the conjunction "causal" or "consecutive"? Or does ὅτι serve merely to introduce an object clause as it does so often in the New Testament?

Consider three paraphrases of the thought that will help to clarify the question:

(1) He preached peace to you that were far off and to us who were near, [the peace being] *that* we both have access to the Father in one Spirit. (This is the meaning if ὅτι introduces an object clause.)

(2) He preached peace to you that were far off and to us who were near, *because* we both have access to the Father in one Spirit. (This is the meaning if ὅτι is causal.)

(3) He preached peace to you that were far off and to us who were near, *so that* we both have access to the Father in one Spirit. (This is the meaning if ὅτι is consecutive.)

The use of ὅτι to introduce an object clause is often found following verbs of communication (writing, speaking, etc.) and verbs of perception (seeing, hearing, thinking, knowing, etc.). In Ephesians 5.5, 6.8, and 6.9, we see ὅτι used after verbs of "knowing," introducing what is known. In Ephesians 2.11–12 ὅτι serves to introduce a clause explaining what Paul wants his readers to remember. In this instance, Paul repeats the ὅτι because prior to completing the object clause, he elaborated on the subject in the clause, spelling out exactly what he meant by "Gentiles." *Wherefore remember that* (ὅτι) *then, you, the Gentiles in flesh, those called uncircumcision by those called circumcision, in flesh, wrought by hands, that* (ὅτι) *you were at that time without Christ.*

In Ephesians 2.18, ὅτι might be construed as introducing an object clause, the object of the verb εὐηγγελίσατο, explaining what was preached. But Paul has already told us what was preached. He preached *peace.* So in this instance, the object clause would be a further explanation of what was preached, a further explanation of the peace, the explanation being that we have access to God. At the same time, of course, Paul is emphatically making the point that both Jew and Gentile have this same peace, this same access to the Father.

The causal use of ὅτι also occurs frequently in the NT. Here in Ephesians, we see this use at 4.25, *speak truth each one with his neighbor, because* (ὅτι) *we are members of one another.* See also Ephesians 5.16, 5.23, 5.30, 6.12.

In Ephesians 2.18, ὅτι is probably to be construed as causal, though the access itself can hardly be thought of as the cause of the preaching (he preached because we have access?). The emphasis of the second clause (verse 18) is not on the access itself nor is the emphasis of the first clause (verse 17) on the mere fact that he preached peace. Paul's point is not merely that he preached peace, but more specifically that he preached peace both to those far off and those who were near. ὅτι serves to connect the fact that peace was preached to Gentiles as well as Jews (vs. 17) with the fact that through Jesus, *both groups* have access in *one* Spirit (vs. 18). He proclaimed peace to both groups, because through him they both have entrance in one Spirit to the Father. This is the meaning indicated by the KJV, NKJV, NIV, ESV, NAS, RSV, ASV, all of which translate ὅτι by means of the word "for."

The consecutive use of ὅτι is unusual in the NT, but may be illustrated by 1 Timothy 6.7. The fact that the use there is unusual probably accounts for the variant readings in the manuscripts, readings introduced by scribes who felt that ὅτι itself did not adequately explain the connection between the two clauses in 1 Timothy 6.7. The only other examples cited in BDAG are questions (Jn 7.35, 14.22, Heb 2.6). Robertson noted examples also in Mark 4.41 and Luke 4.36,[112] again both in questions. Hoehner has the consecutive use in mind when he translates, "so that." However, the causal meaning for ὅτι occurs much more frequently, and in Ephesians 2.18, it yields a sense that is perfectly in keeping with the overall message of the first three chapters.

The mention of one Spirit (ἐν ἑνὶ πνεύματι) is a further development of the idea of the unity that will be most comprehensively stated in 4.4–6. Gentiles' access to the Father was not through a back door, nor was it on a lower level. Gentiles had access to God by the very same means and in the very same way as did Jews—through Christ, in one Spirit.

προσαγωγὴν (*access*) is found again in 3.12, and also in Romans 5.2. BDAG says "a status factor is implied," citing an occurrence of the word

---

[112] Robertson, p. 1001.

in Xenophon's Cyropaedia. Xenophon described an occasion when Cyrus, having taken Babylon, decided to make himself available to the public. The first day he did so, there were so many people clamoring to see him that his closest friends were unable to speak with him. The next day, he met with his friends to discuss this problem and explained that he supposed people would seek access to him through them: Xenophon has Cyrus saying, ἐγὼ δὲ ἠξίουν τοὺς τοιούτους, εἴ τίς τι ἐμοῦ δέοιτο, θεραπεύειν ὑμᾶς τοὺς ἐμοὺς φίλους δεομένους προσαγωγῆς.[113] "But I was expecting such ones, if someone sought something of me, to ingratiate themselves to you who are my friends, seeking access."

While it would be wrongheaded to stand in a pulpit and, with a knowing air, assert that Paul used a special Greek word that indicated privileged access to some important dignitary (προσαγωγή is often used otherwise), in Ephesians 2 the context itself seems to suggest that this is exactly what Paul had in mind. As through one of Cyrus' friends some resident of Babylon might have hoped to gain an audience with the king, so we have access to God through Jesus Christ.[114]

2.19–22   Gentiles are Part of the House of God

Now therefore, no longer are you strangers and sojourners, but you are fellow citizens with the holy ones and members of the household of God, having been built upon the foundation of the apostles and prophets, Christ Jesus himself being the cornerstone, in whom every building being fit together grows into a holy sanctuary in the Lord, in whom you also were built together into a dwelling place of God in Spirit.

2.19   *Now therefore, no longer are you strangers and sojourners, but you are fellow citizens with the holy ones and members of the household of God* (Ἄρα οὖν οὐκέτι ἐστὲ ξένοι καὶ πάροικοι ἀλλ᾽ ἐστὲ συμπολῖται τῶν ἁγίων καὶ οἰκεῖοι τοῦ θεοῦ) This is in contrast to the earlier description of the former status of the Gentiles, that being, *without Christ, alienated from the polity of Israel, and estranged from the covenant of the promise, not having a hope, and godless in the world.* But it also especially calls to mind the Old Testament regulations concerning the sojourner who dwelt among the Israelites.

In the LXX, the words that so often occur are πάροικος (*sojourner*)

---

[113] Cyropaedia 7, 5, 45.

[114] Compare the verb cognate προσάγω as used in 1 Pt 3.18.

for the Hebrew *gar* and ἀλλότριος (*alien*) for *nakᵉri*. In 2.11, Paul used the word ἀπαλλοτριόω, a compounded verb cognate of ἀλλότριος, to say that the Gentiles had been alienated from the polity of Israel (ἀπηλλοτριωμένοι τῆς πολιτείας τοῦ Ἰσραὴλ). Now he says they are no longer aliens, although he uses the word ξένος rather than ἀλλότριος. ξένος is rarely found in the LXX, although it is used of Ruth (Rth 2.10) where it translates *nakᵉri*, and it is used of Ittai the Gittite (2 Sam 15.19) where it again translates *nakᵉri*.

But now Paul also uses the word πάροικος (*sojourner*), found in Deuteronomy 14.21 (LXX) in conjunction with ἀλλότριος and referring to those who were not Israelites but who lived among the Israelites. Under the Mosaic law, such people enjoyed certain protections, but they were not included as part of the "holy people to the Lord."

The Lord's holy people enjoyed protections and privileges that did not accrue to the alien. Of course the foreigner (ἀλλότριος, *nakᵉri*) could not be king (Dt 17.15). Every seven years, debts incurred by Israelites were forgiven, but the foreigner (ἀλλότριος, *nakᵉri*) could be compelled to pay his debt even in the seventh year (Dt 15.3). According to Dt 23.20, Israelites were not to charge interest to one another, but were permitted to charge interest to a foreigner (ἀλλότριος, *nakᵉri*). While an Israelite who might of necessity sell himself to another was not to be subjected "to a slave's service," was not to be treated "with severity," and had other protections (Lev 25.39–43), these did not accrue to the sojourner (the LXX has πάροικος for *tošab*, or rather τῶν παροίκων τῶν ὄντων ἐν ὑμῖν for *hatošabim haggarim 'immakem*) who became enslaved (Lev 25.45). It is even said that the enslaved sojourner could be bequeathed to one's sons, but in contrast to this, "in respect to your countrymen, the sons of Israel, you shall not rule with severity over one another" (Lev 25.46).

In short, the alien living in Israel was a second class resident. But to the Gentiles who have been reconciled along with Jews in one body unto God, Paul stresses that they are not merely strangers and sojourners living among God's people. They are not second class citizens. They are fully citizens, fellow citizens, and, in contrast to Deuteronomy 14.21, fellow citizens with the holy people! That is, they too are holy.

Interestingly, under the law, the Israelites themselves had been described as merely προσήλυτοι καὶ πάροικοι before God, the promised land not being truly theirs, but God's (Lev 25.23).

2.20 ἐποικοδομηθέντες (*having been built upon*) is a plural participle. It is an adverbial modifier of ἐστε, *you are*, and therefore we understand Paul means to say that his readers have been built upon the foundation of the apostles and prophets. Thus Paul changes the figure, and in so doing, carries the idea of proximity to God even further. Now, beyond having full access to the house of God, the Gentiles themselves (together with Jews) are the house of God. The Old Testament notion of God dwelling in the midst of his people, then represented by a tent and thereafter by a building, is now realized in the church of Jesus Christ which is the house of God (1 Tim 3.15). This sort of change of figure, or mixing of metaphors as we might say, is not unusual. Peter does very much the same thing, but in reverse, first describing the saints as the stones that comprised the spiritual house, and then as the priests who serve therein (1 Pt 2.5).

This house is built upon the foundation of the apostles and prophets. Jesus spoke of Peter as the rock upon which he would build his church (Mt 16.18).[115] But the binding and loosing authority that Jesus gave to Peter (Mt 16.19) was not given to Peter exclusively (Mt 18.18–20). This binding and loosing authority consisted of binding and loosing what had been bound or loosed in heaven (ἔσται δεδεμένα = *shall have been bound*, ἔσται λελυμένα = *shall have been loosed*). And such was not the exclusive province even of the apostles. God's word was also revealed through others who had the gift of prophecy (Acts 13.1), and through these, the church was built up.

Christ Jesus himself being the cornerstone (ὄντος ἀκρογωνιαίου αὐτοῦ Χριστοῦ Ἰησοῦ). When a participial clause is syntactically independent of the rest of the sentence, it is said to be absolute. A frequently occurring sort of participial phrase is the "genitive absolute," so called because it is in the genitive case. In its purest form, the subject of the participle has no syntactical connection to the main clause. That is, it is not identified with either the subject or the object, or any other substantive in the main clause. ὄντος ἀκρογωνιαίου αὐτοῦ Χριστοῦ Ἰησοῦ is such a clause. The subject of the genitive participle ὄντος (*being*) is the genitive Χριστοῦ. Neither the

---

[115] Many, including this writer in times past, have argued that Jesus made a distinction between Peter and the rock upon which he would build his church. That distinction may have gained popularity partly from a desire to rebut the Roman Catholic attempt to establish Peter as its first Pope. But in view of (1) Peter's prominence in the early church (Acts 2, Acts 3, Acts 4, Acts 9, Acts 10–11, Acts 12, Acts 15), (2) Satan's singling Peter out as a target (Luke 22.31), and (3) Jesus' confidence that Peter would resist the devil and would turn and strengthen his brethren (Luke 22.32), it is fitting that Jesus identified Peter as the rock upon which the church would be built.

participle ὄντος nor its subject, *Christ*, is grammatically connected with anything in the main clause.

αὐτοῦ is a rare (in the NT) example of an intensive use of the pronoun in the genitive case. Usually, an intensive pronoun is the subject in a clause, and in most instances the subject will be in the nominative case. But here, because the subject is genitive, the intensive pronoun is also genitive—"Christ himself being the cornerstone."

There is a question as to whether the word ἀκρογωνιαίου refers to a *foundation stone* at the corner, or a *capstone* at the corner (and some have even suggested a keystone in the middle of an arch). Most of the ancient commentators understood the passage to speak of a foundation stone, and this was the prevailing understanding until the 20th century. Then Joachim Jeremias argued that the reference is actually to a capstone. And now it is not unusual to find commentators favoring that understanding.

ἀκρογωνιαίος is an adjective not found prior to the LXX. The word itself speaks only of the extreme corner,[116] but in Isaiah 28.16 where it translates *pinnah*, the ἀκρογωνιαίος consists of a stone that the Lord lays in Zion as a foundation. Perhaps a similar architectural figure is in view in Job 38.6 where the Lord asks Job about the earth, "Who laid its cornerstone?"[117] In Jeremiah 51.26, the Lord warns Babylon of its coming demise and says, "they will not take from you even a stone for a corner nor a stone for foundations."[118] In all three of these passages, the Hebrew lying behind the English "corner" is *pinnah*.

Jeremias based his conclusion that in Ephesians 2.20 a capstone, rather a foundation stone, is in view primarily on The Testament of Solomon. Therein, Solomon is described as seeking the assistance of a demon to get an ἀκρογωνιαίον placed εἰς κεφαλὴν γωνίας τῆς πληρώσεως τοῦ ναοῦ τοῦ θεοῦ, *at the head of a corner of the completion of the santuary of God*. All of Solomon's craftsmen and demons had worked together in an attempt to place it at τὸ πτερύγιον τοῦ ναοῦ, *the pinnacle of the temple*, (cf. τὸ πτερύγιον τοῦ ἱεροῦ , in Mt 4.5, Lk 4.9), but had been unable to accomplish the task.

From these expressions and others in the narrative, it is clear enough that the story depicts Solomon as ultimately using the stone as a cap-

---

[116] ἀκρογωνιαίος is from ἄκρον (*high point, extreme end, tip*) and γωνιαῖος, related to γωνία (*corner*).

[117] LXX: τίς δέ ἐστιν ὁ βαλὼν λίθον γωνιαῖον ἐπ' αὐτῆς;

[118] LXX 28.26 (= Masoretic 51.26) has λίθον εἰς γωνίαν, *stone for a corner*, and λίθον εἰς θεμέλιον, *stone for a foundation*.

stone, not as a foundation stone. But the question remains as to whether it is called an ἀκρογωνιαίον in view of its ultimate use, or in view of its originally intended use. In other words, are we to understand that ἀκρογωνιαίος means capstone here, or are we to understand that Solomon found a discarded foundation cornerstone (an ἀκρογωνιαίον) which he then used ("re-purposed") as a capstone?

The part of the story involving this stone is brought to a conclusion with Solomon's triumphant assertion that in placing this stone at the pinnacle of the sanctuary, scripture is fulfilled. Solomon says, "Truly now the scripture is fulfilled that says, 'This stone which the builders rejected has become the head of the corner.'"[119] It is clear that the writer understands Psalm 118.22 to be speaking of a stone that becomes a prominent capstone, and it seems he intended to provide the back story for the fulfillment of the passage. Perhaps, then, we are to understand that the writer speaks of a stone that has been rejected by the builders and not used for its original purpose, namely, to serve as a foundation stone. In that case, we would assume it was referred to as an ἀκρογωνιαίον with its original purpose in view. Solomon ambitiously saw this stone as suitable for another purpose, a capstone, but needed supernatural help to accomplish the transformation.

On the other hand, it may be that Jeremias was correct in understanding the passage to refer to the stone as an ἀκρογωνιαίον in view of its ultimate use, and that we are therefore to understand that ἀκρογωνιαίον can be used of a capstone rather than a foundation stone. But even if it be so, this does not mean we should understand Paul to say Jesus is a capstone.

The Testament of Solomon was composed sometime between AD 100 and AD 400, perhaps in the early part of the third century.[120] It was probably also early in the third century or late in the second century that Symmachus made his Greek translation of the OT. Both at 2 Kings 25.17 and Psalm 118.22 where the Hebrew text has *pinnah*, Symmachus used the word ἀκρογωνιαίος.[121] Certainly in 2 Kings 25.17, if not in Psalm 118.22, a capstone is in view. So we can grant that ἀκρογωνιαίος was used of a

---

[119] ἀληθῶς νῦν ἐπληρώθη ἡ γραφὴ ἡ λέγουσα, λίθον ὃν ἀπεδοκίμασαν οἱ οἰκοδομοῦντες οὗτος ἐγενήθη μὲν εἰς κεφαλὴν γωνίας.

[120] McCown, p. 108.

[121] At Ps 117.22 (=Masoretic Text 118.22), the LXX has οὗτος ἐγενήθη εἰς κεφαλὴν γωνίας, *this one became head of the corner.* At 4 βασ. 25.17 (=Masoretic Text 2 Kings 25.17), the LXX has ὀκτωκαίδεκα πήχεων ὕψος τοῦ στύλου τοῦ ἑνός, καὶ τὸ χωθαρ ἐπ' αὐτοῦ τὸ χαλκοῦν, καὶ τὸ ὕψος τοῦ χωθαρ τριῶν πήχεων, σαβαχα καὶ ῥοαὶ ἐπὶ τοῦ χωθαρ κύκλῳ, τὰ πάντα χαλκᾶ· καὶ κατὰ τὰ αὐτὰ τῷ στύλῳ τῷ δευτέρῳ ἐπὶ τῷ σαβαχα.

capstone, at least certainly by Symmachus, and perhaps in the Testament of Solomon as well.

For those who assign a second century date to Ephesians, Symmachus and Testament of Solomon might be significant. But if we believe Paul wrote the letter in the first century, Symmachus' usage and the Testament of Solomon are not determinative for our understanding of Ephesians 2.20. And there are a number of arguments in favor of understanding Paul's language as referring to a cornerstone that is part of the foundation.

First of all, the stone in Isaiah 28.16 is laid for the "foundation." If there is any ambiguity about that,[122] the context speaks of a coming flood[123] (28.15, cf. 8.7–8), and the stone is one that will not be washed away because it is "firmly placed" (28.16). McKelvey devoted an entire appendix to discussion of the Rabbinical writings pertaining to Isaiah 28.16, showing that they viewed the stone laid in Zion as "the foundation not only of the temple but of the universe."[124] While Paul does not quote Isaiah 28.16 in Ephesians, he does quote the passage at Romans 9.33 (and quotes the last part of the verse again at 10.11). And as McKelvey noted, "Eph. 2.20 belongs…to a cluster of 'stone' texts which has as its scriptural proof Isa. 28. 16."

McKelvey notes that Paul's conception is of a building that is growing,[125] which seems more consistent with the imagery of a building rising upon a foundation stone than with a building already completed and its wall topped off by a capstone.

So then, understanding a foundation stone to be in view, it is important to consider for a moment the significance of identifying Christ Jesus with such a stone. McKelvey describes the process of building as follows:

> Unlike modern architecture, which places the first cornerstone on the top of the foundation, which is dug and filled with mortar, ancient architecture began by laying the cornerstone. It was often placed near ground level, and together with the other stones that were placed next to it, served as the foundation (1 Kgs. 5. 17; 7. 10; Isa. 28. 16; Jer. 51. 26; Job 38.6). Whether the

---

[122] Jeremias (TDNT vol 1, p. 792) argued that only in the LXX is Is 28.16 made to refer to a foundation stone.

[123] Literally translated, an "overflowing scourge." Isaiah mixes his metaphors here. See Alexander, p. 453f., Young, vol. 2, p. 283.

[124] McKelvey, The New Temple, p. 192.

[125] McKelvey, Christ the Cornerstone, NTS 8, p. 358.

stones were placed end to end in a line, as was normally the case, or side by side in platform fashion, it was the practice to begin at one corner with the cornerstone. Since this stone was the one that gave the line of the building it was carefully selected, dressed, squared, and tested (cf. Isa. 28. 16).[126]

Most especially we want to notice that this stone "gave the line of the building." The walls would be lined up with this stone, and if it were not square, they would not be square. If its top were not flat and level, the next course would be askew and the wall would not be vertical. Jesus Christ is the cornerstone. For the church, the house of God, to be true, it must have that true cornerstone. As Paul wrote in 1 Corinthians 3, using a slightly different figure wherein Christ is the whole foundation, "other foundation can no man lay." There, his point is to draw a contrast between building on Christ Jesus and building upon any other man. The foundation must be, can only be, Christ Jesus, and cannot be any other man.

2.21 πᾶσα οἰκοδομὴ is difficult. First, just as is true of "building" in English, οἰκοδομὴ can mean either the process of building, as in 4.12, or the structure that has been built. Here, it must be the structure that has been built. The difficulty arises if we consider this phrase according to the stricter standards of classical Greek, for then we must understand it to mean "every building." But that seems to suggest many buildings that are components of the house of the Lord, and yet in the context, the only buildings that come to mind are two, the Jews and the Gentiles. It can hardly be that Paul has in mind each individual as a building, nor can we suppose he has in mind each congregation being a building as some (e.g., Meyer) have supposed.

Another reading found in several manuscripts seems to better suit the context, and that is πᾶσα ἡ οἰκοδομή, "all the building." The idea would be that the building that is the result of Jews and Gentiles assembled together now grows into a holy temple in the Lord.

But one of the axioms of textual criticism is that, all else being equal, the more difficult reading is likely the original reading. Corollary to that is another axiom, namely, that the reading that can account for the existence of other readings is more likely the original. A difficult reading easily accounts for the existence of a more understandable reading inasmuch as scribes often tried to clarify the text. But scribes did not intentionally

---

[126] McKelvey, The New Temple, p. 198.

change a passage with a clear meaning so as to make it incomprehensible. In the present passage, the more difficult reading is πᾶσα οἰκοδομὴ. If that were the original reading, it would be easy to see that the other reading, πᾶσα ἡ οἰκοδομή, could have arisen when scribes found the original reading to be difficult to understand exegetically. In an attempt to help the passage say what scribes believed was clearly the intent, scribes added the definite article ἡ. But if, on the other hand, the original reading had been πᾶσα ἡ οἰκοδομή, it would be difficult to account for the significant number of manuscripts containing πᾶσα οἰκοδομὴ. If the ἡ were inadvertently omitted, the resultant difficult meaning would surely have been noticed and corrected in most of the flawed manuscripts. (So for example, Codex Sinaiticus originally had πᾶσα οἰκοδομὴ, but a scribe later "corrected" this to πᾶσα ἡ οἰκοδομή by inserting the letter *eta* between the words πᾶσα and οἰκοδομή just above the line.) And therefore we should suppose the original reading was πᾶσα οἰκοδομὴ. Or so goes the theory.

Codex Sinaiticus, Ephesians 2.20b–2.21a, courtesy of the British Library

Even aside from considerations of how likely it is that each reading might have arisen if the other were original, the weight of the manuscript evidence favors the reading πᾶσα οἰκοδομή. This is the reading found in the earliest and most significant manuscripts as well as in the Byzantine manuscripts (the body of manuscripts that lies behind the so called majority text).

Alford argued against insisting upon classical standards and took πᾶσα οἰκοδομὴ to mean "all the building," while allowing that πᾶσα ἡ οἰκοδομή would have been the more proper way to say that. "To a *classical Greek ear*, any other rendering of πᾶσα οἰκ. than '*every building*,' seems preposterous enough."[127] But Alford argued for "all the building" on the basis of (1) context, and (2) other examples where πᾶς with anarthrous referent is used to mean "all," namely Colossians 1.15 and 1.23.

Just as in English, the definite article in Greek serves to specify. But also in Greek, although less so than in English, proper nouns might be deemed sufficiently specific so as to mitigate the need for a definite article. So in Matthew 2.3, we find πᾶσα Ἱεροσόλυμα which clearly means "all Jerusalem" rather than "every Jerusalem." (Notice that similarly in English, we do not need to say "all *the* Jerusalem.") See also Acts 2.36 where we have πᾶς οἶκος Ἰσραήλ which means "all the house of Israel," not "every house of Israel."[128] Alford's suggestion is that "gradually other words besides proper names became regarded as able to dispense with the article after πᾶς." On the basis of the examples cited, I would suggest these were generally nouns that took on a status approaching that of a proper noun. For example, Thucydides has πᾶσα γῆ for "all the earth" (i.e., the whole world, as we might say), not "every earth."[129]

συναρμολογουμένη (*being fit together*), from συναρμολογέω, is used here and in Ephesians 4.16, but is not used elsewhere in the New Testament, nor is it found often elsewhere in ancient Greek.[130] But its meaning seems not to have changed much over two millennia. In modern Greek, the word is used for toys that are already "assembled," an example being a scale model of a jet fighter airplane advertised as a μοντέλα συναρμολογούμενα, "an assembled model." Instructions for replacing a diaphragm in a bilge pump include this:

Diaphragm Replacement
Unscrew bolt separating diaphragm assembly, reassemble (συναρμολογήστε) new diaphragm, diaphragm plate, washer and bolt onto connecting rod.

ἐν πνεύματι should be regarded as the opposite of ἐν σαρκὶ in 2.11. The phrase κατοικητήριον τοῦ θεοῦ ἐν πνεύματι calls attention to the contrast

---

[127] Alford's Greek Testament, vol. 3, p. 101.

[128] Zerwick cites Rom 11.26 (πᾶς Ἰσραὴλ, found often in the LXX,=*all Israel*) in addition to Mt 2.3 and Acts 2:36. p. 61f, §190.

[129] Thucyd. 2.43

[130] Hoehner supposes that "Paul coined this word." However, there was no need for Paul to coin such a word given the existence of συναρμόζω/συναρμόττω which had essentially the same meaning. Moreover, given the modern day usage of συναρμολογέω in precisely that sense which would account for Paul's use of it had it been an existing word, I think it unlikely that Paul "coined" it.

between the Old Testament temple, of which Solomon said, "heaven and the highest heaven cannot contain thee, how much less this house which I have built" (2 Kings 8.27), and the New Testament temple made up of living stones (1 Pt 2.5). The Old Testament temple was a symbol for the presence of God in the midst of his people, and thus a symbol for the reconciliation that would be achieved between God and his people. But it was after all just a symbol. God does not dwell in temples made with hands (Acts 17.24). But spiritually, ἐν πνεύματι, God dwells in the house that is his people, the church of Jesus Christ.

The great message of this section is that these Gentiles, whose estrangement from God was palpably manifested in the temple complex in Jerusalem where they were kept away from the house of God by a barrier between the inner and outer courts, that they had now been raised up with Christ and made to sit in heavenly places and were now not only able to enter the house of God, but did themselves comprise the house of God. They were previously dead by their trespasses and sins had been made a holy dwelling place for God in the Spirit.

3.1–7   A Prayer Delayed by Gratitude

On account of this, I Paul, the prisoner of Christ [Jesus] on behalf of you the Gentiles—if indeed you heard about the stewardship from God's favor that was bestowed upon me for you (namely that according to revelation the mystery was made known to me just as I previously wrote in a few words, with reference to which you are able, when reading, to appreciate my understanding in the mystery of Christ, which in other generations was not made known to the sons of men as it has now been revealed to his holy apostles and prophets in spirit) the Gentiles being fellow-heirs and fellow members of the body and joint partakers of the promise in Christ Jesus through the gospel of which I was made a servant according to the gift of God's grace that had been given to me according to the working of his power.

Chapter three is Paul's prayer on behalf of the Gentiles. He begins by explaining what prompts his prayer: "On account of this." On account of what? On account of the Gentiles having been made fellow citizens with the saints and of the household of God, as described in the preceding chapter.

He identifies himself as the prisoner of Christ on behalf of the Gentiles that they might be reminded of the degree to which he had invested himself in their salvation. And then beginning in verse 14, he describes what he prays on their behalf. But in between his self-identification as a prisoner and the beginning of his description of his prayer, he elaborates on his own work on behalf of the Gentiles and how great a favor he considered it to be that he was given the privilege of bringing the gospel to the Gentiles.

Paul's description of the inception of his ministry is consistent with Luke's account. Luke tells us that through revelation (Acts 26.14*ff*, *cf.* Ga 1.11) Paul was given the privilege of preaching the gospel (Acts 26.16) for Gentiles' benefit (Acts 26.17). The revelation made to Paul included the explanation that the Gentiles could receive an inheritance among the saints by faith in Jesus (Acts 26.18). These are the same ideas that Paul sets forth in Ephesians 3.1–7.

In regard to the question of authorship, the digression found in verses 2 through 13 should be considered. Such a digression is the work of someone whose words flow from his thoughts, not the work of someone who has carefully contrived.[131] If a later writer were to pass himself off as Paul, mentioning such things as being a prisoner, as being an ambassador in chains, and as sending Tychicus, he would not be writing from the heart but would be carefully contriving. Does it seem likely that someone thus contriving would have begun a prayer, digressed at length, and then resumed the prayer? Or is it more likely that such a digression is the writing of Paul himself?

But just as this section serves as an argument in favor of Pauline authorship, it also serves to illustrate the latitude of inspiration. Though moved by the Holy Spirit, and though not writing his own interpretation of what was revealed to him,[132] the writer of scripture was often permitted the latitude to convey the message in his own voice and by means of his own thought pattern. Though the message was of God and not from men, truly it was delivered in earthen vessels. This does not undermine the authority of scripture, for the same God who could use Caiaphas to communicate a great truth by words that in his own mind were designed to oppose Jesus[133] could also certainly use the thoughts and words of an

---

[131] Even Best, though he leaned toward the view that Ephesians was written by someone other than Paul, says of this section, "it is not a carefully planned digression," and sees it as evidence that the writer "had not cleverly planned what he was going to write" (ICC Commentary, p. 295).

[132] Cf. 2 Pt 1.20–21.

[133] Jn. 1.49–52.

apostle Paul to communicate his infallible will. Just as the Holy Spirit is capable of using a man's research skills (Lk 1.1*ff*), a man's occupational skills (Ps 23), a man's speaking style (Mark's urgency seen in his vocabulary and routine use of the present tense to bring events vividly to mind), so also the Holy Spirit can use a man's thought processing. We ought not look to manifestations of personal style in the sacred writings as justification for doubting the reliability of scripture, but rather to see in such things the subtle power of a God who can work effectively within the realm of his creatures, through his creatures.

3.1 *On account of this, I Paul, the prisoner of Christ [Jesus] on behalf of you the Gentiles* (Τούτου χάριν ἐγὼ Παῦλος ὁ δέσμιος τοῦ Χριστοῦ [Ἰησοῦ] ὑπὲρ ὑμῶν τῶν ἐθνῶν). With these words, it seems that Paul begins a thought which he does not finish until after he picks it up again in verse 14. The introductory τούτου χάριν is found again in 3.14, giving support to the idea that there he resumes the thought. The thought Paul begins, and subsequently resumes, is a description of his prayer, as becomes evident when in verse 14 he says, "I bow my knees."

Τούτου χάριν, found also at Titus 1.5, is an idiom roughly equivalent to διὰ τοῦτο (*on account of this*), the expression more frequently found in the New Testament. Perhaps the accusative case χάριν should lead us to think of the expression as something like, "in view of the favor of this" or "with an eye toward the favor of this," *i.e.*, "thanks to this,"[134] and thus, "on account of this." This use of χάριν is found at Luke 7.47, Galatians 3.19, 1 Timothy 5.14, Titus 1.5,11, 1 John 3.12, and Jude 16.

As far as grammar is concerned, the words ἐγὼ Παῦλος ὁ δέσμιος τοῦ Χριστοῦ may be understood as having an implicit verb, "I, Paul, *am* the prisoner of the Christ," or not, "I, Paul, the prisoner of Christ." Without the verb, the words "prisoner of Christ" are in apposition to "Paul" and serve merely to provide an incidental (though not trivial) description of him who describes the blessings bestowed upon the Gentiles.

To construe the phrase as having an implicit verb simplifies our understanding of the grammatical structure of the larger context, but leaves us wondering why Paul thought it important to assert his status as a prisoner.

Against inferring the verb,

(1) Paul's point is not to talk about his own circumstance as a prisoner, as would seem to be the case if he began this section with a declara-

---

[134] MHT, p. 331.

tive sentence saying, "I, Paul, am the prisoner of the Christ." As Eadie wrote, "The apostle does not mean to magnify the fact of his imprisonment: he merely hints in passing that it originated in the proclamation of those very truths which he had been discussing."[135]

(2) If Paul had intended such, it would be more likely that he would have used δέσμιος anarthrously and thus qualitatively ("I am a prisoner") rather than articularly ("I am the prisoner").[136]

But if we do not infer the verb, then it seems that the words represent an uncompleted thought, or rather, a thought not completed until it is resumed in verse 14. Paul did not always plan out the structure of his sentences in advance, but instead sometimes began a sentence in one direction only to change course before completing all of the grammatical requirements of a sentence. In Ephesians 2.1–5, we saw him begin a sentence with the direct object ("you being dead in your trespasses and sins") apparently having in mind the subject and verb—"God made alive"—but then revising his thought to include Jews also as those who were made alive before completing the sentence, so that by the time he arrived at the end of the sentence he had to revise the object from *you* (ὑμᾶς) to *us* (ἡμᾶς). So here, Paul begins a thought with the words Τούτου χάριν ἐγὼ Παῦλος ὁ δέσμιος τοῦ Χριστοῦ [Ἰησοῦ] ὑπὲρ ὑμῶν τῶν ἐθνῶν –, then interrupts his thought to expound upon his readers' understanding of his work on their behalf, and then in verse 14 resumes his original thought, beginning again with Τούτου χάριν. There, however, he does not reiterate the reference to himself as a prisoner of the Christ, but progresses directly to state what it is that he, the prisoner of the Lord, does.

3.2 *If indeed you heard about the stewardship from God's favor that was bestowed upon me for you* (εἴ γε ἠκούσατε τὴν οἰκονομίαν τῆς χάριτος τοῦ θεοῦ τῆς δοθείσης μοι εἰς ὑμᾶς). Having referred to his work on behalf of the Gentiles (3.1), Paul now digresses to discuss that work, and especially to describe it as a great privilege in view of the momentous import of the message that Gentiles are fellow heirs of the gospel.

The words *if indeed you heard* (εἴ γε ἠκούσατε) seem to point to an audience that does not personally know Paul, but only knows of Paul. And yet Paul's relationship with the church at Ephesus is well documented.

---

[135] Eadie p. 210.
[136] Hoehner p. 418.

His departure from the Ephesian elders, described by Luke, was accompanied by great demonstrations of affection (Acts 20.37). This adds to the evidence that the saints at Ephesus were not the unique recipients of this letter. But if, as supposed in this work, Paul is not addressing the church at Ephesus either peculiarly or entirely, but is rather writing specifically to those Gentiles who have become Christians (whether at Ephesus or elsewere in Asia), then it may well be that a large number of those in his audience have become Christians since he last visited the area.[137]

However, not all agree that the words εἴ γε ἠκούσατε indicate an audience that was unfamiliar with Paul's history. Some who believe this letter was intended especially and specifically for the church at Ephesus (where the saints would certainly have known of Paul's history) suggest that εἴ γε can mean "since."[138] Ephesians 4.21 and Colossians 1.23 are cited in support of this meaning. In effect, these commentators argue that Paul uses γε to indicate certainty that his readers knew about his dispensation rather than uncertainty that they knew.

γε is an intensifying particle. It may intensify certainty, or it may intensify uncertainty, or various other ideas, but exactly what it intensifies will be determined by the word or words with which it is used. "Its function is to bring into prominence the particular word with which it occurs."[139] Being postpositive, the word with which it occurs would be the preceding word.[140] Here, that would be εἴ (*if*). But we do well to note Smyth's remark about γε influencing "a whole clause" and citing in particular the construction εἴ γε as an example.[141]

When used with εἴ (*if*), as in Ephesians 3.2, γε does not eliminate the conditional idea. Whether that conditional idea represents actual doubt will have to be determined by the context. We may think of a number of expressions in English (*if in fact you heard, if indeed you heard, if you actually*

---

[137] See the introduction for further discussion of the identity of Paul's intended audience.

[138] Hoehner, who translates εἴ γε ἠκούσατε as "surely you have heard" (p. 421), regards the words "in Ephesus" (1.1) as authentic, but supposes the audience might have included "many house churches in the city of Ephesus and western Asia Minor." Lincoln, who also takes the words as an affirmation of the audience's familiarity with Paul but does not believe Paul wrote the letter, sees εἴ γε as "part of the device of pseudonymity" (p. 173).

[139] Robertson, Manual Grammar, p. 1147.

[140] "In the case of γε it follows naturally the word with which it belongs…" Robertson, Manual Grammar, p. 425.

[141] Smyth, §2823, p. 642.

heard, if truly you heard, especially if you heard) that might approximate the tone of εἴ γε ἠκούσατε depending on the context, and these may allow for a spectrum of nuances on the part of the writer ranging from "I'm not sure you heard" to "I think you probably heard."

But that is not at all to say the force of εἴ (*if*) disappears. Certainly there are contexts wherein γε intensifies some other word and the resultant meaning is a strong affirmation, *e.g.*, ἀλλά γε (*but indeed*), καὶ γε, (*assuredly*). Here, however, γε is used with εἴ (*if*). If we suppose Paul's εἴ γε ἠκούσατε means "surely you heard," we may not be sufficiently acknowledging the word εἴ (*if*).[142]

It is possible that the language is used as a sort of understatement. Even in Ephesians 3.2, if indeed Paul supposed his audience did know of his story, it could be that he wrote as he did to avoid making himself the focal point of the passage. Robertson, for example, saw in the construction "a delicate touch."[143] In this way, in Ephesians 4.21 Paul could write, εἴ γε αὐτὸν ἠκούσατε καὶ ἐν αὐτῷ ἐδιδάχθητε (*if you actually heard him and were taught in him*), knowing full well that they did hear and were taught in Christ.

But allowing that εἴ γε may be used in a "delicate" way is not the same thing as affirming that εἴ γε means *assuredly* rather than *if*. A writer may say *if* knowing full well that his audience will be reminded of a certainty (as in 4.21), but just as it is the tongue in the cheek that gives the hearer the clue that a speaker means something other than what he says, so in Ephesians 4.21 it is the overall context and tone, and not the phrase εἴ γε itself, that gives the reader the clue that there is no doubt that they heard and were taught in Christ. In Ephesians 3.2, there is nothing that calls for us to understand Paul as having his tongue in his cheek.

To be sure, in the same sentence Paul goes on to say, "just as I previously wrote in a few words" (3.3), indicating that his readers *could have* known the story of the revelation given to Paul. As will be argued below,

---

[142] We see γε used both in a clause expressing doubt and in an affirming clause in Acts 17.27. We read εἰ ἄρα γε (*if indeed then*) contemplating the doubtful prospect of the Gentiles successfully feeling after God and thus finding him, and then we read καί γε affirming that God is indeed not far from each of them. This contrast illustrates the significance of the conjunction with which γε is used. The other NT passages where we see εἴ γε (excluding those where the expression includes a negative particle) are Ac 17.27a, 2 Co 5.3, Ga 3.4, Eph 3.2, Eph 4.21, and Co 1.23. Some few mss have either εἴ γε or εἰ γάρ γε at Rom 5.6, but these readings are very doubtful.

[143] Robertson, Word Pictures, vol. 4, p. 530.

this must refer to a previous communication, very possibly the letter to the Galatians, and Paul must be supposing that that letter was widely distributed among many, including those of his present audience. The conclusion then is that Paul is indeed writing to people who *could have* heard of his dispensation to the Gentiles, including no doubt many who had heard and some who had not heard. On the whole, however, they were not his personal acquaintances, even if many individuals among them may have been.

Some would say that the aorist ἠκούσατε is here used as a perfect tense verb. Better I think to simply acknowledge that in English, we tend to want to express some ideas using a perfect tense where Greek speakers were content to communicate the same information simply as a past event. When we use the English equivalent of ἠκούσατε as Paul uses it here, we are typically asking "are you aware of," and thus are focused on the present result, presently being aware of something. Accordingly, we use the perfect tense and say "have you heard of..." more often than "did you hear of..." However, when we use the preposition *about* rather than *of* while meaning exactly the same thing, we are often content to use a simple past verb, "did you hear about..." Thus we see that what governs the tense choice in these phrases (perfect vs. simple past) is really convention—the phraseology has become stereotyped.[144]

The case of the object of the verb ἠκούσατε is also worthy of note. ἀκούω may take either an accusative object or a genitive object. In English, we would say (and indeed our translations do say), if you *heard of* the stewardship, and therefore, we might have expected genitive τῆς οἰκονομίας (*of the stewardship*) rather than accusative τὴν οἰκονομίαν (*the stewardship*). But ἀκούω was regularly used with an accusative object even when the meaning was *hear about*, or *hear of*, as in Galatians 1.13 (ἠκούσατε τὴν ἐμὴν ἀναστροφήν), in Colossians 1.4 (ἀκούσαντες τὴν πίστιν... καὶ τὴν ἀγάπην), and in Philemon 5 (ἀκούων... τὴν ἀγάπην καὶ τὴν πίστιν).

On οἰκονομίαν (*stewardship*), see the comments on 1.10. Paul uses this word of his responsbility, yea, privilege, to preach even to the Gentiles the

---

[144] A Google search (8/9/2010) indicated a great preference for the simple past rather than the perfect tense when using the preposition "about" (searching for "did you hear about" yielded 21,500,000 results, while searching for "have you heard about" returned only 7,490,000 results). On the other hand, there was an overwhelmingly greater preference for the perfect tense as opposed to the simple past when using the preposition "of" (searching for "have you heard of" yielded 12,000,000 results, while "did you hear of" returned only 1,490,000 results).

unsearchable riches of Christ, thus making known what had previously been a mystery, although it was part of God's eternal purpose. The word οἰκονομία itself points to his responsibility as a steward (*cf.* 1 Cor 4.1, "*Let a man count us as stewards...of God's mysteries*"). In the following remarks, I will aim to show that the word χάρις points to the privilege that he considered this stewardship to be.

There are several difficulties in nailing down the precise meaning and interrelation of the words οἰκονομίαν and χάριτος in this context. But let us start with this observation: In verse eight, Paul will use the word χάρις not specifically with reference to the grace of God in Christ Jesus whereby we are forgiven of our sin, but with reference to the *favor* bestowed upon Paul to be the bearer of wonderfully good news to the Gentiles. The *favor* in view is not the content of the message he proclaims, but the privilege of proclaiming the message. Should we also understand the same meaning for χάρις here in verse two?

The answer to that question affects (or is affected by) our understanding of the relationship between the two words οἰκονομίαν (*stewardship*) and the genitive form χάριτος (*of favor*). If we view the favor as God's choosing Paul to be the messenger to the Gentiles, then the genitive is either a genitive of reference, or it functions as an ablative, indicating source; the stewardship *arises out of* the favor. But if we view the favor as the forgiveness of sin, then the stewardship is a responsibility to proclaim the favor of forgiveness, i.e., to proclaim God's grace in Jesus, and Paul sees himself as a steward dispensing God's grace. In the latter case, we are interpreting χάριτος as an objective genitive. We will come back to this momentarily.

τῆς χάριτος...τῆς δοθείσης μοι is *the favor that has been bestowed upon me (the favor, the having-been-given-to-me)*. Grammatically, it is the *grace/favor* that was given to Paul—the genitive participle δοθείσης describes the genitive χάριτος, not the accusative οἰκονομίαν. Paul says this was given μοι εἰς ὑμᾶς (*to me for you*). The favor bestowed upon Paul was ultimately to the benefit of the Gentiles.

We see a similar expression in Romans 15. There, Paul also speaks of God's favor in connection with his mission to preach to the Gentiles. Romans 15.15 has τὴν χάριν τὴν δοθεῖσάν μοι, *the favor that was given to me*. Paul explains this favor as εἰς τὸ εἶναί με λειτουργὸν Χριστοῦ Ἰησοῦ εἰς τὰ ἔθνη, *unto my being a minister of Christ Jesus unto the Gentiles* (Rom 15.16).

Clearly χάρις is the favor God bestowed upon Paul to be a minister of Christ unto the Gentiles.

Again at Galatians 2.9, we see a similar use of χάρις. The *grace/favor* perceived by James, Cephas and John was not the salvation in Jesus Christ, but the privilege bestowed upon Paul to be a messenger of that salvation to the Gentiles. Just as in Ephesians 3.2, we have an attributive construction telling us that the favor is that which was given to Paul: τὴν χάριν τὴν δοθεῖσάν μοι (*the favor, the having-been-given-to-me*). Notice especially the expressions in both passages indicating the purpose of this grace: In Galatians 2.8, the favor was ἐμοὶ εἰς τὰ ἔθνη (*to me for the Gentiles*), and in Ephesians 3.2, we see μοι εἰς ὑμᾶς (*to me for you*).

But if the favor is the privilege bestowed upon Paul to be God's messenger, we must understand the genitive χάριτος either as a genitive of reference ("the stewardship *pertaining to* God's favor that was bestowed upon me for you") or as indicating source ("the stewardship *arising out of* God's favor that was bestowed upon me for you"). In view of the parallel at Colossians 1.25, it is possible that the genitive indicates source. The relationship of τὴν οἰκονομίαν to τῆς χάριτος τοῦ θεοῦ in Ephesians 3.2 is the same as the relationship of τὴν οἰκονομίαν to τοῦ θεοῦ in Colossians 1.25. In both instances, the genitive expression could indicate the source of the stewardship, though in Colossians the source is God while in Ephesians it is God's favor. However, in both passages the genitive could be explained as genitive of reference—a stewardship with reference to God (Col 1.25) or with reference to God's favor (Eph 3.2).

In Colossians 1.25 it is the stewardship that is described as having been given to Paul. But whether Paul says the stewardship was given to him, or, as in Ephesians, the favor was given to him, there is no great difference in the truth being communicated; the essential meaning is the same. But understanding the precise significance of χάρις in Ephesians 3.2 helps us appreciate what Paul is doing in this context. He is for the moment distracted from his prayer as he rejoices in the privilege he has, the favor God has bestowed upon him, to be the one who proclaims the good news to the Gentiles. Even though Paul reckoned himself to be the least of all saints, he was given the privilege of preaching the gospel (Acts 26.16) for the benefit of the Gentiles (Acts 26.17*f*), and he revels in the joy of being the one to bring the good news. (See the comments on verse 8 below.)

Paul's Interrupted Prayer

Paul begins his prayer of thanksgiving (3.1):

> *On account of this, I Paul, the prisoner of Christ [Jesus] on behalf of you the Gentiles—*

but turns his attention to the privilege bestowed upon him, as his readers may have heard (3.2–13):

> *if indeed you heard about the stewardship from God's favor that was bestowed upon me for you*

before resuming the prayer which he had only barely begun (3.14–21):

> *On account of this I bow my knees to the Father…*

3.3 *namely that according to revelation the mystery was made known to me* The NA28 text has [ὅτι] κατὰ ἀποκάλυψιν ἐγνωρίσθη μοι τὸ μυστήριον, the brackets indicating doubt regarding the authenticity of ὅτι (*that*). Either way the meaning is the same. If ὅτι is authentic, its function here is to introduce an explanatory clause. *"If then you heard about the dispensation of the grace of God that has been given me toward you, namely that according to revelation the mystery was made known to me…"* If ὅτι is not authentic, the relationship of the following clause to the preceding is still the same: *"If then you heard about the dispensation of the grace of God that has been given me toward you—according to revelation the mystery was made known to me…"*

just as I previously wrote in a few words (καθὼς προέγραψα ἐν ὀλίγῳ). Does προέγραψα (*previously wrote*) refer to something earlier in this same epistle, or does it refer to some other document? Both uses of the word can be illustrated. Occurrences of προγράφω meaning *aforementioned*, with reference to something previously mentioned within the same document, are found in literary Greek[145] as well as in non-literary

---

[145] Plutarch, On the Generation of the Soul, 1018c, wherein Plutarch discusses the number 36, and writes, τὸ γὰρ ἓν καὶ τὰ ὀκτὼ καὶ τὰ εἰκοσιεπτὰ συντεθέντα ποιεῖ τὸν

Greek.[146] But in the first century, the word was also used of something written on a previous occasion. In the 12th year of Tiberius, one Chaireas wrote to his friend, Τύρρανος, προέγραψά σοι ἀνδραγαθῖν[147] καὶ ἀπαιτεῖν (*I previously wrote to you to be firm and demand payment*).[148]

προγράφω is found elsewhere in the New Testament three times: Romans 15.4, Galatians 3.1, and Jude 4. In Romans 15.4, the reference is to the Old Testament scriptures, things written outside of the letter to the Romans. In Jude 4, it is possible that the word is used without pointing to a literal writing. Almost certainly must this be the case in Galatians 3. But in both instances, it is clear that the reference is to something outside the document wherein the word is used.

Nonetheless, most modern commentators suppose that in Ephesians 3.3, Paul is not referring to some writing other than the present epistle, but rather to something previously written in this epistle, something in chapters one or two, or in both. In earlier centuries, however, the usual understanding was that Paul referred to some prior document. (So, according to Eadie, was it understood by Hunnius, Marloratus, Chrysostom, and Calvin.) Calvin described the view that Paul's words refer to an earlier epistle as the "general opinion" and as the "prevailing opinion." Theodoret is a notable exception.

Given Paul's description of what he says he previously wrote, it hardly seems possible to find anything in Ephesians that would justify taking καθὼς προέγραψα ἐν ὀλίγῳ as a reference to the present epistle. The mostly modern attempts to construe Paul's words as referring to something he had just previously written here in Ephesians end up grasping at straws. Eadie thought he found in Ephesians 1.9 (so also Alford) and in 2.13 the few words previously written.[149] Blakie supposed he found them in 1.9 and 2.18.[150] Blakie acknowledged that these passages may seem "rather vague and general," but appealed to Paul's characterization of his previous writing as being ἐν ὀλίγῳ as justification for making the connection anyway. But Paul says he previously wrote about the mystery

---

προγεγραμμένον ἀριθμόν, *for one and eight and twenty-seven added together make the aforementioned number.*

[146] P. Petr. iii. 104, τὸ προγεγραμμένον ἐκφόριον, *the aforementioned payment.*

[147] ἀνδραγαθῖν for ἀνδραγαθεῖν.

[148] P. Oxy. 2.291.

[149] Eadie, p. 214.

[150] Pulpit, p. 104.

having been made known by revelation specifically to *him*, and this in connection with the unique dispensation given him toward the Gentiles. Ephesians 1.9 refers to a revelation made to *us*, not one made specifically to Paul. Ephesians 2.13 and 2.18 say nothing at all about the *revelation* of the mystery. And none of these passages calls attention to Paul's unique dispensation toward the Gentiles, the very thing about which Paul affirms that he previously wrote.

Several have supposed the reference is to the whole section 2.11–22,[151] but the inadequacies remain: There is nothing in 2.11–22 about the revelation of the mystery being made known to Paul, and that is the very thing of which Paul says he previously wrote.

On the other hand, a strong case can be made for taking καθὼς προέγραψα ἐν ὀλίγῳ as a reference to some earlier document such as Galatians. In Galatians, Paul not only wrote that he received the gospel by revelation of Jesus Christ (1.11), in a few words he adamantly rebutted any claim to the contrary (1.11–24). Moreover, he specifically wrote that he was to preach Jesus "among the Gentiles" (1.16), that he was "intrusted with the gospel of the uncircumcision" (2.7).

And notice this: After saying, "as I previously wrote in a few words," Paul goes on to mention his audience *reading* (ἀναγινώσκοντες) what he wrote. The reference to reading must be taken in connection with προέγραψα (*I wrote*). That is, the reference is to reading what Paul previously wrote (προέγραψα ἐν ὀλίγῳ). Those who received Paul's present letter had read or could read what Paul previously wrote. So we may conclude that Paul refers to something that he wrote to an audience that was at least in part the same as his present audience. Certainly, Galatians was manifestly written to a Gentile audience just as was Ephesians. It appears from what Paul says here in Ephesians 3.3 that the churches of Galatia comprised a significant part of the present epistle's audience. (For discussion of this point, see the Introduction.) But even without that insight, we may revert to the knowledge that Paul's letters were circulated—Colossians 4.16, as well as the very existence of these writings far and wide for the last two millennia, attests to this—and given that Galatians was written a few years earlier than Ephesians, it is not too great an assumption that Paul's Asian readers, and specifically those in the Lycus and Maeander valleys (see the Introduction) would have been familiar with his

---

[151] *E.g.,* Stoeckhardt p. 160, Hoehner p. 428, Schnackenburg p. 132, Lincoln p. 175.

previous letter to neighboring Galatia, and about the revelation that was made to him (ἐγνωρίσθη μοι) as described therein.

Ernest Best faults taking Ephesians 3.3 as a reference to the letter to the churches of Galatia. He asks, "could it be described as brief?"[152] It is certainly brief compared with Romans, being often described as a short version of Romans. But more to the point, what Paul says he wrote briefly need not be the whole letter of Galatians, but merely the description of the revelation to Paul of the mystery. Paul certainly elucidated the common salvation of Jew and Gentile in Galatians, but he only briefly described the revelation that was given to him (Gal 1.11–12, or 11–24 if we include his rebuttal of claims to the contrary).

One final observation: The contrast between older and more recent expositors, the older ones seeing a reference to an earlier epistle and the more recent ones seeing a reference to something in the present epistle, loosely corresponds to the difference in opinion concerning authorship. The correlation is not so strong that we may suppose one who defends Paul as the author will see a reference to an earlier epistle. Many defenders of Pauline authorship have understood καθὼς προέγραψα ἐν ὀλίγῳ as a reference to the present epistle.[153] And on the other hand, Goodspeed, who did not believe Paul wrote Ephesians, took 3.3 as a reference to an earlier letter.[154] But it may be said that those who deny Paul as the author generally do not see a reference to an earlier epistle. Best acknowledged the correlation of which I speak when he wrote, "Some who equate AE with Paul believe that he refers here to his earlier letters."[155] ("AE" is Best's abbreviation for "Author of Ephesians.")

3.4 *with reference to which you are able, when reading, to appreciate my understanding in the mystery of Christ* (πρὸς ὃ δύνασθε ἀναγινώσκοντες νοῆσαι τὴν σύνεσίν μου ἐν τῷ μυστηρίῳ τοῦ Χριστοῦ). Again, it is important to begin with the observation that ἀναγινώσκοντες (*reading*) must be taken in connection with προέγραψα in verse 3. That is, the reference is to reading what Paul previously wrote.

πρὸς ὃ (*to which*) is to be understood as meaning *(with reference) to which* and amounts to *concerning which*. The relative pronoun refers to the whole of

---

[152] Best, ICC Ephesians, p. 302.

[153] *E.g.*, Stoeckhardt, Alford, Patterson, Westcott, Eadie.

[154] Goodspeed, p. 43.

[155] Best, p. 302.

the preceding thought.[156] The neuter gender[157] is the appropriate gender for such an abstract reference (see comments on 2.8). The sum of the preceding thought is the account of the mystery being made known to Paul by revelation and the dispensation being given to him to preach to Gentiles and make known to them the riches of God's grace. Paul's point seems to be that any of his present readers who had read in his previous writing about the mystery being made known to him by revelation would have gained insight into his perspective, that he was one who understood the mystery of the Christ.

This passage has been a favorite proof text for use in showing that the word of God is comprehensible, as if Paul had meant, "By reading what I am writing, you can understand what I understand." But that does not seem to be Paul's point here. Rather he seems to be saying, "If you read what I previously wrote, you can understand *that* I understand."

On *"the mystery of Christ,"* see below.

The foregoing interpretation of verses two through four is perfectly in harmony with what we know of Paul. He was given the privilege of preaching the gospel (Acts 26.16). This was especially to benefit the Gentiles (Acts 26.17). This was all done by revelation (Gal 1.11, Acts 26.14*ff*). It included the explanation that the Gentiles could receive an inheritance among the saints by faith in Jesus (Acts 26.18).

3.5–6 At the beginning of verse 5, the relative pronoun ὅ (*which*) refers back to the word μυστηρίῳ (*mystery*).[158] "The mystery of the Christ" is what was not made known to the sons of men in other generations as it has now been revealed.

The mystery was not the idea of a coming Messiah. The OT clearly spoke of a coming Messiah. Even Herod understood this (Mt 2.2). The priests and the scribes were able to point to the OT prophet Micah in order to tell the king where the Messiah would be born, and this much seems to have been fairly common knowledge among Jews (Jn 7.42).

---

[156] Compare, οὐκ ἔχω, ὦ Σώκρατες, ἀποκρίνασθαι πρὸς ὃ ἐρωτᾶς· οὐ γὰρ ἐννοῶ, "I have nothing, O Socrates, to answer concerning what you ask; for I do not know."Πλάτωνος Κρίτων 50a.

[157] Though the relative pronoun ὅ is neuter, its antecedent is not the neuter τὸ μυστήριον, for the meaning would then be "When reading the mystery you are able to understand my understanding of the mystery," which makes no sense.

[158] We might have expected attraction to occur such that the relative pronoun would agree with the case of its antecedent. But in the New Testament, it is especially when the relative pronoun functions as an object in its own clause that it is attracted to the case of the antecedent. Here, the relative pronoun functions as a subject of the verb ἐγνωρίσθη.

Even the prospect of a blessing for Gentiles was not itself a mystery, having been revealed to Abraham. God had promised Abraham that he would be a blessing for all nations (Gen 12.3), and in repeating that promise to Isaac (26.4) and then to Jacob (28.14), the Lord had specified that this would be accomplished in their descendants. In Isaiah in particular, but also in other prophets, it was revealed that Gentiles would be welcomed in the house of the Lord (Is 2.2ff, 56.6–8), that Gentiles would come to the light of God's people (Is 60.3), and that Gentiles would assist in the building up of the city of God (Is 60.10). In Psalm 87, there is even clear indication that Gentiles would be naturalized as citizens of the city of God, an idea that comes very close to the concept of Gentiles becoming Abraham's seed, heirs according to promise (Gal 3.29). When the circumcision controversy erupted in Jerusalem, it was on the basis of the Old Testament scriptures that James argued for Gentile equality, specifically on the basis of the LXX rendering of Amos 9.12.[159]

But what had been a mystery, now revealed, was the means whereby Gentiles would be included in the blessings of God. For one thing, from an OT perspective it was not clear that Gentiles and Jews would be reconciled in one body to God. And it was also not clear that Gentile believers would counted as children of Abraham.

What Paul describes as having been a mystery, now revealed, is in part the fact that Gentiles would be joint heirs, fellow members of the body, and sharers of the promise in Christ Jesus through the gospel. In 1 Corinthians 15, Paul summarized the gospel as being essentially the following facts: Christ died for our sins, was buried, was raised on the third day, and appeared. While even in that very passage, Paul mentions that Christ's death, burial and resurrection were "according to the scriptures," *i.e.*, the OT prophecies, it had been a mystery that Gentiles' status as joint heirs, fellow members of the body, and sharers of the promise would be accomplished in the gospel as essentially summarized in these facts. No one had understood that by a death and resurrection, indeed the humiliation of the very one anticipated as the Messiah, Gentiles would be reconciled to God along with Jews, in one body. That had been a mystery.

Regarding the second idea, that of being counted as children of Abraham, it is true that Paul does not bring Abraham into the picture in this

---

[159] Acts 15.15–18.

letter. But he thoroughly did so in Galatians, the letter which we have already suggested Paul had in mind when he said, *"just as I previously wrote in a few words."* And here in Ephesians, Paul does speak of being "heirs" (specifically, "joint heirs") and refers to "the promise" (3.6), language that harks back to the promises to Abraham and reminds us of Galatians 3.29, "if ye are Christ's, then are you Abraham's seed, heirs according to promise."

Had it been a mystery that the Gentiles would be counted as Abraham's children? Though in Romans we learn that the words "I will make you the father of a multitude of nations" (Gen 17.5, *cf.* Rom 4.17) meant Abraham would be reckoned as the father of Gentiles as well as of Jews, this was not made explicitly clear in the OT. From an OT perspective, one could have supposed Abraham's natural descendants would satisfy the promise that he would be a father of many nations. (Remember that besides the Israelites, Abraham's descendants included the Ishmaelites, Midianites, Medanites, Asshurim, Letushim, Leummim, and Edomites.) From the OT perspective, though it was promised that there would be a *blessing* for Gentiles through Abraham's seed, it was not clear that Gentiles would be counted as Abraham's children.

Paul enlists three words, each a compound involving the preposition σύν. Compounds in σύν highlight the shared aspect of some thing or activity.

The first is συγκληρονόμος, which Peter uses of husbands and wives who are *joint heirs* of the grace of life. Paul uses this word to describe the standing of Gentiles and Jews as joint heirs.

The second is σύσσωμα. Unknown prior to Ephesians 3.6, the word clearly indicates parts of one body, which is what Paul says Gentiles and Jews are. Paul could have said μέλη τοῦ σώματος (*members of the body*) as he did in 1 Corinthians 12.12, but he chose the unusual word σύσσωμα (Hoehner suspects Paul coined the word[160]) to repeat and reinforce this theme of Gentiles being fully equal to Jews in Christ.

And then, whereas it might have been sufficient to say μέτοχα τῆς ἐπαγγελίας (*sharers of the promise*), Paul again makes use of the preposition σύν, describing the Gentiles as συμμέτοχα τῆς ἐπαγγελίας (*joint sharers of the promise*).

---

[160] Hoehner, p. 446. Lincoln also thinks the writer may have coined the word, though he does not acknowledge Paul as the writer, p. 180.

Paul is emphasizing the idea he developed in chapter two, that Gentiles are full partners, fully equal partners, in Christ, and that it is through the gospel that they are such.

3.7 *of which I was made a servant according to the gift of God's grace that had been given to me according to the working of his power* (οὗ ἐγενήθην διάκονος κατὰ τὴν δωρεὰν τῆς χάριτος τοῦ θεοῦ τῆς δοθείσης μοι κατὰ τὴν ἐνέργειαν τῆς δυνάμεως αὐτοῦ). The antecedent of οὗ (*of which*) is εὐαγγελίου (*gospel*). Paul is a *servant* (διάκονος) of the gospel, as in Colossians 1.23. But is the point to say he serves it up, corresponding to his dispensation, *i.e.*, stewardship? Or is it that he has given himself entirely to the gospel as a slave of it? Trench long ago noted that "διάκονος represents the servant in his activity *for the work*...not in his relation...*to a person*"[161] while δοῦλος describes one who "is in a permanent relation of servitude to another."[162] A διάκονος might be a slave but is not necessarily so (Rom 16.1). Even in the event that he is a slave, the word διάκονος does not point to that fact.

Elsewhere, Paul says he is indeed a slave of Christ (Rom 1.1, Gal 1.10, Phil 1.1), of God (Tit 1.1), and affirms that we must be either slaves of sin or of righteousness (Rom 6.16–18). But in the present context, his purpose is to extol the great gift that was given to him (τὴν δωρεὰν τῆς χάριτος τοῦ θεοῦ τῆς δοθείσης μοι), and he will go on to speak with gratitude of the opportunity bestowed on him to perform the service.

3.8–13 Paul, Privileged to Proclaim Good News to Gentiles

This grace was given to me, the least of all saints, to proclaim to the Gentiles the unfathomable wealth of the Christ, and to enlighten all men what is the dispensation of the mystery that had been hidden from eternity in God who created all things, that now through the church might be made known to the rulers and the powers in the heavenlies the exceeding wisdom of God, according to a purpose from eternity which he accomplished in Christ Jesus our Lord, in whom we have the boldness and access in confidence through his faith. Wherefore I ask that you not be discouraged by my tribulations on your behalf, which is your glory.

In this exultant and simultaneously self-deprecating passage, Paul stipulates that God favored him with two responsibilities, which Paul re-

---

[161] Trench, p. 32.
[162] Trench, p. 30.

gards as privileges, these being to proclaim something to the *Gentiles* and to enlighten *all men* in regard to something. *To the Gentiles*, Paul's privilege was to proclaim "the incomprehensible wealth of the Christ."[163] And then he was to enlighten *all men* concerning "the dispensation of the mystery that had been hidden." This latter task probably consisted of explaining to all men, both Jews and Gentiles,[164] the very thing that Paul has been saying in the first half of Ephesians, that is, that Gentiles are included in the house of God. Paul had been graced with the privilege/responsibility of announcing the wealth of Christ to the Gentiles, and of enlightening all men (both Jews and Gentiles) of the fact that this wealth was available not only to Jews but also to Gentiles.

Then there is a purpose clause, the statement of the ultimate goal, "*that now through the church might be made known to the rulers and the powers in the heavenlies the exceeding wisdom of God.*" Although some have supposed the purpose clause is to be connected with the words "had been hidden," as if Paul is stating the reason for the hiding,[165] it seems clear that the purpose clause is giving the reason for the proclaiming and the enlightening. And that purpose is that the rulers and the powers in the heavenly places might know the wisdom of God. This would be accomplished by the existence of the church which would come about by means of the proclaiming and enlightening.

So then the structure of these phrases is:

This grace was given to me, (the least of all saints)

>*(1) to proclaim to the Gentiles the incomprehensible wealth of the Christ,*
>
>*and*
>
>*(2) to enlighten all men what is the dispensation of the mystery that had been hidden from eternity in God who created all things,*
>
>*that now (through the church) might be made known to the rulers and the powers in the heavenlies the exceeding wisdom of God...*

---

[163] Best is probably correct when he suggests that articular Χριστοῦ in this passage may be designed to present "Jesus as the Jewish Messiah in whose riches the Gentiles participate," (p. 318).

[164] Meyer objected to taking "all men" as meaning Jews in addition to Gentiles on the ground that had this been his meaning, Paul would have written πάντας φωτίσαι (rather than φωτίσαι πάντας) to maintain symmetry with τοῖς ἔθνεσιν εὐαγγελίσασθαι in the preceding clause (p. 412). But that is to dictate a rigidity in style to which Paul's writings did not always conform.

[165] E.g., Meyer, p. 414.

Notice that the beneficiaries are the rulers and the powers in the heavenlies. It is they who come to understand the wisdom of God as the result of the proclamation to Gentiles and enlightenment of all men. It had been a mystery even to them how God would achieve the things prophesied in the OT. We may think of Peter's statement that even angels desired to comprehend the meaning of the things prophesied by OT prophets (1 Pt 1.12), an indication that it was a great mystery even to them, as well as to the prophets themselves. But now in Christ Jesus, wherein Jew and Gentile are reconciled to God in one body, God's wisdom is evident. That is, it is made known "through the church." The church, one body made up of Jew and Gentile, is the realization of the plan God had foreordained from eternity, and is now, by its very existence, the demonstration of his wisdom.

3.8 *To me the least of all saints* (Ἐμοὶ τῷ ἐλαχιστοτέρῳ πάντων ἁγίων) No doubt, Paul's estimation of himself as the least of all saints derived from his past persecution of God's people (cf. 1 Tim 1.12–15, 1 Cor 15.9). He mentions this here in order to highlight the great contrast between his past conduct and the privilege he has been granted (*to proclaim to the Gentiles the incomprehensible wealth of the Christ*).

The words ἡ χάρις αὕτη (*this grace*) must be understood in the immediate context. In the previous verse, Paul called the grace of God that was given to him a gift. The gift in view here, the grace of God given to Paul, is not the forgiveness of sin in Christ Jesus, but the privilege of proclaiming to Gentiles the good news of their inclusion in Christ. The opportunity to announce good and favorable news is a great joy. When a wife tells her husband they are expecting, when a teacher tells a struggling student that he has done very well on a test, when a businessman tells an employee that he is getting a raise—all of these things are occasions of joy to the one who announces the news. So Paul, who considers himself the least of all saints, delights to be the one chosen by God to proclaim to Gentiles the incomprehensible wealth of Christ Jesus.

Chapter three really amounts to a benediction prompted by all that has been said in chapters one and two. The benediction seemed to be in Paul's mind when he began with the words τούτου χάριν (*on account of this*) in verse one. But because Paul considers himself exceedingly favored in having been chosen to bring the good news to Gentiles, his thoughts veered off to express his great joy before resuming the benediction in verse 14, once again beginning with the words τούτου χάριν.

to proclaim to the Gentiles the unfathomable wealth of the Christ (τοῖς ἔθνεσιν εὐαγγελίσασθαι τὸ ἀνεξιχνίαστον πλοῦτος τοῦ Χριστοῦ) In the NT, ἀνεξιχνίαστον is found only here and at Romans 11.33. In the LXX, the word is found at Job 5.9, 9.10, 34.24, and in the apocryphal Prayer of Manasseh.[166] In all of these passages, the word is used of things of God that are beyond human investigation. Inasmuch as rarely used words can better be remembered if one can make some sense of the parts, it may be worthwhile to notice that ἀνεξιχνίαστον is related to ἐξιχνιάζω = ἐξιχνεύω. The stem ἰχνευ- pertains to tracking or hunting.[167] The compound ἐξιχνεύω is found in Judges 18.2, where the sons of Dan sent some of their number to spy out the land and *to investigate* (ἐξιχνιάσαι) it. When Eliphaz tried to advise Job and explain the doings of God to him, he concluded with the words, *"we investigated* (ἐξιχνιάσαμεν) these things, these things are what we have heard."*[168] When Job inquires of God concerning the cause of his suffering, he rhetorically asks if God is as a man that he should have to *search out* (ἐξιχνίασας) Job's sin[169] (and then Job affirms his innocence). ἀνεξιχνίαστον shows the *alpha privative* (αν preceding a vowel), and thus *un*searchable. The wealth of Christ that Paul is to proclaim is beyond man's ability to fathom.

The precise relationship Paul intends to indicate between the "wealth"[170] and "Christ" may be that the wealth comes from Christ (so Meyer, p. 412), or that the wealth *is* Christ (so Lincoln, p. 183).

3.9 πάντας (*all men*) is put in brackets in NA28. It was not included in the NA text prior to the 27th edition. It was included in the UBS 3rd edition but only in brackets, and with a "D" rating ("very high degree of doubt"). In the UBS 4th ed., πάντας was included, but again only in brackets and with a "C" rating ("the committee had difficulty in deciding"). That continues to be the status of the reading in UBS 5th ed.

The uncertainty regarding the inclusion of πάντας (*all men*) is a little surprising. The manuscript evidence in its favor is strong, and Hoehner

---

[166] Ode 12:6 in Rahlfs' edition of the LXX.

[167] ἴχνος is *track*, or *footprint*.

[168] Job. 5:27, LXX.

[169] Job 10:6, LXX τὰς ἁμαρτίας μου ἐξιχνίασας, lit., *having searched out my sins*.

[170] Paul writes πλοῦτος as neuter here (hence the def. article τό) and so also at 2 Cor 8.2, Eph 1.7, 2.7, 3.16, Phil 4.19, Col 1.27, and Col 2.2, but he treats it as masculine in Rom 2.4, 9.23, 11.33, Eph 1.18, 1 Tim 6.17.

notes that the support is from "all text types."[171] The most significant argument against its authenticity seems to be that, were it not original, one could account for its insertion as an attempt to provide the expected object of the verb φωτίσαι. But if indeed πάντας were not original and arose merely as an attempt by some well-meaning scribe to complete the thought of the preceding infinitive, why is it the only attempt? One could expect that other similarly well-meaning scribes would have inserted alternative objects, *e.g.* αὐτούς (*them*),[172] τὰ ἔθνη (*the Gentiles*), ἀνθρώπους (*men*), or ὑμᾶς (*you*). However, such is not evidenced in the extant manuscripts.

Really, were it not for the absence of πάντας in the original hand of Sinaiticus,[173] we may suspect that πάντας would have been included with little question. But it must be accepted that often, corrections in Sinaiticus were warranted.

Paul does not say *to enlighten all men what is the mystery*, but *to enlighten all men what is the dispensation of the mystery*. Remember that Paul is talking about the grace that was given to him, namely the privilege to do two things, first to proclaim to the Gentiles the incomprehensible wealth of Christ, and second, to enlighten all men concerning the dispensation of the mystery. The point of contrast between these two goals is twofold. First, it is the audience. In the first clause, the audience is the Gentiles. In the second clause, it is all men. And then there is a contrast in task. Paul was privileged to proclaim wonderful news to Gentiles, and additionally his work was to enlighten all men, Jew and Gentile, concerning the dissemination of God's grace such that all men might understand the egalitarian nature of the gospel. Certainly, we see Paul accomplishing the latter goal in his letter to the saints in Rome (especially in the first four chapters), in Galatians, and so also here in Ephesians.

On the word οἰκονομία, see comments at 1.10.

The description of God as Creator of all things serves to underscore the message that the gospel is for all.

3.10 *that now through the church might be made known to the rulers and the powers in the heavenlies the exceeding wisdom of God* (ἵνα γνωρισθῇ νῦν ταῖς ἀρχαῖς καὶ ταῖς ἐξουσίαις ἐν τοῖς ἐπουρανίοις διὰ

---

[171] Hoehner, p. 455, n. 1.

[172] Metzger, *Textual Commentary*, p. 603.

[173] In Sinaiticus, πάντας is inserted above the line by a corrector.

τῆς ἐκκλησίας ἡ πολυποίκιλος σοφία τοῦ θεοῦ) We have already seen ἀρχή (*ruler*) and ἐξουσία (*power*) used together in Ephesians 1.21. Here, clearly Paul refers to spiritual entities; they are *"in the heavens."* As the message that Jew and Gentile are reconciled to God in one body through the cross is proclaimed, not only do men come to understand the wisdom of God, but so also spiritual entities come to understand what had been a mystery to them as well. As previously noted, it was no mystery that God had a blessing in mind for all families (not just for Jews) of the earth, but exactly how He was going to accomplish that was not understood. Peter speaks of the perspective of OT prophets in regard to the coming salvation and notes that not only were they unenlightened concerning the specifics of this plan, but even "angels desire to look into such things" (1 Pt 1.10–12).

Some have supposed that Paul here charges the church with the responsibility for making known the wisdom of God. But Paul's point here is not to say the church needs to proclaim the wisdom of God to the world, but rather that the very existence of the church demonstrates the wisdom of God to heavenly beings. Specifically, the existence of the church, including Gentiles as well as Jews, demonstrates the wisdom of God. The culmination of God's eternal purpose vindicated all that had gone before.

3.11 *according to a purpose from eternity which he made in Christ Jesus our Lord* Again, keeping in mind the Gentile convert's perception of himself and his standing *vis à vis* Jewish believers, keeping in mind the degradation of the Gentile world and the Gentile's full awareness of Jewish disdain for it,[174] Paul's statement that the inclusion of Gentiles was God's purpose all along serves as another means of assuring the Gentile convert that through Christ Jesus he stands on the same footing with God as does the Jewish believer. His inclusion is no mere afterthought. God did not reluctantly acquiesce to the inclusion of Gentiles. This was God's plan all along.

3.12 *In whom we have the confidence and access through his faith* For προσαγωγὴν (*access*) see the comments on 2.18.

διὰ τῆς πίστεως αὐτοῦ is *through the faith of him*, or *through his faith*. But does this speak of the faith that we have in Christ, or the faith that Christ had? If genitive αὐτοῦ is understood as being objective, that is, *him* is the

---

[174] See the introduction.

object of *the faith,* the meaning is equivalent to "faith in him." But if genitive αὐτοῦ is understood as being subjective, that is, *he* is the one who had faith, then *the faith of him* would mean "Christ's faith."

In English translations of Paul's writings, there are eight occurrences of "faith of Christ" or something equivalent. These are Galatians 2.16 (πίστεως Ἰησοῦ Χριστοῦ and πίστεως Χριστοῦ), 2.20 (πίστει…τῇ τοῦ υἱοῦ τοῦ θεοῦ), 3.22 (πίστεως Ἰησοῦ Χριστοῦ), Romans 3.22 (πίστεως Ἰησοῦ Χριστοῦ), 3.26 (πίστεως Ἰησοῦ), Philippians 3.9 (πίστεως Χριστοῦ), and Ephesians 3.12 (πίστεως αὐτοῦ). The literature[175] pertaining to this expression has grown over the past 60 years and a strong case has been made for understanding Χριστοῦ/Ἰησοῦ Χριστοῦ/αὐτοῦ subjectively, making the phrase speak of Christ's faith. However, there is no suggestion that an objective meaning (Christ is the object of the faith, i.e., "faith in Christ") is a grammatical impossibility, though D. W. B. Robinson has argued that usage argues against an objective meaning in the absence of an introductory preposition (εἰς or ἐν).[176]

Were it not for the supposition that the similar phrase in Romans 3.22 is made redundant by understanding it to mean *faith in Christ,* the present debate might not have become so robust. It is that passage that served as a starting point for several who have argued for interpreting the various passages wherein we see "faith of Christ" or something similar as meaning Christ's faith. They suppose that in that passage, if we reckon the expression διὰ πίστεως Ἰησοῦ Χριστοῦ to mean faith in Jesus Christ, we

---

[175] With reference to Eph. 3:12 specifically, among those who have argued that the genitive is subjective: Gabriel Hebert "'Faithfulness' and 'Faith'" Theology 58.24 (Oct. '55), 373–79; George Howard "On the 'Faith of Christ'" HTR 60(1967), 459–484, and ExpTims 85 (p. 212f); Luke Timothy Johnson, "Romans 3:21–26 and the Faith of Jesus," CBQ 44 (1982) pp. 77–90; Morna Hooker, NTS, 35 (1989), p. 322; Sam K. Williams, "Again Pistis Christou,"CBQ, 49, p. 432. C.F.D. Moule ("The Biblical Conception of Faith," *ExpTim* 68 [February 1957]:157) did not think highly of this interpretation. Arland Hultgren ("The Pistis Christou Formulation in Paul," NovTest 22, (1980) p. 248–263) argued that in the various passages of Paul's letters where πίστις is followed by a genitive referring to Christ, the meaning is "faith in Christ." But Hultgren did not discuss Eph. 3:12 inasmuch as he considered Ephesians to have been written by someone other than Paul. Thomas Torrance tried to have it both ways, interpreting the genitives subjectively as speaking of Christ's faithfulness, but also "suggesting the answering faithfulness of man" (Torrance, "One Aspect of the Biblical Conception of Faith," ExpTim 68 (January 1957):113.) In the standard grammars, there is a tendency to come down on the side of the objective genitive, though with some caveats. See Robertson, p. 499–501. BDF, p. 90. Turner, p. 210–212. BGAD, p. 663.

[176] Robinson, RTR, p. 78.

are at a loss to understand why Paul in that passage would redundantly add εἰς πάντας τοὺς πιστεύοντας (*to all that believe*).[177]

Perhaps this perception of a difficulty in Romans 3.22 has been unfortunate, giving undue impetus to the perception of a need to rethink the meaning of "the faith of Christ." In Romans 3.22 Paul's εἰς πάντας τοὺς πιστεύοντας is not at all redundant even if we understand Ἰησοῦ Χριστοῦ objectively. The phrase διὰ πίστεως Ἰησοῦ Χριστοῦ affirms that the righteousness of God is through faith in Christ, and then, in keeping with the theme of the immediate context as well as the whole letter, the words *unto all that believe*, with emphasis on *all*, are added to make clear that this is true of both Jews and Gentiles. In other words, Paul's *unto all that believe* is not a pleonastic restatement of what he has just said, but an elaboration upon what he has just said, emphasizing that the rightousness through faith which he has just mentioned is available to *all*, whether Jew or Gentile.

In Ephesians 3.12, there is little in the immediate context to incline the reader one direction or the other. But given the several times that Paul uses this or an equivalent phrase in contexts where he is discussing our justification as being through faith and not through the law, it has the feel of a stock phrase with a stereotyped signficance. And given that in those contexts there is a corollary point being made that Gentiles have equal access to God along with Jews (Rom 3.22, 29f, Gal 2.14ff, 3.28f), a point that is perfectly in keeping with the theme of Ephesians 2–3, we should suppose that the phrase here in Ephesians 3.12 does indeed mean the same thing that it means elsewhere in Paul's writings. In Romans where Paul has argued that justification is by faith using the phrase in question twice (Rom 3.22,26), he goes on in chapter four to set forth Abraham as the prototype of justification by faith. Clearly there, he is talking about Abraham's *own* faith. Paul's point is that we are justified the same way Abraham was. Therefore in Romans 3, we should understand that Paul has in mind *our* faith, not Jesus' faith. And therefore we should understand the expression in Ephesians 3.12 in the same way.

---

[177] Hebert, Johnson, and Hooker all argued from the idea that an objective genitive in Rom 3.22 would make the relevant phrase redundant. Though D. W. B. Robinson (p. 72, "Faith of Jesus Christ"—a New Testament Debate," (p. 72, The Reformed Theological Review, 29 (1970) pp. 71–81) did not ultimately pronounce a verdict on the meaning in Eph. 3:12, he also cited the seeming redundancy in Rom 3.22 as a factor in the evolution of his thinking about the expression πίστις Χριστοῦ.

3.13 *Wherefore I ask that you not be discouraged by my tribulations on your behalf, which is your glory* (διὸ αἰτοῦμαι μὴ ἐγκακεῖν ἐν ταῖς θλίψεσίν μου ὑπὲρ ὑμῶν, ἥτις ἐστὶν δόξα ὑμῶν) The word *you* is not present in the Greek text. μὴ ἐγκακεῖν is a negated infinitive, *not to be discouraged,* and the question must be asked, who is not to be discouraged? Does Paul ask that he himself not be discouraged or does he ask that his readers not be discouraged?

Paul does on occasion write of his own circumstances and state of mind, but generally with some aim that is in the interest of his readers. In Romans, Paul speaks of his own deep sorrow for his kinsmen (Rom 9.1*ff*) in order to introduce the topic of the true Israel that is defined by faith. In 1 Corinthians, Paul speaks of his need to buffet his own body (1 Cor 9.26*f*) as a means of instructing his readers to be similarly self-discplined. In 2 Corinthians, he writes of his own trials and persistence, first to contrast the thriving inner man with the dying outer man (2 Cor 4.7*ff*) and then to put to shame those who failed to rightly regard his credentials (2 Cor 11.16*ff*). In Galatians, Paul tells of his own experience (Gal 1.11*ff*) as a means of defending his apostleship. In Philippians, Paul speaks of his own contentment as an instructive example to his readers. In 1 Thessalonians and 2 Thessalonians, he speaks of his own integrity and labor (1 Thess 2.1*ff*, 2 Thess 3.7*ff*) as a way of encouraging his readers to conduct themselves in similar fashion.

In none of these instances can Paul's description of his own sentiments, trials, or yearnings be considered self-indulgent. Truly, Paul did not preach himself. While in his second letter to Timothy he talked of his approaching death and of those who had disappointed him (4.6–18), his letters generally and especially his letters to churches were not characterized by the self-absorbed testimony that plagues our society and our religious expression today.

In Ephesians, Paul does indeed speak of himself as least of all saints and therefore exults in the privilege bestowed upon him to bring good news to the Gentiles (Eph 3.8*f*). But he does this as part of his effort to exclaim the riches of the grace that has been showered upon his readers.

At the conclusion of the letter, Paul will ask for prayers that he might be bold in proclaiming the gospel. But here in the climax of the first half of the letter, where the whole message is so much about motivating his readers, it is difficult to imagine that Paul turned aside from that message to make a request on his own behalf, namely that he not be discouraged, with no apparent connection to his readers' needs.

by my trials (ἐν ταῖς θλίψεσίν μου)   No doubt Paul was referring specifically to his imprisonment and the charges that would be brought against him before Caesar. See the Introduction, The Place of Composition.

which is your glory (ἥτις ἐστὶν δόξα ὑμῶν)   The fact that ἥτις is feminine points to θλίψεσίν even though the latter is plural while ἥτις is singular. Robertson noted this passage (along with 1 Cor 3.17) as an example where the pronoun agrees in number with the predicate rather than with its antecedent.[178]

3.14–19   Paul's Prayer

On account of this I bow my knees to the Father from whom every family in the heavens and upon earth is named in order that he might give to you, according to the wealth of his glory, to be strengthened with power through his Spirit in the inner man, that Christ might dwell, through faith, in your hearts, you being rooted and founded in love, that you might be made strong to receive with all the saints what is the breadth and length and height and depth, and to know the love of Christ that surpasses knowledge in order that you might be filled unto the fullness of God.

3.14   *On account of this I bow my knees to the Father* (Τούτου χάριν κάμπτω τὰ γόνατά μου πρὸς τὸν πατέρα)   With the words Τούτου χάριν, Paul resumes the thought, the description of his prayer, begun in verse one. On the meaning of this expression, see the comments on verse one.

3.15   *from whom every family in the heavens and upon earth is named* (ἐξ οὗ πᾶσα πατριὰ ἐν οὐρανοῖς καὶ ἐπὶ γῆς ὀνομάζεται)   This is a reminder that God is over all, and is not merely the God of the Jews. Indeed, his rule extends even beyond the earth. The words πᾶσα πατριὰ (*every family*) hark back to the promise made to Abraham, Isaac, and Jacob. That promise was that a blessing would come through Israel but would not be only for Israel—it would be for all families of the earth. In Genesis 12.3 and 28.14, the LXX wording of that promise was that all *tribes* (φυλαί) of the earth would be blessed, and in Genesis 18.18, 22.18, 26.4 it was that all *nations* (ἔθνη) would be blessed. However, when Luke records Peter's reference to this promise in Acts 3.25, he has Peter saying *"all the families*

---

[178] Robertson, A Gramar., p. 729.

(πατριαί) *of the earth.*"[179] Certainly the Hebrew word used in Genesis 12.3 and 28.14, *mishpᵉchoth,* can as well be translated πατριά as φυλαί. Here in Ephesians where Paul is assuring the Gentiles of their place in the scheme of redemption, an allusion to the promise to the patriarchs of a coming blessing for all peoples is utterly fitting.

In 1.21, we saw the expression ὑπεράνω...παντὸς ὀνόματος ὀνομαζομένου, *above...every name that is named.* The verb ὀνομάζεται here in 3.15 is used in a similar sense. It is not the activity of bestowing a name upon a person or family, but is the acknowledgement, and in the present context perhaps even authorization, of existence. If one says, "Name the Presidents in order," he is not asking you to decide by what name each shall be called, but rather to list them by name. But the one *from whom every family in the heavens and upon earth is named* not only lists them, but in fact created them. Still the focus is not upon the actual giving of a name by which they shall be designated, but upon the existential defining of them.

3.16 *in order that he might give to us, according to the wealth of his glory, to be strengthened with power through his Spirit in the inner man* (ἵνα δῷ ὑμῖν κατὰ τὸ πλοῦτος τῆς δόξης αὐτοῦ δυνάμει κραταιωθῆναι διὰ τοῦ πνεύματος αὐτοῦ εἰς τὸν ἔσω ἄνθρωπον) Zerwick supposed it is justifiable to retain the strict sense of εἰς in contrast to ἐν and understand Paul to mean "be strengthened so as to produce" the inner man rather than merely be strengthened *in* the inner man.[180] However, it seems to me the grammatical structure then becomes cumbersome with one purpose awkwardly leading to another (*in order that he might give, so as to produce*) and finally leading up to an anticlimactic "the inner man" as the goal of it all—*that he might give us to be strengthened so as to produce the inner man.* Maybe this would make sense if some resultant attribute of the inner man were named as being produced. But as it is, it seems better to understand the purpose expression to be simply ἵνα δῷ (*in order that he might give*) and the goal to be *the inner man being strengthened.* If we understand

---

[179] This leads us to wonder if perhaps in Greek speaking circles in the first century, a version of the promise using the word *families* (πατριαί) might have gained currency. To be sure, Paul uses the word *nations* (ἔθνη) in Gal 3.8, where, just as here, he was writing to a Gentile audience. Hoehner supposes Paul preferred to use the word πατριαί in Eph. 3.15 as a sort of play on the word πατέρα in verse 14. In any event, in the context of the promise to Abraham, Isaac, and Jacob, all three words, *tribe, nation,* and *family,* have the same significance.

[180] Zerwick, p. 36f, §110.

this to be the meaning, then we have no choice but to understand εἰς in this passage as equal to ἐν, from which it evolved.

3.17–18 *that Christ might dwell, through faith, in your hearts, you being rooted and founded in love that you might be made strong to receive with all the saints what is the breadth and length and height and depth* When Paul speaks of Christ dwelling in our hearts through faith (κατοικῆσαι τὸν Χριστὸν διὰ τῆς πίστεως ἐν ταῖς καρδίαις ὑμῶν), he does not have in mind a version of the power of positive thinking, the sort of thing whereby if one really believes something, then it must be true—"I just know Christ is in my heart because I believe it so strongly." Rather, he means that when one puts his faith in Jesus, abiding in Jesus' word, following in Jesus' steps, sanctifying in his heart Christ as Lord, then in this way Christ dwells in his heart.

The phrase σὺν πᾶσιν τοῖς ἁγίοις (*with all the saints*) is a reference to those of the Jews who had already been God's holy people. As in 2.19, the Gentiles are viewed as now being of equal status with a previously identified people of God. They may now be made strong to receive, along with all the saints, the profound blessings of God in Christ. This way of speaking of Gentiles as being added to a previously identified people of God is akin to Paul's picture of wild branches being grafted into an existing olive tree (Rom 11.17). And again in Romans 15.27, Paul had spoken of the Gentiles becoming partakers of the spiritual things of the Jews.

3.19 *And to know the love of Christ that surpasses knowledge in order that you might be filled unto the fullness of God* What does Paul mean when he speaks of love that surpasses knowledge (τὴν ὑπερβάλλουσαν τῆς γνώσεως ἀγάπην)? The word γνῶσις (*knowledge*) is found in the NT 29 times, 23 of which are in Paul. Outside of Paul, only Luke and Peter use the word, both in a positive sense. But in Paul, the picture is different. Excluding the five occurrences where the word is used by Paul with reference to divine revelation associated with spiritual gifts (1 Cor 1.5, 12.8, 13.2, 13.8, 14.6), γνῶσις is something negative or inadequate almost as often as it is something positive.

It is a good thing in Romans (three times), throughout 2 Corinthians (six times), and in Philippians 3.8. And then there is the occurrence in Colossians 2.3, which we will need to revisit.

In 1 Corinthians 8, where the word occurs five times, it is associated with an arrogant lack of love. γνῶσις was a source of false confidence for the Corinthians—it puffed up (8.1), in contrast to love which built up. Although it is desirable to have the γνῶσις that there is one God and no idol is anything, Paul's description of the man who has knowledge while he sits at the feast in the idol temple (1 Cor 8.10) is a picture of self-centeredness that is indifferent to another's spiritual well-being. Indeed, it is destructive (1 Cor 8.11).

The γνῶσις mentioned in 1 Timothy 6.20 was "falsely so-called" and consisted of profane babblings and oppositions.

Returning to Colossians 2.3, where certainly the word is used in a positive sense—all the treasures of wisdom and γνώσεως are hidden in Christ—Paul nonetheless has that false knowledge in mind, that Gnostic error which he will begin to describe shortly, and he means to contrast the true knowledge that is in Christ with what is falsely called knowledge. He appropriates a number of the Gnostics' words, τέλειος (1.28), ἀποκεκρυμμένην (2.3), στοιχεῖα (2.8), πλήρωμα (2.9), using them against their error. So even though Colossians 2.3 is an instance where γνῶσις is used in a positive sense, the γνῶσις associated with the Gnostic error was in view.

And with that, we return to the use of the word in Ephesians 3.19. Even though we have said that Ephesians, in contrast to Colossians, is undisturbed by forays into Gnostic error, we do see at least brief allusions to the error even here in Ephesians. Paul is writing to Gentile believers throughout Asia and perhaps beyond, but within the environs of his readers, there was at least one locale where Gnostic influence had taken root. This probably accounts for the mention of a love that surpasses knowledge here in Ephesians 3.19. As Paul's exultant prayer reaches its climax, he draws a contrast between the love of Christ that has been so abundantly showered upon the Gentiles and the self-serving "knowledge" in which some had taken pride.

Later, in Ephesians 4.9–10, we will again see language indicating that the Gnostic error is on Paul's mind even though in this letter, addressed to a broad audience, he did not need to confront that error so directly and forcefully as he does in the letter to the church at Colossae. It should be remembered that at a later time, the Gnostic error would be found in Asia outside of Colossae. Specifically, it would be found at Ephesus, as is evidenced by Paul's letters to Timothy.

3.20–21 Doxology

To the one who is able to do surpassingly above all that we ask or think according to the power that is worked in us, to him be the glory in the church and in Christ Jesus unto all the generations forever, Amen.

The prayer was initiated in verse 1, was interrupted as Paul contemplated the great privilege bestowed upon him to bring the good news to the Gentiles (verses 2–13), was resumed in verse 14, then included a plea that God might strengthen the Gentiles through his Spirit and that Christ might dwell in their hearts, and rose to a climax in verses 18 and 19. Now, with words of praise to God, Paul concludes the prayer.

3.20 ὑπερεκπερισσοῦ (*surpassingly*) is an adverb. The adjective περισσός is *abundant* and the simple adverb περρισῶς is *abundantly* or *exceedingly*. But the prepositions ὑπερ (*above*) and ἐκ have been prefixed to the root in the form ὑπερεκπερισσοῦ.

Lincoln calls attention to the "build up of thought reflected" in the language.[181] It was not enough to say God is able to do πάντα (*all*) that we ask or think. More than that, God is able to do ὑπὲρ πάντα (*above all*) that we ask or think. But that is still insufficient. Paul could have said, ὑπὲρ πάντα περρισῶς (*exceedingly above all*). But that too was insufficient. He could have intensified the word περρισῶς (*exceedingly*) and said, ὑπὲρ πάντα ἐκπερρισῶς. But he went even beyond that and said ὑπὲρ πάντα ὑπερεκπερισσοῦ. This is the language of exultant praise. If we are not naturally effusive, we do well to look to Paul's example to learn how to extol the greatness of our God.

αἰτούμεθα (*we ask*) must be understood as middle here, for the passive voice makes no sense. In view of Paul's use of this verb in the middle voice in 3.13, perhaps no great significance is to be attached to the middle voice here. On the other hand, the middle voice could indicate an emphasis on the purpose of the request, "ask for ourselves," or it could be akin to νοοῦμεν (*we think*), indicating inner contemplation, "ask within ourselves." Given the redundant character of the language within the prayer, not to say superfluous character, but redundant for the purpose of emphasis (*strengthened with power, rooted and founded, breadth and length and height and depth*), taking αἰτούμεθα and νοοῦμεν to mean essentially the same thing is not a stretch. But most likely, Paul meant to distinguish between what we might consciously request and what we might merely imagine ("be-

---

[181] Lincoln, p. 216.

yond our wildest dreams"), saying that God is able to provide above and beyond them both. Compare Mathew 6.8,32.

The genitive relative pronoun ὧν in 3.20 is difficult to explain. Hoehner suggests that it may be genitive due to attraction to the case of ὑπερεκπερισσοῦ (*surpassingly, beyond, more abundantly*) and mentions Matthew 18.19 as being similar. But the two passages are not truly similarly constructed. ὧν αἰτούμεθα ἢ νοοῦμεν is a relative clause, *which we ask or think*. Within the clause, the relative pronoun ὧν (*which*) is the direct object of the verb, or in this instance, of both verbs. In such constructions, rather than being in the accusative case as might be expected, the relative pronoun often agrees in case with its antecedent, especially if the antecedent is either genitive or dative. This is called "attraction to the case of the antecedent." In Matthew 18.19, the word to which the pronoun is attracted, πράγματος, is indeed the antecedent of the relative pronoun. But here in Ephesians 3.20, the antecedent of the relative pronoun is not ὑπερεκπερισσοῦ. ὑπερεκπερισσοῦ is not a substantive, but an adverb describing the extent to which God is able to act.

Robertson supposed the relative pronoun ὧν has been attracted to the case of an unexpressed antecedent, τούτων.[182] The same view is offered in BDAG.[183]

Alford is probably correct in observing that ὧν αἰτούμεθα ἢ νοοῦμεν (*which we ask or think*) is a second clause "that repeats the first in a more detailed and specified form."[184] Paul firsts says God is able to do exceedingly above all, and then he elaborates to say specifically that God is able to do exceedingly above all that we ask or even imagine.

3.21 Verse 20 began with the words, *"To the one who is able"* (Τῷ δὲ δυναμένῳ). Now in verse 21, Paul will say what it is that is to him. It is glory. The αὐτῷ (*to him*) is resumptive, picking up the thought he began in verse 21. *To him be the glory in the church and in Christ Jesus unto all the generations forever.*

Not all chapter divisions properly reflect the flow of the text. But this is a good place for a chapter division. Up to this point, Paul has labored to impress upon his readers the great blessing that God has bestowed upon them, the standing that they have as part of the holy habitation of God

[182] Word Pictures, vol. 4, p. 534. A Grammar, p. 647.
[183] BDAG, p. 1033, *s.v.* ὑπερεκπερισσοῦ.
[184] Alford, vol. 3, p. 111.

in the Spirit. Paul has shown that they have been the object of God's plan all along. Paul has shown that they do not come one step behind the Jews who have been saved by grace. And Paul has emphasized that this salvation is indeed by grace, for apart from Christ his readers were dead by sin. Paul will next turn to discuss the manner in which such people should walk. But here he concludes his description of God's great blessing with a prayer of thanksgiving, and the prayer he concludes with *"Amen."*[185]

---

[185] Compare 1 Cor. 14:16.

PART TWO

Chapters 4–6

Paul Calls upon the Gentiles to Walk Worthily of Their Calling

The second half of the letter begins with *therefore,* that is, in view of what has been said about the great grace of God bestowed on us in Jesus Christ, let us walk worthily of the calling with which we have been called. Verses 4–16 may be regarded as a digression but only mildly so, before the theme of walking worthily is resumed in verse 17. As Hamman has observed, "if we had never seen vv 4–16, we would read 4:1–3,17 and the following verses as if they belonged naturally together….The section beginning with v 17 would act as a negative counterpart to the positive directions of vv 1–3 to walk worthy of the calling to be Christians…"

The section that is inserted is not unrelated to the larger point. The larger point is how to walk worthily. The inserted material, the "digression," calls attention to the importance of walking worthily such that the body might truly be united, and explains the means whereby the Gentile saints can learn to walk worthily that the whole body might be united.

4.1–10   Walk Worthily in Unity

Therefore I, the prisoner in the Lord, beseech you, walk worthily of the calling with which you were called with all humility and meekness, with longsuffering, forbearing one another in love, giving diligence to maintain the unity of the spirit in the bond of peace; one body and one spirit, just as you were also called in one hope of your calling, one Lord, one faith, one baptism, one God and Father of all, the one over all and through all and in all. But to each one of us was given the favor according to the measure of the gift of Christ. Wherefore he says,

> *Having ascended on high,*
> *he led captivity captive,*
> *he gave gifts to men.*

Now what is the, "He ascended," except that he also descended into the lower parts of the earth? The one who descended is also himself the one who ascended above all the heavens that he might fulfill all things.

4.1 *Therefore I, the prisoner in the Lord, beseech you, walk worthily of the calling with which you were called* The word *therefore* connects all that follows with all that has preceded. Far be it from us to suggest that Paul should have worded this differently, but it is worth noting that in Colossians, Paul prays for the brethren *to walk worthily of the Lord* (Col 1.10), a thought that would go very nicely with the affirmation that they have become a habitation for God in the Spirit (Eph 2.22). Inasmuch as God's elect have been called collectively to be a "holy temple" for a holy God, they have been called individually to be saints, holy ones (cf. Rom 1.7, 1 Cor 1.2). Paul urges them to walk worthily of this calling.

Eight times in this letter, we see the word *walk* (περιπατέω). The Gentile readers had formerly *walked according to the age of this world, according to the ruler of the power of the air, the spirit that now works in the sons of disobedience* (2.2). But, in Jesus, they have been created for good works in which they should *walk* (2.10). Having previously referred to *the hope of his calling* (1.18), Paul now urges the Gentiles to *walk worthily* of their calling (4.1). He will use the word twice, warning them how not to *walk* (4.17), and then he will urge them to *walk in love* (5.2), *as children of light* (5.8), and *carefully, as wise* (5.15).

4.2–3 *with all humility and meekness, with longsuffering, forbearing one another in love with all humility and meekness, with longsuffering, giving diligence to maintain the unity of the spirit in the bond of peace* These words call to mind the message of 2.14ff. The unity described there, the one body in which both Jew and Gentile are reconciled to God through the cross, the peace between Jew and Gentile, must be diligently pursued.

We probably ought to understand συνδέσμῳ τῆς εἰρήνης (*bond of peace*) in relation to Paul's description of himself as a δέσμιος (*prisoner*) in verse one. He was a prisoner in the Lord, using his imprisonment as an opportunity to serve the Lord. If one is going to be a prisoner, what better than to be a prisoner in the service of the Lord? If one is going to be bound, what better than to be bound in peace?

4.4 *one body and one spirit, just as you were also called in one hope of your calling* To underscore the goal of unity, Paul emphasizes what is shared. Not only do Jews and Gentiles comprise one body, and not only are they led by one spirit, but they share the same hope.

4.5 *one Lord, one faith, one baptism* The fundamental significance of baptism should not be overlooked here. Paul is not itemizing trivialities. He is talking about the fundamental aspects of Christianity that are shared by all. There were sometimes differences between Jews and Gentiles regarding eating meats or observing days (Rom 14), but they served the same Lord, they stood in the same faith, they aspired to the same hope, and they entered into one body through that same act of baptism. In the church of Jesus Christ then and now, baptism was no mere ceremony; it was a burial with Christ and resurrection to new life, and was thus the introduction to this relationship with God and with one another through Jesus Christ. See the comments on 5.26.

4.6 *one God and Father of all, the one over all and through all and in all.* And finally, as Paul brings his litany of unity to a conclusion, he appeals to the one God and father of all, the one who is over all and through all and in all. Reminiscent of Acts 17 where Paul also spoke to Gentiles (ὁ θεὸς ὁ ποιήσας τὸν κόσμον καὶ πάντα τὰ ἐν αὐτῷ... αὐτὸς διδοὺς πᾶσι ζωὴν καὶ πνοὴν καὶ τὰ πάντα, *the God who made the world and all the things in it...he himself giving to all life and breath and all things*), as there, these words are especially appropriate for an audience of Gentiles whose religious heritage was one of national gods and frail gods and competing gods. The unity to which Paul calls his readers, a unity that binds together Jew and Gentile, is all the more appropriate in view of the fact that it is the result of the work of a God who is over all things and all people.

With this emphasis on unity, Paul takes time to describe the means whereby unity throughout the body of Christ can become a practical reality rather then merely a theoretical conception. Ultimately, that practical unity "with all the saints" (3.18) can only be achieved if the Gentiles cease living as Gentiles (4.17) , put away the former manner of life (4.22), and put on the new man (4.24). But they will need to be taught how to do that. And the means whereby that will be accomplished is the point of Ephesians 4.7–16. Specifically, the Lord gave gifts, apostles prophets, evangelists, shepherds and teachers, who would teach the Gentiles how to walk worthily of the their calling. The result would be a unity of the faith (4.13), a body fitly framed and knit together (4.16).

4.7–8 *But to each one of us was given the favor according to the measure of the gift of Christ. Wherefore he says,*
>**Having ascended on high,**
>**he led captivity captive,**
>**he gave gifts to men.**

The words are taken from Psalm 68.18, but they follow neither the Hebrew text nor the LXX.

Psalm 68.18	as quoted in Ephesians 4.8
You ascended on high, You led captive captivity, You received gifts among men. [LXX Ps 67.19] ἀνέβης εἰς ὕψος, ᾐχμαλώτευσας αἰχμαλωσίαν, ἔλαβες δόματα ἐν ἀνθρώπῳ	Having ascended on high, he led captivity captive, he gave gifts to men. ἀναβὰς εἰς ὕψος ᾐχμαλώτευσεν αἰχμαλωσίαν, ἔδωκεν δόματα τοῖς ἀνθρώποις.

The change from second person verbs to third person would not be too great a problem by itself. We could simply reckon Paul's quotation to be indirect rather than direct, a paraphrase. However, with the change from ἔλαβες (*you received*) to ἔδωκεν (*he gave*), the meaning is changed. Moreover, Paul builds his ensuing point on this word *gave*, describing the apostles, *et al.* as what is given.

Chrysostom wrote, "The prophet says in the psalm, 'You received gifts among men,' but he himself [i.e., the Apostle Paul] says, 'he gave gifts among men.' This is the same as that."[1] It seems he was in fact arguing that Paul did not change the meaning of the psalm, that ἔλαβες (*received*) and ἔδωκεν (*gave*) amount to the same thing. But the very fact that he felt the need to say this indicates an awareness of the problem.

Some interpret Psalm 68 as being utterly messianic with no historical reference at all. Were that the case, what need would there have been to alter the wording for the messianic application? But in fact, the difference in the wording at Psalm 68.18 and as quoted by Paul in Ephesians is significant.

By those who see a historical reference, Psalm 68 is variously inter-

---

[1] Homily 11. Ὁ μὲν Προφήτης φησὶν ἐν τῷ ψαλμῷ· Ἔλαβες δόματα ἐν ἀνθρώποις· αὐτὸς δέ φησιν· Ἔδωκε δόματα ἐν ἀνθρώποις. Τοῦτο ταυτόν ἐστιν ἐκείνῳ.

preted as a celebration of the Ark's entry to Zion (2 Sam 6), of a military victory, or of the return from captivity.

The nature of the gifts is variously understood. On the basis of Numbers 8.16 ("I have taken" the Levites) and 8.19 ("I have given the Levites as a gift to Aaron and to his sons") Smith sees the gifts as being the Levites.[2] While there may be seen a precedent in God's provision of the Levites for service just as he later provides the Apostles, *et al.* for service, the reference to the Levites is not clear in Psalm 68.

But if the psalm was occasioned by a military victory, God may be pictured as a conquering king, the gifts possibly being from the king's subjects in honor of his victory. Or, in view of Psalm 68.12 ("she who remains at home will divide the spoil"), they may be the spoils of war brought back and divided among the king's subjects (*cf.* Jdg 5.30, 1 Sam 30.24–31). If this is correct, then the gifts, though *received* from the vanquished, are then *given* (by implication) to the subjects of the conquering king. In this picture of a conquering king bestowing gifts on his people, the ultimate conquering King being God himself, Paul could easily see a theme that would be ultimately realized in the conquering Christ who would bestow gifts upon his people. (For the idea of Christ taking spoils, see Mt 12.29.)

In addition to the possible indication that the gifts received are the spoils distributed, there are other aspects of the psalm that make it a suitable device for Paul's point in Ephesians 4. The unquoted final line of Psalm 68.18 is, "Even among the rebellious also, that the LORD God may dwell there." Given that Ephesians is addressed to Gentiles in light of their new standing in the household of God, who along with Jewish believers, are built together for a habitation of God in the Spirit (Eph 2.19), and given that the message of the second half of Ephesians is a call to these formerly rebellious people (Eph 2.2, 4.17–19) to walk worthily of the calling with which they have been called, the remarkable thing is not so much that Paul adapted the first three lines of Psalm 68.18, but rather that he did not go on to quote the perfectly suited last line.

Psalm 68 pictures God:

    1. as having vanquished his enemies (68.1–2, 11–14)

    2. as having ascended to a place of honor (68.15–18)

    3. and as beneficent toward his subjects (68.5–6).

---

[2] Smith, 187.

Paul, by the Holy Spirit, sees in the words of Psalm 68.18 (with some adaptation) an application to the Christ, who has:

1. vanquished *his* enemies (Compare Col 2.15: "having despoiled the principalities and the powers, he made a show of them openly, triumphing over them in [the cross]")
2. ascended to a place of honor
3. and is beneficent toward *his* subjects.

Does Paul merely borrow language that is suitable to his purpose, or does he indicate that language was used in the psalm with a view to the Messiah, or does he in fact appeal to the psalm as proof of his teaching that Christ gave gifts?

Gary Smith said, "Paul's awareness of the word 'gifts' in Psalm 68.18… caused him to use this verse as a proof of his statement in Ephesians 4.7 that 'each one of us is given grace according of the measure of the gift of Christ.'"[3] But a proof is exactly what it is not. Thinking of the citation as a proof contributes to the problem we have in reconciling Paul's use of the passage with our understanding of scripture as inspired. For if Paul's quotation were intended to be a proof (*i.e.*, it was prophesied that Christ would give gifts and therefore we can believe that he did so), it would be necessary that Psalm 68 could be rightly comprehended *per se* as describing dispensing of gifts by the Christ.

For the believer, who needs not be convinced that David wrote by the Spirit, nor that Jesus is the Christ, Paul has as much right to say "he gave" as David had to say "you received." Both David and Paul are speaking from God. The purpose of the quotation is neither to prove that fact nor to prove that what Paul wants to say must be true because it was already said by David. The purpose of the quotation is to use again the imagery of the victorious king and with it, make a new application. Compare the use Paul makes of Deuteronomy 30.11–14 in Romans 10.6–10.

There should be no doubt that the psalm could have been inspired with a view to the future King who would bestow gifts. But that is not the immediately apparent meaning of the psalm. In order to make that meaning clear, Paul found it necessary to alter the wording.

But notice that Paul does not say, "Psalm 68 said…therefore we may believe…" Rather Paul says, "Christ gave gifts, wherefore the Psalm said…" Paul consciously gives us a *retrospective* interpretation of the psalm. He

---

[3] Smith, p. 182.

tells us that the Lord gave gifts to us; he does not prove to us that the Lord gave gifts to us. He says, *Wherefore it says* (διὸ λέγει). Paul is explaining why the psalm said what it said, not why we can know Christ gave gifts. Paul is telling us about a meaning that we likely would not have seen in the psalm. He tells us what the Lord did and then says, "and by the way, this was anticipated in Psalm 68, and let me show you how."

We can put this psalm in the same category as so many others. It describes Old Testament events that were *typical* of the coming Christ. Themes are contained therein that will be ultimately realized in the Messianic kingdom.

4.9–10 *Now what is the, "He ascended"?* (τὸ δὲ ἀνέβη τί ἐστιν) In NA28, ἀνέβη (*He ascended*) is italicized to indicate that it is a quotation. The UBS Greek text capitalizes it, Ἀνέβη, to indicate it is the first word of a quotation. The quotation consists of only that one word. The neuter definite article τὸ introduces the quotation. We can represent this in English, *"Now what is the 'He ascended'?"* The idea is more completely expressed in English if we say, *"Now what is the significance of the statement, 'He ascended'?"*

Of course, Paul has in mind the language of Psalm 68.18, though neither the LXX nor Paul's quotation of the psalm in verse eight had precisely this form. In the LXX (Ps 67.19), the second person form ἀνέβης (*you ascended*) is used, following the Hebrew. Paul's quotation of the passage in Ephesians 4.8 has the participle ἀναβάς (*having ascended*). Hoehner supposes Paul departed from the participle he used in verse eight, changing "it into a finite verb in order to make a corresponding comparison with the following finite verb κατέβη 'he descended'."[4]

Regarding the phrase *he also descended into the lower [parts] of the earth* (καὶ κατέβη εἰς τὰ κατώτερα [μέρη] τῆς γῆς), we need to discuss the textual issue, and then concern ourselves with whether this refers to a descent to earth at the incarnation or on the other hand, a descent into death at the crucifixion.

First, the textual issue: In 𝔓⁴⁶, codices D, F, and G, some of the ancient versions, and in numerous patristic citations, the word μέρη (*parts*) is absent. But given the presence of the word not only in the chief uncials but also in the Byzantine tradition (the mss behind the so-called majority text), it is a little surprising that the editors of the UBS5 give the in-

---

[4] Hoehner, p. 531.

clusion of the word no better than a C rating. While it might be easier to explain the insertion of the word as a scribal attempt to clarify the text than to explain the omission of the word, it should be noted that the mss that include the word are of wide geographic origin. With the exception of 𝔓⁴⁶ and the ancient Sahidic Coptic version (cop^sa), the witnesses that omit the word are all western.

Now let us turn to the meaning. There is a similarity between Paul's use of Psalm 68 here and his use of Deuteronomy 30 in Romans 10. In both Ephesians 4 and Romans 10, Paul is discussing Christ's ascent and descent, and he adapts OT language to make his point. However, in Romans 10, Christ's implied descent is his incarnation and his implied ascent is his resurrection, whereas here in Ephesians, Christ's descent is his death and his ascent is his return to the Father (Acts 1.9, 2.33–34).

Here in Ephesians, Paul specifies not merely the earth, but *the lower parts* of the earth as that to which Jesus descended. Zerwick took τῆς γῆς (*of the earth*) as an epexegetic genitive, an explanation of the prior τὰ κατώτερα [μέρη] (*the lower parts*), thus understanding Paul to say that Christ descended to the lower parts, *viz.*, the earth, which is lower "with respect to heaven."[5] But in the LXX at Psalm 62.10 (=63.9 in English), we see εἰσελεύσονται εἰς τὰ κατώτατα τῆς γῆς (*they will go into the lower parts of the earth*) where the meaning is certainly death, the grave. It is not earth in contrast to heaven that is described as low, but some realm that is low as compared with earth generally. See also Psalm 85.13 (=86.13), ἐρρύσω τὴν ψυχήν μου ἐξ ᾅδου κατωτάτου (*deliver my soul out of lowest hades*). Paul is referring to Jesus' death, and yes, his descent into Sheol/Hades.[6]

---

[5] Zerwick, p. 46, §45.

[6] So Chrysostom in Homily 11 on Ephesians: Ὁ καταβὰς, αὐτός ἐστι καὶ ὁ ἀναβὰς ὑπεράνω πάντων τῶν οὐρανῶν, ἵνα πληρώσῃ τὰ πάντα. Ταῦτα ἀκούων, μὴ μετάβασιν νόμιζε. Ὅπερ γὰρ ἐν τῇ πρὸς Φιλιππησίους Ἐπιστολῇ κατασκευάζει, τοῦτο καὶ ἐνταῦθα. Καθάπερ ἐκεῖ περὶ ταπεινοφροσύνης παραινῶν παράγει τὸν Χριστὸν, οὕτω δὴ καὶ ἐνταῦθα, λέγων· Εἰς τὰ κατώτερα μέρη κατέβη τῆς γῆς. Εἰ γὰρ μὴ τοῦτο ἦν, περιττὸς οὗτος ὁ λόγος ὅνπερ λέγει· Ὑπήκοος γενόμενος μέχρι θανάτου. Ἀπὸ δὲ τοῦ ἀναβῆναι τὴν κατάβασιν αἰνίττεται. Τὰ δὲ κάτω μέρη τῆς γῆς, τὸν θάνατόν φησιν, ἀπὸ τῆς τῶν ἀνθρώπων ὑπονοίας, καθάπερ καὶ ὁ Ἰακὼβ ἔλεγε· Κατάξετε τὸ γῆράς μου μετ' ὀδύνης εἰς ᾅδου· καὶ πάλιν ἐν τῷ ψαλμῷ, Ὁμοιωθήσομαι τοῖς καταβαίνουσιν εἰς λάκκον· τουτέστι, τοῖς ἀποθανοῦσι. Διὰ τί τοῦτο τὸ χωρίον ἐπεξεργάζεται ἐνταῦθα; καὶ ποίαν αἰχμαλωσίαν φησί; Τὴν τοῦ διαβόλου· αἰχμάλωτον γὰρ τὸν τύραννον ἔλαβε, τὸν διάβολον λέγω, καὶ τὸν θάνατον, καὶ τὴν ἀρὰν καὶ τὴν ἁμαρτίαν. Ὁρᾶς σκῦλα καὶ λάφυρα; "The one who descended, he himself is also the one who ascended above all the heavens, in order that he might fulfill all things"' Hearing these things, do not think (merely) of transition. For what he maintains in the epistle to the Philippians, this same also he does here. Just as there he

Hoehner sees a distinction between the grave and Hades, arguing that the passage likely refers to Jesus' burial in the earth, but dismissing the notion that it refers to his descent into Hades.[7] Hoehner goes so far as to say, "there is no indication in the Gospel narratives that after the burial of Jesus he went to Hades."[8]

But this is to miss the point that both Jews and Gentiles understood Hades to be the realm of all the dead. While the Gentile conception may have been somewhat different than the Jewish conception, it was the general understanding that when one dies, his spirit is relegated to the Hadean realm.

When Jacob mourned the loss of Joseph, he said, "Surely I will go down to Sheol in mourning for my son." It's not unlikely that he meant exactly what the Statler brothers meant when they sang, "I'll go to my grave loving you, loving you." Neither they nor he had in mind merely the burial plot or the cave that would become the site of the decomposition of the physical body, but death abstractly. Sheol is the Hebrew word that corresponds to the Greek Hades. David often spoke of the pit and of Sheol when talking about God's deliverance, but it was not merely deliverance from having his body sealed in a tomb. It was deliverance from death itself.

And while David knew that one day his death would come, he anticipated awakening from death, *i.e.*, a resurrection (Ps 17.15), at which time he would behold the face of God. And so he could say, "Thou will not abandon my soul to Sheol" (Ps 16.10). But Peter tells us that when David did say that, he was in fact speaking of the Christ, that the Christ was not left in Hades (Acts 2.31). Jesus died. His body was placed in a tomb. But his spirit was disembodied (2 Cor 5.8), and hence unclothed, naked (2 Cor 5.3–4), just as we all will be after death, awaiting the resurrection when we receive a heavenly body. But Jesus was to conquer death and

---

brings forward the Christ in urging (his readers) concerning humility, so also he does here, saying, "into the lower parts of the earth." For if this were not (his meaning), this statement he makes, "becoming obedient unto death," would be superfluous. But from the ascending he intimates the descent. And he calls death the lower parts of the earth, from the notions formed by men, just as also Jacob was speaking, "Then shall you bring down my old age with sorrow unto hades." And again in the psalm, "I will be like those who go down into a pit," that is, those who die. Why does he elaborate upon this region here? And of what captivity does he speak? The one of the devil. For He took captive the tyrant, the devil I say, and death, and the curse and sin. Do you see spoils and trophies?

[7] Hoehner, p. 536.

[8] Hoehner, p. 535.

hades, not merely death, but death and hades (Rev 2.18). And he would conquer them by experiencing them but escaping. He experienced both death and Hades, which are really inseparable. He was raised, reunited with his body that had lain in the tomb.

Even in Romans 10, where Paul did indeed speak of Christ's incarnation as, by implication, a descent—"Do not say in your heart, 'Who will ascend into heaven?' that is, to bring Christ down," for Christ has already come down to earth—there is evidence that at death Christ descended to Hades. That evidence is in the next verse where Paul says there is no need to ask, "'Who will descend into the abyss?' that is, to bring Christ up from the dead" (Rom 10.7). Paul speaks of Christ's already accomplished resurrection from the dead as being a raising up from the *abyss* (ἄβυσσος), a word chosen because it can refer both to the sea, thus maintaining a connection with the language of Deuteronomy 30 which Paul is referencing, and can also refer to Sheol, from whence Christ was raised. In Deuteronomy 30, the (unnecessary) question was "who will cross the sea (LXX, θαλάσσης)...?" For θαλάσσῃ Paul substitutes ἄβυσσος, which can indeed mean the depths of the sea (Gen 1.2, 7.11, 8.2, Ps 106.9, Is 51.10), but is also used for the realm of the dead (Ps 70.21 in the LXX,[9] Luke 8.31, Rev 9.1–2, 9.11, 11.7, 17.8, 20.1,3). Thus Paul tweaks the wording found in Deuteronomy 30.12 to make it fit the Christ who was not brought from across the sea, but was rather brought up from death. For our purposes, the significant point is simply that in connection with death, ἄβυσσος, from whence Christ was brought up, speaks not merely of the literal grave, but of a spiritual realm, the hadean realm. It is equivalent to Sheol.

We may well ask why this foray into the matters of ascending and descending is necessary when Paul's point is to connect the description of the conquering king of Psalm 68 with with the victorious Jesus. In Colossians, the companion epistle, the Gnostic doctrine is addressed head on. Apparently, at Colossae, this was much needed. Ephesians is written to a broader audience, but an audience that included Colossae (see the Introduction). For the Gnostics, the idea that there could be an identity between the crucified Jesus and the exalted Christ was unthinkable. And so as an aside to his main point, an aside probably having in view the Gnostic doctrine, Paul says, *He himself who descended is also the one who ascended above all the heavens.*

---

[9] In Ps. 70:21(= 71:20), the LXX has καὶ ἐκ τῶν ἀβύσσων τῆς γῆς πάλιν ἀνήγαγές με.

4.11–16   Gifts for Achieving Unity

And he himself gave the apostles, and the prophets, and the evangelists, and the shepherds and teachers for the perfecting of the saints, unto a work of service, unto edification of the body of Christ, until we all arrive at the unity of the faith and of the knowledge of the Son of God, unto a full-grown man, unto the measure of the stature of the fullness of Christ in order that we might be children no longer, tossed about and carried around by every wind of doctrine in the dice game of men, in trickery with the scheming of deception, but speaking truth in love, we might grow in every way unto him who is the head, Christ, from whom all the body, being put together and held together through every ligament of support in accordance with the working in measure of each individual part, makes for itself the growth of the body for building of itself in love.

4.11   *And he himself gave* (Καὶ αὐτὸς ἔδωκεν)   Nominative αὐτὸς is not always intensive, but here the intensive force seems very much intended as it was in verse 10.

The list of gifts given by the Lord is fourfold:

1. apostles
2. prophets
3. evangelists
4. shepherds and teachers.

Shepherds and teachers constitute one category, shepherds being also teachers, and not two separate categories. This is made clear by the conjunctions used in the list, μὲν prior to ἀποστόλους (*apostles*) and then δὲ prior to each subsequent item in the list:[10]

τοὺς μὲν ἀποστόλους,
τοὺς δὲ προφήτας,
τοὺς δὲ εὐαγγελιστάς,
τοὺς δὲ ποιμένας καὶ διδασκάλους.

Notice the similar introductory μὲν followed by listed items separated internally by δὲ in Matthew 13.23:

ὃ μὲν ἑκατόν,
ὃ δὲ ἑξήκοντα,
ὃ δὲ τριάκοντα.

---

[10] Cf. Smyth, §2905.

In both Ephesians 4.11 and Matthew 13.23, the construction μὲν...δὲ... δὲ... is used to differentiate between the listed groups, "Some...others..."[11] Again in Jude 8 (σάρκα μὲν μιαίνουσιν, κυριότητα δὲ ἀθετοῦσιν δόξας δὲ βλασφημοῦσιν), we see the first item in a list introduced by μὲν and then succeeding items separated by δέ. And then again in Jude 22–23, we see the same pattern:

> οὓς μὲν ἐλεᾶτε διακρινομένους,
> οὓς δὲ σῴζετε ἐκ πυρὸς ἁρπάζοντες,
> οὓς δὲ ἐλεᾶτε ἐν φόβῳ.

In Ephesians 4.11, the final τοὺς δὲ precedes ποιμένας καὶ διδασκάλους (*shepherds and teachers*). There is no τοὺς δὲ between ποιμένας (*shepherds*) and διδασκάλους (*teachers*).[12] We should therefore reckon τοὺς δὲ ποιμένας καὶ διδασκάλους as one category, pastors being also teachers, and not two separate categories.[13]

Why the two terms, ποιμένας καὶ διδασκάλους, for the one category? We will return to that thought momentarily, in the discussion of the *service*, or *ministry*, mentioned in verse 12.

4.12 *for the perfecting of the saints, unto a work of service, unto edification of the body of Christ* (πρὸς τὸν καταρτισμὸν τῶν ἁγίων εἰς ἔργον διακονίας, εἰς οἰκοδομὴν τοῦ σώματος τοῦ Χριστοῦ) In three prepositional phrases, Paul explains what is to be accomplished by the apostles, prophets, evangelists, pastors and teachers. It is a mistake to parse the interrelation of these phrases so as to see the work of ministry as being accomplished by the perfected saints rather than by the apostles, prophets, evangelists, pastors and teachers themselves. It is important to

---

[11] Zerwick/Grosvenor, Grammatical Analysis, vol 2, p. 585.

[12] There is a similar construction in Clement of Alexandria at the very beginning of "*To the Newly Baptized.*" The exhortation begins, ἡσυχίαν μὲν λόγοις ἐπιτήδευε, ἡσυχίαν δὲ ἔργοις, ὡσαύτως δὲ ἐν γλώττῃ καὶ βαδίσματι. Though talking and walking are distinct things, here these two words, γλώττῃ and βαδίσματι, comprise one category involving bodily activity, and are together set off as distinct from works (ἔργοις) and even words (λόγοις). That they comprise one category is evidenced by the single preposition ἐν as well as the adverb ὡσαύτως which must apply to the whole phrase ἐν γλώττῃ καὶ βαδίσματι. And so, just as in Eph 4.11, we have a list consisting of several items, the first introduced by μὲν and the subsequent items introduced by δέ.

[13] Lincoln's argument to the contrary (p. 250) is based not on the intrinsic grammatical indications, but on Lincoln's suppositions about teachers who were not shepherds, and especially upon Lincoln's implicit assumption that whatever is said about teachers here must be true of all teachers.

see that all three accomplishments (perfecting of the saints, work of ministry, building up of the body) are attributed directly to the apostles, *et al.*[14] So older translations punctuated the verse, treating the three prepositional phrases as grammatically parallel. In this manner Chrysostom[15], and more recently Meyer, Alford, and Barry, understood the passage, with minor variations.

But the NASB, NIV, NKJV, ESV, and some others render so as to have the apostles *et al.*, being given for the perfecting or equipping of the saints, and in turn, the saints doing the work of ministry.

Our understanding of who performs the work of ministry that Paul has in mind—whether apostles, prophets, evangelists, pastors and teachers, or on the other hand, those perfected by their efforts—will partly be determined by the sort of ministry we imagine.

Some will think of charitable acts wherein one provides for others' mundane needs. Others will think of the ministry of the word, *i.e.*, service of the gospel. In the NT, we see both. διακονία (*ministry, service*) is used of charitable acts, acts of service in material things, such as providing for impoverished believers in a number of passages (Lk 10.40, Acts 6.1, 11.29, 12.25, Rom 15.31, 1 Cor 16.15, 2 Cor, 8.4, 9.1,12*f*). Some of these passages give examples of an apostle (Paul) instructing saints (at Corinth) in the matter of performing a service (providing funds). But διακονία is also used frequently of the work of preaching, or specifically, of the work of an apostle (Acts 1.17,25, 6.4, 20.24, 21.19, Rom 11.13, 2 Cor 6.3, 11.8, Col 4.17, 1 Tim 1.12, 2 Tim 4.5, 4.11).

One who performs service, or ministry, is a διάκονος. In contexts discussing someone whom a church designates to be responsible for service,

---

[14] One of those who previewed this work and assisted by offering criticisms supposed the point of the exegesis presented here was to deny the role of every Christian in building up the body of Christ. However, that is not the intended conclusion. The point is merely that here, in this particular passage, the ministry in view is that of the apostles prophets, evangelists, shepherds and teachers. Certainly all members of the body of Christ contribute to the building up of the body, as Paul will say in Ephesians 4.16.

[15] In Homily 11 on Ephesians, after discussing the differences in rank among the gifts (the apostles, prophets, *et al.*) while noting that the subordination or precedence of one with respect to another is evident only from another epistle but cannot be made out from the present letter, and that here Paul simply says of them all, "He gave," Chrysostom concluded, Πρὸς καταρτισμὸν τῶν ἁγίων, εἰς ἔργον διακονίας, εἰς οἰκοδομὴν τοῦ σώματος τοῦ Χριστοῦ. Ὁρᾶς τὸ ἀξίωμα; Ἕκαστος οἰκοδομεῖ, ἕκαστος καταρτίζει, ἕκαστος διακονεῖ. "For the perfecting of the saints, unto a work of service, unto building the body of Christ. Do you see the worth? Each one builds, each one perfects, each one serves."

this word is sometimes translated *deacon* (1 Tim 3.8, 3.12, 3.13, Rom 16.1, Phil 1.1). But when the service to be performed is the work of teaching, διάκονος is often translated *minister* or *servant* (1 Tim 4.6, 2 Cor 3.6, Eph 3.7, 6.21, Col 1.23,25, 4.7).

In Acts 6, the apostles charged the multitude of the disciples with the task of choosing seven men who could oversee the daily διακονία of providing meals for widows so that the apostles themselves could remain focused on the διακονία of the word. See there two very different services, one providing for the nourishment of the physical body and one providing for the nourishment of the spirit. Which sort of service is in view in Ephesians 4.12?

In Ephesians 4.12, the service is part of that process that leads to the "unity of the faith," to being "no longer tossed to and fro and carried about with every wind of doctrine," to "speaking the truth in love." The kind of ministry that leads to this result is the kind that especially characterizes the work of the apostles, prophets, evangelists, pastors and teachers. It is teaching. It is "the ministry of the word," as in Acts 6.4.[16]

Hence, it is most natural to understand the ministry mentioned in 4.12 to be the work of the apostles, *et al.* themselves, *whereby* the saints are perfected. The giving of the gifts (vs. 11) was unto the work of ministry and building up of the body of Christ, with the outcome being the perfecting of the saints, which is to say the same thing as the arriving *at the unity of the faith and of the knowledge of the Son of God, unto a full-grown man, unto the measure of the stature of the fullness of Christ.*

Now this sheds some light on why Paul used two words, ποιμένας καὶ διδασκάλους (*shepherds and teachers*), for one category. The work of shepherds extends beyond teaching, but Paul meant to highlight their work as teachers in this particular passage because it would be through that work, shared with apostles, prophets, and evangelists, that an understanding of how to walk worthily and a resulting unity could be achieved.

But against this understanding is the objection that the three prepositional phrases do not all begin with the same preposition. The idea is that if Paul had meant to say the apostles, *et al.*, are themselves responsible for καταρτισμὸν τῶν ἁγίων (*perfecting the saints*) for ἔργον διακονίας (*a work*

---

[16] Best spoke of "five different ministries" in 4.11, using the phrase "leadership role" as interchangeable with "ministry" (p. 160). But it is better to understand the one ministry, that being the ministry of the word, as being the work in which all four (not five) groups are involved.

of service), and for οἰκοδομὴν τοῦ σώματος τοῦ Χριστοῦ (*building the body of Christ*), he would have used the same preposition to relate each of the three activities (*perfecting, work of service,* and *building*) to the apostles *et al.* It is supposed that the fact that he did not do so suggests that there is a progression in view: The apostles, *et al.*, are intended πρὸς perfecting the saints, and then the saints, having thus been perfected, are prepared εἰς a work of service, and as a result of all this the body of Christ is built up. Westcott argued, "The change of preposition shews clearly that the three clauses (πρὸς...εἰς...εἰς...) are not coordinate."[17] Robinson a bit more cautiously wrote, "The phrase εἰς ἔργον διακονίας is most naturally taken as dependent on καταρτισμόν. The change of prepositions (πρὸς...εἰς) points in this direction, but is not in itself conclusive."[18]

Indeed it is not. Elsewhere in Paul we see prepositional phrases introduced with a mixture of prepositions but all referring equally back to the same thing. In Ephesians 1.5f, we have προορίσας ἡμᾶς <u>εἰς</u> υἱοθεσίαν διὰ Ἰησοῦ Χριστοῦ εἰς αὐτόν, <u>κατὰ</u> τὴν εὐδοκίαν τοῦ θελήματος αὐτοῦ, <u>εἰς</u> ἔπαινον δόξης τῆς χάριτος αὐτοῦ. The prepositional phrases introduced by εἰς, κατά, and then εἰς again all refer equally back to προορίσας ἡμᾶς (*having predestined us*). In Romans 3.25f we see nine prepositional phrases, three of which have the same relationship to the verb προέθετο. The relationship of the phrases may be represented as follows:

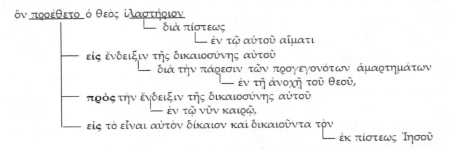

Clearly it is not the repetition of like prepositions or the variation in prepositions *per se* that informs us as to the grammatical hierarchy of the various phrases, but their substance. In the end, we do best to understand Ephesians 4.12 as did Chrysostom rather than to attempt to discern some sort of domino effect in the three prepositional phrases.

---

[17] Westcott, p. 63.

[18] Robinson, p. 182.

4.13 *until we all might attain unto the unity of the faith and of the knowledge of the Son of God, unto a mature man, unto a measure of the stature of the fullness of the Christ* The result of the perfecting of the saints, the work of ministry, the edification of the body, is to be a unity of the faith, a body wherein Jew and Gentile have come to be truly one, having attained a maturity commensurate with Christ. The maturity in view here is the corporate maturity. The mature man is the church, the one body, not the individual Christian. Once previously in this epistle, at 2.15, Paul spoke of the church as a man, though there he used the word ἄνθρωπος. But the imagery is familiar (*cf.* 1 Co 12.12–27). Of course the body as a whole cannot mature apart from individual Christians behaving as they ought, and accordingly the words *unto a measure of the stature of the fullness of the Christ* give meaning to the challenge to *walk worthily of your calling*.

4.14–15 *in order that we might be children no longer, tossed about and carried around by every wind of doctrine in the dice game of men, in trickery with the scheming of deception, but speaking truth in love, we might grow in every way unto him who is the head, Christ* Paul continues to move back and forth between discussion of the one body as a whole and the individual members who comprise that body. In verse 13, it was a plurality, *we all*, that came to be a singularity, *a mature man* (ἄνδρα τέλειον). But now in verse 14, the individuals are again in view, the goal being that we might no longer be *children* (νήπιοι, plural).[19] This really makes perfect sense inasmuch as the maturity of the one new man which is the church is dependent upon the ἐνέργειαν ἐν μέτρῳ ἑνὸς ἑκάστου μέρους, *the working in measure of each individual part* (4.16).

In the midst of his metaphor of the growing body, Paul inserts the imagery of a ship tossed about in a stormy sea. κλυδωνίζομαι (BDAG: "be tossed here and there by waves") is found at Isaiah 57.20 and Antiquities 9.239. The expression περιφερόμενοι παντὶ ἀνέμῳ (*carried about by every wind*) has a close parallel at Acts 27.15. Enroute to his present imprisonment, Paul himself had experienced this very phenomenon, and Luke described the effect of the storm upon the ship in words similar to those Paul uses: τῷ ἀνέμῳ ἐπιδόντες ἐφερόμεθα (*given over to the wind, we were carried along*). περιφερόμενοι and ἐφερόμεθα are both compounds of φέρω (*I carry*).

---

[19] BDAG, as well as Bertram in TDNT (v. 4, p. 912), indicates the word was used of children prior to puberty. Bertram says that it was generally used of "small children from 1 to 10," and mentions burial inscriptions in particular as evidence for this age range.

But Paul's imagery becomes yet more diverse. Having begun with a mature man in contrast to a child, and then having turned to a storm-tossed ship, he now enlists the imagery of a crooked dice game. The English word *cube* comes from the Greek κύβος, a *die*. The word Paul uses, κυβεία, was the word for games played with dice, games of chance. In Xenophon's Memorabilia, we read "To pray for gold or silver or sovereignty or any other such thing, was just like praying for a gamble (κυβείαν) or a fight or anything of which the result is obviously uncertain."[20] Then as now, these games were not always on the level. In a fragment of a play by Menander, lingering too long in life is compared to lingering too long in a city where there are thieves, dice games (κυβεῖαι), and amusements to which one will lose his money and come to ruin. That Paul has in mind not merely a dice game as an amusement, but a crooked game, is indicated by the ensuing language, ἐν πανουργίᾳ πρὸς τὴν μεθοδείαν τῆς πλάνης— *in trickery with the scheming of deception.* πανουργία is a compound of two stems, παν- (*all*) and ἐργ- (*work*). The resultant meaning was "ready to do anything," but was usually used with a negative connotation. Danker uses the word "rascally" to elaborate on the glosses "cunning, craftiness, trickery." μεθοδείαν also speaks of *crafty scheming*, and πλάνης is *deceit*.

So then, the gifts, *viz.*, the apostles, prophets, evangelists, and shepherds who are teachers, are given to the church so that it might become united and likened to a mature man rather than a child, that the saints might not be tossed about doctrinally like a ship in a stormy sea, that the saints might not be deceived like a man in a crooked dice game.

4.16 On συναρμολογούμενον (*being put together*), see the comments at 2.21.

4.17–24 The New Man
This therefore I say and testify in the Lord, that you must no longer walk just as the Gentiles also walk, in the emptiness of their mind, being darkened in their thoughts, alienated from the life of God on account of the ignorance that is in them, on account of the hardness of their hearts, who having become calloused gave themselves over to reckless impulsiveness to the practice of all uncleanness in covetousness. But you did not so learn Christ, if indeed you heard him and were taught in him, just as truth is in Jesus, regarding your former manner of life to put away from yourself the old man that is being destroyed according to the desires of deceit, and

---

[20] Xenophon, Memorabilia 1.3.2, Loeb vol. IV, p. 44–45, translated by E.C. Marchant.

to be renewed in the spirit of your mind, and to clothe yourself with the new man that has been created according to God in righteousness and holiness of truth.

As Paul urges his readers, Gentiles, to no longer walk as the Gentiles walk, he first reminds them of the lifestyle they have rejected and then encourages them to live as new men in Christ. The life they have rejected is futility. Desires are deceitful. Truth is in Christ.

The same is true today. The worldly life today is futility. We seek meaning in pleasure, education, career, and when we have acquired sufficient financial resources, we seek it again in pleasure. And yet we do not find complete satisfaction, and indeed, for many, the problems of life outweigh whatever fleeting satisfaction we may attain. Our desires prove to be "lusts of deceit." Hence the warnings, "be not deceived..." (1 Cor 6.9, *et al.*). So then we turn to alcohol, or some drug, or perhaps illicit sexual indulgence, for distraction and escape. But these do not address our problems, but rather increase them. Moreover, the initial pleasure that we found in such things, fleeting as it was, no longer provides even that measure of relief that it did at the first. And so more alcohol, a more dangerous drug, more perverse sexual stimulation is sought. But there is no true escape, only even greater pain. As in Ecclesiastes, all is vanity, all is futility. Desires are deceitful. Truth is in Christ.

Paul says, "you did not so learn Christ." Life in Christ is not merely forgiveness for past sins, but a new way to live. It is the point Paul develops more thoroughly in Romans 6 as Paul answers the question, "Shall we continue in sin?" And the answer is no, because you died to sin, indeed, were baptized into Christ's death so that you might be raised to walk with him in newness of life. Therefore, do not let your desires continue to govern you (Rom 6.12). Or as Paul will say it here, "Put away the old man that is according to the former manner of life." To "learn Christ" is not merely to learn about Christ, but to learn to live in accordance with the example and teaching of Christ.

Moreover, these changes would be necessary for Jews and Gentiles to become united in one body in a practical sense. The same could be said for many Jews, but Paul is writing to Gentiles whose lifestyles were then, as always, characterized by the ills associated with following after the lusts of men.

When Paul first began his admonition to them to walk worthily of their calling (4.1), he quickly veered off into an explanation of the means whereby the Lord would provide for their instruction in the will of God so that they, with all the saints, might indeed comprise a mature man in Christ.

Having concluded his discussion of the means whereby instruction in the unifying doctrine would be given, now in verse 17, Paul returns to take up again, in practical terms, the admonition to walk worthily. Paul is writing to Gentiles, and yet calls upon them not to walk as Gentiles walk. In our modern era of sensitivity, of decrying negative stereotypes, of avoiding saying anything negative about some particular culture, it may be hard for us to understand how Paul could be addressing Gentiles and yet so speak. But his audience needed not only to understand but to come to grips with the fact that their culture, yea their own heretofore lifestyle, was depraved. There was no value in soft-pedaling that fact. There was no value in affirming that lifestyle as having validity. Paul's words were direct, and tantamount to a messenger from God saying to us today, "Don't live as Americans live!" Indeed, our world is a world of people living according to our own lusts. And everything that Paul says hereafter is immediately applicable to us as we come to Christ out of this world.

4.17–18 *This therefore I say and testify in the Lord, that you must no longer walk just as the Gentiles also walk* (Τοῦτο οὖν λέγω καὶ μαρτύρομαι ἐν κυρίῳ, μηκέτι ὑμᾶς περιπατεῖν, καθὼς καὶ τὰ ἔθνη περιπατεῖ) The inferential conjunction οὖν is repeated (τοῦτο οὖν λέγω), but whereas in the first instance (4.1), Paul's admonition was stated positively—ἀξίως περιπατῆσαι (*walk worthily*)—it is now stated negatively: μηκέτι ὑμᾶς περιπατεῖν. As in English, so in Greek the subject of an infinitive is in an objective case. In Greek the accusative case is used. Here, accusative ὑμᾶς is the subject of περιπατεῖν. Blass supposed that the imperatival infinitive is found in only two passages in the New Testament, those being Romans 12.15 and Philippians 3.16.[21] But the infinitive περιπατεῖν clearly has an imperative force here, and this is not an unusual phenomenon in Greek. Whether this phenomenon is to be explained as the result of ellipsis, *i.e.*, a governing verb has been omitted (Blass, p. 196, §389), or not (Moulton, Prolegomena, p. 179, Robertson, p. 944), the use of the infinitive as an imperative is familiar to readers of non-Biblical Greek. But it is easy to think of the expression as being elliptical, λέγω καὶ μαρτύρομαι ἐν κυρίῳ, μηκέτι ὑμᾶς περιπατεῖν for λέγω καὶ μαρτύρομαι ἐν κυρίῳ ὅτι δεῖ μηκέτι ὑμᾶς περιπατεῖν.

---

[21] Blass, Debrunner, p. 196, §389.

As mentioned in connection with 4.1, Paul repeatedly instructs his readers in their walk. His use of περιπατέω (*walk*) is frequent enough to constitute a theme in Ephesians. First, there is the reminder of the Gentiles' former walk, or manner of life, in Ephesians 2.2, followed by the assertion in 2.10 that God foreordained that his people should walk in good works, a hint of what lies ahead in Paul's epistle. But it is not until chapter four that Paul focuses his audience's attention on that new walk. There in verse one, he calls upon them to walk worthily of their calling in Christ (Eph 4.1), and after a discussion of the means whereby the Lord has provided for instruction in that walk that the goal of unity in the body might be achieved, Paul reiterates the call, but this time in negative form: *"no longer walk just as the Gentiles also walk"* (4.17). Rather they are to *"walk in love"*(5.2) and *"as children of light"*(5.8). In general, he says to them, *"watch carefully how you walk"*(5.15).

in the emptiness of their mind (ἐν ματαιότητι τοῦ νοὸς αὐτῶν) ματαιότητι itself means *futility*, or *emptiness*, and is used in this sense by Paul in Romans 8.20. Peter also used the word in this sense, juxtaposing the lofty sound of false teachers' words with their emptiness (2 Pt 2.18). It is the word so often used in the Septuagint in Ecclesiastes where a number of English translations use the word *vanity*. Psalm 93.11 in the Septuagint (94.11 in Hebrew and in English) uses the related adjective μάταιος. The passage reads, κύριος γινώσκει τοὺς διαλογισμοὺς τῶν ἀνθρώπων ὅτι εἰσὶν μάταιοι, *The Lord knows the thoughts of men, that they are empty.*

But it is also possible that we should think of another use of the word and its cognates in the Septuagint where it stood specifically for the emptiness of idolatry, the futility of serving gods that were nothing.[22] The similarity of Ephesians 4.17–18 to Romans 1.21 may also suggest that idolatry is the particular futility in view. We see the words ματαιότητι (*futility*) and ἐσκοτωμένοι (*darkened*) in Ephesians 4.17–18, and in Romans 1.21, we see ἐματαιώθησαν (*were made futile*) and ἐσκοτίσθη (*was darkened*). In Romans, Paul spoke of their senseless heart (ἡ ἀσύνετος αὐτῶν καρδία), and in Ephesians, he says they are darkened in mind

---

[22] καὶ ἐπορεύθησαν ὀπίσω τῶν ματαίων καὶ ἐματαιώθησαν καὶ ὀπίσω τῶν ἐθνῶν τῶν περικύκλῳ αὐτῶν (LXX: 4 Kings 17.15, cf. 17.16); ἐπορεύθησαν ὀπίσω τῶν ματαίων καὶ ἐματαιώθησαν (Jer 2.5); διὰ τί παρώργισάν με ἐν τοῖς γλυπτοῖς αὐτῶν καὶ ἐν ματαίοις ἀλλοτρίοις; (Jer. 8.19, *"why did they provoke me with their carved images and foreign vanities?"*); ἵνα τί ἀγαπᾶτε ματαιότητα καὶ ζητεῖτε ψεῦδος (Ps. 4.3).

(τῇ διανοίᾳ), similar thoughts though expressed in different words. In Romans, the context is manifestly about the futility of idolatry.

Earlier, Paul described Gentiles apart from Christ as ἀπηλλοτριωμένοι τῆς πολιτείας τοῦ Ἰσραὴλ, *alienated from the polity of Israel* (2.12). Now, Paul uses the same word, ἀπηλλοτριωμένοι (*alienated*), to say that Gentiles (those not in Christ) are alienated from the life that is of God. This is on account of the ignorance that is in them, and that on account of the πώρωσιν of their hearts.

In the KJV, πώρωσιν is translated "blindness." There is little doubt that πώρωσιν indicates an insensibility, but the metaphor by which that meaning is conveyed is in doubt: Is it insensibility due to blindness, or is it insensibility due to a hardening?[23]

The verb πωρόω, used in Mark 6.52, 8.17, Romans 11.7, and 2 Corinthians 3.14, is *petrify*. Hippocrates used the verb in discussing kidney stones which form when impurities solidify into something that at first is small but then "grows and hardens (πωροῦται)."[24] The noun πώρωσις is found at Mark 3.5, John 12.40, and Romans 11.25, as well as here in Ephesians 4.18. Hippocrates uses the noun for the calcification/ossification where there has been a break in a bone. In discussing the proper positioning of the heel when setting a broken leg, he notes that if bones are not in their natural positions during the healing process, the πωρώσιες (*calcification*) will be weaker.[25] In speaking of the healing of a particular type of collarbone break, he says, "the shoulder and arm left to themselves will bring the fragments together. Any ordinary dressing will suffice and callus (πωρώσιος) will form in a few days."[26]

However, see Joseph Armitage Robinson, p. 264ff. Based on the use of the verb by Athenaeus, Robinson argued that insensibility, not hardness, is the point of Paul's statement in Ephesians 4.19. According to Athenaeus, Nymphas of Heracleia described a tyrant named Dionysis as being so fat that he had difficulty breathing and would be in danger of suffocating when he fell into a deep sleep. On such occasions, his physicians would

---

[23] See the discussion found in four letters to the editor of Theology, 69 (69:547 Jan. '66, Lord Fisher of Lambeth, p. 25–6; 69:549 Mar. '66, Barnabas Lindars p. 121; 69:550 Apr. '66, Colville of Culross, p. 171; 69:551 May '66, C. H. Dodd p. 223–4.

[24] Concerning Airs, Waters, Places, 9.

[25] On Fractures, 23. On the form πωρώσιες, see Smyth 268 D. 1 (p. 67).

[26] On Joints, 15; translation by E.T. Withington, LCL, 1927, p. 243. On the form πωρώσιος, See Smyth 268 D. 1 (p. 67).

insert long needles into his sides in an attempt to rouse him. But "up to a certain point his flesh was so callous (πεπωρωμένης) by reason of the fat, that it never felt the needles."[27] Here, the meaning seems to be lacking in sensation rather than hardened.

Again, it is clear that Paul's point is ultimately that Gentiles have largely come to be characterized by hearts that are insensible. It is only the mechanics involved as the metaphor is conceived by Paul that is unclear.

4.19 *who having become calloused gave themselves over to reckless impulsiveness to the practice of all uncleanness in covetousness* (οἵτινες ἀπηλγηκότες ἑαυτοὺς παρέδωκαν τῇ ἀσελγείᾳ εἰς ἐργασίαν ἀκαθαρσίας πάσης ἐν πλεονεξίᾳ) ἀπηλγηκότες is a perfect participle of ἀπαλγέω, for which BDAG offers two meanings. First, there is the possibility that it means "become callous" so as to be "dead to feeling." Alternatively, it is suggested the idea might mean "be despondent," a related idea but having more to do with the psyche. The hopelessness of Ephesians 2.12 is offered in support of this alternative. And it may be noted that some copyists apparently understood the meaning to be "despondent" as evidenced by their substitution of the word ἀπηλπικότες (perfect participle of ἀπελπίζω, *I despair*, from ἀπό and ἐλπίζω) for ἀπηλγηκότες.[28] Polybius can be cited for both uses of ἀπαλγέω,[29] illustrating the fact that we must look at the immediate context rather than general lexicography in order to determine the meaning here. If we understand πώρωσιν in verse 19 to mean *hardening*, we do best to understand ἀπηλγηκότες as meaning *having become callous*.

ἀσέλγεια, rendered *reckless impulsiveness* in the foregoing translation, is of uncertain etymology. It and its cognates were variously explained in the 12th century work, *Etymologicon Magnum*. On the one hand, ἀσέλγεια was explained as being derived from Selge, "a city of Cilicia, whose citizens are temperate," and so with the alpha privative, ἀσέλγεια was thought to indicate the opposite character.[30] ἀσελγεῖς was explained similarly: "Selgoi, a people most temperate; whence therefore ἀσελγεῖς,

---

[27] Athenaeus, The Deipnosophists, 549, transl. by C.D. Yonge.

[28] ἀπηλπικότες is found in 𝔓⁹⁹, D, and a few other mss, and ἀφηλπικότες, alternate spelling of the same word, is found in F and G. To my eye, 𝔓⁴⁹ seems likely to be another ms where the reading was ἀπηλπικότες. A lacuna leaves only the first five letters visible and the fifth letter is very unclear, but seems more likely to be π than γ.

[29] Polybius 16.12.7 has ἀπηλγηκυίας ἐστὶ ψυχῆς, roughly, *numbskulled*, or *thick-headed*. But Polybius 1.35.5 has τὰς ἀπηλγηκυίας ψυχὰς for *the souls having despaired*.

[30] ἀπὸ τῆς Σέλγης πόλεως Κιλικίας, ἧς τινος πολῖται σώφρονες (EM, *s.v.* ἀσέλγεια).

those not temperate."[31] On the other hand, ἀσελγής was said to be derived either from Selge, "a city of Pisidia, where the people were living maliciously,"[32] with a prefixed alpha that is said to intensify the meaning, or alternatively, from θέλγω (*enchant, be a witch*) again assuming the prefixed alpha is an intensifier. Craig Gibson cites an early papyrus indicating that the word came from the name of a city in Italy.[33] Looking in an entirely different direction, Donaldson cited Hesychius and supposed ἀσέλγεια shares a root with "σελαγέω ('to lighten up, to illume') so that ἀσελγής primarily means 'dark, dirty, foul, unclean, defiled.'"[34]

As to its meaning, although in several NT contexts, ἀσέλγεια seems especially to have a sexual connotation, the word itself is not limited to this. According to Trench, it is "wanton lawless insolence."[35] Demosthenes, having received an unprovoked blow to the head from a wealthy bully named Meidias, prepared a speech which began with a reminder of Meidias' reputation for ἀσέλγειαν and ὕβριν[36] (*arrogant insolence*; think of *hubris*).

As did Demosthenes, so also Plutarch used the word in a context where insolent behavior was manifested in an unprovoked blow. He used it of the conduct of Alcibides, who "once gave Hipponicus a blow with his fist…not that he had any quarrel with him, or was a prey to anger, but simply for the joke of the thing, on a wager with some companions. The wanton (ἀσελγείας) deed was soon noised about the city, and everybody was indignant, as was natural."[37] We see this behavior in our world today. In recent years, there have been news reports of teens in various cities violently assaulting strangers as a game, in an attempt to knock them out

---

[31] Σέλγοι, ἔθνος σωφρονέστατον· ἀσελγεῖς οὖν ἐντεῦθεν, οἱ μὴ σώφρονες (EM, *s.v.* ἀσελγεῖς).

[32] ὅτι Σέλγη πόλις ἐστὶ τῆς Πισιδίας, ὅπου κακῶς ἔζων οἱ ἄνθρωποι (EM, *s.v.* ἀσελγής).

[33] In P. Lond. 179, someone commenting on Demosthenes, likely writing near the beginning of the 2nd century, said (as translated by Gibson), "The Selgoi are a people of Italy, just and reverent; So those who overstep justice would naturally be called *aselgeis* (un-Selgoi-like)." The Greek text, as quoted by Gibson, is Σέλγοι ἔθνος ἐστὶν ἐπὶ τῆς Ἰταλίας, δίκαιον καὶ ὅσιον· οἱ οὖν παραβαίνοντες τὸ δίκαιον εἰκότως ἂν κληθεῖεν ἀσελγεῖς. Craig A. Gibson, Interpreting a Classic: Demosthenes and His Ancient Commentators, University of California Press, 2002, p. 203.

[34] Donaldson, John William, The New Cratylus, 4th ed., Longmans, Green, and Co., 1868, p. 692.

[35] Trench, Synonyms, p. 56.

[36] Demosthenes 21.1, against Meidias.

[37] Plutarch, Alcibiades 8.1. Loeb, transl. by Bernadotte Perrin.

cold with one blow. This sort of mindless disregard for humanity, even for basic rules of decent behavior, plagues our society.

Another occurrence of ἀσέλγεια is found in Josephus. About the time that Paul was preaching in Macedonia and Achaia (Acts 17–18), there was a disturbing event in Jerusalem during the Days of Unleavened Bread. Josephus reports that tens of thousands of Jews died as they attempted to flee the temple, crushed to death in the narrow passageways through which they fled. The panicked worshipers had supposed they were being set upon by the Roman soldiers sent as reinforcements by Cumanus, predecessor to Felix as procurator. He had sent the reinforcements because he feared an uprising might be imminent. This whole affair began when the Jews became outraged by the behavior of one of the Roman soldiers routinely stationed in the temple porticoes during the Jews' annual feasts. As recounted in Jewish Wars, on the fourth day of this particular feast, "one of the soldiers having pulled up his raiment and having bent over shamefully turned his backside to the Jews and made a sound in accordance with his posture."[38] As recounted in Antiquities, "he displayed his genitals to the crowd."[39] Josephus described the soldier's conduct as ἀσέλγεια.[40] It is not difficult to think of examples of similar conduct in our society. This is the world out of which Gentile Christians were coming. This is the world out of which we come to Christ.

So then ἀσέλγεια is conduct lacking in restraint, conduct that disregards the concerns of others or of morality in general, and is not limited to sexual licentiousness. While insolence may not be especially in view at Ephesians 4.19, the lack of restraint Paul has in mind does seem to go beyond lack of sexual restraint. Those who have given themselves up to ἀσέλγεια have done so to work all uncleanness in greediness.

On ἀκαθαρσία, see the comments on 5.3.

4.20 *you did not so learn Christ* a simple and pointed affirmation that Paul's readers learned a different way of life as they came to Christ.

4.21–24 The gist of this section is that just as truth is in Jesus, those who are his put on a new man that is created in things of truth, and they put away the old man associated with deceitful lusts.

The section is built around three infinitives: ἀποθέσθαι (*to put away from*

---

[38] Josephus, Wars 2.224.

[39] Josephus, Antiquities, 20.108.

[40] Josephus, Antiquities, 20.112.

yourself), ἀνανεοῦσθαι (*to be renewed*), and ἐνδύσασθαι (*to be clothed with*, or *to put on*). A question arises concerning the function of these infinitives. Are they to be understood as infinitives, functioning as objects of the verb ἐδιδάχθητε (*you were taught*)? Or are they to be understood as imperatives?

If we understand them to be objects of the verb ἐδιδάχθητε, each infinitive serves to explain part of what Paul's readers had been taught. The meaning is, you were taught to put away the old man, to be renewed in the spirit of your mind, to put on the new man.[41]

If we understand them to function as imperatives, then we would read the whole section as an if/then construction, a protasis containing the condition (if you were taught) followed by an apodosis containing the commands (then put away, etc.). So the translation, abridged, would run, "If you heard him and were taught in him (just as truth is in Jesus), then put away the old man, be renewed in the spirit of your mind, put on the new man."[42]

Certainly it is true that the Greek infinitive was at times used as an imperative.[43] As noted above, we see an example of such (though in a

---

[41] Lincoln (p. 283*f*) discusses three distinct meanings that could be indicated by the infinitives, assuming they are not to be regarded as imperatives. We can summarize them as follows: The infinitives may be final ("you were taught so that you might put away, etc."), they may be consecutive ("you were taught such that you did put away, etc."), or they may be epexegetical ("you were taught to put away, etc."). It is this last meaning that is advocated in the present commentary.

[42] I think there is some confusion in the various commentaries about what this passage would mean if we suppose Paul intended to use the infinitives as imperatives. Alford speaks of the infinitives as having "an imperative force," but interprets the passage as meaning they were taught to do these things, which really makes them infinitives functioning as objects of the verb ἐδιδάχθητε, just as if they were accusative nouns. The fact is, in a logical sense, there is an imperative force involved in the very act of teaching conduct, and thus the passage will yield a logical imperative regardless of what we think of the significance of the infinitives. But that is not the same thing as an infinitive used as a grammatical imperative. Again, when some commentators speak of infinitives as imperatives, they have in mind infinitives of indirect discourse, meaning an infinitive that follows and completes a finite verb of speech, desire, will, etc., explaining what was spoken, desired, willed, etc. So for example, 1 Tim 2:8 (βούλομαι οὖν προσεύχεσθαι τοὺς ἄνδρας), Mk 6:39 (ἐπέταξεν αὐτοῖς ἀνακλῖναι πάντας). But in these examples, the infinitive is not a *grammatical* imperative. There may be a logical imperative, but grammatically, the infinitive is simply the object of the finite verb. However here in Eph 4.22, it is not that logical imperative that is at issue. The question is whether or not the infinitives themselves function as *grammatical* imperatives, as does the infinitive in Phil 3.16 (πλὴν εἰς ὃ ἐφθάσαμεν, τῷ αὐτῷ στοιχεῖν).

[43] See the discussion of χαίρειν in the comments on 1:2. Also, see Smyth, p. 448, §2013. For NT examples, see Moulton, Prolegomena, p. 179, and Robertson, A Grammar, p. 943f.

prohibition) in verse 17, unless we regard the expression μηκέτι ὑμᾶς περιπατεῖν as elliptical.

But in the immediate context of verses 21–24, where Paul is speaking of what his readers have already done, namely having put off the old man and having put on the new man, the stronger argument can be made for taking the infinitives not as imperatives but as objects of ἐδιδάχθητε. They were taught to put off the old man and put on the new man, and this they did. That putting off the old man and putting on the new man was something they had already done is established by the similar passage in Colossians 3.9 where Paul writes, "Lie not one to another, having put off the old man with his practices, and having put on the new man that is being renewed unto knowledge..."[44]

Finally, it is important to see the contrast between the truth that is in Jesus and the deceit of walking in lusts. This contrast underpins the whole point about what Paul's readers had been taught. Because truth is in Jesus and walking in lust is deceit, they should put on the things associated with truth. We might summarize as follows so as to highlight the words *truth* and *deceit*: "You were taught, just as *truth* is in Jesus, to put away the things associated with *deceit*, and to put on the things being created in holiness of the *truth*!"

On εἴ γε (*if indeed*) see the comments on 3.2.

4.25–5.5   Practical Instructions for Holy Ones

Wherefore putting away the lie, speak truth each one with his neighbor, because we are members of one another. In your anger, do not sin. Let not the sun set on your anger. Neither give place to the Devil. The one who steals, let him no longer steal, but rather let him labor, working with his hands that which is good in order that he might have something to give to the one who has need. Do not let any vile word come out of your mouth, but rather what is good for edification as needed that it might give grace to those who hear. And do not grieve the holy Spirit of God, by which you were sealed unto a day of redemption. All bitterness and wrath and anger and clamor and denigrating speech, let them be taken away from you, with everything evil. Be kind one to another, compassionate, forgiving one another just as God also in Christ forgave you. Therefore as beloved children, be imitators of

---

[44] For a more thorough discussion of various interpretations of 4.20–24, see Hoehner, pp. 593–602.

God and walk in love just as Christ loved us and gave himself on behalf of you as an offering and a sacrifice to God as a pleasing aroma. But fornication and every uncleanness or covetousness, let it be unnamed among you just as is appropriate for saints; also shameful talk and foolish talk or risqué witticisms which are not appropriate, but rather thanksgiving. For this you know, knowing that every fornicator or unclean person or coveteous person, who is an idolator, does not have an inheritance in the kingdom of Christ and of God.

Paul begins to talk about the practical implications of walking worthily of our calling, taking direct aim at the kinds of misconduct typical of a society estranged from God in the first century, which are the same as in every century.

The first two specific admonitions are introduced by means of statements from the OT, and in each case, Paul elaborates with an explanatory statement of his own. It is worth noting that even though Paul is writing to Gentile Christians, in quoting the Jewish scriptures Paul assumes familiarity with them, as he also does in other letters. Christianity was taught to Gentiles not as a new religion, but as the culmination of all that was contained in the Old Testament. We conclude that Gentiles who became Christians were taught the Old Testament scriptures as part of their foundational instruction.

4.25 *Wherefore putting away the lie, speak truth each one with his neighbor, because we are members of one another* (Διὸ ἀποθέμενοι τὸ ψεῦδος λαλεῖτε ἀλήθειαν ἕκαστος μετὰ τοῦ πλησίον αὐτοῦ, ὅτι ἐσμὲν ἀλλήλων μέλη) Διὸ *(wherefore)* connects the present thought with the one immediately preceding. In effect, Paul says the new man has been created in holiness of truth, and consistent with that, we must speak truth. In addition to the logical connection established by the word διό, there is a thematic connection in the vocabulary, the use of the word ἀποτίθημι (*put away*). Just as they were taught *to put away* (ἀποθέσθαι) the old man of deceit, they must now be about the business of putting this into practice, *putting away* (ἀποθέμενοι) the lie.

πλησίον is an adverb meaning *near*, used substantively in the NT (with the exception of Jn 4.5) for one who is near, *i.e., neighbor.* μετὰ τοῦ πλησίον αὐτοῦ is "with the [one] near of him," i.e., *with his neighbor.*

At Zechariah 8.16, the Septuagint has λαλεῖτε ἀλήθειαν ἕκαστος πρὸς τὸν πλησίον αὐτοῦ. Paul's quotation of the passage diverges from the Septuagint in that Paul replaces πρὸς τὸν with μετὰ τοῦ, but the meaning is the same. Hoehner thinks Paul's Greek better represents the Hebrew than does the Septuagint.[45]

The passage in Zechariah is a broad admonition to integrity in interpersonal speech and in judicial proceedings inasmuch as falsehoods are injurious. Paul's explanation as to why we must speak truth is that *"we are members of one another."* Paul particularly has in view conversations among and interactions between God's people, not because we have no obligation to speak truth with others, but because Paul's admonition is rooted in the unity of Jew and Gentile in one body, as discussed in chapter two.

4.26 *In your anger, do not sin* (ὀργίζεσθε καὶ μὴ ἁμαρτάνετε) This is verbatim from Psalm 4.5 as translated in the Septuagint. Perowne translated the Hebrew, "Tremble and sin not," and then explained, "TREMBLE *i.e.* before *God*, not before me, and sin not against *Him*."[46] Meyer also saw the LXX rendering as at variance with the Hebrew, but interpreted the psalm as David's demand that his enemies should "tremble on account of their iniquities towards him, the favorite of God, and not further sin."[47] However, Delitzsch reckoned the LXX to have it right. He reckoned the words to be a warning to Absalom's partisans, "if ye will be angry be aware of sinning."[48]

If we understand the second stich to be parallel to the first, the first part of each stich indicating the internal state of mind and the second part of each stich indicating the resulting stance toward God, the KJV seems to have it about right: "Stand in awe" as you "commune with your own heart"; "be still" and "sin not." This would be in keeping with Perowne's take on the passage.

Setting aside the meaning of Psalm 4.5, ὀργίζεσθε can hardly be taken in its own right to mean anything like "stand in awe" or "tremble before God." Paul takes the thought suggested by the LXX and, unrelated to the context in Psalm 4, makes his own point. This is evident inasmuch as he adds the thought, *"let not the sun go down upon your wrath."*

Imperative ὀργίζεσθε in Ephesians 4.26 may be understood as concessive, "be angry (if you must)."[49] In John 2.19, the imperative λύσατε ("de-

---

[45] Hoehner, p. 616.

[46] Perowne, p. 128.

[47] Meyer, 478, n. 2.

[48] Delitzsch, p. 114.

[49] Zerwick, Analysis, vol. 2, p. 587

stroy this temple") obviously must be understood in this manner. Meyer (following Bengel) noted that it is especially where one imperative follows another, as in ὀργίζεσθε καὶ μὴ ἁμαρτάνετε, that the force of the imperative may accrue only to the second verb, and paraphrased, "in anger do not fall into transgression."[50]

let not the sun set on your wrath (ὁ ἥλιος μὴ ἐπιδυέτω ἐπὶ [τῷ] παροργισμῷ ὑμῶν) The point of Paul's words is clear enough—do not carry a grudge. If you get angry with someone, resolve the matter quickly. But it is possible that there is an allusion to the ordinance that the corpse of a condemned man not be left hanging on a tree overnight (Dt 21.23). Philo paraphrased the legislation, "let not the sun set on those who have been hung on a stake, but having been taken down, let them be buried before sunset" (μὴ ἐπιδυέτω ὁ ἥλιος ἀνεσκολοπισμένοις, ἀλλ' ἐπικρυπτέσθωσαν γῇ πρὸ δύσεως καθαιρεθέντες).[51] Righteous anger had inflicted the ultimate penalty, but by sundown, it was to be over; the body was buried. If Philo's μὴ ἐπιδυέτω ὁ ἥλιος (identical to Paul's ὁ ἥλιος μὴ ἐπιδυέτω except in word order) was a common way of stating the legislation in Deuteronomy (and the language of Joshua 8.29, καὶ ἐπιδύνοντος τοῦ ἡλίου, is further evidence that it was), given that Paul has twice borrowed Old Testament language immediately prior to this, it would not be too far-fetched to think that Paul has done so again here.

More likely, however, we should simply understand that it was a proverbial expression. We see it in Deuteronomy 24.15 [52] with reference to paying a poor man his wages, as well as in Plutarch, who speaks of the Pythagoreans who resolved their occasional differences πρὶν ἢ τὸν ἥλιον δῦναι "before the setting of the sun."[53]

4.27 *Neither give place to the Devil* Continuing to be angry, holding a grudge, is to give place to the devil. When Cain was disconsolate be-

---

[50] Meyer, 478. See also Robertson, 949.

[51] Philo, *Special Laws 3.152.*

[52] If it is a proverb, it did not uniquely belong to Greeks of the hellenistic age, for the LXX literally represents the Hebrew of Dt. 24:15.

[53] Plutarch, De fraterno amore, 17, εἶτα μιμεῖσθαι τοὺς Πυθαγορικούς, οἳ γένει μηθὲν προσήκοντες 6 ἀλλὰ κοινοῦ λόγου μετέχοντες, εἴ ποτε προαχθεῖεν εἰς λοιδορίαν ὑπ' ὀργῆς, πρὶν ἢ τὸν ἥλιον δῦναι, τὰς δεξιὰς ἐμβαλόντες ἀλλήλοις καὶ ἀσπασάμενοι διελύοντο. Then we ought to imitate the Pythagoreans, who, not being related by race but partaking of a common discipline, if they should happen to be led by anger to berating speech, before the setting of the sun, they were parting, grasping one another's right hand and saluting one another.

cause his offering had not met with God's approval, he was warned, "sin is crouching at the door." When we allow our mood to have its way with us, rather than the other way around, we are giving place to the devil.

4.28 *The one who steals, let him no longer steal, but rather let him labor, working with his [own] hands that which is good in order that he might have something to give to the one who has need* (ὁ κλέπτων μηκέτι κλεπτέτω, μᾶλλον δὲ κοπιάτω ἐργαζόμενος ταῖς [ἰδίαις] χερσὶν τὸ ἀγαθόν, ἵνα ἔχῃ μεταδιδόναι τῷ χρείαν ἔχοντι)   ὁ κλέπτων is *the one who steals*, or simply, *the thief.* Concerning the present participle κλέπτων, Lincoln's remark is probably on the mark: "with the definite article the present participle virtually becomes a noun and has a timeless force."[54] The primary significance of the present tense is not *present time*, but *kind of action*, namely, ongoing action. Outside of the indicative mood, we can almost make that statement without including the qualifier "primary." So we need not suppose Paul's admonition here indicates that some of the brethren were actively stealing even as Paul writes this letter, although we can not exclude that possibility. But the admonition may be viewed as one of several that those coming from the world must heed: Fornicators, no longer fornicate; liars, no longer lie; thieves, no longer steal. Paul's admonition neither assumes the activity has ceased or continues, but merely acknowledges that what is a way of life (hence the present tense) among some cannot be a way of life for the new man created in righteousness and holiness of truth.

4.29 *Do not let any vile word come out of your mouth, but rather what is good for edification as needed that it might give grace to those who hear* (πᾶς λόγος σαπρὸς ἐκ τοῦ στόματος ὑμῶν μὴ ἐκπορευέσθω, ἀλλὰ εἴ τις ἀγαθὸς πρὸς οἰκοδομὴν τῆς χρείας, ἵνα δῷ χάριν τοῖς ἀκούουσιν)   Third person Greek imperatives defy the conventions of English grammar. We routinely translate them by means of the word "let." *Do not let any vile word come out of your mouth.* πᾶς...μὴ is effectively *not any.* Singular στόματος (*mouth*) is used with plural ὑμῶν (*of you = your*).

Hoehner argues that inasmuch as a prohibition utilizing a present tense imperative "has the force of cessation of activity in progress,"[55] we

---

[54] p. 303.

[55] Hoehner, p. 629, citing Wallace, p. 724. But Wallace rightly qualifies his comment with the modifier, "frequently."On the same page, Wallace notes that "The present prohibition can also have the force of a general precept. This kind of prohibition really makes no comment about whether the action is going on or not." As an example, Wallace cites Eph 6.4

should understand Paul to be telling his audience to stop doing some-thing rather than merely warning them to avoid doing something, the implication being that they were using unwholesome speech. It very well may be that they were, but the distinction between the present imperative and the aorist subjunctive in prohibition is overblown. It is a distinction that would usually hold true if a speaker intended to indicate one idea or the other ("stop doing what you are doing" vs. "don't start doing what you aren't doing"), but it is not necessary to suppose that a writer assumed one or the other every time he wrote a prohibition. In those instances when nothing is assumed about the current activity of the audience, a writer might choose either form of prohibition.

The distinction Hoehner makes is based on the fundamental idea of the tenses and moods, specifically the aspect of the present tense as op-posed to that of the aorist tense, and the contingency associated with the subjunctive mood. The present tense is a tense of ongoing activity, where-as the nature of the activity (ongoing or not) is undefined when the aor-ist tense is used (*aorist* from ἀόριστος, *indeterminate, indefinite*). A negated present imperative is the natural construction if a writer has in mind an ongoing activity and intends to prohibit its continuance. A negated aorist subjunctive avoids implying the activity is currently ongoing and merely posits the possibility of the activity and prohibits it. Accordingly, the aor-ist construction is an appropriate choice when a writer wants to warn against possible future activity that is not now known to be occurring.

But the semantic difference between the negated aorist subjunctive and the negated present imperative has been exaggerated in not a few grammars, including some notable ones.[56] Specifically, it has been said that the present imperative is used in prohibition when the intent is "stop what you are doing," and the aorist subjunctive is used in prohibi-tion when the intent is "do not start doing it." For a less simplistic but more accurate analysis, see McKay (NovT 27 [1985] 201–26) Naylor (Clas-

---

where the present imperative prohibition μὴ παροργίζετε (*do not provoke*) does not imply that Paul's readers were in fact provoking their children to wrath. Wallace concludes his discussion of prohibition expressed by the present imperative with this spot-on comment: "In many of the NT letters the force of a particular present prohibition will not always be focused on the cessation of an activity in progress. It is *not*, then, safe to say that when an author uses the present prohibition the audience is being indicted for not heeding this com-mand. Other factors—especially the overall context and *Sitz im Leben* of the book—must be taken into account" (p. 725).

[56] Robertson , p. 851, Moulton, p. 240, D&M, etc.

sical Review 19, [1905] 26–30), and Mounce (p. 309), Wallace (p. 715), or Fanning (325–388).

If we keep in mind the fact that the present tense is fundamentally characterized by ongoing action and the aorist tense is used without defining kind of action, we will discern what distinction there is. Given that the present tense is fundamentally characterized by ongoing action, a negated present imperative verb could be used to prohibit the continuation of an activity that is already in progress (e.g., Jn 8.11), but it could also be used to prohibit habitually engaging in some activity though the audience is not presently engaging in that activity. In 1 Peter 4.15, there is no need to suppose the readers were presumed to be suffering already as murderers, thieves, evildoers, and meddlers in other men's matters, even though a present imperative is used in the prohibition: μὴ γάρ τις ὑμῶν πασχέτω ὡς φονεὺς ἢ κλέπτης ἢ κακοποιὸς ἢ ὡς ἀλλοτριεπίσκοπος·

Not only does Paul prohibit vile and abusive speech, but he also charges us to speak constructively—*but rather what is good for edification as necessary that it might give grace to those who hear.*

4.30 *And do not grieve the Holy Spirit of God, by which you were sealed unto a day of redemption* The ideas of redemption and sealing were previously introduced in 1.7 and 1.13 respectively. As noted in the comments at 1.13, God's inheritance is sealed by the Holy Spirit, thus identifying it as his. Here, as Paul describes the life of the new man that has been created in righteousness and holiness of truth, having been sealed by the Holy Spirit, in that connection he says, "Do not grieve the Holy Spirit of God."

4.31 *All bitterness and wrath and anger and clamor and denigrating speech, let them be taken away from you, with everything evil (*πᾶσα πικρία καὶ θυμὸς καὶ ὀργὴ καὶ κραυγὴ καὶ βλασφημία ἀρθήτω ἀφ' ὑμῶν σὺν πάσῃ κακίᾳ) Perhaps *blasphemy* (βλασφημία) is popularly regarded primarily as speech against God. But speaking in a denigrating way about one's fellow man is also considered βλασφημία. See the use of the verb βλασφημέω in Rom 3.8, 1 Cor 10.30, and Tit 3.2.

4.32 *Be kind one to another, compassionate, forgiving one another just as God also in Christ forgave you.* Notice that God's forgiveness as compelling their own is mentioned in Ephesians rather than in the parallel exhortation in Colossians (3.13). This is natural in that it is in Ephesians (chapters 1–3) that Paul so thoroughly developed the thought of forgiveness on account of the great grace of God in Christ Jesus.

"Forgiving" represents the verb χαρίζομαι. In the gospels, ἀφίημι is used for forgiving sin, but Paul prefers χαρίζομαι in all his letters. In the story of the sinful woman at Simon's house (Luke 7), the two words have a nexus in viewing forgiveness of sin as a cancellation of debt (7.42f where χαρίζομαι is used, and 7.47ff where ἀφίημι is used).[57] But Paul's use of χαρίζομαι is probably due to its etymological connection with χάρις, the word so prominent in Paul's writings. Here in Ephesians, χάρις is God's *grace* in Christ (1.6–7, 2.5–8), God's *favor* in choosing Paul as a messenger to the Gentiles (3.2–8), and the *grace* with which we are to speak to others (4.29). Forgiveness is a *gift* rooted in kindness and compassion.

Though primarily a reflexive pronoun, ἑαυτοῖς is here (as also in the parallel Col 3.13, and in Eph 5.19 and Col 3.16) used for the reciprocal pronoun. The reciprocal pronoun is used in the beginning of this sentence and its repetition would have created a nice symmetry. It appears, however, that variety trumped symmetry.

The manuscript tradition reflects a tension between understanding Paul to be pointedly speaking of Christ's sacrificial death on behalf of *the Gentiles*, or, on the other hand, speaking of Christ's sacrificial death on behalf of *us all*. This is seen in the three statements, *God in Christ forgave you/us*, *Christ loved you/us*, and *gave himself on behalf of you/us*, all found in 4.32–5.2.

In 4.32, there is strong support for the reading ἐχαρίσατο ὑμῖν (*forgave you*, 𝔓[46], ℵ A, F, G, *et al.*), but there is also strong support for the reading ἐχαρίσατο ἡμῖν (*forgave us*, 𝔓[49] B, D, and many others including the bulk of the Byzantine manuscripts).

𝔓[49], Eph 4.32–5.1a. The critical apparatus in UBS5 cites 𝔓[49] as supporting the reading ἡμῖν. In this image, the bottom line picks up with the latter part of the word ἐχαρίσατο. The line appears to read ρίσατο ἡμ[ῖ]ν γίνεσθ]ε οὖν μιμηταὶ τοῦ θεοῦ "(θεοῦ is abbreviated as θΥ)" before dissolving in shreds. Beinecke Rare Book and Manuscript Library, Yale University.

In 5.2, both Vaticanus and Alexandrinus have ἠγάπησεν ὑμᾶς (*loved you*). So also Codex Sinaiticus originally had ἠγάπησεν ὑμᾶς (*loved you*),

---

[57] Philo used χαρίζομαι when he spoke of "forgiving (χαριζομένων) fellow tribe members their debts in the seventh year." τὰ δάνεια ἑβδόμῳ ἔτει τοῖς ὁμοφύλοις χαριζομένων (Spec. Leg. 2.39).

but a scribe changed the reading to ἡμᾶς (*us*). However, ἡμᾶς (*us*) is the reading found in 𝔓⁴⁶, as well as in D, F, G, and the bulk of the Byzantine manusripts. The reading in 𝔓⁴⁹ is indiscernable due to a lacuna, a vertical tear in the middle of the page.

In the latter part of 5.2, 𝔓⁴⁶, 𝔓⁴⁹, ℵ, A, D, F, G and the bulk of the Byzantine manuscripts, all agree in the reading παρέδωκεν ἑαυτὸν ὑπὲρ ἡμῶν (*gave himself on behalf of us*). But Codex Vaticanus has παρέδωκεν ἑαυτὸν ὑπὲρ ὑμῶν (*gave himself on behalf of you*).

The manuscript evidence is strongest in the third instance, clearly pointing to the originality of *us* in the phrase, *gave himself on behalf of us*. There, we see agreement between the papyri, the Western tradition, the Byzantine manuscripts, and with the notable exception of Vaticanus, the Alexandrian tradition.

But if Paul had originally written *us* in all three instances, there would have been little impetus to change the reading to *you*. On the other hand, it is not difficult to imagine a scribe seeing *you*, finding that unsatisfactory, and feeling the need to affirm the comprehensive work accomplished in Christ, that in him God forgave us all, not just the Gentiles of Paul's audience. So then, the existence of variants points to the originality of *you* in at least one of these places. But because *us* is so strongly supported in the third instance, we must suppose that if a *you* were originally present in one of the three instances, it would have been in the first and/or second of the three phrases. Even if *you* had been original in only one of the three phrases, that could have been sufficient to induce some scribe to attempt to bring the other two phrases into conformity, changing *us* to *you*.

On 4.32, Metzger, describing the thinking of the committee behind the USB Text (3rd edition) wrote, "In the light of the earlier part of the sentence the reading ὑμῖν…seems to be required by the sense." His point is that Paul implores his readers to forgive one another, and that it makes more sense to suppose Paul appealed to God's having forgiven *them* as the reason they should forgive each other, rather than to God's having forgiven *us* as the reason. That is not a compelling argument, and it also runs counter to the axiom that the more difficult reading is to be preferred because the easier reading can readily be explained as an attempt to fix the difficult reading, whereas there is a lower likelihood of a difficult reading arising if the original were easy. Metzger also suggests the possiblity of a variant arising due to the "similar pronunciation of υ and η in later Greek."

However, we apparently see divergent readings in 𝔓⁴⁶ (c. 200) and 𝔓⁴⁹ (late 3ʳᵈ century), both of which are very early.

5.1–2 *Therefore as beloved children, be imitators of God and walk in love just as Christ loved us gave himself on behalf of you as an offering and a sacrifice to God as a pleasing aroma.* In view of Jesus' teaching in Matthew 5.44f, where he connects the responsibility to love with the status of being children of God, the point being that sons of God will imitate their father and love as their father loves, we ought to consider the possiblity that walking in love here in Ephesians 5.2 is intended to be the means whereby we imitate God. We may paraphrase, "As children loved by God, imitate God, by walking in love." Parallels to the two imperatives connected by καί, where the second explicates the first, may be seen in Matthew 11.29, Matthew 19.14, Mark 10.14, Luke 18.16, John 11.44 and Acts 5.38.

On the distinction between offering and sacrifice, etymologically, προσφορά (cognate of the verb προσφέρω, *bring to*) emphasizes the act of offering, the *bringing to* God (though in classical literature, the word was also used in non-religious contexts), while θυσία (cognate of the verb θύω, *kill, sacrifice*) more especially brings to mind the thing offered itself. These two ideas, represented by the phrase προσφορὰν καὶ θυσίαν (*offering and sacrifice*), are also found together with reference to Jesus in Hebrews 10.12, but there as a verb (προσενέγκας, aorist participle of προσφέρω) and its object (θυσίαν) rather than as two nouns. The verb προσφέρω and the noun θυσία are used together frequently in the LXX, especially in Leviticus and Numbers.[58] In the OT, a worshiper brought his offering to the priest (*e.g.*, Lev 2.8) or the priest brought it, or presented it, to God (*e.g.*, Lev 21.6). But inasmuch as Paul says, *"gave himself on our behalf as an offering"* (παρέδωκεν ἑαυτὸν ὑπὲρ ἡμῶν προσφοράν), Paul pictures Christ as offering himself, as the one who lays down his life for his friend (Jn 15.13). It is such love as this in which we are to walk.

for an odor of a fragrance (εἰς ὀσμὴν εὐωδίας) Accusative case ὀσμὴν (*smell, odor*) is the object of the preposition, and genitive case εὐωδίας (*of a fragrance*) specifies the kind of odor, the quality of the odor. The expression is anthropomorphic, describing the offering as pleasing to God in terms that we can understand.

The expression occurs frequently in the LXX. It is used not only of animal sacrifices, but also of an animal sacrifice in combination with a

---

[58] Lev 2.8, 14; 9.17; 21.6; 21.21; 22.21; 23.16; Nu 15.4; 15.9; 28.26.

grain offering (Lev 23.18), and also of a grain offering alone (Lev 6.14, 6.21 in English). Upon exiting the ark, Noah offered burnt offerings and "the Lord smelled the soothing aroma" (LXX: καὶ ὠσφράνθη κύριος ὁ θεὸς ὀσμὴν εὐωδίας). The precise phrase εἰς ὀσμὴν εὐωδίας is found 26 times in the Septuagint.[59]

Paul's use of such language in a letter most specifically addressed to Gentiles is a testament to the extent to which the OT, not only its stories but indeed its concepts and its very language, was expected to serve as the foundation for the faith of all Christians, Gentiles as well as Jews. On this point, we might observe that it is incumbent upon the disciple of Jesus Christ to familiarize himself with all of God's word, and thus being schooled in the customs and language of the OT, to be better prepared to understand the teachings of the NT.

5.3 *But fornication and every uncleanness or covetousness, let it not be named among you.* Apart from the Jewish context, the NT, and related writings, the word πορνεία was not frequently used.[60] When it was used in classical Greek, it meant prostitution. Therefore it has been argued that the condemnation of πορνεία in the Bible does not extend to premarital sexual relations, but only has in view prostitution.

However, "Later Judaism shows us how the use of πορνεία etc. gradually broadened."[61] In the LXX, in rabbinical writings, and in the NT itself, πορνεία came to be used of sexual unchastity generally.[62] For example, in Acts 15.29, the Jerusalem letter uses πορνεία as the one-word summation of the various sexual sins mentioned in Lev 18, including homosexuality and bestiality.[63] With that in mind, let us consider πορνεία and cognates as used by Paul.

As in Ephesians 5.3, so also in Colossians 3.5, Galatians 5.19, and 2 Corinthians 12.21, πορνεία occurs in a list of sins without much in the context to help us determine the precise meaning of the word. In 1 Corinthians 5.1, it is clearly not prostitution. There it is used of the relationship be-

---

[59] Ex 29.18, 29.25, 29.41, Lev 2.12, 4.31, 8.21, 17.4, 17.6, Nu 15.7, 15.13, 15.24, 18.17, 28.2, 28.6, 28.8, 28.24, 28.27, 29.1, 29.6, 29.8, 29.11, 29.13, 29.36, Jdth 16.16, Ezek 16.19, Dan 4.37.

[60] According to Harper, "Πορνεία occurs in only four classical authors" p. 369.

[61] Hauck/Schulz, TDNT, vol. 6, p. 587.

[62] Kyle Harper provides a thorough discussion of the development of the meaning in "Porneia: The Making of a Christian Sexual Norm" JBL 131:2(2012) pp. 363–383.

[63] Smelser, Is It Lawful? A Comprehensive Study of Divorce, p. 40.

tween a man and his father's wife.[64] Within the immediate context of 1 Corinthians 6.13 and 6.18, there is little to preclude the possibility that it might specifically refer to sexual relations with a prostitute. But again in 1 Corinthians 7.2, the word must mean extramarital sexual relations generally, for the antidote is marriage. If only sexual relations with prostitutes is condemned, then marriage, with all it entails, would not seem to be the easiest solution to the problem. Relations between "consenting adults" outside of marriage would suffice quite well. Again, in 1 Thessalonians 4.3, the context seems to point to marriage as the means of abstaining from fornication, and fornication is denounced not as an unseemly financial transaction, but as giving oneself over to the passion of lust.

The verb πορνεύω is used by Paul in 1 Corinthians 6.18, where as mentioned above, it would be possible to suppose prostitution is in view. But it may mean something more in 1 Corinthians 10.8, where it occurs twice. Paul warns his readers not to do what the Israelites did, and the example is the event described in Numbers 25.1–18 and further explained in Numbers 31.14–18. It appears that the sexual sin of the Israelites involved seduction and may have been associated with idolatrous rituals, but it is not clear that prostitution was involved.

Usually in ancient Greek, πορνή is prostitute.[65] Paul uses this word in 1 Corinthians 6.15*f* and uses the related πορνός in 1 Corinthians 5.9*ff*, 1 Corinthians 6.9, and 1 Timothy 1.10. The last passage does not provide any explanatory context. In 1 Corinthians 6.9, πορνοί are grouped with other sexually immoral people, none of whom are described as prostitutes. One could argue that this makes it more likely or, alternatively, less likely that the πορνοί in view are prostitutes. But in 1 Corinthians 5.9*ff*, Paul's assertion that one would have to go out of the world to avoid associating with πορνοί leads us to the conclusion that there, πορνοί means fornicators generally, and not only prostitutes. One does not have to go out of the world to avoid associating with prostitutes. Moreover, the context is that wherein Paul is denouncing the sin of the man who was cohabiting with his father's wife.

So we can say this with confidence: While it would be possible, if we considered 1 Corinthians 6 in isolation from the rest of Paul's writings, to suppose that Paul is only condemning prostitution, when we consider

---

[64] Some point to 1 Cor 5:1 as an instance where πορνεία is used as a technical term for incest. Against this, see Smelser, *Is it Lawful*, pp. 37–42.

[65] Hauck/Schulz say that πορνή is "from πέρνημι, 'to sell,'." TNDT vol. 6, p. 580.

all of the contexts wherein Paul uses this word group we come to the inescapable conclusion that he condemns all sexual relations outside of marriage.

Moreover, given the continuity from 1 Corinthians chapters five through seven, it seems hardly reasonable to suppose that even in chapter six Paul has in mind only prostitution unless he addresses it as related to sexual sin in general. The word group from πορν- (πορνεία, πόρνος πόρνη) forms a thread through this section. In chapter five, the issue was πορνεία and as noted above, was clearly not prostitution. Paul urges that the Corinthians address the issue by not associating with the πόρνοις (5.9). He then expands the instruction, saying they should take the same approach to dealing with a brother who is committing any of various sins. First in the list is the πόρνος (5.11), apparently because this is the sort of person that has been in view, which fact argues against taking πόρνος in the limited sense of prostitute. Then in chapter six, Paul warns the Corinthians against a litany of sins which proves to be the same list as that found in 5.11, but with two items broken out into subcategories. Whereas the list in 5.11 includes the πλεονέκτης, the list in 6.9–10 has along with πλεονέκται, κλέπται, which is merely one who practices applied covetousness. Similarly, whereas the list in 5.11 includes the πόρνος, the list in 6.9–10 has μοιχοὶ, μαλακοὶ, and ἀρσενοκοῖται along with πόρνοι, thus particularizing various practitioners of πορνεία.

1 Corinthians 5.11	1 Corinthians 6.9–10
πόρνος	πόρνοι, μοιχοὶ, μαλακοὶ, ἀρσενοκοῖται
πλεονέκτης	κλέπται, πλεονέκται
εἰδωλολάτρης	εἰδωλολάτραι
λοίδορος	λοίδοροι
μέθυσος	μέθυσοι
ἅρπαξ	ἅρπαγες

Seeing the list in 6.9–10 as another form of the list in 5.11 helps us understand that the theme of πορνεία begun in 5.1 is still in view. So then when we come to 6.12–13 and Paul begins to address the Corinthian mindset whereby πορνεία was thought to be justified ("all things are permitted to me," "food for the belly and the belly for food"), we should see this as a continuation of the context begun in 5.1, where the πορνεία clearly was not prostitution. And then in chapter seven, Paul turns to the first of several questions posed by some at Corinth and discusses marriage as the antidote to πορνεία, which as noted above must be more than just prostitution, else less entangling antidotes would have been available. Therefore, in 6.15 and 6.18 when Paul uses the term πορνή, we can only suppose he has in mind the narrow meaning of "prostitute" if we acknowledge that Paul sees this as related to the problem of sexual sin in general which has been the theme of the preceding context.

That πορνεία is used in the New Testament of sexual sin generally and not merely of prostitution specifically has been well understood throughout the ages. But in our day, at least in Western culture where sexual relations are routinely assumed to be freely enjoyed independent of marriage, we are seeing the arguments made that God's word does not condemn such. Once again, we see that as a society, we are as was the Gentile world of Paul's readers, and that we who have been saved by the grace of God must recognize that we must shake off the assumptions and conduct of the society from which we have escaped. But some who fail to do that attempt to re-interpret God's word so as to accommodate the old man, that they might continue to walk as the Gentiles walk.

Fornication is regarded as an example of uncleanness, as indicated by the subsequent expansion, καὶ ἀκαθαρσία πᾶσα (*and every uncleanness*). ἀκαθαρσία was literally *filth*. A lease agreement for a cellar and additional storage space stipulated that at the end of the lease period, the vacated areas were to be handed over to the lessor clean, without "refuse and any ἀκαθαρσία.»[66]

But Demosthenes used the word ἀκαθαρσία for unethical behavior, wickedness.[67] So too in Epictetus we see ψυχῆς ἀκαθαρσία (*impurity of soul*).[68]

In the LXX, it is used generally of whatever is defiling, as is the adjective ἀκάθαρτος.[69]

---

[66] Oxyrhynchus 912.

[67] 21.119.

[68] Discourses 4.11.8, cf. 4.11:5, 2.8.12–13.

[69] In the New Testament, the adjective ἀκάθαρτος is used most frequently to describe spirits, otherwise referred to as demons. It is used with the same breadth of meaning it generally has in the OT in 2 Cor 6.17 (where Is 52.11 is quoted) and probably with the same breadth of meaning in Rev 17.4. In Acts 10.14 and 11.18, it is used with specific reference to defiling food. It is also used with reference to Gentiles, who from the Jewish perspective, were unclean (Acts 10.28). By extension, under the law, the children born to mixed marriages had been considered unclean (1 Cor 7.14, cf. Ezra 10.3, Neh 13.24), although Paul's

In the New Testament, we see ἀκαθαρσία used with similar breadth of meaning. While in Matthew 23.37 ἀκαθαρσία is used of the uncleanness associated with decaying bodies, the word is used broadly in Romans 6.19 and 1 Thessalonians 2.3.

To be sure, in several passages the noun ἀκαθαρσία is used especially with reference to sexual sin. The use of ἀκάθαρτος with a sexual connotation is illustrated outside the New Testament by Plutarch's description of Tigellinus, who was a prefect of the Praetorian Guard under Nero. Plutarch described Tigellinus' proclivity for prostitutes as unclean.[70] In 1 Thessalonians 4.7, ἀκαθαρσία is set opposite ἁγιάσμος, which in the context has been explicitly described as abstaining from fornication. So then in that context, the particular ἀκαθαρσία in view is fornication. Similarly, ἀκαθαρσία seems to have a sexual connotation in Galatians 5.19 and 2 Corinthians 12.21.

But here in Ephesians 5.3, it seems to be broader, encompassing not only sexual sins already summed up in the word πορνεία, but anything at all that defiles a person. Keeping in mind the fact that what is κοινός is ἀκάθαρτος (Acts 10.14*f*), we may think of Jesus' statement, "For out of the heart come evil thoughts, murders, adulteries, fornications, thefts, false witness, slanders. These are the things which defile the man" (Matt 5.19*f* NAS*)* The words *the things which defile* represent τὰ κοινοῦντα. Paul's ἀκαθαρσία πᾶσα (*every uncleanness*) extends as far as Jesus' list of things that defile so as to go beyond sexual sin and include all those defiling things in the heart, including such as lead to evil thoughts, murders, thefts, false witness, slanders, etc.

The construction "fornication and all uncleanness, or covetousness" pairs the first two sin categories in contrast to the third.[71] Let neither fornication (and all other uncleanness) nor covetousness be named among you. Paul is making a distinction between two categories of sin, sin of impurity and sin of misplaced priority. Covetousness (πλεονεξία) is greed, that craving for more that can characterize a seemingly upstanding, moral

---

point in 1 Cor 7.14 is to say that is no longer the case.

[70] ἐν γυναιξὶ πόρναις καὶ ἀκαθάρτοις ἐγκυλινδήσεις, Plut. De Othone, 2.2.

[71] This is evident not only because πορνεία should be seen as an example of ἀκαθαρσία, but also because of the singular verb ὀνομαζέσθω. The singular is the appropriate number for a compound subject with a disjunction. But if ἀκαθαρσία were regarded as a distinct category separate from πορνεία, not only would the change from καὶ to ἢ be inexplicable, but the singular verb would also be a glaring error.

man. The man who asked Jesus to intervene in a sibling dispute about an inheritance prompted a warning against πλεονεξία and a parable about a man whose only noted flaw was a preoccupation with acquisition (Lk 12.13*ff*). The rich young ruler who asked about eternal life (Mt 19.16*ff*, Mk 10.17*ff*, Lk 18.18*ff*) was the sort of man who could hardly be charged with uncleanness—in regard to laws about murder, adultery, theft, false witness, honoring parents, loving one's neighbor, he could say "all these have I kept from my youth up"—but he was covetous. His wealth was more important to him than was the Lord, and he well illustrates Paul's point that covetousness is idolatry (Eph 5.5, cf. Col 3.5). So covetousness, the heart problem of the seemingly upstanding man, is set off against fornication and all uncleanness.

Paul admonishes, *let it not be named among you.* ὀνομάζω must have a different connotation than it carries in Ephesians 1.21, *every name that is named* (παντὸς ὀνόματος ὀνομαζομένου). There, the meaning is more or less every powerful entity so *designated*, or *acknowledged*, or really, just *named*, as when a student might be called upon to "name the presidents." In 5.3, Paul is not prohibiting the listing of certain sins.

But there are two other possibilities. Some suppose Paul means to prohibit the *occurrence of* such sins—there should be no cause to name them, *i.e.*, *report them*, because they should not occur. Others suppose Paul is in fact saying, *do not talk about* such sins. Of course this would not be an absolute prohibition, for Paul himself mentions the fornicator at Corinth (1 Cor 5.1), and even here, mentions the sin of fornication in warning against it.

Lincoln argues, almost convincingly, that all three sins should be understood as being sexual in nature, and that the point really is to discourage casual conversation of these things.[72] But construing πλεονεξία as a sexual sin is problematic in a context where, as discussed above, this sin is grammatically set apart from "fornication and all uncleanness," and more especially, is alone reckoned as idolatry (5.3). If Paul had intended πλεονεξία in a sexual sense, such that all of these sins are of the same (sexual) nature, it would make no sense to single out the (sexually) covetous man as the only idolator in the group.

---

[72] p. 322. Lincoln mentions the 10th commandment and 1 Thess 4.6 as evidence in favor of seeing a sexual reference in πλεονεξία. He cites the reference to things of which it is shameful even to speak (5.12) as evidence that μηδὲ ὀνομαζέσθω ἐν ὑμῖν indicates that "these sins should not even be talked about."

Necessarily then, we must understand covetousness in the usual sense of greed, as discussed above. But then there is no reason to suppose Paul would say that discussion of this sin should be avoided, as he might warn against casual conversation of sexual perversions. And yet covetousness, just as certainly as fornication and all uncleanness, is in view when Paul warns, *let it not be named among you*. Therefore we must conclude that *let it not be named* is not a prohibition against mentioning these sins, but is rather an admonition that such things should not need to be named for they ought not occur.

Lincoln's interpretation would require that we understand ὀνομάζω to mean nothing more than *talk about*, or *mention*. Certainly the verb is used where it does not mean precisely, *give a name to something or someone*.[73] But clear examples of its use to mean merely *talk about* or *mention* are elusive.[74] In 2 Timothy 2.19, ὀνομάζω is not merely *mention*, but approaches *call on*.[75]

However much truth there is in the principle that things casually discussed become casually regarded,[76] it seems that this is not Paul's point

---

[73] *E.g.*, Herodotus 6.129.

[74] One passage that may illustrate ὀνομάζειν in the sense of *mention* is found in Dio Chrysostom 48.16. A new proconsul is coming and the speaker wishes to warn the members of the assembly to exhibit their best behavior, and to reserve airing dirty laundry for a later time. The relevant text is στάσιν δὲ οὐδὲ ὀνομάζειν ἄξιον παρ᾽ ἡμῖν μήτε λεγέτω μηδείς, and might be translated, *To name discord is not worthy among us, neither let anyone mention it.* Did Dio Chrysostom mean to say two different things about discord in the city (it was not to be named for it was not to occur, and it was also not to be the subject of conversation), or did he mean to equate *naming it* and *mentioning it*, while distinguishing between the fact that *it was unworthy* of being named/mentioned and therefore people *ought not* name/mention it. If the latter is the point, the difference between the two clauses is not a distinction between naming and mentioning, but is rather the distinction between reckoning such mentioning *to be unworthy* and (therefore) *prohibiting* such mentioning. If that is correct, we have here a passage wherein ὀνομάζειν essentially means *mention*. However, I think there is a better way of understanding this passage in light of an earlier remark, where Dio Chrysostom says his own purpose is to speak on behalf of like-mindedness (ὑπὲρ ὁμονοίας λέγειν, 48.14) but then considers the possibility that someone might object to his reasoning. This possibility that someone would speak in favor of airing grievances may be the key to understanding the words μήτε λεγέτω μηδείς. The whole phrase could be understood, "To name discord is not worthy among us, neither let anyone reason for it." With this interpretation, there is no justification in taking ὀνομάζειν as a synonym for λέγειν, no justification for taking ὀνομάζειν to mean merely *talk about* or *mention*.

[75] BDAG, p. 714.

[76] When Herodotus described this very principle as it prevailed among the Persians, he used the verb λέγειν, not ὀνομάζειν (1.138): ἄσσα δὲ σπι ποιέειν οὐκ ἔξεστι, ταῦτα οὐδὲ λέγειν ἔξεστι, and whatever is not permitted to them to do, neither is it permitted to speak of these things.

here. Rather, he means that neither fornication and all uncleanness, nor covetousness, should be found among God's people. This is precisely the use of ὀνομάζω found in the so-called majority text at 1 Corinthians 5.1,[77] καὶ τοιαύτη πορνεία ἥτις οὐδὲ ἐν τοῖς ἔθνεσιν ὀνομάζεται (*and such fornication as is not even named among the Gentiles*).

καθὼς πρέπει ἁγίοις *just as is fitting to holy ones*   It is fitting to holy ones that the sins Paul has discussed not be named among them. Remember that in the first three chapters, Paul laid out God's riches to the Gentiles in Christ. As that theme was developed, either the readers, or all of God's people, were described as ἅγιοι (*holy*) seven times (1.1, 1.4, 1.15, 1.18, 2.19, 3.8, 3.18). Then beginning in chapter four, Paul called upon his readers to walk worthily of their calling. Here we may remember that in writing to the Corinthians, Paul said they were κλητοῖς ἁγίοις, *called holy ones*. So here, the calling of which Paul urges his readers to walk worthily is a calling to holiness. And it is fitting that people aspiring to holiness should be untainted by fornication and all uncleanness, or covetousness.

Paul will come back to fornication, uncleanness and covetousness in verse five. But first, he warns against three things that all seem to have to do with our talk, our banter. 𝔓[49] has a colon after the phrase καθὼς πρέπει ἁγίοις, indicating that the copyist supposed the ensuing words began a new thought. But the imperative prohibition μηδὲ ὀνομαζέσθω ἐν ὑμῖν is still in view. The vices now introduced are additional things that ought not be named among holy people.

5.4 *shameful talk and foolish talk, or risqué witticisms* (καὶ αἰσχρότης καὶ μωρολογία ἢ εὐτραπελία)   Etymologically, the word εὐτραπελία pertains to a "well-turned" phrase, being derived from the adverb εὖ (*well*) and the verb τρέπω (*turn*). Here, it is clearly used of risqué or lewd witticisms.

5.5 *For this you know, knowing that every fornicator or unclean person or coveteous person, who is an idolator, does not have an inheritance in the kingdom of Christ and of God* (τοῦτο γὰρ ἴστε γινώσκοντες ὅτι πᾶς πόρνος ἢ ἀκάθαρτος ἢ πλεονέκτης, ὅ ἐστιν εἰδωλολάτρης, οὐκ ἔχει κληρονομίαν ἐν τῇ βασιλείᾳ τοῦ Χριστοῦ καὶ θεοῦ)   Now Paul returns to the three categories of verse three, sexual sin, all uncleanness and covetousness. The expression ἴστε γινώσκοντες (*you know, knowing*) is explained by some as a Hebraism, an expression influenced by Hebrew

---

[77] This reading is also found in 𝔓[68], ℵ[2], Ψ and 1881.

idiom. An example of this sort of expression is found in Genesis 2.17, *mot tamut* (*to die, you shall die*, but meaning *you shall certainly die*). It consists of a Hebrew infinitive *to die* (*mot*) followed by a cognate finite verb *you shall die* (*tamut*). Another example is found in Genesis 15.13, "knowing, you shall know." The Hebrew infinitive *yadoa'* (*to know*) together with the verb *teda'* (*you shall know*) means "you shall certainly know."[78] We do indeed see this sort of Hebraism in the NT quotations of the OT (εὐλογῶν εὐλογήσω, Heb 6.14; βλέποντες βλέψετε, Acts 28.26).[79] But the expression in Ephesians 5.5 is different in a couple of ways. First, two unrelated verbs are used together, ἴστε and γινώσκοντες. However, Hoehner notes that we see something similar in the LXX rendering of 1 Samuel 20.3 where the Hebrew *yadoa' yada'* (*certainly knows*) is represented in Greek as γινώσκων οἶδεν. But the expression in Ephesians 5.5 also differs from other examples of this Hebraism in that the participle is the second word in the phrase rather than the first.[80]

If the expression is a not a Hebraism, we can understand the first of the two verbs (ἴστε) as looking back to verse four and the second (γινώσκοντες) as looking forward: "For you know this (what I have just said, *viz.*, that the aforementioned things ought not be named among you) knowing that (with the knowledge that) such ones will have no inheritance in the kingdom of Christ and of God.[81]

5.6–21 Walking as Children of Light

Let no one deceive you by empty words, for on account of these things the wrath of God comes upon the sons of disobedience. Therefore do not become participants with them, for you were then darkness, but now you are light in the Lord. Walk as children of light—for the fruit of the light is in all goodness and righteousness and truth—demonstrating what is pleasing to the Lord. Therefore do not become par-

---

[78] Although Gesenius opined that here the construction was more euphonic than emphatic, p. 342, §116 o.

[79] Zerwick, §61, p. 21.

[80] Zerwick also mentions the variation wherein the Hebrew infinitive is represented in Greek by an instrumental dative, as in Lk 22.15, Ἐπιθυμίᾳ ἐπεθύμησα; Jn 3.29, χαρᾷ χαίρει; Acts 5.28, παραγγελίᾳ παρηγγείλαμεν; Acts 28.26 Ἀκοῇ ἀκούσετε, §61, p. 21. But again, in all these examples, the Greek represents the Hebrew infinitive first, either by means of a dative case noun or a participle, and then represents the Hebrew finite verb by means of a Greek finite verb.

[81] Porter suggests that evidence for this understanding might be found in a chiastic structure which he sees in the passage.

ticipants with them, for you were then darkness, but now you are light in the Lord. And do not share in the unfruitful works of the darkness, but rather even expose them. For the things being done secretly by them are shameful even to speak. And all things being exposed by the the light are manifest, for everything being made manifest is light. Wherefore it says,

> Arise, sleeping one,
> And rise up from the dead
> And the Christ will shine on you.

Therefore see that you walk carefully, not as foolish ones, but as wise men, buying time, because the days are evil. On account of this, do not be unwise, but understand what the the will of the Lord is. And do not be drunk with wine in which is dissipation, but be filled with the Spirit, speaking to each other in psalms and hymns and spiritual songs, singing and making music with your heart to the Lord, always giving thanks to the God and Father for all things in the name of our Lord Jesus Christ, subjecting yourselves one to another in reverence of Christ.

5.6 Μηδεὶς ὑμᾶς ἀπατάτω κενοῖς λόγοις *Let no one deceive you by empty words* μηδεὶς is used here rather than οὐδείς because the verb (imperative ἀπατάτω) is not indicative. Justifications of living as the Gentiles do are "empty words." Peter says, "For uttering great swelling words of vanity (ματαιότης, cf. Eph 4.17) they entice in the lusts of the flesh, by lasciviousness." The consequence is God's wrath. *for on account of these things* (διὰ ταῦτα γὰρ) *i.e.,* the sins mentioned in the preceding section (verses 3–5) *the wrath of God comes upon the sons of disobedience.*

5.7 *Therefore do not become participants with them* (μὴ οὖν γίνεσθε συμμέτοχοι αὐτῶν) The οὖν (*therefore*) connects the present admonition with the preceding statement of the dismal end of the sons of disobedience. Because the wrath of God comes upon them, do not share with them in their lifestyle. The implication is that if you share in their lifestyle, you will become an object of the wrath of God with them.

5.8 *for you were then darkness, but now you are light in the Lord. As children of light, walk* (ἦτε γὰρ ποτε σκότος, νῦν δὲ φῶς ἐν κυρίῳ· ὡς τέκνα φωτὸς περιπατεῖτε) Those coming to Christ today from this increasingly pagan world need to take this to heart. When one is baptized into Christ, he is not merely forgiven; he passes from darkness to light (cf. 1 Pt 2.9), and a commensurate change in his conduct must occur. Westcott noted that the wording is ἧτε γάρ ποτε σκότος (*you were then darkness*) rather than ἐν σκότει (*in darkness*) and commented, "The thought is dominantly not of individual character but of social influence."[82] We will return to this observation in connection with verse 10.

5.9 *for the fruit of the light* The whole of verse nine must be construed as parenthetical inasmuch as the following participle, δοκιμάζοντες, is nominative plural and is to be read in connection with the subject of nominative plural περιπατεῖτε in verse 8. So then, the thought, "You all be sure to walk as children of light proving/approving what is pleasing...," is interrupted by the parenthetical description of the fruit of the light, the description of the things that will characterize the saints' walk and will thus appear as light to the world. Paul's remarks here bring to mind Philippians 2.14–16.

The mss that have φωτός (*light*) rather than πνεύματος (*spirit*) include the 3rd century 𝔓49, and 4th century codices Sinaiticus and Vaticanus. Early evidence for πνεύματος is found in 𝔓46 (c. AD 200). The language is more clearly connected with the preceding and the following if καρπὸς τοῦ φωτός is read. But perhaps the reason that consensus swings in favor of φωτός is because it is easy to imagine a copyist replacing καρπὸς τοῦ φωτός with the familiar phrase καρπὸς τοῦ πνεύματος (*fruit of the spirit*; cf. Gal 5.22).[83]

is in all goodness and righteousness and truth (ἐν πάσῃ ἀγαθωσύνῃ καὶ δικαιοσύνῃ καὶ ἀληθείᾳ) The prepositional phrase serves as a predicate. The copulative is inferred.

5.10 *approving what is pleasing to the Lord* (δοκιμάζοντες τί ἐστιν εὐάρεστον τῷ κυρίῳ) δοκιμάζω is found in ancient Greek generally as well as in the LXX and NT with the meaning *test, try* (Lk 12.56, 14.19,1 Cor 3.13, 11.28, 2 Cor 13.5, Gal 6.4, 1 Tim 3.10, 1 Pt 1.7, 1 Jn 4.1). A related meaning is not merely test, but "to accept as tested or proved,"[84] *to consider something to be tried and true.* So we see in Romans 14.22, *Happy is the one who does not condemn himself in what he approves.* See also 1 Corinthians 16.3, 2 Corinthians 8.22, Philippians 1.10, 1 Thessalonians 2.4a. δοκιμάζω is sometimes used in contexts where the sense seems to be *choose* (test and validate and therefore select). So for example, a husband discussing

---

[82] Westcott, p. 77.

[83] Lincoln, p. 317.

[84] TDNT, vol. II, p. 256.

with his wife the organization of the household goods says, χώραν τε δοκιμασώμεθα τὴν προσήκουσαν ἑκάστοις ἔχειν, *Let us choose an appropriate place for each thing to have.*[85] Perhaps we see this usage in Romans 1.28, καὶ καθὼς οὐκ ἐδοκίμασαν τὸν θεὸν ἔχειν ἐν ἐπιγνώσει, *and just as they did not choose to have God in their knowledge...*" So then we might translate Ephesians 5.10, *choosing what is pleasing to the Lord.* This is perhaps close to Tyndale's "Accept that which is pleasinge to the Lorde."

Some versions translate as if Paul would have his readers find out what is pleasing to the Lord. The NIV has "find out what pleases the Lord," the ESV has "try to discern what is pleasing to the Lord," and the NASB has "trying to learn what is pleasing to the Lord." Presumably, translators have been led to this thought by the presence of the interrogative pronoun τί (*what?*), a pronoun we first think of as indicating a question. Certainly, in most of the NT occurrences of the phrase τί ἐστιν, this is the case.[86] Often, τί represents an indirect question. If that were the case here, the implied direct question would be, "What is pleasing to the Lord?" With δοκιμάζοντες (*testing*) then, one can see why translators might end up with "try to discern what is pleasing to the Lord." And to be sure, a similar thought may be seen in 1 Thessalonians 5.21, "try all things, hold to that which is good."

But in Ephesians 5.10, the renderings found in the NIV, ESV, and NAS introduce a thought that is at odds with the context. The second half of Ephesians is not an exhortation to find out what is pleasing to the Lord. The section begins with a reminder that gifts have already been provided that will result in building up the body of Christ. Furthermore, the second half of Ephesians is itself an instruction in what is pleasing to the Lord. Ephesians 4–6 is an exhortation to walk worthily, to walk in love, to walk carefully, and in the present section, Paul is in essence saying, "Here is how to do that."

But we need not suppose the language requires a meaning such as "try to discern" or "find out what pleases the Lord." Sometimes τί functions as a relative pronoun.[87] Indeed, that seems to be the case in Ephesians 5.17.

---

[85] Xenophon Economics, 8.10

[86] The occurrences of τί ἐστιν (interrogative with copulative, *"what is"*) in the NT are Mt 9.13, 12.7, Mk 1.27, 2.9, 5.14, 9.10, Lk 5.23, Jn 6.9, Jn 16.17, 16.18, 18.38, Acts 10.4, Acts 21.33, Ac 23.19, Eph 4.9, Eph 5.10, Heb 2.6.

[87] E.g., Mk. 14.36, Mt. 15:32, Lk 17:8, Mk. 2.25 (cf. Lk 6:3), Mt 10.19 (cf. Lk. 12.12). See Robertson, p. 737, BDF §298(4).

So then in 5.10, rather than seeing an implied question ("What is pleasing to the Lord?"), but instead taking δοκιμάζοντες as approving, or even choosing, we can understand the text to mean "approving what is pleasing to the Lord" = "approving that which is pleasing to the Lord." We probably see the same phenomenon, τί as a relative pronoun, in Romans 12.2 (εἰς τὸ δοκιμάζειν ὑμᾶς τί τὸ θέλημα τοῦ θεοῦ), the passage in Paul most similar to this one.

5.11 *And do not share in the unfruitful works of the darkness, but rather even expose them* (καὶ μὴ συγκοινωνεῖτε τοῖς ἔργοις τοῖς ἀκάρποις τοῦ σκότους, μᾶλλον δὲ καὶ ἐλέγχετε)   A similar warning is found in 1 Timothy 5.22, "neither share in others' sins." The very first sin was the result of deception, but the second was simply a matter of someone sharing in the sin of the first: "She gave also to her husband with her, and he ate." Often, deception is not necessary where there is the desire to please a companion.

Taking care not to share in someone else's sin means also taking care to avoid enabling someone else's sin, for one who enables something shares in it (Phil 4.15–17). John commends Gaius who by virtue of his hospitality was a fellow-worker with those who experienced his hospitality as they went forth preaching the gospel (3 Jn 3–8). But John warns against even offering an encouraging greeting to someone whose mission is to spread a doctrine that is not the teaching of Christ, because by encouraging him one would become a partaker in his evil works (2 Jn 9–11).

In the New Testament, ἐλέγχω is usually *rebuke, confute, convict,* or *convince.* But there is a close relationship between convicting the criminal and bringing a crime to light. A letter written about 250 BC instructed a subordinate, "Come to Talao at once, bringing also *the shepherd who can give evidence* [τὸν ποιμένα τὸν ἐλέγξοντα] concerning the things you related to me."[88] Xenophon tells of Socrates offering advice as to how a bad flautist could pass himself off as a good one, but warning that he should never accept an engagement or else *"he will be exposed* [ἐλεγχθήσεται] to ridicule."[89] In the NT, this meaning is illustrated in John 3.20, "for everyone who does evil hates the light and does not come to the light in order that his works *might* not *be exposed* (ἐλεγχθῇ)."

The whole passage is intended to encourage each saint to draw a stark

---

[88] παραγενοῦ εἰς Ταλαὼν ἤδη ἄγων καὶ τὸν ποιμένα τὸν ἐλέγξοντα περὶ ὧν μοι εἶπας, P. Hibeh I, 55.

[89] Xenophon, Mem., 1.7.2.

line of demarcation between his new life in Christ and the former life that characterized his old man: Do not participate in the works of darkness; rather expose them by your light. You must walk as children of light and thus evidence what is pleasing to God, that being the fruit of light as seen in goodness and righteousness and truth.

Walking in the light while not participating in the works of darkness yields two complementary results: The saints demonstrate what is pleasing to the Lord and expose as evil what is not.

5.12–14 *For the things being done secretly by them are shameful even to speak. And all things being exposed by the the light are manifest. For everything being made manifest is light. Wherefore it says,*

> *Arise, sleeping one,*
> *And rise up from the dead*
> *And the Christ will shine on you.*

In these lines, Moule saw a parallel structure "comparable to that of Hebrew poetry." [199] Presumably, he had in mind the first two lines wherein *arise* (ἔγειρε) and *rise up* (ἀνάστα) would be parallel to each other, as would *sleeping one* (ὁ καθεύδων) and *the dead* (τῶν νεκρῶν), such that both lines call upon one to rise from sleep/death. The semblance to Hebrew poetry would be consistent with the idea that these lines were part of a well-known hymn, introduced by the words, διὸ λέγει, *wherefore it says.*

Others have tried to account for the introductory διὸ λέγει by supposing what follows is a quotation from the Old Testament, as in 4.8. But there is no passage in the Old Testament that stands out as being sufficiently similar to Paul's language here such that it can be identified as the source of the quotation. Alford confidently affirmed that Paul was paraphrasing Isaiah 60.1–2, "Arise, shine; for your light has come and glory of the LORD has risen upon you…And His glory will appear upon you." At first glance, both Ephesians 5.14 and Isaiah 60.1–2 speak of the Lord and someone or something shining or appearing, but beyond that there is little similarity. Moreover, the vocabulary Paul uses has almost nothing in common with the Greek of the LXX at Isaiah 60.1–2. To find any more similarity than that, Alford had to reach back to Isaiah 59.10 where Judah was compared to dead men.

But whatever may be the source of these lines, they constitute an exhortation that is continued in the following words.

5.15–16 *Therefore see that you walk carefully, not as foolish ones,* *but as wise men* (Βλέπετε οὖν ἀκριβῶς πῶς περιπατεῖτε μὴ ὡς ἄσοφοι ἀλλ' ὡς σοφοί) βλέπετε as an imperative[90] is often used in contexts where the imperative is a warning, much as we might say, "watch out!" In various contexts, the idea may range from "see to it that you..." "be sure to" or "take care to...", or when used with ἀπὸ, it is "be wary of..." (though we see this meaning without ἀπὸ in Phil 3.2). For βλέπετε...πῶς, see 1 Corinthians 8.9, and especially Luke 8.18 where we see βλέπετε οὖν πῶς ἀκούετε (*therefore watch how you hear = listen carefully!*), which is alternatively represented at Mark 4.23 as εἴ τις ἔχει ὦτα ἀκούειν ἀκουέτω (*if one has ears to hear, let him hear*). In Mark 13.9, Jesus warns, "*Watch yourselves* (βλέπετε δὲ ὑμεῖς ἑαυτούς); *they will deliver you to councils.*" And then in Mark 13.23, after warning that some would attempt to deceive the elect, Jesus again warns, "You watch!" (ὑμεῖς δὲ βλέπετε). In these passages, the word is used much in the same way as ἀγρυπνεῖτε, with which it is joined in Mark 13.33.

5.16 *buying time, because the days are evil* (ἐξαγοραζόμενοι τὸν καιρόν, ὅτι αἱ ἡμέραι πονηραί εἰσιν) There is probably no thought of *redeeming*, i.e., buying *back*, in the use of ἐξαγοραζόμενοι in this context. When Nebuchadnezzar's Chaldeans pleaded to know what the king had dreamed before venturing to offer an interpretation of the king's dream, Nebuchadnezzar rebuked them, and the LXX translates his rebuke, οἶδα ὅτι καιρὸν ὑμεῖς ἐξαγοράζετε, "I know that you are buying time," that is, stalling, or trying to prolong a conclusion.[91]

But buying time in the sense of stalling is certainly not the idea in Ephesians 5.16 (nor in Col 4.5). In trying to catch the sense of Paul's exhortation here, perhaps it is best to turn our attention to the word καιρός as distinct from χρόνος.

First, a word of caution: We do not want to leave the impression that Greek was a language with rigid semantic barriers between near synonymyms any more so than English is such a language. The fact is there is much overlap such that καιρός as well as χρόνος may be used simply of time. Paul used καιρός with reference to "the present time" in both

---

[90] Mt. 24:4, Mk. 4:24, 8:15, 12:38, 13:5, 13:9, 13:23, 13:33, Lk. 8:18, 21:8, Ac. 13:40, 1 Co. 8:9, 1 Co. 16:10, Gal. 5:15, Phil. 3:2 (3x), Col. 2:8, Heb. 3:12, 12:25, 2 Jo. 8. Βλέπετε may also be imperative in 1 Cor 1:26 and 10:18.

[91] Although as we shall see καιρός is not always merely "time," perhaps the LXX translators intended merely "time" here. Or perhaps they intended to represent Nebuchadnezzar as accusing the wise men of attempting to buy, not merely time, but an *opportunity* to turn the difficult situation in their favor.

Romans 3.26 (τῷ νῦν καιρῷ) and 8.18 (τοῦ νῦν καιροῦ). It is not immediately apparent that the time being considered is an especially propitious moment in either instance.

However, there is a distinction to be made between the semantic sphere of the two words.[92] Trench showed that the meaning of καιρός is more specific than χρόνος and is entirely encompassed by the meaning of χρόνος such that χρόνος might always be used in place of καιρός but καιρός cannot always be used in place of χρόνος.

Trench cautions against supposing that *opportunity* sufficiently covers the ground of καιρός inasmuch as not every καιρός is convenient; sometimes a καιρός is noteworthy because of its inconvenience rather than its convenience. Matthew 8.29 could illustrate the truth of this observation. *Occasion* might often be an apt translation, indicating some time with a particular character without leaning toward either favorability or unfavorability.[93]

In any event, it can be said that while every καιρός exists within χρόνος, the use of the word καιρός often points to some character of the time in question, not that the word defines that character, but that the word alerts the hearer or reader to the fact that the time in view is of some particular character. When the devil departed from Jesus ἄχρι καιροῦ (Lk 4.13), it was not merely "for a season" (ASV), but "until an opportune moment."[94] At first glance, it is not easy to see anything that would account for the use of καιρός rather than χρόνος in Acts 13.11. However, even there, Luke does not use the accusative expression πρὸς χρόνον which, the accusative being the case of extent, would mean "for a time."[95] Rather, Luke uses

---

[92] According to Delling, καιρός is the "'decisive or crucial place or point,' whether spatially, materially or temporally," and in the temporal sense, is the "decisive moment."(TDNT, v. 3, p. 455.) As suggested above, καιρός is sometimes used where it can hardly be distinguished from χρόνος, and Delling notes several passages in the Septuagint and in Theodotian where it means "stretches of time." But he says that in these instances, "the original sense is quite lost."

[93] Delling notes that καιρός, as the "decisive moment," occurs as "neutral, positive and negative," but is most often positive (TDNT, v. 3, p. 455).

[94] Marshall, 174; Horst and Schneider, Exegetical Dictionary of the New Testament, p. 186.

[95] So for example, when Dio Cassius writes of emperor Marcus Aurelius Antoninus (Epitome of Book LXXI.19.1) that he did not receive all foreign ambassadors on the same terms, but gave some citizenship, some permanent exemption from tribute, and some an exemption *for a time* (πρός χρόνον τινά), the accusative case points to the *duration of the exemption* for a certain time, not to the *nature of the particular occasion* on which the exemption would come to an end. See also Ant. 8.63.

the genitive expression ἄχρι καιροῦ, and the genitive case being the case of kind, this points to a time that in some way would be appropriate for Elymas to have received his sight again.

Paul was certainly capable of using καιρός with its particular nuance in mind. So in Galatians 6.10, he writes, "as we have opportunity (καιρόν), let us work that which is good toward all men, and especially toward them that are of the household of the faith." He does not mean merely *time*, in the sense that we all lead busy lives and it is difficult to find time to do good. Rather, he means, as we have suitable occasions for doing good, i.e., opportunities, let us do so.

Therefore, even if in such a passage as Romans 8.18 there seems to be little reason for the use of καιρός rather than χρόνος, nonetheless we ought to be quick to recognize the particular connotation of καιρός whenever the immediate context affords us reason to do so. So in Romans 3.26, while at first blush we might suppose the meaning is simply, "the present time," upon further consideration we may realize that Paul is indeed calling attention to the vindication of God's righteousness as being *occasioned* by the propitiating sacrifice of Jesus; *for the showing of his righteousness at this occasion*. In Matthew 11.25, we ought to understand that Jesus thanked the Father on that particular *occasion* (not, "at that season"as in the ASV). It was *à propros* to do so at that moment, given the preceding discourse and the particular thing for which Jesus gave thanks, and the relationship between the two. Jesus had spoken of those who failed to repent though they had witnessed more mighty works than had others who did repent, and on that occasion, and in that connection, at that καιρός, he thanked the Father that the Father had hidden things from the wise and understanding and revealed them to the babes (Cf. 1 Cor 1.26*ff*).[96]

So then, if in Ephesians 5.16 it makes sense to give to καιρός its expected import, we should understand Paul to speak of buying the occasion, the

---

[96] At first glance, it might appear that Matthew uses ἐν ἐκείνῳ τῷ καιρῷ as nothing more than a transition device, and that καιρῷ simply means χρόνῳ. But in Mt 12.1, the particular occasion on which Jesus plucked the grain on the Sabbath is recounted immediately after Jesus said, "my yoke is easy and my burden is light" (cf. Mt 23.4). In Mt 13.30, the point of καὶ ἐν καιρῷ τοῦ θερισμοῦ is that the harvest provides the appropriate occasion for separating the tares from the wheat. In Mt 14.1, it was Jesus' aforementioned return to "his own country" that accounted for Herod's attention to Jesus' activities and speculation that this was John, risen from the dead. In Mt. 16:3, the times are those of particular characteristics that can be signified, and not merely time in the abstract. In Mt 21.34, 21.41, and 24.45, the point is again the appropriate time. And in Mt 26.18, the reference is to the particular time for which Jesus had come to earth.

moment, the opportunity. The days are evil, so be careful how you walk in them, taking opportunity when you see an opportunity. We might say, "taking advantage of the opportunity." The idea then seems to be, the days are evil, that is, we live in wicked times—when you have an opportunity, when an occasion arises in which you must make a choice between wisdom and folly, take advantage of the opportunity to follow wisdom. That kind of decision-making characterizes one who walks in wisdom.

ὅτι αἱ ἡμέραι πονηραί εἰσιν With this phrase, Paul calls attention once again to the world out of which these Gentile believers have come, and the contrast that should be manifest between their new lives and the world around them. In 2.2, Paul had written of *the power of the air, the spirit now working in the sons of disobedience.* After having said, *you must no longer walk just as the Gentiles also walk,* and after having spelled out specific behaviors wherein their lives must now be different, he offers a spiritual pep talk: "Wake up! Watch carefully how you walk! Take advantage of the opportunity to walk as wise rather than as unwise. The opportunity is here, because the days are evil. For example, rather than resorting to the revelry and escapism in drink, be filled with the Spirit, and find joy in singing psalms and hymns and spiritual songs. That is to say, let your heart and your life be lifted above these evil days."

5.17–18 *On account of this, do not be unwise, but understand what the the will of the Lord is.*   That is, on account of the preceding, the fact that the days are evil, understand what the will of the Lord is.

And then Paul offers an example of the kind of choice he has in mind: *And do not be drunk with wine in which is dissipation, but be filled with the Spirit.* Whereas the Gentiles seek pleasure by being drunk with wine which leads to ἀσωτία (*dissipation*), Paul tells those who have become the house of God, πληροῦσθε ἐν πνεύματι.

ἀσωτία has to do generally with lack of restraint. We see the cognate adverb in Luke 15.13. The *"prodigal* son" wasted his inheritance *living loosely* (ζῶν ἀσώτως). You can hear him asking himself, "Where did it all go?" and having no answer because he spent it with such little thought. He had scattered (διεσκόρπισεν, as one broadcasts seed) his substance to no purpose. Aristotle said of ἄσωτος, "Really it denotes the possessor of one articular vice, that of wasting one's substance."[97]

---

[97] Ethic. Nic. iv.1.5, Loeb Classical Library, London: William Heinemann 1926. Translated by H. Rackham.

Paul calls his audience to no longer walk as the Gentiles walk (4.17), and Peter describes the way of life among Gentiles as one of dissipation,

> For the time already past is sufficient for you to have carried out the desire of the Gentiles, having pursued a course of sensuality, lusts, drunkenness, carousing, drinking parties and abominable idolatries. In all this, they are surprised that you do not run with them into the same excesses of dissipation (ἀσωτίας), and they malign you (1 Pt 4.3–4).

Intoxicating drink often results in squandering financial resources, both directly as money is spent on alcohol, and more especially indirectly as financial troubles mount in the life of the person who is given to drink. Compare Proverbs 23.21.

In form, πληροῦσθε (*be filled*) could be either indicative or imperative. But it is set over against the prior μεθύσκεσθε which we understand to be imperative not only because the context demands it, but also because the negative particle μὴ is used rather than οὐ which would have been used had the indicative been intended. So then as the alternative to the prohibition *be not drunken*, we understand πληροῦσθε as an imperative, *be filled*.

Should we understand the dative construction ἐν πνεύματι as a locative, *in spirit*, or as an instrumental dative, *with the Spirit*? The instrumental use of ἐν is found in Hellenistic Greek,[98] and is perhaps even more predominately found in the New Testament due to Semitic influence.[99] To be sure, our tendency to attempt rigid differentiation between locative and instrumental overlooks the fact that there is often ambiguity, at least in the mind of the hearer if not also in the mind of the speaker, and yet the meaning of the phrase is clearly communicated. And this is because very often the same reality can be described with a view to location or

---

[98] Robertson, p. 73, 91.

[99] Robertson, p. 102, 452, 533*f*, 590. At one time, the instrumental ἐν was deemed a Hebraism, but Moulton says it was "rescued from the class of 'Hebraisms' by the publication of the Tebtunis Papyris (1902), which presented us with half-a-dozen Ptolemaic citations for it." (Moulton, Prolegomena, p 12). NT examples of instrumental ἐν include ἐν τίνι ἁλισθήσεται (Mt 5.13), ἐν ᾧ γὰρ κρίματι κρίνετε κριθήσεσθε, καὶ ἐν ᾧ μέτρῳ μετρεῖτε μετρηθήσεται ὑμῖν (Mt 7.2), ἐν τῷ Βεελζεβοὺλ (Mt 12.24), καὶ εἰ ἐγὼ ἐν Βεελζεβοὺλ ἐκβάλλω τὰ δαιμόνια, οἱ υἱοὶ ὑμῶν ἐν τίνι ἐκβάλλουσιν (Mt 12.27), εἰ δὲ ἐν πνεύματι θεοῦ ἐγὼ ἐκβάλλω τὰ δαιμόνια (Mt 12.28), εἰ πατάξομεν ἐν μαχαίρῃ (Lk 22.49), ἐν πυρὶ ἀποκαλύπτεται (1 Cor 3.13), οὐ στενοχωρεῖσθε ἐν ἡμῖν, στενοχωρεῖσθε δὲ ἐν τοῖς σπλάγχνοις ὑμῶν (2 Cor. 6.12), ἀποκτεῖναι ἐν ῥομφαίᾳ καὶ ἐν λιμῷ καὶ ἐν θανάτῳ (Rev 6.8).

instrumentality. Indeed, Robertson says, "all the N.T. examples of ἐν can be explained from the point of view of the locative."[100]

Certainly this ambiguity is also present in English. Whether I say, "I went to Texas in a car," or "I went to Texas by car," I am describing the same reality. If we say, "He was elected in a landslide," is the "in" locative or instrumental? If the speaker is especially conscious of the metaphor, and visualizes the candidate coming down the hillside amidst sliding dirt, rocks and trees which represent the many votes in his favor, then it's easy to see the locative idea. But if the expression has become so familiar that the metaphor is forgotten and the thought of a literal landslide no longer comes to mind, then the speaker is probably thinking instrumentally: The candidate was elected "by" a large majority.

In the present instance, however, being filled in spirit can mean something very different than being filled by the Spirit. The locative idea would point to one's own spirit being filled[101] whereas the instrumental idea would point to his being filled by God's Spirit.

Taking ἐν πνεύματι as instrumental permits a tight parallel to οἴνῳ—do not be drunken *with wine*, be filled *with the Spirit*. So then the admonition is not merely "be full in spirit" as if to say, "have a heart of happiness" or "be upbeat." It is rather an instruction to be filled with, or by, the Spirit of God.

While there is no definite article, πνεῦμα was often used as we would use proper nouns, just as was θεός. In Greek, proper nouns were sometimes articular, but often were not. Therefore the absence of the article is no obstacle to our understanding the phrase to mean, "with the Spirit."[102]

Luke often describes someone as being filled with the Spirit without the article, though he always uses a genitive construction. Jesus was πλήρης πνεύματος ἁγίου (Lk 4.1). On the day of Pentecost, the disciples ἐπλήσθησαν πάντες πνεύματος ἁγίου (Acts 2.4). In Acts 6.3, seven men who were πλήρεις πνεύματος were to be chosen. Then Stephen, one of the seven, was particularly described as being πλήρης πίστεως καὶ πνεύματος ἁγίου (Acts 6.5). Stephen was again described as being πλήρης πνεύματος ἁγίου just before he was stoned to death (Acts 7.55). Barnabas was πλήρης πνεύματος ἁγίου (Acts 11.24).

---

[100] Robertson, p. 590.

[101] This seems to be Wescott's interpretation, p. 81*f*.

[102] We have anarthrous πνεῦμα used of the Holy Spirit in Lk 4.1. In Mt 12.28 (ἐν πνεύματι θεοῦ) and again in Mt 22.43 (ἐν πνεύματι) we have instrumental ἐν with anarthrous πνεῦμα referring to the Spirit of God.

Meyer well noted the obvious but too often overlooked implication of the passive imperative: "the possibility of resistance to the Holy Spirit."[103] Paul's instruction to be filled with the Spirit calls for an obedient response, and that implies a choice. Those who attribute a changed life to the Holy Spirit as if they had no choice in the matter are deluded. Indeed, their repudiation of any choice on their part leaves them subject to the impulses of the flesh.

5.19 *speaking to each other in psalms and hymns and spiritual songs* (λαλοῦντες ἑαυτοῖς [ἐν] ψαλμοῖς καὶ ὕμνοις καὶ ᾠδαῖς πνευματικαῖς) Music was already well developed prior to the first century. In "Concerning Music," a work attributed to Plutarch but thought to have actually been written much earlier by someone else, the narrator gives an account of a feast during which learned men recounted the history of music (both vocal and instrumental), and discussed the prior development of rhythms, harmonies, musical scales, semitones and tetrachords. Specifically, three kinds of scales are discussed, the enharmonic (being the oldest), the diatonic, and the chromatic. One would need to know quite a bit about music theory to comprehend all that is said. The respective merits of simple and complex melodies and rhythms are discussed. One speaker distinguishes between the music of the theater and the music appropriate for the praise of the gods and of great men, and reckons different types of music as having different moral character.

In the phrase λαλοῦντες ἑαυτοῖς (*speaking to one another*), we see the reflexive ἑαυτοῖς for the reciprocal.[104] The idea is not necessarily antiphonal,[105] but is perhaps merely the Spirit-led counterpart to the convivial affairs of the pagans. God's people, no less than others, have a communal need. But their communion should be in things that edify (1 Cor 14.26).

The word ψαλμός is found in Euripides for the sound of a bowstring when an arrow is released.[106] LSJ cite occurrences where it is used of "the sound of the cithara or harp." But in the LXX, the word was used for

---

[103] Meyer, p. 505.

[104] Robertson, p. 690, cf. Moulton Prol. p. 87.

[105] It need not be antiphonal here any more than in the phrase χαριζόμενοι ἑαυτοῖς (*forgiving one another*) in 4.32, or the phrase γίνεσθε εἰς ἀλλήλους χρηστοί (*be kind to one another*) in the same verse.

[106] Ion, 173: As Ion goes about the business of cleaning the temple at Delphi and shooing away birds, he warns a bird, ψαλμοί σ᾽ εἴρξουσιν τόξων, *twangs of bows will keep you away*.

miz^emor (*melody*) 57 times in Psalm titles. Additionally, it was used for cognates of *miz^emor* in 2 Kings 23.1 (=2 Sam 23.1 in English Bibles), Psalm 80.2 (=81.2), Psalm 97.5 (=98.5) and Psalm 146.1 (=147.1).[107]

The plural ψαλμοί came to be the name not only for those designated by the term *miz^emor*, but for the entire collection. So for example, in Codex Sinaiticus, after the last psalm, there is a subscription, "Psalms of David."[108] When Jesus spoke of "the law of Moses and the prophets and the psalms" (Lk 24.44), he either had in mind the collection of psalms that we know as the book of Psalms, or perhaps as some suppose, he used the word even more broadly to refer to the third part of the OT scriptures known as the *ketuvim*, the writings, which included the Psalms. Luke knows the Psalms as a collection such that he quotes from the "book of Psalms" (Lk 20.42, Acts 1.20). Paul knows the Psalms arranged in order, so that he can quote from the "second Psalm" (Acts 13.33).

Really, only 1 Corinthians 14.26 stands as an obstacle to understanding all NT occurrences of ψαλμός as references to the OT book of Psalms. Someone has argued that inasmuch as the context there suggests a Spirit-directed psalm, it would necessarily not be one from the OT. But this is a *non sequitur*. Why could not the Spirit of God direct a worshiper to sing a particular song from the OT, and even give him perfect remembrance of that psalm? So then in the end, it is most natural to suppose that Paul does indeed have in mind the Psalms of the OT.

A hymn (ὕμνος) was especially a song *"in praise* of gods or heroes."[109] In the aforementioned work "Concerning Music," it is said, "for to sing hymns (ὑμνεῖν) is pious and primary to men, the gods having graciously given to them alone articulate voice."[110] The same work disparages the music of the theater as decadent[111] in contrast to the ancient music that was primarily designed to honor gods and to praise good men, such as is called ὕμνος earlier in the work.[112]

In the NT, the noun is used only here and in the very similar Colos-

---

[107] In ten other places, it translates unrelated words.

[108] The subscription reads, ΨΑΛΜΟΙ ΔΑΑ, the second word being a misspelling of the frequent abbreviation, ΔΑΔ.

[109] LSJ p. 1849.

[110] On Music, 2. ὑμνεῖν γὰρ εὐσεβὲς καὶ προηγούμενον ἀνθρώποις τοὺς χαρισαμένους αὐτοῖς μόνοις τὴν ἔναρθρον φωνὴν θεούς.

[111] On Music, 27, ἐπιδέδωκεν τὸ τῆς διαφθορᾶς εἶδος, *has given way to a form of corruption.*

[112] E.g., On Music, 3.

sians 3.16. The verb ὑμνέω is found at Matthew 26.30, Mark 14.26, Acts 16.25, and Hebrews 2.12.

The fact that songs of praise to God are indicated by the words ψαλμός and ὕμνος is not at odds with the emphasis on speaking one to another, or as in Colossians 3.16, "teaching and admonishing one another." One may teach others by proclaiming God in their hearing and by acknowledging one's dependence upon God to them. We often see this connection in the OT Psalms, as in Psalm 17.50 (=18.49, quoted at Rom. 15.9), διὰ τοῦτο ἐξομολογήσομαί σοι, κύριε, ἐν τοῖς ἔθνεσιν καὶ ἐν τῷ ὀνόματί σου ψαλῶ, (*on account of this I will confess you, Lord, among the nations, and in your name I will make music*).[113]

ᾠδαῖς πνευματικαῖς is *spiritual songs*. In almost all witnesses, the noun is accompanied by the adjective πνευματικαῖς (*spiritual*). It is absent only in 𝔓[46], B, and in a couple of old Latin translations. The critical apparatus in NA28 and UBS5, as well as Metzger's Textual Commentary, curiously indicate that the word is also absent in Ambrosiaster. Ambrosiaster is the name given to an unknown fourth century author who wrote, among other things, commentaries on Paul's letters. However, Ambrosiaster's commentary on Ephesians, as published in Migne, quotes 5.19 as follows: *Sed impleamini Spiritu sancto, loquentes vobismetipsis, in psalmis, et hymnis, et canticis spiritualibus.* Clearly the adjective is present—*canticis spiritualibus* is "spiritual songs."

In contrast to the words ψαλμός and ὕμνος, ᾠδή (*song*) carried no reverent or religious connotation. Other than here and at Colossians 3.16, it is found only in Revelation (5.9, 14.3 twice, and 15.3). The feminine adjective agrees only with feminine ᾠδαῖς. Lincoln cites BDF §135.3 to the effect that when there are disparate nouns, an adjective need agree only with the nearest, and concludes that πνευματικαῖς (*spiritual*) describes all three of the preceding nouns. But Hoehner rightly points out that "the first two nouns normally have specific reference to the praise of God, whereas the last noun is more general, suggesting that Paul wanted to ensure that believers sang spiritual songs, that is, songs that issued from hearts filled by the Holy Spirit rather than produced by wine."[114]

These three terms are not to be thought of as mutually exclusive, for when Josephus spoke of Jewish scriptures as being composed of the

---

[113] See also Ps. 56:10 (ἐξομολογήσομαί σοι ἐν λαοῖς, κύριε, ψαλῶ σοι ἐν ἔθνεσιν), κ.τ.λ.
[114] Hoehner p. 709.

books of Moses, the prophets, and the hymns (ὕμνους),[115] the hymns surely included the Psalms, as well as other poetic books. When Philo mentions hymns (ὑμνούς)[116] in connection with the laws and sayings delivered through prophets, he possibly has reference to the Psalms.[117] And of course many ψαλμοί are, in fact, ὕμνοι. A particular song might be a psalm, a hymn, and also an ode (ᾠδή).

But this is not to suggest that the three words are merely "another example of this writer's fondness for piling up synonyms."[118] They represent three categories of songs, though there is easily overlap among them. Josephus sees fit to mention ὕμνοις and ψαλμοῖς distinctly in Ant. 12.7.7, "honoring God with hymns (ὕμνοις) and psalms (ψαλμοῖς)." And in another passage where Josephus speaks of things composed by David and therefore must have in mind Psalms, he speaks distinctly of ὕμνους (hymns) and ᾠδάς (odes).[119] So then a particular psalm may be an ᾠδή, and another may be a ὕμνος. And there were also hymns and odes that were not among the Psalms.

The conclusion is that Paul first mentioned psalms, probably having in mind the Psalms of the OT, and then in addition he mentioned hymns, meaning songs of praise and mentioned separately so as to include songs not from the OT, and finally songs that were not necessarily songs of praise, but such as were nonetheless spiritual and therefore edifying. Certainly an OT psalm of praise to God could be aptly described by all three terms. But not every spiritual song could be so described.

singing and making music with your heart to the Lord (ᾄδοντες καὶ ψάλλοντες τῇ καρδίᾳ ὑμῶν τῷ κυρίῳ) The meaning of ψάλλοντες, from ψάλλω, is much discussed. It is undisputed that originally, the word meant "to pluck" as "to pluck a string," and, accordingly, was used for playing a stringed instrument. It is also clear that the meaning of the word evolved, for in modern Greek, ψάλλω indicates only the use of the voice, meaning *chant* or *sing*. But this evolution was not monophonic. In the middle of the evolution, its use was (if we may use a musical analogy) more like a song with multiple parts rather than a single melody. That is, in the middle of the evolution, the word might be used in one context to

---

[115] Against Apion, 1.8.

[116] The Contemplative Live, 25.

[117] Colson, Appendix to *De Vita Contemplativa*, p. 520, Philo, vol. 9 in the Loeb series.

[118] Lincoln, p. 346.

[119] Ant. 7.12.3, ᾠδὰς εἰς τὸν θεὸν καὶ ὕμνους συνετάξατο.

mean merely *sing*, and in the same time period might otherwise be used to mean *play an instrument*, and by another writer might be used of singing that was accompanied by a musical instrument.

In the LXX, translated during the third and second centuries BC and in the midst of this evolution, ψάλλω is very often used of singing praises,[120] sometimes used of singing where the context clearly indicates the accompaniment of an instrument, and at the same time also still used specifically of playing an instrument in a dozen instances.[121] A clear example is LXX 1 Kings 16.23 (=1 Sam 16.23), *And David took the kinnor and played* (ἔψαλλεν) *it with his hand.*[122] And then there are a half dozen passages in the LXX where a musical instrument is mentioned but ψάλλω represents *zamar* which sometimes means *sing* and sometimes means *play an instrument.*[123] And finally, there is one passage where ψάλλω represents *nagan* but clearly the meaning is sing and not play.[124]

The evolution continued. Kurfees was mistaken when he wrote, "at the opening of the New Testament period…this change had been completely effected."[125] Late in the first century, Josephus described the remedy for Saul's discomfiture as someone who was able to play upon a kinnor

---

[120] Usually when representing *zamar*. Ps. 65.4 (66.4 in English Bibles) is a good example: πᾶσα ἡ γῆ προσκυνησάτωσάν σοι καὶ ψαλάτωσάν σοι, ψαλάτωσαν τῷ ὀνόματί σου, Let all the earth worship you and sing praise to you, let them sing praise to your name. Another is Ps. 70.23 (=71.23). ἀγαλλιάσονται τὰ χείλη μου, ὅταν ψάλω σοι, My lips will rejoice whenever I sing praise to you. Often in the Psalms, ψάλλω is associated with confessing, i.e., acknowledging God, as in Ps. 56.10 (=57.9): ἐξομολογήσομαί σοι ἐν λαοῖς, κύριε, ψαλῶ σοι ἐν ἔθνεσιν, I will acknowledge you among peoples, Lord, I will sing praise to you among nations. Passages where ψάλλω probably means *sing* are Jd 5.3, 2 Ki 22.50 (=2 Sam 22.50), Ps 7.17, 9.2, 9.12 (=9.11), 17.50 (=18.49), 20.13 (=21.13), 26.6 (=27.6), 29.5 (=30.4), 29.13 (=30.12), 46.7 (=47.6), 46.8 (=47.7), 56.7 (=57.7), 56.10 (=57.9), 58.18 (=59.17), 60.9 (=61.8), 65.2 (=66.2), 65.4 (=66.4), 67.5 (=68.4), 67.33 (=68.32), 70.23 (=71.23), 74.9 (=75.9), 91.2 (=92.1), 97.4 (=98.4), 103.33 (=104.33), 104.2 (=105.2), 107.1 (=108.1), 107.4 (=108.4), 134.3 (=135.3), 137.1 (=138.1), 145.2 (=146.2), 12.6 (=13.6), 67.34 (=68.33), 100.2 (=101.2), Sir 9.4.

[121] 1 Ki 16.16 (=1 Sam 16.16) 2x, 1 Ki 16.17 (=1 Sam 16.17), 1 Ki 16.18 (=1 Sam 16.18), 1 Ki 16.23 (=1 Sam 16.23), 1 Ki 18.10 (=1 Sam 18.10), 1 Ki 19.9 (=1 Sam. 19.9), 4 Ki 3.15 (=2 Ki 3.15) 3x, Ps 32.3 (=33.3), Ps 67.26 (=68.25). In all of these passages, ψάλλω represents *nagan*.

[122] καὶ ἐλάμβανεν Δαυιδ τὴν κινύραν καὶ ἔψαλλεν ἐν τῇ χειρὶ αὐτοῦ.

[123] Ps 32.2 (=33.2), 70.22 (=71.22), 97.5 (=98.5), 143.9 (=144.9), 146.7 (=147.7), 149.3 (=149.3). In all these, ψάλλω represents *zamar*. BDB reckons *zamar* in all six of these passages as examples where it is used "of playing musical instruments."

[124] Ps. 68.13 (= 69.12), *and those who drink wine were singing to me* (καὶ εἰς ἐμὲ ἔψαλλον οἱ πίνοντες τὸν οἶνον). The parallelism with "those who sit in the gate talk about me" is conclusive for the meaning.

[125] Kurfees, p. 97.

(ψάλλειν ἐπὶ κινύρᾳ),[126] and then tells of David as the one who served as Saul's only physician by *singing the hymns and playing the kinnor* (λέγων τε τοὺς ὕμνους καὶ ψάλλων ἐν τῇ κινύρᾳ).[127] Late in the first century or early in the second, Plutarch used ψάλλω for playing an instrument.[128] Even after the writing of the NT, Lucian in the second century was still using ψάλλω to mean *play a stringed instrument*, saying it is impossible *to play* (ψάλλειν) without a lyre just as it is impossible to go horseback riding without a horse or to pipe without flutes.[129]

So then when we come to the New Testament, we cannot determine the meaning of ψάλλω simply by the date of the composition. Danker is responsible for the comment in both BGAD and BDAG that "those who favor 'play' (e.g. L-S-J-M; ASouter, Pocket Lexicon, 1920; JMoffatt, transl. 1913) may be relying too much on the earliest mng. of ψάλλω."[130] Both Lincoln and Hoehner make reference to this comment and conclude that the word is used for singing here. (Hoehner specifies that it means singing psalms.) Notwithstanding the observations of these learned commentators, we must give due consideration to the phrasing in Ephesians 5.19 which, as we shall see, suggests the usage of ψάλλω as found in Psalm 32 and Psalm 146 of the LXX is in view.

To be sure, the other four NT occurrences of ψάλλω (Rom 15.9, twice in 1 Cor 14.15, James 5.13) all seem to mean "sing" in view of the respective contexts. But the occurrence in Ephesians 5.19 must be considered on its own merit.

The language here is reminiscent of Psalm 32.2 in the LXX (=Ps. 33.2 in the MT and in English translations). There, we see the imperative

---

[126] Ant. 6.166.

[127] Ant. 6.168. Josephus also used ψάλλειν twice in this context for "play" without a named object.

[128] Pericles 1.5, ὁ δὲ Φίλιππος πρὸς τὸν υἱὸν ἐπιτερπῶς ἔν τινι πότῳ ψήλαντα καὶ τεχνικῶς εἶπεν· "Οὐκ αἰσχύνη καλῶς οὕτω ψάλλων;" ἀρκεῖ γάρ, ἂν βασιλεὺς ἀκροᾶσθαι ψαλλόντων σχολάζῃ, καὶ πολὺ νέμει ταῖς Μούσαις ἑτέρων ἀγωνιζομένων τὰ τοιαῦτα θεατὴς γιγνόμενος. "And so Philip once said to his son, who, as the wine went round, plucked the strings charmingly and skilfully, 'Art not ashamed to pluck the strings so well?' It is enough, surely, if a king have leisure to hear others pluck the strings, and he pays great deference to the Muses if he be but a spectator of such contests." Plutarch Lives, vol. 3, Loeb Classical Library, English Translation by Bernadotte Perrin. Cambridge, MA. Harvard University Press. London. William Heinemann Ltd. 1916, reprint 2001.

[129] Καὶ αἱ μὲν ἄλλαι τέχναι χωρὶς ὀργάνων οὐδαμῶς τῷ κεκτημένῳ ὑπηρετεῖν δύνανται· οὔτε γὰρ αὐλεῖν ἔνι χωρὶς αὐλῶν οὔτε ψάλλειν ἄνευ λύρας οὔτε ἱππεύειν ἄνευ ἵππου. Concerning a Parasite, 17.

[130] BDAG, p. 1096. Cf. BAGD, p. 891.

ψάλατε, while here in Ephesians 5.19 Paul uses the participle ψάλλοντες. There, the music is directed to αὐτῷ (*him*), the antecedent of which is κυρίῳ (*Lord*), just as here, the music is τῷ κυρίῳ (*to the Lord*). There, the instrument, the thing with which one makes the music, is indicated by the instrumental dative, (ἐν ψαλτηρίῳ δεκαχόρδῳ, *with the ten stringed lyre*), as also here (τῇ καρδίᾳ, *with the heart*). Similar parallels can be drawn between the phrase here in Ephesians 5.19 and Psalm 146.7 in the LXX (ψάλατε τῷ θεῷ ἡμῶν ἐν κιθάρᾳ).[131]

To be sure, in the LXX, the preposition ἐν (*in*) represents the Hebrew בְּ, in which case one might suppose the translator's thought was locative rather than instrumental. But Delitzsch says, "The בְּ is *Beth instrum*." In any event, as discussed in connection with the previous verse, the locative and instrumental ideas are often closely related. Whether one thinks of playing music on a harp or playing music with a harp, in both Hebrew and Greek this could be expressed using the same preposition.

The point here is that the language of Ephesians 5.19 is very much reminiscent of the language of the LXX, and in particular, of passages where ψάλλω was used for instrumental music. We need not doubt that the word was well on its way to meaning merely "sing" and that this was the meaning in most of its NT occurrences. But the similarity to the language of Psalm 32.2 and 146.7 suggests that in Ephesians 5.19, Paul uses the word ψάλλω in the older sense of playing an instrument, and then identifies the heart as the instrument.

So then this is a metaphorical use of the word ψάλλω. Notwithstanding the attempts to argue that ψάλλω in and of itself cannot mean play but must mean sing, the instrumental dative here is probably best understood, by way of analogy to these OT passages, as viewing the heart as being in place of the ψαλτηρίῳ or the κινύραν, such that the imagery is playing a musical instrument. But the fact that the heart is the instrument is in keeping with the worship of the New Testament church wherein the things made with hands, the mere copies and shadows, have been replaced by the spiritual things that are indeed the true, the real.

---

[131] In view of the language, "made with hands" in Heb 9.11,24, it is also possible that the contrast Paul has in mind is between the heart and the *hands* rather than between the heart and the *musical instrument*. The phrase ψάλλοντες τῇ καρδίᾳ ὑμῶν could be contrasted with ἔψαλλεν ἐν τῇ χειρὶ αὐτοῦ (1 Ki 16.23, LXX; = 1 Sam 16.23). In both instances, we see the instrumental dative, but in the OT passage, David took the κινύραν and made music ἐν τῇ χειρὶ αὐτοῦ (*with his hand*), whereas here in Eph 5.19, Paul urges his readers to make music τῇ καρδίᾳ ὑμῶν (*with your heart*).

When Paul substitutes the heart as the instrument in place of the ten-stringed lyre or the cithara, we see the same sort of contrast between the OT and NT worship that is developed in Hebrews 9. The former involved things made with hands. The latter is spiritual. Calvin caught this contrast and called attention to the pedagogical purpose of the musical instruments, incense, and other physical elements of OT worship, as well as their impropriety in NT worship, in his comment on Psalm 33.2:

> There is a distinction, however, to be observed here, that we may not indiscriminately consider as applicable to ourselves, every thing which was formerly enjoined upon the Jews. I have no doubt that playing upon cymbals, touching the harp and the viol, and all that kind of music, which is so frequently mentioned in the Psalms, was a part of the education; that is to say, the puerile instruction of the law...But when [believers today] frequent their sacred assemblies, musical instruments in celebrating the praises of God would be no more suitable than the burning of incense, the lighting up of lamps, and the restoration of the other shadows of the law.

We should note that Paul does not have in view only the sacred assemblies of New Testament Christians. Paul's point is not to prescribe the manner of conducting an assembly as much as it is to contrast the spiritual focus of the Christian's joyful life with the empty, dissolute revelry of the pagan's life. But in borrowing the language of the OT to make this point, modifying it only to substitute the heart for the instrument made with hands, he underscores the contrast between the worship that characterized the old covenant and the worship that characterizes the new covenant.

This is not to say that Christians should shun entertainment by musical instruments or secular entertainment altogether. Nor is it to say that the NT focus on the spiritual rather than a mechanism made with hands should constitute some rigid rule stipulating that a reverent word and mechanically produced note must never occupy the same air space. As Calvin said of believers under the new covenant, "even now, if believers choose to cheer themselves with musical instruments, they should, I think, make it their object not to dissever their cheerfulness from the praises of God." How far removed would it be from Paul's point if believers were to conclude that when they exult in the joys of life they must think only secular thoughts.

But it is to say that the purposeful use of instruments made with hands in worshiping God belonged to a time of instruction that utilized physical objects to teach spiritual concepts. The instruments produced a joyful sound that served as a hint of the joy that one might truly find in the coming Christ. But the Law had merely a shadow of the good things to come, not the very image. The body is Christ. Why now turn back to the weak and beggarly elements that were merely a shadow? In fact, the use of the instrument in worship today is sometimes a sign that the worshipers are no more advanced in their spirituality than many in OT Israel, and that they must have the instrument to have any joy, for their hearts have not found it in Christ.

Paul describes the Spirit filled man using four participles, λαλοῦντες (*speaking*), ᾄδοντες καὶ ψάλλοντες (*singing and making music*), and εὐχαριστοῦντες (*giving thanks*). These function as adverbial participles, but can more specifically be described as participles indicating attendant circumstances.

These participles all have to do with joyful expression. The first three in particular pertain to mutual edification through singing. This is in contrast to the empty revelry of the Gentiles. Peter describes the Gentiles in their dissipation as "having pursued a course of sensuality, lusts, drunkenness, carousing, drinking parties and abominable idolatries." My nephew, a young man in his twenties not too far removed from undergraduate life, recently paraphrased the middle of this description in a way that brings home the similarity between the worldly life of the first century and the worldly life we must leave behind today: "1 Pet 4:3 is saying (paraphrased), 'don't drink to get drunk, don't go to frat parties, and don't participate in cocktail parties.'" The difference Paul is describing is the difference between the person who lives for the weekend when he can get drunk and sleep off his hangover and the person who finds recreation in joyfully singing praises to God with other saints.

5.20 *Always giving thanks to God for all things in the name of our Lord Jesus Christ* (εὐχαριστοῦντες πάντοτε ὑπὲρ πάντων ἐν ὀνόματι τοῦ κυρίου ἡμῶν Ἰησοῦ Χριστοῦ τῷ θεῷ καὶ πατρί) We might have supposed ὑπὲρ πάντων means *on behalf of all* rather than *for everything*, interpreting ὑπὲρ in accordance with its usual meaning with the genitive and taking πάντων as masculine rather than neuter. But there are a couple of good reasons for translating ὑπὲρ πάντων "for all things." Hoehner prefers "for all things" in part because of the parallel passage at Colossians 3.17 where the preceding "do all in the name of the Lord" would more likely be followed by an admonition to give thanks for all things than by an admonition to give thanks on behalf of everyone. It may also be noted that in Hellenistic Greek, ὑπὲρ was encroaching upon the uses of περί.[132] We see an earlier example of this phenomenon in this very letter and, moreover, in a phrase about giving thanks. At Ephesians 1.16, we read οὐ παύομαι εὐχαριστῶν ὑπὲρ ὑμῶν (*I cease not giving thanks for you*), where clearly the meaning is not giving thanks on behalf of you, as if they should be giving the thanks but Paul does it for them. Paul can only mean he is grateful for the saints to whom he writes and expresses this to God.

5.22–6.9   Haustafel, or Household Code

Attempts have been made to find a secular source for what is called the household code, the instructions for household members found in Ephesians 5–6, Colossians 3, 1 Peter 2–3, 1 Timothy 2 and 6, and Titus 2.[133] For example, according to Hoehner, Dibelius saw Colossians 3.18–4.1 as "a lightly Christianized version of a Stoic code."[134] Caird went so far as to turn Paul's purpose on its head, suggesting (again, according to Hoehner) that Paul was urging conformity with societal norms because many of his readers' husbands and masters "may not have been a part of the believing community."[135] But we should keep in mind that Paul's purpose is to encourage his readers to walk not as the Gentiles walk. His instructions are designed to point them in a different direction.

While there were secular discussions of household management that had certain things in common with the instructions given by Paul,[136] Hoehner sees significant contrasts between the Hellenistic concept of household management and Paul's discussion of the same. Hoehner writes, "Greek literature addresses those in the positions of authority (e.g., the husband, father and master) but not those who are asked to submit to authority (e.g.,

---

[132] BDF §231, p. 121.

[133] For a discussion of the history of these efforts, see Hoehner, 720ff.

[134] Hoehner, p. 721.

[135] Ibid. p. 726.

[136] E.g., Aristotle wrote, "Household management falls into departments corresponding to the parts of which the household in its turn is composed...the primary and smallest parts of the household are master and slave, husband and wife, father and children," *Politics* 1.2.1. Translated by H. Rackham, Loeb Classical Library, Harvard University Press.

the wife, children, and slave), whereas the NT addresses both the husbands and the wives, the fathers and the children, the masters and the slaves."[137]

Furthermore, not only do the NT passages address those who are instructed to submit, but at least in the case of wives and slaves, the NT does so with complete acknowledgement that they are fully the intellectual equals of their husbands or masters, and that their submission is to be chosen as a matter of their will and as a reflection of their submission to the Lord.

Greek writings portrayed the subordinate members of these relationships as inferior, and therefore subjected, by nature. Regarding women, Aristotle wrote, "the male is by nature superior and the female inferior, the male ruler and the female subject."[138] Regarding slaves and in response to some who objected to slavery on the grounds that it was contrary to nature and therefore unjust, Aristotle wrote, "the manager of a household must have his tools, and of tools some are lifeless and others living." He said, "a slave is a live article of property."[139] And further, "he is by nature a slave who is capable of belonging to another (and that is why he does so belong), and who participates in reason so far as to apprehend it but not to possess it."[140] Aristotle went on to compare slaves to animals, having strong bodies and therefore being serviceable for the necessities of life, whereas those who by nature are freemen have been made "serviceable for a life of citizenship."[141]

In discussing the free/slave, male/female, man/child relationships, Aristotle spoke of the one who rules as having reason (τοῦ λογον ἔχοντος), and the one who is ruled as being irrational (τοῦ ἀλόγου).[142] He allowed that all (whether free or slave, male or female, man or child) "possess the various parts of the soul," but opined that they "possess them in different ways; for the slave has not got the deliberative part at all, and the female has it, but without full authority....Hence the ruler must possess intellectual virtue in completeness...while each of the other parties must have that share of this virtue which is appropriate to them."[143]

---

[137] Hoehner, p. 724.

[138] Politics 1.2.12. Translated by H. Rackham, Loeb Classical Library, Harvard University Press.

[139] Ibid., Politics 1.2.4.

[140] Ibid., Politics 1.2.13.

[141] Ibid., Politics 1.2.14.

[142] Ibid., Politics 1.5.5.

[143] Ibid., Politics 1.5.6–7.

From such a perspective, one can hardly imagine an appeal such as Paul's being addressed to women, let alone to slaves, wherein they are called to submit as a rational choice in response to a gracious God. Remember that Paul's appeal is part of the "therefore" section of Ephesians (chapters 4–6); it is based on the prior discussion of the great blessings God has bestowed on the Gentiles in Christ (chapters 1–3). Aristotle regarded the submission of the woman or of the slave as simply a matter of course due to their nature, and would have seen any attempt to reason with the woman or with the slave, any attempt to present a rationale to the woman or to the slave, as a pointless exercise. Indeed, he viewed the ruled to have virtue, but only of an irrational sort. But for Paul, submission to others in some capacity is not due to natural inferiority to others, but corresponds to our submission to Christ who has saved us, having given himself up for us.

In the New Testament, the wife is a joint heir of the grace of life (1 Pt 3.7). Specifically in Paul's remarks, she is one flesh with her husband, and therefore his body for whom he is to give himself up, just as Christ gave himself up for the church. The slave is not inferior to his master by nature, but is to choose to submit to his master as part of his servitude to Christ. His submission is not to be a response merely to compulsion, but a response to the grace of God that offers him the promise of a reward— *"knowing that whatsoever good thing each one does, the same shall he receive again from the Lord."* In the case of Onesimus, his return to his master Philemon was to be not merely as a slave, but as a brother (Phm 16).

So then, Paul's remarks about the household relationships differ from what prevailed in the Gentile world not only in terms of the attitude toward and treatment of those in a subordinate position, but also in terms of the motivation of those who are subordinate. Do not live as the Gentiles live: Submit joyfully, from the heart, because it is the Lord's will, and because submission is fundamental to our very identity as children of a God on whom we are dependent for all things. Do not live as the Gentiles live: Do not take for granted the submission of those whom you are over, but recognize your responsibility for them, and pattern your care for them after Jesus' care for his church.

5.21–32 Wives and Husbands, the Church and Christ

Wives submit yourselves to your own husbands as to the Lord, because a husband is head of the wife as Christ is head of the church, himself being savior of the body. But as the church submits itself to Christ, thus also the wives to the husbands in all things. Husbands, love [your] wives, just as Christ loved the church and gave himself on its behalf, that he might sanctify it by the word, having cleansed it by the washing of water, that he himself might present to himself the church as glorious, not having spot or wrinkle, or any such things, but that it might be holy and blameless. Thus also the husbands ought to love their wives as their bodies. The one who loves his wife loves himself, for no one ever hates his own flesh, but nourishes and cares for it; just as Christ also does for the church because we are members of his body. For this cause a man will leave father and mother and will be joined to his wife and the two shall be as one flesh. This mystery is great, but I speak with reference to Christ and the church. Even so you also, each one of you, let him thus love his wife, and the woman that she might reverence the husband.

STRUCTURE AND TEXTUAL PROBLEM

Both the NA28 and UBS5 have a paragraph break between verse 20 and verse 21, thus connecting "submitting yourselves one to another" with the following discussion of the marriage relationship. This is a change from earlier editions. As recently as the 25th edition of Nestle Aland (so also in WH and Souter), the text was printed so as to suggest that verse 21 was the conclusion of the preceding section and verse 22 marked the beginning of the discussion of marriage.

The evidence seems to support the older arrangement, the conclusion of the preceding section and the beginning of the new section being as follows:

> *And do not be drunk…but be filled with the Spirit*
> *speaking to each other in psalms and hymns and spiritual songs,*
> *singing and making music with your heart to the Lord,*
> *always giving thanks to the God…in the name of our Lord Jesus Christ,*
> *submitting yourselves one to another in reverence of Christ.*
> *Wives submit yourselves to your own husbands as to the Lord…*

A difficult textual issue in verse 22 has some bearing on our thinking about where the preceding thought ends and the new one begins. The textual issue pertains to the presence or absence of a verb in verse 22. If it is absent, we must suppose the verb of verse 21, ὑποτασσόμενοι (*submitting yourselves*), is taken up implicitly in verse 22, and then of course verse 22 must be read with verse 21—"*submitting yourselves to one another, wives to your own husbands as unto the Lord.*" But if there is an explicit finite verb in verse 22, it is possible to see verse 21 as the conclusion of Paul's previous remarks and to see verse 22 as the beginning of a new (though related) thought.

In regard to the verb in verse 22, the textual tradition shows three possibilities: (1) no verb, (2) the verb ὑποτάσσεσθε (*submit yourselves*), and (3) the verb ὑποτασσέσθωσαν (*let them submit themselves*). Among the manuscripts that have a verb in verse 22 (possibilities 2 and 3), there is some variation in the position of that verb.

The manuscripts that have no explicit verb in verse 22 read, αἱ γυναῖκες τοῖς ἰδίοις ἀνδράσιν ὡς τῷ κυρίῳ (*the women to their own husbands as to the Lord*). These include 𝔓⁴⁶ and Vaticanus, as well as some others cited by Jerome that are no longer extant. Clement also quotes the passage without a verb,[144] and the passage is found without a verb in the Latin work of Theodore.

The second person imperative ὑποτάσσεσθε (*submit yourselves*) is found in two positions. Many mss have ὑποτάσσεσθε following the words γυναῖκες τοῖς ἰδίοις ἀνδράσιν (*wives to your own husbands*). This is the Byzantine reading and therefore the reading found in the great bulk of the manuscripts, but apparently none that predate the ninth century. A few mss have ὑποτάσσεσθε (*submit yourselves*) prior to the words *to your own husbands*, γυναῖκες ὑποτάσσεσθε τοῖς ἰδίοις ἀνδράσιν. This reading is found earlier, in codices D (sixth century), F, and G, all three considered part of the Western text tradition.

---

[144] Stromata 4.8. It is worthwhile to note that Clement was indeed quoting and not paraphrasing, and worthwhile to evaluate the care with which he did so by considering the entirety of the quotation: διὸ καὶ ἐν τῇ πρὸς Ἐφεσίους γράφει· ὑποτασσόμενοι ἀλλήλοις ἐν φόβῳ θεοῦ· αἱ γυναῖκες τοῖς ἰδίοις ἀνδράσιν ὡς τῷ κυρίῳ, ὅτι ἀνήρ ἐστι κεφαλὴ τῆς γυναικὸς ὡς καὶ ὁ Χριστὸς κεφαλὴ τῆς ἐκκλησίας, αὐτὸς ὁ σωτὴρ τοῦ σώματος. ἀλλ' ὡς ἡ ἐκκλησία ὑποτάσσεται τῷ Χριστῷ, οὕτως καὶ αἱ γυναῖκες τοῖς ἰδίοις ἀνδράσιν ἐν παντί. οἱ ἄνδρες, ἀγαπᾶτε τὰς γυναῖκας, καθὼς καὶ ὁ Χριστὸς ἠγάπησεν τὴν ἐκκλησίαν· οὕτω καὶ οἱ ἄνδρες ὀφείλουσιν ἀγαπᾶν τὰς ἑαυτῶν γυναῖκας ὡς τὰ ἑαυτῶν σώματα. ὁ ἀγαπῶν τὴν ἑαυτοῦ γυναῖκα ἑαυτὸν ἀγαπᾷ· οὐδεὶς γάρ ποτε τὴν ἑαυτοῦ σάρκα ἐμίσησεν. There are some minor variations from the text as it stands in the UBS5 and NA28 (articular σωτὴρ in vs. 23, addition of ἰδίοις in vs. 24, the transposition of ὀφείλουσιν and καὶ οἱ ἄνδρες in vs. 28). But the only major difference is the omission of vss. 25b-27 which may be an intentional ellipsis.

And finally, some early and significant manuscripts have the third person plural form of the present imperative[145] verb ὑποτασσέσθωσαν following ἀνδράσιν, or in one manuscript, following γυναῖκες. In either position, with this form of the verb the meaning of the clause would be, *Let the wives submit themselves to their own husbands.* This reading has early and strong support in the Alexandrian text type, most notably from Sinaiticus, but also from Alexandrinus and numerous others.[146]

Scribal habits also enter into the discussion. There is often a bias in favor of reckoning the shortest reading as the original inasmuch as scribes sometimes added words to assist the reader, but usually did not intentionally omit words. In this particular instance, if the verb were originally present, there is no good explanation as to how it fell out in some manuscripts. On the other hand, it is easy to argue that the verb was originally absent and those manuscripts that include the verb are the result of scribal attempts to clarify the text, perhaps looking to Colossians 3.18 as a model.

Also, the variety of readings containing a verb, with variations both in person and position, is the sort of variety that occurs when the word was not originally present at all. In this scenario, while different scribes would see a need to clarify the passage by adding a verb, they would make different choices as to what verb should be added and where it should be added. So it may be argued that the textual evidence favors the absence of the verb in verse 22, and this would seem to require that we take verse 21 with verse 22.

But in the absence of ὑποτάσσεσθε or ὑποτασσέσθωσαν in verse 22, the passage is structurally amorphous; there is no finite verb and no clearly identifiable main clause to begin the discussion of the marital relationship. The passage is just a mass of dependent clauses unless we go all the way back to the instruction to be filled with the Spirit (verse 18). If we do that, the passage, abridged, is, "Do not be drunk but be filled with the Spirit, speaking one to another in psalms, hymns, and spiritual songs, giving thanks to God, subjecting yourselves one to another, women to their husbands because the husband is the head of the wife as Christ is the head of the church." Those are some rather disparate thoughts. If indeed the original text had no verb in verse 22, it is very easy to see why a

---

[145] Hoehner mistakenly identifies ὑποτασσέσθωσαν as a subjunctive, p. 730.

[146] ὑποτασσέσθωσαν is found in uncials ℵ, A, I, P, Ψ (following γυναῖκες); in minuscules 6, 33, 81, 104, 256, 263, 365, 424ᶜ,436, 459, 1175, 1241, 1319, 1573, 1739, 1881, 1962, 2127, 2464; in several lectionaries and in numerous ancient versions and patristic quotations.

scribe or scribes would have been inclined to insert one and thus break up the passage into separate sentences. So much is this so that we have to ask whether Paul would have written the passage with the participle of verse 21 being carried over by implication in verse 22.

There is no question that verse 22 is acceptable Greek without an explicit verb. Certainly it is. The question arises not because understanding the participle of verse 21 to be implied in verse 22 is any sort of grammatical problem in and of itself, but because of what that understanding would do to the flow of the thought in the whole passage. The thought moves from admonitions related to being filled with the Spirit to discussion of the husband and wife relationship. Even though the idea of submitting oneself to another provides a nice segue, the content of verses 22–33 is significantly different from that of the preceding section. Given this, it seems a near necessity that there be a new main clause as the topic of the husband and wife relationship is introduced. That new main clause does not begin in verse 21, for the verb therein is a participle, a continuation of the series of participles from verse 19, all subordinate to the finite verb in verse 18. So then the only place the new main clause could begin is in verse 22. And the manuscripts that contain either ὑποτάσσεσθε or ὑποτασσέσθωσαν in verse 22 provide strong textual support for a new main clause as the discussion moves to the marital relationship.

Supposing, then, that a finite verb belongs in verse 22, we can read verse 21 as the conclusion of the preceding section. The preceding section is summed up with the exhortation to be filled with the Spirit, and that thought enhanced by five participles, λαλοῦντες (*speaking*), ᾄδοντες καὶ ψάλλοντες (*singing and making music*), εὐχαριστοῦντες (*giving thanks*), and ὑποτασσόμενοι (*submitting*). Then in verse 22 a new sentence would begin, picking up the last thought of the preceding verse, namely, submitting oneself, and apply this specifically to wives with reference to their husbands.

If the correct reading is second person imperative ὑποτάσσεσθε, we would regard αἱ γυναῖκες is an example of an articular nominative being used for a vocative.[147] The grammatical construction of the ex-

---

[147] Wallace, p. 58. If indeed αἱ γυναῖκες is an articular nominative used as vocative, we should perhaps understand a tone that would best be conveyed in English by retaining the definite article in translation, perhaps, "The women, submit yourselves." Moulton (Prolegomena, p. 70) tried to convey the nuance of the articular nominative as vocative by inserting the second person pronoun in translation: "Fear not, you little flock!" (Lk 12.32), and "Hail, you 'King'!"(Jn 19.3).

hortation would be similar to that of the subsequent instruction to the husbands in verse 25, Οἱ ἄνδρες, ἀγαπᾶτε τὰς γυναῖκας. There again we see an articular nominative used as a vocative and a second person imperative verb. This parallel is a strong argument in favor of the reading ὑποτάσσεσθε in verse 22.

But third person imperative ὑποτασσέσθωσαν (*let them submit themselves*) has earlier manuscript support than does second person imperative ὑποτάσσεσθε (*submit yourselves*). With ὑποτασσέσθωσαν, the text flows very naturally. And if ὑποτασσέσθωσαν were the original reading, the presence of ὑποτάσσεσθε in later manuscripts could easily have arisen as a result of conscious or unconscious assimilation to Colossians 3.18.

In the end, it may be impossible to know with certainty what the correct reading is here. But the internal evidence favors the presence of either ὑποτάσσεσθε or ὑποτασσέσθωσαν. Between the two, though there is a difference in grammar, there is no difference in the meaning of the passage. With ὑποτάσσεσθε, the text means "Wives, submit yourselves," and with ὑποτασσέσθωσαν, the text means "Let the wives submit themselves."

5.22 *Wives submit yourselves to your own husbands as to the Lord.* (For discussion of the textual issue, see above, STRUCTURE AND TEXTUAL PROBLEM.) The language τοῖς ἰδίοις ἀνδράσιν (*to their own men*) makes it abundantly clear that the submission of the woman herein discussed is to her husband, and not to every man.

It has become popular, even the *norm de rigueur*, to begin discussion of this instruction by noting that Paul has just previously said we must all submit ourselves to one another (ὑποτασσόμενοι ἀλλήλοις),[148] and to conclude that Paul is talking about a submission that is mutual and therefore nothing unique is being said about the wife's submission to her husband. But this is to ignore the point of the paragraph. This is really an attempt to accommodate Paul's instruction to the prevailing thought of the modern world. It is to lose sight of the fact that this whole context is about *not* living as those of the world around us live! If it is anathema to society at large to expect a wife to submit to her husband, so be it. But society at large is alienated from the life of God. Those who are God's holy house will live in accordance with God's will.

While God has given the woman great natural ability to influence the

---

[148] Whether ὑποτάσσεσθε or ὑποτασσέσθωσαν should be regarded as middle (*submit yourselves*) or passive (*be subjected*) is of no great consequence in this context. In either case, the instruction is directed to the one who is to submit.

man (whether for good as in the case of Abigail, Esther, and the Shunam-
mite woman who inclined her husband to provide for Elisha, or for evil
as in the case of Eve, the Midianite women, Jezebel, Solomon's wives, and
Salome and Herodias) the plain teaching of the Bible is that God has legislated for the man a position of influence over the woman. Where God's
word is followed, all of this results in a nice balance in marriage such
that there is leadership without annulling the voice of the one who is being led. Had God merely legislated the headship of the husband without
giving the woman a natural ability to sway him, the woman would be in
a dismal position. Had God given the woman such a powerful allure as
she has without legislating the husband's responsibility to lead, the man
would be in a dismal position.

   **5.23   *because a husband is head of his wife as Christ is head of the
church, himself being savior of the body.*** Here Paul introduces the
parallel between the relationship of the woman to her husband and the
relationship of the church to Christ. The imagery of God's people as his
spouse is an old one, found often in the OT, *e.g.*, Ezekiel 16, Jeremiah 3,
Hosea 1–3, and everywhere that idolatry is described as harlotry.

   But here the imagery is complex, the church being simultaneously pictured as both the wife of Christ and the body of Christ. This combination
of images is rooted in the creation story. The woman created from a rib
of the man was bone of his bones, flesh of his flesh. With this in view, the
marital union was described as becoming one flesh. From one came two,
and in marriage, the two became one again, one body. So then Christ's
wife, the church, is his body. Similarly, the man and his wife are one body,
the man being the head, the wife his body.

   **5.24–25   *But as the church is subject to the Christ, so also the wives
are to their husbands in everything. Husbands, love your wives, just as
Christ also loved the church and gave himself on its behalf.*** The Greek
text has αἱ γυναῖκες τοῖς ἀνδράσιν (*the women to the men*). As noted above,
the context has indicated the marriage relationship is in view, *wives to their
husbands*, though this meaning is demanded by the preceding and ensuing context and not by the language of verse 24 itself.

   The church is subject to Christ because it is made up of people who
have chosen to be subject to Christ. In drawing a parallel to the church, the
wife's subjection is seen as her choice. It is, of course, the only right choice,
but it is nonetheless her choice.

The godly wife who recognizes that for every Christian, a willingness to submit to others and ultimately to God is fundamental, and who recognizes that for her this submission is demonstrated practically especially in relation to her own husband, will do much to enhance her marriage.

Turning to the instruction to husbands in vs. 25, in οἱ ἄνδρες we see an articular vocative used for a nominative. As previously noted, if the correct reading in verse 22 is second person imperative ὑποτάσσεσθε, then the instruction to the men is grammatically parallel to the instruction to the women.

Jesus did not conquer those whom he would save and force them into submission. They are not the enemy. Rather his enemies are their enemies (6.11*ff*, 4.12, 4.14.). He is on their side. He leads the church to be subject to himself by his self-sacrifice. This whole letter to the Gentiles reflects this very motivation. Remember that the first three chapters of Ephesians are all about the great blessing in Christ that has been bestowed upon them. The last three chapters begin with "therefore," calling upon them to respond to the grace of God in Christ by bringing their lives into harmony with their calling: *walk in love just as Christ loved us gave himself on behalf of you*. So here Paul instructs husbands to love their wives, *just as the Christ also loved the church and gave himself on behalf of it* (καθὼς καὶ ὁ Χριστὸς ἠγάπησεν τὴν ἐκκλησίαν καὶ ἑαυτὸν παρέδωκεν ὑπὲρ αὐτῆς). In verses 28*f*, Paul will further develop the parallel principle in regard to the husband's love for his wife.

Those who see the sovereignty of God as precluding the possibility of a human choice to submit might ought to consider this parallel between the church and the wife. Does a Calvinistic husband, in the place of the sovereign Lord, actually compel his wife's submission, and does a Calvinistic wife truly have no choice in the matter?

5.26–27 *In order that he might sanctify it, having cleansed it with the washing of the water by word, in order that he himself might present the church to himself, it having no spot or blemish or any such thing, but that it might be holy and blameless.* First we should briefly note that while some translations render the pronouns here and in the preceding verse as "it" and some use the feminine "her," there is no real issue here. αὐτὴν is feminine because the antecedent is the feminine ἐκκλησίαν, and in most contexts we would simply translate the pronoun into English as "it." The possibility of using the feminine "her" in translation arises here only because of the context, and not because of the feminine pronoun. In the context, the church is pictured as the wife, as the bride for whom Christ gave himself and whom he cleansed and sanctified. Only because of this does it make sense to translate using "her." The choice between "her" and "it" is made solely on the basis of whether or not one wishes to play up the analogy in expressing the pronoun. It is impossible to discern which thought was in Paul's mind, and perhaps even unlikely that there would or could have been a distinction in his mind.

The analogy of the husband-wife relationship to the Christ-church relationship is continued, here focusing on the wedding. The bride is presented to her husband in all her glory. But here it is the Christ who has made his bride glorious that he might present her as resplendent bride to himself.

We will take up the significance of ἁγιάσῃ (*might sanctify*) and καθαρίσας (*having cleansed*, or *cleansing*) momentarily, and especially consider the question as to whether these are two different events or two different ways of talking about the same event. But first we will consider the words τῷ λουτρῷ τοῦ ὕδατος (*the washing of water*).

Dative τῷ λουτρῷ is instrumental, *by means of the washing*. Most have seen a reference to baptism in the words τῷ λουτρῷ τοῦ ὕδατος,[149] but some argue strongly against such a reference. The disagreement reflects the controversy concerning the significance of baptism itself. While in ancient times it was generally accepted that Paul did indeed mean to refer to water baptism, Hoehner dismisses that idea, saying, "this is reading patristic and modern liturgy into the first century." But it can as well be argued that first century practice would have led most readers of Paul's letter to think of baptism.

Before his ascension, Jesus charged the apostles with the mission of making disciples, baptizing them in the name of the Father and of the

---

[149] In evidence of the unanimity with which commentators prior to the 20th century have understood the passage to refer to baptism, the testimony of Charles Hodge may stand in place of a lengthy listing of commentators and their views: "Commentators, however, almost without exception understand the expression in the text to refer to baptism. The great majority of them, with Calvin and other of the Reformers, do not even discuss the question, or seem to admit any other interpretation to be possible. The same view is taken by all the modern exegetical writers. This unanimity of opinion is itself almost decisive. Nothing short of a stringent necessity can justify any one in setting forth an interpretation opposed to this common consent of Christians. No such necessity here exists. Baptism is a washing with water. It was the washing with water with which Paul's readers as Christians were familiar, and which could not fail to occur to them as the washing intended." (Ephesians, p. 318)

Son and of the Holy Spirit. The beginning of the church on the Day of Pentecost was marked by the baptism of 3,000 people. In the book of Acts, with the exception of Sergius Paulus, every conversion story sufficiently detailed to identify a converted individual makes note of his or her baptism. In Romans, Paul identified baptism as the point of identification with Christ's death ("baptized into his death"), which of course is what cleanses us. In Galatians, Paul said those who have been baptized into Christ have put on Christ.[150] Paul wrote to the Corinthians of the unity of the Spirit saying, "in one Spirit were we all baptized into one body," and a bit earlier drew an analogy to the Israelites who were "baptized unto Moses in the cloud and in the sea," a reference to the day wherein "the Lord saved Israel."[151] In Colossians, Paul speaks of being "buried with Christ through baptism." It was the Apostle Peter who compared the separation of Noah and his family from a sinful world with our separation from sin at baptism, and whether it accords with one's theology or not, Peter went so far in his language as to say that as they were saved by water, so also "baptism now saves you." Clearly one need not read back into the first century a later mindset to find a reference to baptism in Paul's "washing with water." Whether it fits with one's theology or not, the uniform teaching and practice of the first century would have provided ample basis for seeing such a reference in those words. The truth is, one has to read a 20th century Evangelical mindset [152] back into the passage in order to avoid thinking of baptism when reading Ephesians 5.27.

It is one thing to say baptism would readily come to the mind of Paul's readers, but it is another thing to say that Paul so intended. Of course, the presumption is that Paul, being a capable teacher and writer, and moreover, guided by the Spirit, would be well aware of the ideas that his words would prompt, and would endeavor to choose such words as would bring to mind only those thoughts he intended. But then we remember his first

---

[150] For those who suppose associating baptism with cleansing from sin is opposed to justification by faith, it should be noted that Paul's remark in Galatians 3.27 that his readers had put on Christ when they were baptized into Christ is offered as explanation of his immediately preceding statement that his readers were sons of God through faith! And of course, Romans, wherein Paul points to baptism as the point at which one is identified with the death of Christ, is all about justification by faith.

[151] Ex. 14.30.

[152] I say 20th century rather than 21st century because today, even among Evangelicals, there seems to be a growing recognition and appreciation of the Biblical significance of baptism. See N.T. Wright, Bercot, Stott, etc.

letter to the Thessalonians wherein he spoke of the Lord's future return, and we see evidence in 2 Thessalonians that his meaning may have been misconstrued, some supposing that return was imminent.

So we now turn to the question, did Paul *intend* that his readers think of baptism, as in fact they generally have for most of two millennia (excepting the 20th century)? First in evidence is the same milieu described above. After all, many of the NT references cited above demonstrating the first century understanding of baptism were written by Paul himself. Paul himself had been told, "Arise and be baptized and wash away your sins, calling on the name of the Lord." It should be evident that just as surely as first century readers would have been unlikely to read the words of Ephesians 5.26 without thinking of baptism, so also Paul would have been unlikely to have written them without thinking of baptism.

The second piece of evidence to be considered is the reference to baptism in Colossians. As has been argued in the Introduction, Colossians was written at about the same time as Ephesians, delivered by the same courier, on the same journey. And as all recognize, the two letters are very similar. Given especially the similarities between Colossians and Ephesians, the reference to baptism in Colossians makes it even harder to discount the possibility that Paul intended a reference to baptism here in Ephesians.

Hoehner's suggestion that the reference was to the "bridal bath practiced in the first century" is a testament to the fact that one is naturally drawn to think of some literal washing that Paul used, in Hoehner's words, "as a metaphorical expression of redemption." But baptism itself is such a metaphor. In baptism we participate in Christ's death. We are buried with him. As we come up out of the water of baptism, we arise to a resurrected life as did Christ. It is reasonable to suppose the metaphor Paul had in mind was the very one he himself repeatedly used elsewhere. (This is not to rule out the possibility that baptism is here seen as corresponding to a bridal bath. We will consider that possibility momentarily.)

Hoehner's objection that "the rite of baptism does not cleanse one from sin" ignores the significance Paul himself attaches to baptism, that it is the act wherein we are united with Christ's death which does indeed cleanse us from sin. Throughout the Bible, we see time and again God's unmerited grace extended to man on the occasion of a man's compliance in some outward act, some requisite expression of faith. We see this when Moses threw a tree into the bitter waters and they became sweet,[153] when Moses struck a rock and water poured out,[154] when Israel marched around Jericho in accordance with the Lord's instruction and the walls fell "by faith,"[155] when Naaman dipped in the Jordan seven times and was cleansed of his leprosy,[156] when Israelites looked to the bronze serpent and were saved from the bite of the snakes.[157] Consider especially this bronze serpent raised upon a standard, which Jesus compared to his own being raised upon the cross: We cannot literally turn our eyes to Christ upon the cross as the Israelites could literally look to the bronze serpent. But as the Lord gave them the instruction to look, he has given us the instruction to be baptized. Should we not see baptism as the God-given means whereby we look to Christ, rather than as some liturgical ritual that is incidental to our salvation and really unnecessary? If we would so understand it, we would not suppose that remission of sins at baptism is at odds with faith. We would see baptism as the requisite expression of faith.

But even as we conclude that "the washing of water" refers to baptism, the possibility of a reference to a bridal bath is not excluded. Lincoln, who says, "the readers are scarcely likely to have taken this as anything other than a reference to their experience of baptism," nonetheless allows that "the language of 'washing with water' is likely to have as a secondary connotation the notion of the bridal bath."[158] Meyer saw baptism as the literal reference and the bridal bath as the thing representing baptism in the marriage analogy. He wrote, "We have thus here not simply an *allusion* to baptism, but a *designation* of the same (comp. Tit. iii. 5 ; 1 Cor. vi. 11), and an allusion to the bath of the bride before the wedding-day."[159] In

---

[153] Ex 15.25.

[154] Ex 17.5f.

[155] Heb 11.30.

[156] 2 Kings 5.14.

[157] Num 21.8f. To be sure, in all of these, the required action was in part intended to demonstrate that the benefit was from God, and in some instances that the one acting was the representative of God. If in the eyes of the beneficiaries the benefit had seemed to occur spontaneously, there would have been no compelling reason to conclude it was from God or, more especially in some instances, that Moses was the representative of God. When it occurred only upon compliance with God's instruction, then it was clear that it was from God. So then, part of the reason for the required action was to increase faith in God and his representative. But that it was simultaneously an expression of faith is evidenced by Heb 11.30.

[158] Lincoln, p. 375.

[159] Meyer, p. 513.

a footnote, Meyer mentions Hofmann's objection which apparently was that the bathing of the bride was not the business of the bridegroom.[160] Presumably, Hofmann therefore disputed a reference to a bridal bath that would be administered by Christ to his bride, the church. Meyer retorted that this "is an over-refinement of taste at variance with the context."[161] It may be added that in Ezekiel 16.8ff, the Lord is pictured as washing and adorning his bride.

The fact that the participle καθαρίσας is aorist does not itself necessitate our understanding the cleansing to have been antecedent to the sanctifying. The phrase may mean, "that he might sanctify it, having cleansed…," or it may mean, "that he might sanctify it, cleansing…" Nonetheless, there is an argument to be made for a sequential understanding.

Meyer summed up the meaning of the whole verse this way: "In His sacrificial death, namely, Christ's intention with regard to His future church had this aim, that, after having by baptism brought about for its members the forgiveness of their pre-Christian sins, He would make it partaker of Christian-moral holiness by means of the gospel."[162] In so saying, Meyer distinguished between the cleansing, which he associated with baptism, and the sanctifying, which he understood to be accomplished by the word.[163] He understood the structure to be ἵνα αὐτὴν ἁγιάσῃ (καθαρίσας τῷ λουτρῷ τοῦ ὕδατος) ἐν ῥήματι, *in order that he might sanctify her (having cleansed by the washing of the water) by Word."* Meyer understood Paul to say that Christ cleansed the church at baptism, and then the church is sanctified as it is guided by the word revealed through the Spirit—"this sanctification by means of the gospel constantly influencing the baptized."[164]

This interpretation fits well with the overall structure of the letter, the first three chapters emphasizing the grace of God in Christ that saves us from our sins, and the last three chapters encouraging us to therefore walk worthily of our calling. While the thought seems somewhat awkwardly constructed, commentators who take the cleansing as merely an explana-

---

[160] Meyer, p. 515, n. 2.

[161] Meyer, p. 515.

[162] Meyer, p. 512.

[163] An early interpretation counter to this, associating the baptismal washing with the word, seems to be reflected in Clement of Alexandria, Exhortation to the Greeks, 11. Clement describes as "moistened sword points" those "who have been dipped by the word" (ταῖς ὑδατίναις ἀκμαῖς ταῖς ὑπὸ τοῦ λόγου βεβαμμέναις).

[164] Meyer, p. 512.

tion of the sanctifying, such that both are accomplished simultaneously, end up with something even more awkward. The phrase ἐν ῥήματι (*in word*) is left dangling: *in order that he might sanctify her, (i.e.) cleansing her by the washing of the water, in word*. Various attempts are made to derive some sense out of this, but no compelling explanation is forthcoming. On the other hand, connecting the words ἐν ῥήματι (*in word*, or rather, taken instrumentally, *by word*) with *that he might sanctify* is reminiscent of John 17.17, "Sanctify them in the truth, Your word is truth."

Chrysostom supposed the phrase *"by the word"* was a reference to the phrase, "in the name of the Father and of the Son and of the Holy Spirit," which had become a baptismal formula.[165] But neither the immediate context nor Paul's writings generally offer any support for this interpretation.

The church, having been cleansed by Jesus' atoning sacrifice, is holy and without blemish. J. W. Shepherd thought it obvious that the church cannot now be described as holy and without blemish, and that this "blessed state" would only be achieved at the Last Day.[166] But it is not Jesus' return that will at some future time cleanse the church. It was his sacrifice, his giving himself up on behalf of the church, that has already cleansed the church, and either the same event or the preaching of the word that sanctifies the church. The problem in Shepherd's thinking was he thought of the church as that which he could perceive, not that which God sees. But it is a mistake to start with what we perceive to be the church and draw conclusions about the church based on observation. Not everyone who can claim membership in some outwardly defined religious body is a member of the body of Christ. Too many take consolation in being a part of a church that they see, rather than in being a part of Christ and thus being cleansed by his sacrifice, and thus being a part of that church that God sees.

---

[165] ἐν ῥήματι ποίῳ; ἐν ὀνόματι τοῦ πατρὸς καὶ τοῦ υἱοῦ καὶ τοῦ ἁγίου πνεύματος, "In what word? 'In the Name of the Father and of the Son and of the Holy Spirit'." Homily 20 on Ephesians.

[166] Shepherd added the following note to Lipscomb's comments on Eph 5.27: "there can be no doubt as to when this end is to be attained, for in this life neither scripture nor experience affords an example; still if one should attain this blessed state, it cannot be affirmed of the whole body of believers. It is then when the righteous dead shall be raised in the likeness of the Son of God, and those who shall be alive shall be changed.... When this incorruptible shall have put on incorruption and this mortal shall have put on immortality – it is then that the church shall be made ready as a bride adorned for her husband (Rev. 21.2; 19.6–8)." Likewise Meyer was adamant in saying Christ "presents the church as bride to Himself at His Parousia" (p. 515).

5.28–30 *Thus also the husbands ought to love their wives as their bodies. The one who loves his wife loves himself, for none ever hated his own flesh, but nourishes and comforts it, just as Christ also the church, because we are members of his body.* The husband does not defeat his wife, but gives himself up for her, motivating her to submit to his leadership. His care for his wife should be as his care for his own body, for she is part of him.

ἐκτρέφει καὶ θάλπει αὐτήν (*nourishes and cares for it*) is not language from the nursery as Hoehner supposed,[167] following Martin. Yes, ἐκτρέφω was used of raising up a child. But the fundamental idea was nourishment, as seen in Genesis 47.17, and that is the meaning here. A man nourishes and cares for his body. When he takes a wife, he is to regard her in the same way, nourishing and caring for her. Yes, an allusion to the feeding and caring for a young child would add an element of affection, but that is not the picture Paul chose to use. Yes, θάλπω is used by Paul in 2 Thessalonians 2.7 where there is a tender picture of affectionate care of children. But that is not the picture here. Here, Paul focuses on the analogy of a man's care for his own body, not a man's care for his own children, for Paul is speaking of Christ's church as Christ's body.

In the NA28, the text at verse 30 reads ὅτι μέλη ἐσμὲν τοῦ σώματος αὐτοῦ (*because we are members of his body*). This is the reading found in 𝔓⁴⁶ ℵ* A, B, 048, 6, 33, 81, 424ᶜ, 1739*, 1881, 2464, 1422, itˢ, copˢᵃ,ᵇᵒ eth Origenˡᵃᵗ, Methodius; Jerome Augustineᵛⁱᵈ Ps-Jerome. The text in the KJV (*For we are members of his body, of his flesh, and of his bones*) represents the reading ὅτι μέλη ἐσμὲν τοῦ σώματος αὐτοῦ ἐκ τῆς σαρκὸς αὐτοῦ καὶ ἐκ τῶν ὀστέων αὐτοῦ, found in a number of uncials, many minuscules and various other witnesses ℵ² D,F,G, Ψ in minuscules 075, 104, 256, 263, 365, 424*,436, 459, 1175, 1241, 1319, 1573, 1739ᶜ, 1852, 1912 (omits the first αὐτοῦ) 1962, 2127, 2200, the Byzantine mss generally, itᵃʳ,ᵇ,ᵈ,ᶠ,ᵍ,ᵐᵒⁿ,ᵒ vg, syr⁽ᵖ⁾,ʰ arm geo slav Irenaeusᵍʳ,ˡᵃᵗ Chrysostom Theodoreˡᵃᵗ; Victorinus-Rome Ambrosiaster Ambrose Pelagius.[168] It is noteworthy that corrections go both ways. Sinaiticus was corrected from the shorter reading to the longer one. Minuscule 424 was corrected from the longer reading to the shorter reading. Minuscule 1739 was corrected from the shorter reading to the longer reading.

---

[167] p. 766.

[168] One ninth century minuscule has only the words καὶ ἐκ τῶν ὀστέων αὐτοῦ (*and of his bones*).

If the longer reading is the correct one, the shorter reading likely arose as a result of homoeoteleuton. If the first αὐτοῦ and the last αὐτοῦ were both at the end of different lines in an exemplar, a scribe would have copied up to the first αὐτοῦ, and then when his eye returned to the examplar it could have fallen on the last αὐτοῦ, where he would resume copying, resulting in the omission of the intervening text.

If the shorter reading is the correct one, the addition of the words "of his flesh and of his bones" would likely be explained as a harking back to Genesis 2.23 in view of the ensuing quotation from Genesis 2.24.

5.31 *On account of this a man shall leave his father and mother and shall be joined to his wife, and they two shall be as one flesh.* The introductory ἀντὶ τούτου corresponds to ἕνεκεν τούτου (*for the sake of this = on account of this*) in the LXX (and in Mt 19.5, Mk 10.7). The root idea of ἀντί seems to be *one thing facing another*,[169] and from this, the idea of *correspondence*, and then *equivalency*, arises, such that one thing can be a *substitution* for the other (as in 1 Cor 11.15, Mt 5.38), and thence comes the idea of one thing being *payment for* another, in *exchange for* another, or in *return for* another (Heb 12.16, Mt 12.28, Mk 10.45, Rom 12.17, 1 Th 5.15, 1 Pt 3.9, *et al.*). Once the preposition is used to mean this *for* that, it is easy to see how the use of ἀντί to indicate purpose could arise. Jesus endured the cross *for* (ἀντί) the joy set before him (Heb 12.2). This can be thought of in terms of evaluating the one thing (*joy*) as well worth the other thing (*enduring the cross*). But of course this can also be thought of as enduring the cross *for the purpose of* (and thus, *on account of*) attaining the joy set before him. So then the expression ἀντὶ τούτου is *for this*, or *on account of this*. But why Paul uses ἀντὶ τούτου rather than ἕνεκεν τούτου as in the LXX is a mystery.

In Genesis 2.24, the thought was that woman, having been taken out of man, rightly belonged with man to reconstitute the whole, and on account of this, in marriage the woman and the man come together such that the whole is reconstituted. Two become one.

5.32 τὸ μυστήριον τοῦτο μέγα ἐστίν· ἐγὼ δὲ λέγω εἰς Χριστὸν καὶ εἰς τὴν ἐκκλησίαν. *This mystery is great, but I speak with reference to Christ and the church.* Knox argued that the word "mystery" is used here as it was used in connection with the mystery cults, *viz.*, as a description of a spiritual explanation for "crude and primitive practices of barbarous religion." Knox's meaning is that the writer here is giving a

---

[169] Robertson, 572, Smyth p. 373, §1683.

spiritual interpretation (presumably the relationship between Christ and the church) to human marriage, thus making it "sacred marriage." Knox supposed that this suggests that the writer could not have been Paul inasmuch as Paul always used the word "mystery" in a different sense, namely, the "Palestinian-Jewish sense of a divine secret."[170]

It is better to suppose that the writer (and it is Paul) uses the word just as he did earlier in chapter three. Although Paul is discussing household relationships, the particular relationship between the husband and the wife brings forth the analogy of the relationship between Christ and the church, and this being something that was a mystery, though foreshadowed, in the OT. The nation of Israel was the woman God took to himself and upon whom he bestowed great love and riches (Ezek 16, Hos 1–3, Jer 3, *et al.*). As Paul has earlier described the Gentiles who had been afar off as now being the very house of God, so he now describes them as being the very wife of the Christ. This is that which had been a mystery, to wit, the Gentiles with the Jews reconciled in one body to God through the cross, a body that is the house of God, the bride of Christ.

All of the ethical teaching found in chapters four through six is rooted in what God has done for us in Christ ("forgiving one another, just as God in Christ forgave you"), and especially in the idea that the readers are the body of Christ ("Speak truth each one with his neighbor"—why? —"because we are members of one another"). So now as he discusses the husband's love for his wife and the wife's submission to her husband, it is again rooted in and a reflection of what God has done for us in Christ, and how we should respond in grateful submission. So it is that Paul says, "I speak of Christ and the church."

6.1–4 Children and Parents

Children, obey your parents [in the Lord] for this is just. Honor your father and mother, which is the first commandment with promise, in order that it might be well with you and you might be a long time upon the land. And fathers, do not provoke your children to anger, but nurture them in the discipline and instruction of the Lord.

Isolated from this context, πατέρες (*fathers*) could arguably mean *parents*, as it must in Hebrews 12.23, where we are told Moses was hidden

---

[170] 83f.

three months by his πατέρων.[171] But the context in Ephesians 6 argues against understanding the word to mean *parents* here. Paul instructed that children be obedient to their γονεῦσιν in the first verse, and had he meant to address the parents (mothers and fathers) in verse four, it would seem most natural to have used the same word again. But the fact that he now uses the word πατέρες indicates that he means to speak of fathers in particular.

6.5–9 Slaves and Masters

Slaves, obey those who are your lords according to the flesh with fear and trembling in sincerity of your heart as to Christ, not according to eye-service as sycophants but as slaves of Christ, doing the will of God from the heart, serving with a good attitude, as to the Lord and not to men, knowing that each one, if he should do something good, will receive this back from the Lord, whether slave or free. And lords, practice the same things toward them, abandoning the use of threat, knowing that the Lord of both them and you is in the heavens, and there is no favoritism with him.

6.5 *Slaves, obey those who are your lords according to the flesh with fear and trembling in sincerity of your heart as to Christ* (Οἱ δοῦλοι, ὑπακούετε τοῖς κατὰ σάρκα κυρίοις μετὰ φόβου καὶ τρόμου ἐν ἁπλότητι τῆς καρδίας ὑμῶν ὡς τῷ Χριστῷ)   The word κύριος is used five times in verses five through nine, twice with reference to the human lords or masters of the slaves, and thrice with reference to Christ, who is lord of both masters and slaves. It is important to use the same English word in each of these instances so that the reader sees the point Paul eventually makes—human lords stand on equal footing with their slaves before the heavenly Lord. We could use the word *master* in each instance, but having used *lord* elsewhere in Ephesians, for the sake of consistency, it seems best to continue to use the same word here.

In an age of unbelief, such passages as this become proof texts used by those who understand little of God's word to argue that the Bible cannot

---

[171] Not all of the secular occurrences cited in BDAG as examples of πατήρ meaning *parent* are convincing. In particular, it is not clear to me that the passage in Diodorus Siculus (21.17.2) or the passage in Dionysius of Halicarnassus (multiple occurrences in 2.26) means anything other than *fathers*. And in Apollon. Rhod. 4.1089, it seems most likely that πατρός means specifically *father* rather than *parent*. The reference in Xenophon of Ephesus is arguable. But at least the inscription cited from Kaibel's *Epigrammata Graeca* does seem to be a clear instance where πατέρες means *parents*.

be trusted to lead us in the right way. Does the Bible condone slavery? Well, the truthful answer will have to be yes, but certainly not the sort of slavery that comes to the minds of the American public.

Certainly the evils associated with slavery are contrary to the word of God. The foundation of God's instruction is love. His instructions teach us how to love God and how to love our fellow man (Mt 22.36*ff*, Rom 13.8*ff*, Gal 5.14). In regard to loving one's fellow man, Jesus said, *"Just as you would that men should do to you, do likewise to them"* (Lk 6.31, cf. Mt 7.12). Certainly, that precludes taking a man by force, removing him from his loved ones and from his homeland against his will, treating him like an animal, and imposing onerous tasks upon him with the threat of violence. Elsewhere, Paul himself treats the act of taking captives and enslaving them as of the same class as murder and various other things that are "contrary to the sound doctrine" (1 Tim 1.10). Capturing and selling someone into slavery, at least with regard to Israelites, was condemned in the law of Moses (Ex 21.16, Dt 24.7). The capture itself was regarded as a theft of the most egregious kind, such that the penalty was death.

Now it must be acknowledged that God did allow the nation of Israel to take captives when going to war with other nations (Dt 21.10) and to enslave foreigners (Lev 15.44–45),[172] whether by conquest (Dt 20.11), inheritance (Lev 15.46), or purchase. God also sent the Israelites to war and instructed them to kill their enemies, something that we cannot do if we are to be governed by the principles that we must love our neighbor, that love works no ill to its neighbor, and that we are to love even our enemies. But when God gave instruction to the Israelites, specific instructions *by direct revelation,* to go to war against these particular nations or those particular cities, it was his divine judgment that was being executed, not their own.[173] Our Creator most certainly does have the right to execute such judgments. Hath not the potter power over the clay?

But the slavery in view in Ephesians 6 is not the result of God's people executing divine justice upon condemned societies. And the instruction to slaves to submit is not a punishment. Paul enjoins submission on the

---

[172] Exodus 21.2 does refer to a "Hebrew slave," but such a person was really more comparable to an indentured servant. The Hebrew slave was to be treated as "a hired man" and not "with severity," and was to be given his freedom in the seventh year (Lev 15.39–43). See also Dt 25.12*ff.*

[173] See J.W. McGarvey's article, *"Jewish Wars as Precedents for Modern Wars,"* Lard's Quarterly 5:2, 113–126, April 1868, especially pp. 121*ff.*

part of slaves in accordance with the principle of love for God. He tells them to obey their masters "as slaves of Christ, doing the will of God from the soul, rendering service as to the Lord and not to men."

The principle of yielding one's own will to do the will of another is fundamental to Christianity. This is what Jesus prayed before going to the cross—"not my will, but thine be done." This is what characterized his whole earthly existence—"I came not do my own will, but the will of him who sent me" (Jn 6:38). Jesus took upon himself "the form of a slave" (Phil 2.7). And in doing so, he modeled for us what he expects of every one of us. Indeed, as Peter gives instructions to the slave (οἰκέτης)[174] similar to those given here by Paul, he points to Christ's example: "for unto this you were called, because Christ also suffered on your behalf, leaving you an example that you might follow in his footprints" (1 Pt 2.21). But it is not only in the master/slave relationship that we are to emulate Jesus' submission, but in various ways, including our submission to civil authority, wives' submission to husbands, and ultimately, our submission to God as his slaves, as slaves of righteousness.

In the present age, we find the very notion of slavery fundamentally abhorrent. But the message of Ephesians is that we can no longer walk in accordance with the spirit of this age. And how different the Spirit is by which we are led is seen in the constant use of the term "slave," whereby Paul describes himself and us in our relationship to God.

One may rightly point out that the inception of a master/slave relationship is often fraught with violence and evil. A man engaged in slave trafficking is an ανδραποδιστής (1 Tim 1.10) and as noted before, is classed with murderers, fornicators, homosexuals, *et al.* But here in Ephesians, Paul does not concern himself with how the relationship came to be.

It is similar to the instructions to submit to civil authority or that a wife submit to her husband. Paul does not concern himself with how

---

[174] An οἰκέτης is a household servant. Athenaeus quotes Chrysippus to the effect that the οἰκέτης is property of a master: "But Chrysippus says that there is a difference between a δοῦλος and an οἰκέτης; and he draws the distinction in the second book of his treatise on Similarity of Meaning because he says that those who have been emancipated are still δοῦλοι but that the term οἰκέτης is confined to those who are not discharged from servitude for the οἰκέτης, says he, is a δοῦλος, being actually at the time the property of a master"(Deipnosophists, or Banquet of the Learned, Athenæus, transl. by C.D. Yonge, vol. 1, London: Bohn, 1854, p. 419). Athenaeus himself said it is possible that the οἰκέτης is a free man (The Deipnosophists, 6.93). Generally, however, the οἰκέτης is such by birth and is considered property. See for example Plato Leges 776d–778a.

these relationships came to be, either. Perhaps the civil rulers in power came to be in power through war. Perhaps the citizen had no choice in the matter. Perhaps the wife was deceived by a man who claimed he loved her. Perhaps it was an arranged marriage. Perhaps she herself was not a believer when she agreed to marry a man whom she now recognizes to be a hindrance to her service as a Christian. Paul does not concern himself with any of this.

How did Jesus come to stand before Pilate? Certainly not for just cause. And yet he yielded to the cross, yielded to his inferiors, indeed, to his creatures.

It is possible to acknowledge the duty of the slave to submit to the master without condoning the means by which he was made a slave. It may be that a man became a slave through some immoral means, or it may be that he sold himself into slavery as a means of dealing with his debt. But by whatever means a given man may have been enslaved, the state saw fit to enforce the rights of the master over the slave, lest the whole system fall apart. Paul's teaching in Ephesians 6.5–8 does not address the act of enslaving someone, but merely confronts the parties involved where they are.

One may ask if Paul should have commanded Christians who owned slaves to release them. In some instances, this would have been to the slave's advantage. But, foreign to our thinking as it may be, being set free would not always have been an advantage. In some instances, a man who was illiterate and had no skills could find his needs reliably met in the service of a benevolent master, much more so than if he were free.

In any event, it is simply not Paul's purpose to discuss such things here. When he described the marriage relationship in 5.22–33, he did not venture down the path to explore under what circumstances the relationship might be dissolved or what to do if an unbelieving spouse departs. His purpose was to discuss the husband/wife relationship, not the circumstance under which it might be terminated. So here, his purpose is to discuss the master/slave relationship, not the termination of such a relationship, nor the inception of such a relationship.

6.6 The word rendered *eyeservice* is ὀφθαλμοδουλία, a compound of ὀφθαλμός (*eye*) and δούλεια (*servile*). Used only here and at Colossians 3.22 in the NT, it is unknown outside of the NT. But its meaning is easily discerned. It speaks of insincere service rendered only sufficiently enough to appear to the eye to be compliant. The meaning is similar to that of *lipservice,* though the latter speaks of the profession on the lips of the servant while the former speaks of the appearance in the eye of the master.

sycophants In the NAS, this is *men-pleasers.* It represents ἀνθρωπάρεσκοι which is also unknown in secular Greek. It is found twice in the NT (here and in Colossians 3.22), in the LXX at Psalm 52.6 (53.6 in English), and in the Psalm of Solomon 4.7,8,19. It is a compound of ἄνθρωπος (*man*) and ἄρεσκος, a word that meant *pleasing,* but which usually had a negative connotation such as *obsequious.* So then, even though the two words are unknown in secular Greek, used together the meaning of the whole phrase, κατ᾽ ὀφθαλμοδουλίαν ὡς ἀνθρωπάρεσκοι (*according to eye-service as sycophants*), becomes clear. It speaks of insincere service rendered with a pretense of sincerity.

In contrast to this, Paul admonishes his readers who might be slaves to render their service ἐκ ψυχῆς, *from the soul* (another way of saying what was expressed in the previous verse by the phrase ἐν ἁπλότητι τῆς καρδίας ὑμῶν, *in sincerity of your heart*), reckoning the service as unto Christ. Saints are to be conscientious in their work, whether they be free or slaves. They are to do their work as servants of Christ.

6.9 *And lords, practice the same things toward them, abandoning the use of threat, knowing that the Lord of both them and you is in the heavens, and there is no favoritism with him* (Καὶ οἱ κύριοι, τὰ αὐτὰ ποιεῖτε πρὸς αὐτούς, ἀνιέντες τὴν ἀπειλήν, εἰδότες ὅτι καὶ αὐτῶν καὶ ὑμῶν ὁ κύριός ἐστιν ἐν οὐρανοῖς, καὶ προσωπολημψία οὐκ ἔστιν παρ᾽ αὐτῷ) When Tychicus carried this letter to Asia, apparently he also carried Paul's letter to Philemon[175] wherein Paul urged Philemon to receive him "no longer as a slave, but more than a slave, a beloved brother" (Phlm 16). And yet Onesimus, the formerly unprofitable slave, was being returned to Philemon in accordance with the principle that Philemon's thinking about the matter should be honored (χωρὶς δὲ τῆς σῆς γνώμης οὐδὲν ἠθέλησα ποιῆσαι, *without your mind I did not choose to do anything*)[176], with the expectation that he would now be profitable to Philemon.

This illustrates the delicate balance between being in a position of authority toward a brother in Christ while at the same time recognizing that the subordinate one is indeed a *brother* in Christ. Paul himself, who

---

[175] See the Introduction.

[176] Phlm 14.

was due deference on account of his age, his imprisonment for Christ, his standing as the one who had brought Onesimus to Christ, and his standing as someone to whom Philemon was indebted, did not command that Philemon refrain from recriminations against Onesimus, but rather implored him to do so. Philemon was expected to exercise his own authority over Onesimus according to this example.

6.10–20   Spiritual Warfare

Finally, strengthen yourselves in the Lord and in the power of his strength. Put on the armor of God such that you are able to stand against the methods of the devil. Because the struggle for us is not against blood and flesh, but against the rulers, against the powers, against the world-rulers of this darkness, against the spiritual beings of the evil one in the spiritual realms. On account of this, take up the armor of God that you might be able to resist in the evil day and having accomplished all, to stand. Stand therefore girding your waist in truth and putting on the breastplate of righteousness, and having shod your feet with the firm footing of the gospel of peace, in everything taking up the shield of faith with which you will be able to extinguish the fiery missiles of the evil one. And receive the helmet of salvation and the sword of the Spirit which is the word of God. Through every prayer and supplication praying in every time in the spirit and unto this end, being vigilant in all steadfastness and prayer concerning all the saints, and on my behalf, in order that a word might be given to me in opening my mouth in boldness to make known the mystery of the gospel on behalf of which I am an ambassador in chains, in order that in it I might be bold as is necessary for me to speak.

6.10   Finally, strengthen yourselves in the Lord and in the power of his strength (Τοῦ λοιποῦ, ἐνδυναμοῦσθε ἐν κυρίῳ καὶ ἐν τῷ κράτει τῆς ἰσχύος αὐτοῦ)   According to the NA28 critical apparatus, genitive τοῦ λοιποῦ (literally, *of the rest*, or *of the remaining*) is the reading found in 𝔓⁴⁶, Sinaiticus (original hand), Alexandrinus, Vaticanus, I, 0278, 33, 81, 1175, 1241ˢ, 1739, 1881, and 2464. But in Sinaiticus, in the hand of a later corrector, and also in D, F, G, Ψ, and the Byzantine mss, the reading is τὸ λοιπὸν, which may be construed as either nominative or accusative. The expression, in both the genitive form and nominative/accusative form, is an idiom found in ancient Greek with varying significance. It is said that χρόνου (*time*) is implied in the genitive construction seen in Galatians 6.17 and Ephesians 6.10,[177] so that the phrase literally would be "of the re-

---

[177] BDF §186.

maining time." So then, this would account for the uses where it seems to mean "in the future," or "henceforth."[178] The expression περὶ τοῦ λοιποῦ χρόνου (*concerning the future*) is found in Xenophon[179] and this may be the most complete form of the expression. But this does not account for the nominative/accusative form of the idiom. Given that χρόνος is masculine, it cannot be argued that it is implied in the nominative/accusative construction τὸ λοιπόν, which is neuter. And yet it would seem likely that the expressions τοῦ λοιποῦ and τὸ λοιπόν have a common origin, even if there is some subtle distinction indicated by the case difference.

As to the significance of the case distinction, citing Xen. Cyr. viii.5.24, Drury supposed τὸ λοιπόν "implies a continuous and unbroken time" while "τοῦ λοιποῦ signifies rather the repetition of some circumstance at some future time," illustrated by Herodotus i.11.[180] This is roughly in keeping with the distinction between the accusative of time and the genitive of time.

But Moule supposed that the expression most often meant "finally."[181] Again, we can see how this could be, supposing "of the rest" to be roughly equivalent to "pertaining to the remaining things to be said"[182] and thus serve as a means of introducing the final topic to be addressed. Moule favors "finally" in 2 Corinthians 13.11 (where it is anarthrous), Philippians 4.8, 1 Thessalonians 4.1 (where it is anarthrous), 2 Thessalonians 3.1 as well as here in Ephesians 6.10. In each of these instances, being at or near the end of a letter, "finally" does indeed seem to be the meaning. And we probably ought to add Galatians 6.17 to that list. The only reservation is that taking the expression in Ephesians 6.10 and Galatians 6.17 as having the same significance as in the other passages in this list fails to account for the use of the genitive rather than the accusative. But then, it may be that the accusative reading, τὸ λοιπόν, is authentic in Ephesians 6.10.

6.11 ἐνδύσασθε τὴν πανοπλίαν τοῦ θεοῦ πρὸς τὸ δύνασθαι ὑμᾶς στῆναι πρὸς τὰς μεθοδείας τοῦ διαβόλου· **Put on the armor of God such that you are able to stand against the methods of the devil.** The ex-

---

[178] Compare Thucydides iii.104.2.

[179] Hellenica, iii.2.6.

[180] Herodotus, with Critical and Historical Notes by W. B. Drury, Book 1, pp 14–15.

[181] Moule, Idiom Book, p. 161. He reckons this meaning "to be the commonest" on p. 161, but then on p. 162, he says, "*For what remains* thus appears to be the dominant or underlying meaning."

[182] Compare Meyer, "as concerns the rest" p. 535.

hortation to put on the armor of God is primarily concerned with protection against spiritual threats rather than marching orders to go on the attack. Paul says, *Put on the armor of God such that you are able to stand against the methods of the devil.* On στῆναι (*to stand*), see the comments below on ἑτοιμασία in verse 15. Regarding μεθοδεία, see the comments on its occurrence at 4.14.

6.12 Regarding the identity of the enemies here named, see the comments on 1.21.

against the spiritual beings of the evil one in the spiritual realms That these evil forces are located ἐν τοῖς ἐπουρανίοις (in many translations, "in the heavenly realms" or "in the heavenly places") need not be disconcerting. ἐν τοῖς ἐπουρανίοις means, "in the spiritual realms." It does not in and of itself indicate a realm of purity, holiness and bliss. Even in 1.20*f*, when Paul spoke of the Christ being seated at the right hand of God ἐν τοῖς ἐπουρανίοις, the words ὑπεράνω πάσης ἀρχῆς κ.τ.λ. were not intended to indicate that the spiritual realms are above all rule, etc., but that the Christ himself is above all rule, etc.

6.13 διὰ τοῦτο ἀναλάβετε τὴν πανοπλίαν τοῦ θεοῦ, ἵνα δυνηθῆτε ἀντιστῆναι ἐν τῇ ἡμέρᾳ τῇ πονηρᾷ καὶ ἅπαντα κατεργασάμενοι στῆναι. ***On account of this, take up the armor of God that you might be able to resist in the evil day and having accomplished all, to stand.***

6.14 Stand therefore girding your waist in truth (στῆτε οὖν περιζωσάμενοι τὴν ὀσφὺν ὑμῶν ἐν ἀληθείᾳ) Notice that the exhortation is to stand, rather than to charge or run. We will return to this when we consider verse 15.

and putting on the breastplate of righteousness (καὶ ἐνδυσάμενοι τὸν θώρακα τῆς δικαιοσύνης) This and several of the following spiritual identifications of armor and weaponry are taken from the OT. The breastplate of righteousness (as well as the helmet of salvation in verse 17) is taken from Isaiah 59.17.

Josephus mentions the Roman infantry as being equipped with θώραξιν (breastplates or cuirasses)[183]. Just for the purpose of remembering the word, think of the English *thorax*. This is the part of the body that is covered by the θώραξιν. The Greek soldier was equipped with a cuirass that was designed to look like a muscular human torso. Xenophon describes a conversation between Socrates and an armor maker wherein we

---

[183] *Wars*, 3.93.

learn that the Greek soldier paid a premium for a cuirass that was well-fitted, accurately conforming to his particular anatomy so as not to simply hang from the shoulders but rather having its weight supported by the "collar-bone and shoulder-blades, the shoulders, chest, back and belly."[184]

6.15 *And having feet shod with the firm footing of the gospel of peace* (καὶ ὑποδησάμενοι τοὺς πόδας ἐν ἑτοιμασίᾳ τοῦ εὐαγγελίου τῆς εἰρήνης)   At Isaiah 52.7, the LXX has ὡς πόδες εὐαγγελιζομένου ἀκοὴν εἰρήνης, *as feet of one who brings news of peace.*

The usual meaning of ἑτοιμασία is *preparation*, and certainly not *"firm footing."* But Amalric Buscarlet told of having found an explanation of the use of ἑτοιμασία in *De calceis Hebraeorum*, a seventeenth century work, wherein it is posited that the meaning of ἑτοιμασία here is "basis, foundation," a meaning derived from the use of the word in the Septuagint to translate *kun*. For discussion of the unexpected use of ἑτοιμασία in this sense, see Buscarlet's article. The basic argument is that the Hebrew *kun* has a range of meaning that spans both *prepare* (Gen 43.16), that being the meaning properly reflected in the Greek ἑτοιμάζω, as well as the meaning *establish* (1 Sam 13.13, 2 Sam 7.12, and Ps 65.6 where again we see ἑτοιμάζω in the LXX). Inasmuch as a *basis*, or *foundation*, serves as the *preparation* of that which is built upon it, we can see why in some instances, a Hebrew word pointing to a *foundation* could in context be rendered by a Greek word meaning *preparation*. The Lord would *prepare* David's kingdom by *establishing* it. While ἑτοιμασία does not itself properly mean *establishment*, the LXX usage of ἑτοιμάζω to translate *kun*, which does include the idea of *establishing* or *causing to stand*, accounts for Paul's use of ἑτοιμασία in accordance with this latter sense.

The Hebrew *kun* means *establish*, but is more frequently used in the OT in contexts where the derived meaning *prepare* is operative. (One prepares for a building by laying its foundation.) Given the preponderance of uses of *kun* in the sense of *prepare* and in these instances the use of the Greek ἑτοιμάζω/ἑτοιμασία/ ἕτοιμος to represent the Hebrew, Hatch argued that although the Greek ἑτοιμ- was not used in the sense of *establish* in Classical times, the word group came to be so used, having been associated with the Hebrew expression which fundamentally did mean *establish*. So then, Hatch found that "ἑτοιμάζειν is used interchangeably with ἀνορθοῦν, θεμελιοῦν, κατορθοῦν, στερεοῦν as the translation of כּוּן."

---

[184] Memorabilia 3.10.9–15. Loeb Classical Library, translated by E. C. Marchant.

After citing further evidence from the LXX, Hatch concluded, "It seems clear from these passages that, like ἑτοιμάζειν, ἑτοιμασία and ἕτοιμος had come to have the meaning of the Hebrew words which they were used to translate."[185]

Hatch cited Matthew 20.23, Mark 10.40, Matthew 25.34,41, 1 Corinthians 2.9, and Hebrews 11.16 as instances in the NT where the verb ἑτοιμάζω might best be understood in light of this phenomenon. With reference to the use of the noun ἑτοιμασία in Ephesians 6.15, Hatch concluded, "it seems most appropriate to take it in the sense which it has been shown to have elsewhere in Biblical Greek of 'firm foundation,' or 'firm footing.'"[186]

Whereas many commentators have supposed the function of the footwear is to facilitate movement,[187] Buscarlet was convinced that is not at all the point, but rather the footwear is to assure stability, for, said he, "the sandals used by the ancients were as bands and impediments to all rapid movement, and were considered to be so by them." He quoted Musonius and Clemens Alexandrinus to this effect, makes specific reference to the spiked sandals designed to make the Roman soldier sure-footed, and says, "Now Paul does not wish to teach the Christian solider that he needs to be shod with the gospel of peace so as to propagate it, but he is speaking of the whole armour of God, which is to be 'put on,' that he may *stand*, 'and having done all, may *stand* in the evil day.'" Buscarlet argued convincingly that Paul spoke of the gospel of peace as footwear that aids the Christian in standing "against the wiles of the devil—just as soldiers were shod, not so as to facilitate prompt movements, but so as to stand more firmly, and not slip in wrestling with their foe."[188]

Perhaps the notion that agile movement is in view has been encouraged not only by our own cultural understanding of athletic footwear, but also by the allusion to Isaiah 52.7, which is elsewhere cited by Paul in connection with the preacher who is sent to preach the good news (Rom 10.15). And Isaiah 52.7 itself speaks of one who does not merely stand and announce good news, but who *brings* good news.

But in support of Buscarlet's conclusion, note that the series of participial phrases that includes "having shod your feet" is appended to the

---

[185] Hatch, 52*f.*

[186] Ibid., 55.

[187] As for example, Meyer: "enabling him…to advance against the enemy with agile and sure step," p. 543.

[188] Buscarlet, 38*f.*

imperative "Stand therefore" (vs. 14). How do we stand? By having girded our loins with truth, by having put on the breastplate of righteousness, and by having shod our feet with the cleated shoes of the gospel of peace.

6.16 *in everything taking up the shield of faith* (ἐν πᾶσιν ἀναλαβόντες τὸν θυρεὸν τῆς πίστεως) Josephus mentions the θυρεὸν (buckler, or shield) of the Roman soldier as being oblong,[189] and notes that the cavalry were also equipped with bucklers that rested "obliquely on the horse's flank."[190]

with which you will be able to extinguish the fiery missiles of the evil one (ἐν ᾧ δυνήσεσθε πάντα τὰ βέλη τοῦ πονηροῦ [τὰ] πεπυρωμένα σβέσαι) For βέλη (*missiles*), see in Josephus the story of Sabinus who advanced in spite of the darts that came flying at him. He successfully mounts the wall, but falls and then is killed when buried under βέλεσιν (*missiles*), which seems more likely to be a reference to rocks than to darts.[191] And indeed, a βέλος was anything hurled, whether a dart, or a rock, or anything else.[192] However, Paul speaks of τὰ βέλη... τὰ πεπυρωμένα, *the flaming missiles*. In Aeschylus' Prometheus Bound, we see πύρπνουν βέλος, *fire-breathing darts*.[193] (See also fiery darts elsewhere in Prometheus.) In Psalm 7.13, David wrote of God's arrows with flaming shafts.[194]

6.17 *And receive the helmet of salvation* (καὶ τὴν περικεφαλαίαν τοῦ σωτηρίου δέξασθε) See Isaiah 59.17.

Up to this point, the armor mentioned has been defensive in nature, that we may be able to stand against the wiles of the devil. But now Paul includes the one offensive tool we have: καὶ τὴν μάχαιραν τοῦ πνεύματος, ὅ ἐστιν ῥῆμα θεοῦ, *and the sword of the Spirit which is the word of God.* Our offense is not to consist of our personal testimony about how wonderfully well things have turned out for us since we came to Christ. (Contrast such testimonies with Paul's description of his troubles in 2 Corinthians 11.23*ff*, or with Jesus' warning to his apostles in Matthew 10.16*ff*, or with the hint of greater persecution to come in He-

---

[189] Wars, 3.93, Loeb Classical Library, translation by H. St. J. Thackery.

[190] Ibid.

[191] Ibid., Wars 6.60.

[192] In Lucian's Symposium, the mention of a βέλους (Symp. 2) proves to be a reference to a bowl that was thrown during a food fight.

[193] line 917.

[194] The LXX (Ps 7.14) has τὰ βέλη αὐτου τοῖς καιομένοις ἐξειργάσατο, using the dative case to represent the Hebrew *lamed*, but Symmachus has εἰς τὸ καίειν rather than τοῖς καιομένοις.

brews 12.4, or the promise of greater persecution to come in Revelation 2.10.) Our only offense is the word of God.

In Isaiah 49.2, the Servant of the Lord says his mouth has been made a sword (τὸ στόμα μου ὡσεὶ μάχαιραν). In both Isaiah 11.4 and Hosea 6.5, the mouth of the Lord, or the word proceeding therefrom, is a weapon, though not specifically a sword.

The Roman soldier carried a μάχαιραν which could be of various lengths. Josephus says a Roman infantryman carried two, one on each side (μαχαιροφοροῦντες ἀμφοτέρωθεν, *carried swords on both sides*), while a μάχαιρα μὲν ἐκ δεχιῶν μακρὰ (*long sword on the right side*) was carried by cavalry.[195]

Whereas the previously mentioned pieces of armor have been introduced with participles (περιζωσάμενοι τὴν ὀσφὺν, ἐνδυσάμενοι τὸν θώρακα, ὑποδησάμενοι τοὺς πόδας, ἀναλαβόντες τὸν θυρεόν) that are subordinate to the main verb στῆτε, we now have in imperative δέξασθε, *receive the helmet of salvation and the sword of the Spirit.* Meyer supposed the change is merely a deviation from the preceding construction and is not intended to indicate a new and grammatically unrelated imperative. Meyer understood both the instruction to receive the helmet of salvation and the ensuing words about prayer as grammatically subordinate to the imperative "stand" (vs. 14) just as the various participles were subordinate to the imperative "stand."[196]

6.18   After having introduced an imperative in verse 17, Paul now returns to a participle to elucidate further the instruction to *stand* (v. 14), προσευχόμενοι (*praying*). But while he resumes the use of participles, he departs from the armament metaphor.

through every prayer and supplication praying in every time in the spirit Concerning καιρός, see the notes at 5.16. As discussed there, the use of καιρός often points to some character of the time in view. So then, Paul is not merely saying, "pray all the time," but is rather urging that his readers pray at all kinds of times. Pray when things are going well. Pray when you are overwhelmed with difficulties. Pray ἐν παντὶ καιρῷ.

We have εἰς αὐτὸ in verse 18 and εἰς αὐτὸ τοῦτο in verse 22. These are examples of an idiom that occurs elsewhere in the NT in Romans 9.17, 13.6, 2 Corinthians 5.5, and of course, in Colossians 4.8 where the text runs very

---

[195] Wars, 3.93.
[196] Meyer 548.

much as it does here.[197] In each of these passages, the meaning is *unto this end, for this purpose*. The function of αὐτὸ is probably to be regarded as intensive, *for this itself*.

The relationship of ἀγρυπνοῦντες (*being vigilant*) to what has gone before is difficult to determine. Some suppose the two words προσευχόμενοι and ἀγρυπνοῦντες function together to create one idea (forming a hendiadys, "one idea through two"). But the two participles seem to be serving different functions. While προσευχόμενοι is part of what the Gentiles need to do in order to stand against the principalities, powers, and world rulers, ἀγρυπνοῦντες is unto some particular end (εἰς αὐτὸ) that must be different. It is probably not the same end (*i.e.*, to stand in the evil day), given that the being vigilant is explained in part as being vigilant in supplication on behalf of Paul. It hardly makes sense to suppose that Paul would say part of what the Gentiles need to do in order to stand in the evil day is pray for Paul himself to have boldness while he remains a prisoner in Rome.

The words εἰς αὐτὸ (*unto this end*) must point back to προσευχόμενοι (*praying*) rather than to στῆτε (vs. 14). So then rather than seeing ἀγρυπνοῦντες as part of a hendiadys with προσευχόμενοι, we understand ἀγρυπνοῦντες to be introducing the instruction that will assist the Gentiles in their effort to be praying at all occasions.

On the whole, from verse 14 on, Paul is saying, in order to stand, take up this armor, and also be praying at all occasions; and to this end, namely that you might be praying at all occasions, be vigilant in persistence and entreaty for all the saints and for me. The προσευχόμενοι serves as a pivot point. It is tied to the foregoing context as part of the spiritual defense of the Gentiles, but it is also tied to the ensuing context as a proactive measure on behalf of the saints and of Paul. "Put on this armor, and pray at all occasions. And to the end that you pray at all occasions, be vigilant in persistence and entreaty, and make those entreaties on my behalf as well as on behalf of all the saints."

6.19–20 In verse 19, the particular thing for which Paul needed his readers' prayers was that he might have boldness in making the mystery of the gospel known. Paul has already spoken of the great privilege that it was to be the chosen messenger to the Gentiles and to reveal the mys-

---

[197] In Acts 27.6, though we have the words εἰς αὐτό, the idiom is not the same, for there neuter αὐτό has as its antecedent πλοίον, and the expression merely means "into it," i.e., into the boat.

tery to them (3.2–12). But that does not mean it was always easy for him to fulfill his mission. At Athens, after Paul had been waiting for Silas and Timothy to arrive, "his spirit was provoked with him as he beheld the city full of idols." He had not arrived at Athens proclaiming the message openly and freely. But there came a point at which what he saw compelled him to speak. And we do well to remember he was in Athens because he had just been escorted out of Berea to escape the trouble brewing there, which was just an extension of the previous violence at Thessalonica. No wonder he seemed ready to adopt a low profile for a bit at Athens while he waited for his companions. But as he observed the idolatry, he could hold his peace no longer. Yes, Paul was an eager messenger, but he was not immune to the effects of the violent opposition. Now he is in chains in Rome, but he knows he is there as an ambassador for Christ. His imprisonment is a constant reminder of the price he may pay for speaking boldly. While his Roman audience would likely have little reason to oppose him for their own part, the more boldly Paul spoke, the more likely it was that Jews would be stirred up against him and would make their opposition known to Caesar. And so Paul asks that his readers pray that he might have boldness, in order that he might speak boldly, as it was necessary for him to speak.

6.21–24 Final Instructions

In order that you also might know the things according to me, what I do, Tychicus, the beloved brother and faithful servant in the Lord, will make known all things to you, whom I sent to you unto this end, in order that you might know the things concerning us and that he might comfort your hearts. Peace to the brethren and love with all faith from God , father and Lord Jesus Christ. The Grace be with all who love our Lord Jesus Christ in incorruption.

Finally, Paul tells his readers that Tychicus, who will be carrying this letter (see the Introduction) will explain his circumstances to them.

WORKS CONSULTED

Commentaries

Alford, Henry. *The Greek New Testament: An Exegetical and Critical Commentary*. 5th ed., vol. 3. London: Rivingtons, 1871. Reprint, Grand Rapids, MI: Baker, 1980.

Arnold, Clinton E. *Zondervan Exegetical Commentary on the New Testament: Ephesians*. Grand Rapids: Zondervan, 2010.

Best, Ernest. *A Critical and Exegetical Commentary on Ephesians*. Edinburgh: T&T Clark, 1998.

Caldwell, C. G. *Truth Commentaries, Ephesians*. edited by Mike Willis. Bowling Green, KY: Guardian of Truth Foundation, 1994.

Dunn, James D. G. *The Epistles to the Colossians and to Philemon, a Commentary on the Greek Text*. Grand Rapids: Eerdmans, 1996.

Eadie, John. *A Commentary on the Greek Text of the Epistle of Paul to the Ephesians*. Edinburgh: T&T Clark, 1883.

Goodspeed, Edgar J. *The Meaning of Ephesians*. Chicago: The University of Chicago Press, 1933.

von Harnack, Adolf. *The Acts of the Apostles*. New York: G. P. Putnam's Sons, 1909.

Hodge, Charles. *A Commentary on the Epistle to the Ephesians*. New York: Robert Carter and Brothers, 1860.

Hoehner, Harold W. *Ephesians: An Exegetical Commentary*. Grand Rapids, MI: Baker, 2002.

Kreitzer, Larry. *The Epistle to the Ephesians*. London: Epworth Press, 1997

Lightfoot, J. B. *St. Paul's Epistle to the Colossians and to Philemon: A Revised Text with Introductuions, Notes and Dissertations*. MacMillan, 1879. Reprint, Grand Rapids, MI: Zondervan, 1971.

Lincoln, Andrew T. *Word Biblical Commentary, Ephesians*. Nashville: Thomas Nelson, 1990.

Marshall, I. Howard. *The Gospel of Luke, A Commentary on the Greek Text*. Grand Rapids, MI: William B. Eerdmans Publishing Company, 1978.

Meyer, H.A.W. *Critical and Exegetical Hand-book to the Epistle to the Ephesians*. Translated by Maurice J. Evans. Revised and edited by William P. Dikson. New York: Funk & Wagnalls, 1884.

Patterson, Robert E. *An Exposition of the Epistle to the Ephesians*. Springfield, MO: Particular Baptist Press, 2011.

Robinson, J. Armitage. *St Paul's Epistle to the Ephesians: A Revised Text and Translation with Exposition and Notes*. 2nd ed. London: Macmillan, 1904.

Schnackenburg, Rudolf. *Ephesians, A Commentary*. Edinburgh: T&T Clark, 1991.

Stoeckhardt, G. *Commentary on St. Paul's Letter to the Ephesians*. St. Louis: Concordia. 1952.

Journal Articles

Bowen, Clayton R. "Are Paul's Prison Letters from Ephesus?" *The American Journal of Theology* 24, no. 1 (Jan., 1920): 112–135. http://www.jstor.org/stable/3155941

Bowman, J. W. "The Epistle to the Epheisans." *Interpretation* 8 (1954): 188–205.

Buscarlet, A. F. "The Preparation of the Gospel of Peace." *The Expository Times* 9 (1897): 38–40.

Emmel, Stephen. "Greek Biblical Papyri in the Beinecke Library." *Zeitschrift für Papyrologie und Epigraphik* 112 (1996) 289–294.

Gordon, T. David. "'Equipping' Ministry in Ephesians 4?" *Journal of the Evangelical Theological Society* 37 (1994): 69–78.

Hamann, H. P. "Church and Ministry: An Exegesis of Ephesians 4:1–16." *Lutheran Theological Journal* 16, no. 3 (December 1982): 121–128.

_____. "The Translation of Ephesians 4:12—A Necessary Revision." *Concordia Journal* 14 (1998): 42–49.

Harper, Kyle. "Porneia: The Making of a Christian Sexual Norm." *Journal of Biblical Literature* 131, no. 2 (2012): 363–383.

Hatch, William H. P. and C. Bradford Welles. "A Hitherto Unpublished Fragment of the Epistle to the Ephesians." *Harvard Theological Review*, 51 no. 1 (January 1958): 33–37.

Hebert, Gabriel, "'Faithfulness' and 'Faith'." *Theology* 58, no. 24 (Oct. '55): 373–79.

Hooker, Morna D. "ΠΙΣΤΙΣ ΧΡΙΣΤΟΥ." *New Testament Studies* 35, no. 3 (1989): 321–342.

Howard, George. "On the 'Faith of Christ'." *Harvard Theological Review* 60, no. 4 (October 1967): 459–484.

_____. "The 'Faith of Christ'." *Expository Times* 85 no. 7 (1974): 212–215.

Hultgren, Arland J. "The Pistis Christou Formulation in Paul." *Novum Testamentum* 22 no. 3 (1980): 248–263.

Johnson, Luke Timothy. "Romans 3:21–26 and the Faith of Jesus." *Catholic Biblical Quarterly* 44 no. 1 (January 1982): 77–90.

Kuhn, K. G. "Der Epheserbrief Im Lichte der Qumrantexte." *New Testament Studies* 7: 334–46

Marcus, Joel. "The Circumcision and the Uncircumcision in Rome." *New Testament Studies*, 35 no. 1 (1989): 67–81.

Metzger, B. M. "Literary Forgeries and Canonical Pseudepigrapha." *Journal of Biblical Literature* 91 (1972): 3–24.

McKelvey, R.J. "Christ the Cornerstone," *NTS* 8 (July 1962): 352–59.

Moule, C.F.D. "The Biblical Conception of 'Faith'." *Expository Times* 68 (February 1957): 157.

Murphy-O'Connor, Jerome. "Paul and Gallio." *Journal of Biblical Literature*, 112, no. 2 (Summer, 1993): 315–317.

Novenson, Matthew V. "Can the Messiahship of Jesus Be Read off Paul's Grammar? Nils Dahl's Criteria 50 Years Later." *New Testament Studies*. 56 no. 3 (July 2010): 396–412.

Porter, S.E. "ἴστε γινώσκοντες in Ephesians 5,5: Does Chiasm Solve a

Problem?" *Zeitschrift für die Neutestamentliche Wissenschaft* 81 (1990): 270–76.

Robinson, D.W.B., "'Faith of Jesus Christ'—a New Testament Debate." *Reformed Theological Review*, 29 no. 3 (Sept.–Dec. 1970): 71–81.

Slingerland, Dixon. *"Acts 18:1–18, the Gallio Inscription, and Absolute Pauline Chronology."* Journal of Biblical Literature 110 no. 3 (Autumn, 1991): 439–449.

Smith, G.V. "Paul's Use of Ps. 68:18 in Eph. 4:8." *Journal of the Evangelical Theological Society* 18 no. 3 (1975): 181–89.

Torrance, Thomas F. "One Aspect of the Biblical Conception of Faith." *Expository Times* 68 (January 1957): 111–14.

Williams, Sam K. "Again Pistis Christou." *Catholic Biblical Quarterly* 49 no. 3 (1987): 431–447.

Other Works

Aland, Kurt *Text und Textwert der Griechischen Handschriften des Neuen Testaments, 2, Die Paulinischen Briefe*, Band 3: *Galaterbrief Bis Philipperbrief.* Berlin: Walter De Gruyter, 1991.

Best, E. "Recipients and Title of the Letter to the Ephesians: Why and When the Designation 'Ephesians'?" In *ANRW*. Geschichte und Kultur Roms im Spiegel der neueren Forschung. II: Principat. Band 25 (4. Teilband): Religion (Vorkonstantinisches Christentum: Leben un Umwelt Jesu; Neues Testament [Danonische Schriften und Apokryphen] , Forts.), ed. W Haase. Berlin/New York: de Gruyter, 1987, 3247–79.

Dahl, N.A. "The Particularity of the Pauline Epistles as a Problem in the Ancient Church." In *Neotestamentica et Patristica. Freundesgabe, eine Freundesgabe, Herrn professor Dr. Oscar Cullmann zu seinem 60. Geburtstag überreicht.* Leiden: Brill, 1962, 261–71.

_____. "Die Messianität Jesu bei Paulus." In *Studia Paulina in honorem Johannis de Zwaanseptuagenarii* (Haarlem: Bohn, 1953) 83–95; Eng. trans.'The Messiahship of Jesus in Paul,' *The Crucified Messiah* (Minneapolis: Augsburg, 1974) 37–47; repr. in Dahl, *Jesus the Christ: The Historical Origins of Christological Doctrine* (ed. D. H. Juel; Minneapolis: Fortress, 1991) 15–25.

_____. *Studies in Ephesians Introductory Questions, Text- & Edition-Critical Issues, Interpretation of Texts and Themes*. Edited by David Hellhom, Vemund Blomkvist, and Tord Fornberg. Tübingen:Mohr Siebeck, 2000.

Deissmann, Adolf. *St. Paul, A Study in Social and Religious History*, transl. by Lionel Strachan. London:Hodder and Stoughton.1912

DeWette, W. M. L. *An Historico-Critical Introduction to the Canonical Books of the New Testament*, Translated by Frederick Frothingham. Boston: Crosby, Nichols, & Company. 1858.

Drury, William B. *Herodotus, with Critical and Historical Notes*. Dublin:Milliken and Son. 1835.

Duncan, George S. *St. Paul's Ephesian Ministry, A Reconstruction*. London: Hodder and Stoughton. 1929.

Elliott, James Keith, ed. *New Testament Textual Criticism:The Application of Thoroughgoing Principles, Essays on Manuscripts and Textual Variation*. Leiden: Brill, 2010.

Grenfell, Bernard Pyne and Arthur Surridge Hunt, editors, *The Oxyrhynchus Papyri, Part 6*. London: Egypt Exploration Fund, 1908.

Gruen, Erich S. *Diaspora, Jews amidst Greeks and Romans*. Cambridge, Mass: Harvard University Press, 2002.

Harrison, P.N. *The Problem of the Pastoral Epistles*. London: Oxford, 1921.

Hatch, Edwin. *Essays in Biblical Greek*. Oxford: Clarendon Press, 1889.

Kaibel, Georg, *Epigrammata Graeca ex Lapidibus Conlecta*. Berlin: Reimer, 1878.

Käsemann, E., "Ephesians and Acts" in L. E. Keck and J.L. Martyn (eds.), *Studies in Luke-Acts, FS Paul Schubert,* Nashville: Abingdon Press, 1966, 288–97

_____. *Perspectives on Paul*. London: SCM Press, 1971.

Knox, Wilfred Lawrence, *St. Paul and the Church of the Gentiles*. Cambridge [Eng.] : University Press, 1939.

Lightfoot, J.B. "The Destination of the Epistle to the Ephesians" In *Biblical Essays*. London: Macmillan, 1893, 375–96.

McKelvey, R.J. *The New Temple, The Church in the New Testament.* Glasgow: Oxford University Press, 1969.

MaGee, Gregory S. *Portrait of an Apostle: A Case for Paul's Authorship of Colossians and Ephesians.* Eugene, OR: Wipf and Stock Publishers, 2013.

Metzger, B. M. *The Text of the New Testament.* 2nd ed. New York: Oxford University Press, 1968.

Mitton, C. Leslie. *Ephesians.* Attic Press:Greenwood, S.C, 1976.

Moule, C.F.D. *An Idiom Book of New Testament Greek,* 2nd ed. Cambridge, Cambridge University Press, 1959, reprinted 1998.

Perowne, J. J. Stewart. *The Book of Psalms, A New Translation with Introductions and Notes Explanatory and Critical.* 4th Ed. Revised. George Bell and Sons, 1878. Reprint edition, Grand Rapids: Zondervan, 1980.

Plutarchi Chaeronensis , *Moralis,* Gregorius N. Bernardakis, vol III, Lipsiae, In Aedibus B. G. Teubneri, 1891. http://ia600404.us.archive.org/9/items/moralia03plut/moralia03plut.pdf

Ramsay, Sir William Mitchell. *The Church in the Roman Empire before A.D. 170.* 6th ed. London: Hodder and Stoughton, 1900

_____. *The Historical Geography of Asia Minor.* London: John Murray, 1890.

_____. *A Historical Commentary on St. Paul's Epistle to the Galatians,* 2nd ed. London: Hodder and Stoughton, 1900.

Roon, A. Van, *The Authenticity of Ephesians.* Leiden: E.J. Brill, 1974.

Trench, Richard Chenevix. *Synonyms of the New Testament,* 9th ed. London, 1880. Reprint edition, Grand Rapids: Wm. B. Eerdmans, 1980.

Wallace, Daniel B. *Greek Grammar Beyond the Basics,* Grand Rapids, MI: Zondervan, 1996.

Westcott, Brooke Foss, *Saint Paul's Epistle to the Ephesians: The Greek Text with Notes and Addenda.* Grand Rapids: Eerdmans 1952. publ. by Macmillan, 1906.

Wright, N. T., *Christian Origins and the Question of God, Vol. 4, Paul and the Faithfulness of God, Book II, Parts III and IV,* Minneapolis: Fortress Press, 2013.

Yee, Tet-Lim N. *Jews, Gentiles and Ethnic Reconciliation*, #130 in Society the New Testament Studies Monograph Series, ed. Richard Bauckham. Cambridge: Cambridge University Press, 2005.

Zerwick, Maximilian. *Biblical Greek*, English edition adapted from the 4th Latin Edition by Joseph Smith. Rome: Scripta Pontificii Instituti Biblici, 1963.

More Bible Commentaries by DeWard Publishing

Exposition of Genesis (volumes 1 and 2), H.C. Leupold

The Growth of the Seed: Notes on the Book of Genesis, Nathan Ward

Thinking Through Job, L.A. Mott

Thinking Through Jeremiah, L.A. Mott

Let Us Search Our Ways: A Commentary on Lamentations,
Evan and Marie Blackmore

Original Commentary on Acts, J.W. McGarvey

Uncommon Sense: The Wisdom of James for Dispossessed Believers,
James T. South

The Lamb, The Woman, and the Dragon: Studies in the Revelation of St. John,
Albertus Pieters

*For a full listing of DeWard Publishing
Company books, visit our website:*

www.deward.com

CPSIA information can be obtained
at www.ICGtesting.com
Printed in the USA
LVHW102331090123
736818LV00013B/249/J

9 781936 341948